# PRAISE FOR *EMPATHY ECONOMICS*

"With extraordinary access to an extremely busy Janet Yellen as well her family, close friends, and colleagues, Owen Ullmann traces the path Yellen took from Fort Hamilton High School in Brooklyn to the highest rungs of the US government with exacting detail and insight. Ullmann reveals how Yellen overcame obstacles, outmaneuvered hostile men, and held onto all the values that led her to study economics in the first place—all to the great benefit of the American people. When you finish this book, you really know who Yellen is and why she has been so successful and influential."

—DAVID WESSEL, the Brookings Institution,
author of *Only the Rich Can Play*

"Few people have had as great an impact on America's economy as Yellen, the first woman to serve both as chair of the Federal Reserve and as treasury secretary. In *Empathy Economics*, Ullmann masterfully traces her rise from precocious Brooklyn schoolgirl to the corridors of power in Washington. Ullmann artfully weaves together Yellen's life and career, showing how her lived experience informed her view of economic policies that put American families at the forefront. This deeply human portrait brings to life one of the country's towering trailblazers, who is still paving the way for women in economics and beyond."

—JOANNE LIPMAN, author of *That's What She Said*,
and former editor-in-chief, *USA Today*

"*Empathy Economics* is a terrific read, well researched, and well written. Ullmann captures the characteristics that have made Yellen the leader of three of the nation's key economic-policy institutions, the Council of Economic Advisers, the

Federal Reserve, and the Treasury—the only person to have held all three positions. Yellen combines sharp intelligence, and a deep commitment to fact-based objective economic analysis, with empathy, a big heart, and a deep dedication to public service. She is strong yet humble; she has taken on leadership roles and their onerous 24/7 responsibilities not for prestige or power but to improve the lives of ordinary Americans. No one has brought more knowledge, experience, and empathy to addressing the core economic challenges facing the nation. The book also provides a fascinating history of the evolution of Federal Reserve policy during Yellen's leadership, including the adoption of an explicit inflation target and greater transparency in Fed decision-making."

—LAURA TYSON, distinguished professor, Haas School,
University of California; former chair,
White House Council of Economic Advisers; and
director, White House National Economic Council

"Ullmann's excellent biography of Yellen documents the origins and trajectory of Yellen's remarkable career and what lies behind her success—intelligence, diligence, and deeply held values of equity and inclusion that inform the content of her work as well as her working style. A valuable bonus is that Ullmann's clear explication of the issues that have confronted Yellen provides a thorough overview of the major financial, tax, and growth policies of the past several decades. Yellen's inspiring story of succeeding in a man's world to tweak economic policy at the highest levels and achieve positive outcomes for many is a good read. Every economist should apply her values to our discipline and profession to make economics much more useful and humane."

—HEIDI HARTMAN, research professor,
George Washington University, and president,
Institute for Women's Policy Research

# EMPATHY ECONOMICS

# EMPATHY ECONOMICS

Janet Yellen's Remarkable Rise to Power
and Her Drive to Spread Prosperity to All

## Owen Ullmann

**PUBLIC**AFFAIRS
*New York*

PublicAffairs
Hachette Book Group
1290 Avenue of the Americas, New York, NY 10104
www.publicaffairsbooks.com
@Public_Affairs

Printed in the United States of America
First Edition: September 2022

Published by PublicAffairs, an imprint of Perseus Books, LLC, a subsidiary of Hachette Book Group, Inc. The PublicAffairs name and logo is a trademark of the Hachette Book Group.

The Hachette Speakers Bureau provides a wide range of authors for speaking events. To find out more, go to www.hachettespeakersbureau.com or call (866) 376-6591.

The publisher is not responsible for websites (or their content) that are not owned by the publisher.

Lyrics to "Who's Yellen Now" by Dessa © 2021, reprinted with permission.

Library of Congress Cataloging-in-Publication Data
Names: Ullmann, Owen, author.
Title: Empathy economics : Janet Yellen's remarkable rise to power and her drive to spread prosperity to all / Owen Ullmann.
Description: First edition. | New York : PublicAffairs, [2022] | Includes bibliographical references and index.
Identifiers: LCCN 2022001445 | ISBN 9781541701021 (hardcover) | ISBN 9781541701045 (ebook)
Subjects: LCSH: Yellen, Janet L. (Janet Louise), 1946– | Board of Governors of the Federal Reserve System (U.S.)—Officials and employees—Biography. | Economists—United States—Biography. | Monetary policy—United States. | United States—Economic policy.
Classification: LCC HB119.Y45 U45 2022 | DDC 330.092 [B]—dc23/eng/20220113

LC record available at https://lccn.loc.gov/2022001445

ISBNs: 9781541701021 (hardcover), 9781541701045 (ebook)

LSC-C

Printing 1, 2022

*To Lois, Cara, and Daniel*

# CONTENTS

*Photo insert appears between pages 220 and 221*

# INTRODUCTION

*"She really is the RBG of economics"*

THE MEN WHO HAD LED THE FEDERAL RESERVE BOARD EVER since the nation's central bank system was established by the US Congress in 1913 had always kept their focus on the needs of Wall Street and the financial industry. But when Janet Louise Yellen became the first female chair of the powerful institution in February 2014, she was determined to show that it represented the economic interests of all Americans. To underscore that commitment, she decided to make her first out-of-town speech as chair at a community reinvestment conference on March 31, 2014, in Chicago. The conference, sponsored by the Fed and other banking agencies, was held each year to discuss ways to help economically depressed neighborhoods. Yellen used the forum to highlight the plight of millions who had lost their jobs during the Great Recession of 2007–2009.

"The past six years have been difficult for many Americans, but the hardships faced by some have shattered lives and families," Yellen told the audience. "Too many people know firsthand how devastating it is to lose a job at which you had succeeded and be unable to find another; to run through your savings and even lose your home, as months and sometimes years pass trying to find work; to feel your marriage and other relationships strained and broken by financial difficulties. And yet many of those who have suffered the most find the will to keep trying."

Yellen pointed out that the Fed had taken extraordinary steps to spur economic activity and create jobs by keeping interest rates low to make homes more affordable; to lower the cost of buying a car; to help small businesses build, expand, and hire. She then introduced three unemployed workers and shared with the audience their personal stories of how they struggled to find jobs at decent wages. Dorine Poole had lost her job processing medical insurance claims at the start of the recession. Despite fifteen years of steady employment, Poole found employers unwilling to hire her because she had been out of work for two years. Jermaine Brownlee lost his job as an apprentice plumber when the recession hit and had to settle for a lower-paying job. Vicki Lira lost her full-time job of twenty years at a printing plant when it shut down in 2006. At times homeless, she found part-time work serving food samples to customers at a grocery store.

"I have described the experiences of Dorine, Jermaine, and Vicki because they tell us important things that the unemployment rate alone cannot," Yellen said. "They are a reminder that there are real people behind the statistics, struggling to get by and eager for the opportunity to build better lives. . . . The Federal Reserve is committed to strengthening communities and restoring a healthy economy that benefits all Americans. It is my hope that the courageous and determined working people I have told you about today, and millions more, will get the chance they deserve to build better lives."

It turned out that Dorine Poole and Jermaine Brownlee were convicted felons. Yellen knew that one of them had spent time in prison because she had talked to all three people before her speech to learn their personal stories, and she didn't think a criminal past was something she needed to highlight. But subsequent news stories revealed that Poole had been convicted of felony theft sixteen years earlier, and Brownlee had been convicted of narcotics possession in 2012. The revelations sparked a major controversy, as some opinionated stories concluded it was no wonder the pair struggled to find work.

Rather than feeling embarrassed by the brouhaha, Yellen was upset and angry by the insensitive reaction. "To me these were people whose lives had been badly affected by the recession," she recalled seven years later. "They were really struggling to get back on their feet. Some newspapers made a big deal that these individuals had criminal records. I pointed out that a very large share of Americans— almost a third of adults—have some sort of criminal record. It is a huge impediment to people gaining employment. They are part of a disadvantaged group of Americans who are made to pay their whole lives for a mistake from their past. The truth is that a strong job market increases the chances that those with prison records can get jobs and build careers."

On November 17, 2017, more than three years after she gave that speech in Chicago, Yellen was on a New York–bound Amtrak train from Washington for an appearance at New York University's business school. She was reviewing her notes as a man carrying a restless toddler walked up and down the aisle to soothe the child. Suddenly, he approached Yellen and introduced himself as Sam Bell, founder of Employ America, an economic think tank that promotes full employment policies. "You're Janet Yellen, aren't you," Bell said. "I want to tell you what an enormous difference your monetary policy has made to the life of a close friend of mine who lost his kids after the recession because he had a prison record and was unable to get a job or get his kids back. Now we have this really strong labor market, and he's gotten a job and he's getting part custody of his kids."

In the fall of 2021, then as the first woman to serve as secretary of the Treasury in American history, Yellen reflected on the symbolism of that Chicago speech and Bell's unexpected tribute. "I thought it was really critical to communicate that monetary policy is being made for Main Street and not for Wall Street," she explained. "I tried to use my speeches and meetings as a way of making that clear." When she said "Main Street," she meant everyone, even those who run afoul of the law and have the toughest time getting back on their feet.

Her feelings demonstrated powerfully that Janet Yellen was not your father's Fed chair—or Treasury secretary. Her ability to show empathy toward the disadvantaged in society, including felons, is a signature trait molded throughout her life. She has wielded it during a historic career in public service: not only the first female Fed chair and Treasury secretary but also the second woman to chair the Council of Economic Advisers, and the only person of either gender to hold all three positions—the "trifecta" of economic policymaking. That record, observed Daniel Tarullo, a former Federal Reserve governor who served with Yellen at the central bank, makes her "the most important woman economic policymaker in history, and the most important in the United States by several orders of magnitude."

"Janet Yellen is set to be the most influential secretary of the Treasury in decades," Adam Posen, president of the Peterson Institute for International Economics, wrote after she was named. "Her unmatched qualifications and personal gifts make that attainable." Republicans and Democrats in the US Senate agreed when they confirmed her to the post on January 25, 2021, with an overwhelming 84–15 vote that belied the deep political polarization gripping Congress. Her confirmation was preceded by a unanimous vote of support from the Senate Finance Committee, whose members from both parties hailed her as the most qualified candidate for the job in history even if they didn't agree with all her positions.

Yet, what makes Janet Yellen so remarkable is not just *what* she accomplished, but *how* she rose to such heights, and *why* she devoted her career to such demanding responsibilities.

By almost any measure, she had a comfortable life growing up just after the end of World War II in Brooklyn, New York. Her father was a physician who earned a good living. His family of four lived in an attractive two-story row house above his office on a suburban-like, tree-lined boulevard. Her mother filled the house with antiques and fancy furniture. The Yellens dined at the finest restaurants in New York and went on cruises to Europe and South America—opportunities many of young Janet's working-class friends could only dream about.

Yet on a nearly daily basis during her youth, Yellen saw the dark and troubled side of life in the eyes and gait of patients who trudged into her father's office with a variety of ailments. They were people struggling to provide for their families. Many were unemployed; some were still suffering hard times from the Great Depression of the 1930s. She saw the pain on their faces. She saw the loss of self-esteem that came from being out of work. She saw how her father always treated his patients with respect and compassion and accepted whatever cash they could afford for an office visit. She never forgot.

It was not until her college years that she decided to become an economist—determined to use her training to make the American economy work for everyone, not just for affluent families like hers. Through college, graduate school, teaching, and the highest economic posts in the United States over a fifty-year career, she dedicated her work to that goal: greater prosperity for everyone. It was not a dream of an idealist but rather a realistic outcome she was convinced was possible when government used its powerful tool kit wisely to spread the wealth in a judicious manner.

At the root of that philosophy was a gift she inherited from her father: empathy. Dr. Julius Yellen did not just feel sorry for his patients, he put himself in their shoes, feeling their anguish and pain. Yellen learned to do that, as well. In all her powerful jobs, as she demonstrated in her speech in Chicago in 2014, she embraced the economics of empathy.

She was empowered to use that gift of compassion and understanding to make a difference during her long career. And she became a most unlikely role model as a result.

> *. . . here comes Yellen with that inside voice.*
> *Never mind the mild manner, policies make noise*
> *She's 5-foot nothing, but hand to God*
> *She can pop a collar, she can rock a power bob*
> *Bay Ridge represent!*
> *Brooklyn's in the cabinet!*
> *Damn, Janet, go and get it—*
> *Fifth in line for president!*
> *. . . It only took a couple centuries*
> *The first female secretary of the treasury*

> —"Who's Yellen Now," lyrics by Dessa ©2021,
> reprinted with permission

She's hardly someone you would think of as a pop culture icon. She's short; she's a senior citizen (she turned seventy-six in 2022); her hair is styled in a plain white bob; she prefers tailored, high-collared, solid-color jackets to a glitzy wardrobe; she retains a slight Brooklyn accent from her youth; and she spends most days absorbed in the arcane world of policymaking.

Yet Janet Yellen has nonetheless emerged as a feminist symbol, much as the late Supreme Court Justice Ruth Bader Ginsburg (RBG) had. Both spent lifetimes breaking glass ceilings to become powerful forces for justice, Ginsburg through the law and Yellen through economics.

When president-elect Joe Biden announced her as his pick for Treasury on November 30, 2020, he quipped, "We might have to ask Lin-Manuel Miranda, who wrote the musical about the first secretary of the Treasury, to write another musical about the first woman secretary of the Treasury." *The Late Show with Stephen Colbert* helpfully obliged by producing its own two-minute spoof, "Her name is Janet Louise Yellen," based on the popular musical, *Hamilton*.

"She really is the RBG of economics," said Michele Jolin, a Washington, DC, attorney who served as Yellen's chief of staff at the Council of Economic Advisers (CEA) during the Clinton administration and has remained a close friend ever since. "She is such an amazing role model for young women," added Jolin, also an outside adviser to the Biden administration, who helped Yellen prepare for her Senate confirmation hearing in January 2021. "Her integrity, her compassion, breaking so many glass ceilings. I hear this so often from young women who admire her so much."

That observation is echoed by David Wessel, a Pulitzer Prize–winning reporter and editor at the *Wall Street Journal*. He covered Yellen as part of his economics beat and then became a colleague of hers at the Brookings Institution, a Washington, DC, think tank, where both were resident scholars prior to her joining Biden's cabinet. "I think she was startled—and I was, too—by how much of a rock star she became among young women," he said. "I mean, every time she spoke, they all wanted selfies with her. She *is* like RBG. She's a symbol of progress, someone who played in a man's game and rose to the top of the heap. I think they find her inspiring because they see what she accomplished, and they know it must have been difficult. And it is complemented by her affect, which is very warm and welcoming."

Mary Daly, a protégé of Yellen's who became president of the Federal Reserve Bank of San Francisco in 2018, recalled a similar reaction by young women: "I went to speak to three hundred high school students from low-income neighborhoods. And this group of young women came up to me afterwards, and they're standing in a giant circle around me and saying, 'Do you know Janet Yellen?' And I said, 'I do.' And they asked, 'Have you talked to her?' I said, 'I have.' And they said, 'Oh my gosh, we've met you and you've met Janet. So, we've kind of met Janet.' It was the most wonderful thing. I went on to talk to them about a lot of things she had taught me, and then I called her up and I said, 'Janet, you're helping people even when you don't know it. They touched me, and now they think they've touched you, and you've probably changed their lives.' They're like, 'I can do anything.' Someone should make a bobblehead of Janet. She's that iconic."

Joanne Lipman, a former editor in chief of *USA Today*, who has written about gender discrimination in the workplace, believes Yellen's iconic status is more than her achievements and role as a trailblazer who has led the way for other women. It also is her stamina and grit while in her mid-seventies. "She has endured. I do think there's something about the pioneer status, but also the fact that she's kept at it," explained Lipman, who wrote *That's What She Said: What Men Need to Know (and Women Need to Tell Them) About Working Together*, a guidebook for how men and women can work together on an equal footing. "There's a growing admiration for older women and their achievements."

In a January 2021 interview with *The Current* about her tribute to Yellen, the rapper Dessa said she watched a lot of online tutorials about fiscal and monetary policy because "I wanted to be sure that Janet Yellen was somebody that I feel comfortable [with], even just in a silly song form. And so, I listened to a lot of her speeches. I read about her history as an economist and she's brave, man. Like, she's gone to bat speaking about how the really dramatic and growing inequities in our society run counter to American values." Dessa concluded: "She ends up being a total boss."

"She is so competent," said economist Laurence Meyer, a private consultant who had served with Yellen on the Fed Board of Governors in 1996. "She was so perfect for every position she was going to get. So, if it was a glass ceiling, it was never going to be a problem for her. She was going to shatter it without any question. I don't think of her so much as the first woman to become secretary of the Treasury as her being just a brilliant appointment."

Yellen was not deterred when she saw the smart boys from her junior high school class siphoned off to nearby public high schools reserved only for gifted boys. She fought archaic rules in college that expelled women who secretly spent a night out of the dormitory with male friends. She not only thrived but shined brightly in a nearly all-male environment in graduate school. She put up with a male social network that largely excluded her during her career as an assistant professor. Undaunted, she wrote trailblazing research papers on economics that are still cited today.

In government, she had to put up with bullying and patronizing by men who dominated the Clinton administration. In the Obama administration, she was an obvious choice to chair the Federal Reserve but was not even considered until a group of men and women in the Senate mounted a campaign on her behalf. Through it all, she never acted the part of the victim; instead, she put her head down and did the best she could with no sense of grievance. Dozens of friends and colleagues describe a woman who is kind, cheerful, and funny, but can be as tough as any man when it comes to arguing the merits of economic policy.

Her track record as an economic forecaster is strong, the result of decades of preparation and careful analysis of the facts. As head of the Council of Economic Advisers, she was an early advocate for a plan to combat global warming. Later, as president of the Federal Reserve Bank of San Francisco, she was one of the early voices concerned about growing economic inequality in the United States and the lack of regulation of the reckless financial practices that triggered the subprime housing mortgage crisis in late 2007. Her forecasting abilities were confirmed by a *Wall Street Journal* analysis of top Fed policymakers' predictions from 2009 to 2012: she came out on top.

Yellen certainly had resources to pull from, including her husband of more than four decades, economist and Nobel laureate George Akerlof, as well as a son, Robert "Robby" Akerlof, an associate economics professor at the University of Warwick in England. Yet it is her own sharp analytical skills and unassuming manner that stick with those who know her from her graduate student days at Yale University; her teaching assignments at Harvard University and University of California, Berkeley; and her various federal policy positions.

"First, I would say it's that she's just genuinely smart, understands issues, and is good at explaining them, but that isn't enough to get you all these jobs," said James Wilcox, a longtime colleague at the University of California, Berkeley, Haas School of Business. "It's also the case that she has earned a reputation for being someone you can work with because she's basically a nice person," he added, trying to explain her extraordinary success. Wilcox, who knows Washington from his stints as an economist at the Fed and Treasury Department in the 1990s, observed that some top officials in government "are just not that much fun, no matter how smart. They just make you grind your teeth down to nothing. Not Janet." And, he admitted, she also had luck on her side: "She no doubt benefited from being in the right place at the right time. After all, it's a big country and there are a lot of really talented people."

Donald Kohn, who preceded Yellen as Federal Reserve vice chair, a position she assumed in 2010, recalled her as a junior member of the Board of Governors in the 1990s, homing in on critical issues that all the other members of the Board of Governors missed. "Quite often, she would just go to the heart of the matter. And it struck me that she was able to do that because her mind was so well-organized," he said. "Her thinking was so logical that she could see where the argument was going, where it was strong, where it was weak, despite the fact that all these really smart people who spoke before her missed those points."

When engaged in a debate, whether with a colleague or member of Congress, she revealed another special skill: an ability to listen to the other side of an argument and respond in a respectful way that did not make the other person feel insulted or put on the defensive. In Washington, that is extraordinarily rare. "When she's doing economics, she's very well-grounded empirically, and it's not just about theory," said David Teece, professor in global business who worked with Yellen for many years at Berkeley's Haas School. "She is not doctrinaire. A lot of well-meaning people get captured by elegant analytical models that may be weakly connected to any recognizable reality. Janet's never been that way. She's always been close to the numbers and close to the facts on the ground and very, very willing to listen to people."

"There's a lot of shoes she's never been in, but she seems to have an ability to think about what it would be like to be in somebody else's shoes," added James Wilcox, "whether it's economic plight and financial problems, personal lives and medical conditions, particular pluses and minuses of whatever job or boss they're working with, what the company does. Somehow, she seems to be able to work her way through what other people's prospects and problems are."

As an influential official in government, Yellen employed her ability to put herself in others' shoes to find a remedy for their financial plight. Most often their problems stemmed from poverty, unemployment, job discrimination, or a lack of economic opportunity resulting either from a disadvantaged background or just bad luck. At the Federal Reserve, White House Council of Economic Advisers, and Treasury Department, she emphasized the need to reduce poverty, unemployment, and economic inequality.

When she became Fed chair, she elevated those issues to be more important concerns—problems the central bank traditionally had downplayed. Under her leadership, the Fed kept interest rates low enough to let the economy run a little hotter—at the risk of slightly higher inflation—in an effort to accelerate job and wage growth for lower-income workers.

As Treasury secretary, Yellen doubled down on her conviction that empathy should be at the center of economic policy by providing people the resources they need to build more productive and environmentally friendly lives. The result is more inclusive prosperity and a sustainable climate.

In a virtual appearance at the annual World Economic Forum at Davos, Switzerland, on January 21, 2022, Yellen called for government to pursue "modern supply side economics," which focuses on the need to expand and enhance human capital rather than just monetary capital. Conservative "supply side economics" enacted by the Reagan administration in the 1980s emphasized tax cuts and deregulation to boost output through increased private capital investment. "It is, unquestionably, important to properly implement regulation and maintain a pro-growth tax code, but they are not sufficient and can often be overdone," Yellen said, as she plowed new ground for someone holding her cabinet post. "Modern supply side economics, in contrast, prioritizes labor supply, human capital, public infrastructure, R&D [research and development], and investments in a sustainable environment. These focus areas are all aimed at increasing economic growth and addressing longer-term structural problems, particularly inequality."

Economist Michael Katz, a student of Yellen's at Harvard and later a colleague at Berkeley, sees empathy as the core of his former professor: "I just know from talking to her that she's really concerned with how people are doing, particularly how less advantaged people are doing. I would like to think that people in government are always like that, but I've been in government and I know they're not. That's the thing about her that makes her such a good person to be in public policy. She's very empathetic and extremely smart and knowledgeable, as well. She's also intellectually honest and tries to get to the right answer without fanfare. There are people who are very pleased with themselves for being smart and make pronouncements. Instead, she is just very humble about this stuff."

Yale mentor and longtime friend Joseph Stiglitz observed that Yellen's empathy and keen interest in attacking economic inequality and other social ills was bolstered during the late 1960s, when she was studying for her PhD. "The milieu at Yale back then was one of very strong concern about societal problems," said Stiglitz, who would precede her as chair of President Bill Clinton's Council of Economic Advisers and would later share a Nobel Prize in economics with Yellen's husband, George Akerlof. The terrible toll the Great Depression exacted on society and the persistent problem of inequality were emphasized in economics classes. "Looking back, she fit into that milieu of people who were concerned about these issues. If you remember, this was the sixties, and it was just part of the culture of young people."

Yellen's idealism is something many others arrive with when they first come to Washington. But so many then develop "Potomac Fever," as their desire to do good for society transforms into a drive to do well for themselves. They chase fame, power, status, and wealth.

During the summer of 2020, when election polls showed Joe Biden with a steady lead over Trump, Biden's brain trust for his presidential transition concluded that Yellen would be the best fit for Treasury. She had the experience, credibility with Wall Street, confidence of the progressive wing of the Democratic Party, cordial relations with many Republicans in Congress, and a reputation for collegiality. And, of course, she would bring Biden's promise of diversity to his cabinet.

It took several weeks of self-reflection before she was willing to return to public service. Her initial reluctance to take the Treasury post fit a pattern. She expressed the same hesitation about heading up the Council of Economic Advisers in 1997, becoming president of the Federal Reserve Bank of San Francisco in 2004, and returning to Washington as Fed vice chair in 2010. She was savvy enough to never shut the door entirely when offered the positions, knowing what good career opportunities they were. Yet she first wanted to assess whether she had the appropriate skills, would find the work as satisfying as what she was doing, and could make a difference for the betterment of society. The status did not seem to be the primary allure. Ultimately, she said "yes" to every offer.

Yellen's philosophy and the way she executed it resulted in a strong track record of accomplishments. In 2021, the new administration faced a set of problems that was every bit as historic as was her selection. The ongoing pandemic had caused the steepest economic collapse since the Great Depression—even worse than during the Great Recession—and the recovery was uneven and unfair. Highly educated workers largely kept their jobs, and those with investments profited greatly when the stock market rebounded into record territory. The main economic casualties of the pandemic-triggered crisis were lower-skilled, low-paid workers in the service industry, along with women who lacked childcare at a time when schools and daycare facilities were shuttered.

Yellen underscored this problem on her first day in office, shortly after she was sworn in on January 26, 2021. In a "Day One Message" to the department's eighty-four thousand employees, she implored them to help those in need because of the "K-shaped recovery." That is how economists described a pandemic-scarred economy that produced ever greater wealth for high-income Americans and deepening economic plight for the less fortunate.

"Long before COVID-19 infected a single individual, we were living in a K-shaped economy, one where wealth built on wealth while certain segments of the population fell further and further behind," she wrote. "Our Department can play a major role in addressing [the crisis]. After all, economics isn't just something you find in textbooks. Nor is it simply a collection of theories. Indeed, the reason I went from academia to government is because I believe economic policy can be a potent tool to improve society."

Upon taking office, the Biden administration's proposed response was as historic as the challenge: the biggest expansion of government since President Lyndon Johnson's Great Society of the 1960s. It represented a reversal of the Reagan Revolution of the 1980s that had chipped away at Big Government, a trend continued under Republican and Democratic administrations.

The first step was a $1.9 trillion relief package passed in the spring of 2021. Despite Biden's pleas for a bipartisan plan, it only attracted Democratic votes in Congress. Not a single Republican supported the program, which represented the biggest boost for low-income workers and those living in poverty in fifty years.

The relief package was only the first step. The administration also struggled throughout 2021 to win congressional support for several trillions more in spending to improve the nation's infrastructure and expand other social needs long ignored, including childcare and long-term care for the elderly, job training, clean energy development, affordable housing, and union protections. The immediate response from Republicans, not surprisingly, was to label such ambitious spending as a nonstarter. A sole Senate Democrat hesitant about the high cost denied Biden the bill's passage and forced the president to shelve his Build Back Better program, which appeared dead in 2022. But Biden won bipartisan support for a $1.2 trillion infrastructure package he signed into law on November 15, 2021.

Even at a reduced level, such massive spending during 2021 had few precedents. Would it rapidly heal an otherwise healthy economy that was briefly devastated by the pandemic-forced shutdowns? Or would it prove to be reckless spending that would result in a return to an inflationary spurt unseen since the 1970s? Yellen and Fed chair Jerome "Jay" Powell initially defended the optimistic scenario, as the Fed kept its interest rates near zero until 2022 to ensure a return to full prosperity without letting inflation get out of control.

Many other economists warned that the dark scenario of sharply higher inflation was more likely. They were right, pointing to a rate above 8 percent in 2022, the highest in four decades. Yellen, nonetheless, could take comfort in the fact that 2021 also marked the best year on record for the labor market: record job gains, a historic drop in the unemployment rate, a sharp rise in pay—the largest increase benefiting low-wage workers—and major improvements in working conditions. The result was a narrowing of the economic inequality gap, which brought her great satisfaction. Yes, those gains were being eroded by rising inflation. Yellen believed, however, that temporary supply and labor disruptions caused by the pandemic were principal drivers of higher prices and that inflation eventually would come back down as the pandemic faded and the Federal Reserve did its part by boosting interest rates. Improvements in the labor market, by contrast, would be lasting. Typical of her lifelong economic philosophy, Yellen saw the welfare of workers as a top economic priority.

It likely will take years to determine which economic scenario takes firm hold. Will the economy embark this decade on a long period of growth with a return to low inflation, an expanding job market, rising wages, and greater income equity? Or will the economy be dragged down by stubbornly high inflation, a stock market collapse, a rapidly expanding national debt, or Russia's invasion of Ukraine? The brutal attack led to unprecedented economic sanctions against Russia that roiled the global economy, shocked financial markets, and sent gas prices soaring. Yellen entered her job well aware there are no models that can accurately predict what will occur during her tenure at the Treasury Department. She knew it would take a lifetime of hard work, organization, preparation, and shrewd economic analysis to find the proper course ahead.

For Janet Yellen, it was never enough to leave a legacy as the first female Treasury secretary or as a feminist icon who smashed through glass ceilings. "Who's Yellen now?" to quote rapper Dessa. Her reply would be: a Treasury secretary who employed empathy economics to make society better.

As she well knew, success in achieving that lofty goal could not be guaranteed.

# - 1 -

# IN PURSUIT OF PERFECTION

*"My father . . . had a visceral reaction to economic hardship"*

FOR THE FIRST WAVE OF BABY BOOMERS BORN IN NEW YORK City in 1946, Bay Ridge was an ideal place to grow up. Located at the southwestern tip of Brooklyn with a grand view of New York Harbor, Staten Island, and the Verrazzano-Narrows Bridge from its western ridge, this community was a vibrant melting pot that attracted residents of varying ethnic, religious, and economic backgrounds. Among those who found a safe and comforting childhood in Bay Ridge was Janet Yellen, the second child of a family doctor and former elementary school teacher.

The area had long been inhabited by Native Americans until the Dutch arrived in the seventeenth century—later bringing slaves—and drove out the indigenous residents to form a farming community, according to a 2019 history of the region, *How Bay Ridge Became Bay Ridge*, by Henry Stewart, a Bay Ridge native who has written two other books about this section of Brooklyn. The Dutch called their settlement Yellow Hook after the color of the clay but changed it to a more pleasant-sounding and geographically appropriate name, Bay Ridge, in 1853, perhaps influenced in part by negative publicity about a severe outbreak of yellow fever in New Orleans that year.

The area also was a strategic location for the British, who defeated the Americans in the Battle of Brooklyn on August 27, 1776, one of the early battles of the Revolutionary War. In 1825, the US Army began erecting a military base on the southern tip to guard New York Harbor along with Fort Lafayette, located on a small island just off the coast, and Fort Wadsworth on Staten Island. Completed six years later, the new fortification was named Fort Hamilton after the nation's first secretary of the Treasury. Janet Yellen grew up less than three miles from the fort, never imagining at the time that she would take the same solemn oath of office as Alexander Hamilton had 232 years and seventy-seven male occupants later.

While northern Brooklyn became increasingly cosmopolitan during the nineteenth century, Bay Ridge retained its mostly rural character, according to the introduction to a book of photos published by the Bay Ridge Historical Society. It described "farmhouses, summer cottages and stately homes [that] dotted the shoreline" along the Narrows. Around the turn of the twentieth century, Bay Ridge became a magnet for Norwegian immigrants in part because the seaside hills reminded them of their homeland.

In anticipation of the construction of the subway in 1916, the historical society observed, "Bay Ridge increasingly began to change from its rural setting into a thriving community of row houses, stores and trolley cars." After World War II, it remained heavily Scandinavian and became the largest Norwegian community in the United States, holding an annual Miss Scandinavia contest. But Bay Ridge by then also included a large contingent of Irish, Italian, and German Catholics, Christians from Syria and Lebanon, and a small Jewish population. Economically, it was very diverse:

prosperous residents lived in large homes close to the shoreline, and middle- and working-class families lived in row houses and apartment buildings farther east. Bay Ridge was all white but for a few Blacks stationed at Fort Hamilton. Indeed, for many years the area celebrated its connections to Robert E. Lee and Stonewall Jackson, both of whom spent a few years stationed at Fort Hamilton before the Civil War.

Even as the neighborhood became more cosmopolitan in the postwar years, it retained a sense of a close-knit community, where everyone mingled regardless of economic or ethnic background, crime was rare, homes had front and rear yards where neighbors congregated, and abundant parkland wrapped the shoreline like a green ribbon. "Several of us recently have been talking about how lucky we were to grow up in Bay Ridge at that time," said Susan Stover Grosart, a former classmate and close Yellen friend who has stayed in touch over the years. "Friends' houses were open, people just walked around the neighborhood, we went to the park and played sports or went to the playground," added Grosart, who later worked as a Head Start teacher. "It was in so many ways a *Leave It to Beaver* life."

This is where Julius and Anna Ruth Yellen raised Janet and her older brother, John, who was born four years earlier. "It was wonderful in its way," recalled Yellen, echoing the fond memory of Bay Ridge that her friend, Susan, had described. "I feel like I had a very peaceful, pleasant time growing up there. We went to the public schools, which were excellent. There was a big mix of people and they generally got along. There wasn't much racial diversity at that time, but it was a melting pot. I had a wonderful group of friends, it was a safe residential neighborhood, there was nothing disruptive at all about life."

Today, Bay Ridge looks very much like the way Yellen described it, although the residents and shops reflect far more diverse ethnic and racial backgrounds. Residential streets are tree-lined and quiet; homes and apartments are well maintained; and there has been little new construction in the last sixty years.

❖ ❖ ❖

Yellen's father, Julius, was a first-generation American, the youngest of five siblings whose parents immigrated from a town in Poland west of Warsaw. Julius, who was born in Manhattan, attended City College of New York, the first member of his family to go to college. "He got the break that the other kids didn't," said his son, John. "They wanted to see him succeed." Julius, who worked in the post office to help cover college costs, aspired to be a doctor. However, he could not get into a US medical school, a barrier he blamed on rampant anti-Semitism in the 1920s and 1930s. So, along with several Jewish acquaintances who encountered the same discrimination, he traveled to the University of St. Andrew's in Scotland to get his medical degree.

Anna Ruth Blumenthal, a native of Jersey City just across the Hudson River from New York, was the only child of proud and proper German Jews. She went to Hunter College and became an elementary school teacher. She and Julius met while taking a summer course together. When they decided to get married, "they had two weddings, a secret wedding before my father went off to medical school and a nonsecret wedding," according to John. "I guess it was because they were young, they wanted to be able to sleep together, and they came out of a background where you just don't do that."

"That was an age where there was a very traditional morality, and that's the background that both my parents came out of," explained John. "In terms of our growing up, that morality was really important." Julius and his secret wife, Ruth, who went by her middle name, were officially married on March 29, 1934, the year he finished medical school.

Julius became what his son described as a "real old-time country doctor," working out of an apartment on Colonial Avenue, where John spent the first years of his life. Around the time Janet was born, the family moved to a spacious two-story attached brownstone on more upscale Ridge Boulevard, a tree-lined thoroughfare three blocks east of the shoreline. The family occupied the main and second floors, and Dr. Yellen's office was in a lower floor partially below street level with its own stairs to the entrance.

It wasn't a huge house but quite spacious compared to the apartments where many of Janet's and John's classmates lived. The first floor above Julius's office had a large living room; a formal dining room; and a small, narrow kitchen with a table where Julius and Ruth would have coffee in the morning. The kitchen led to a small backyard, where Julius tended to hydrangeas he grew there. The second floor had three bedrooms; a fourth room that served as a combination den, workroom, and playroom; and the home's sole bathroom. Ruth had fine taste and decorated the home with high-quality mahogany furniture and antiques that included a Federal-style mirror, a mantle clock, a crystal chandelier, and fine china. She collected toby jugs, pottery of seated figures dating back to the eighteenth century. Ruth also decorated the house with wallpaper with borders wrapped around the tops of the walls. One pattern was of flowers connected by vines that young Janet hated because they reminded her of snakes.

Being a family doctor in Bay Ridge made Julius and his family among the most prosperous people in the neighborhood, and that had a huge impact on the elder Yellens' self-esteem, outlook on life, and expectations for their children. "From his and my mother's perspective, they were really successful," said John. "My father wasn't a specialist. He was just an ordinary GP [general practitioner]. But that was a step up for them, I think an extremely important step where you 'move up' in the world. I think my parents were extremely satisfied, and I was really proud that my father was a doctor respected in this working-class community.

"Looking back, I realize I grew up with a sense of real privilege, that I was at the top of that status hierarchy in my world." And in this mainly working-class community, privilege also meant that John and Janet would be among the minority of residents to go on to college and graduate school, achievements their parents just assumed for their children.

Both proved their parents' assumption correct. John received a PhD in anthropology at Harvard University and became a renowned archeologist who has spent many years doing research in Africa with his equally distinguished wife, Alison Brooks, a paleo-anthropologist at George Washington University. He became program director for archaeology at the National Science Foundation and the founder and president of the Paleoanthropology Society. His sister got her PhD in economics at Yale University en route to a groundbreaking career in government. "I was a good boy and Janet was a good girl, too," said John. "Neither of us ever rebelled against our family in the slightest. We just did what they wanted." And their parents were immensely proud of their success.

Julius Yellen was highly regarded in Bay Ridge as a good man and a caring physician, although he didn't want patients to know what was wrong with them. "This is a very old-fashioned way of looking at the world. I'm your doctor. You ought to trust me," explained John. He made house calls twice a day and felt compassion for patients who were down on their luck, many still scarred physically or emotionally by bad times in the 1930s and by World War II. For those who couldn't afford to pay, he waived his charge.

At the end of the day, son John remembered, he would talk to his family about what work meant to his patients, the loss of dignity and self-worth that followed when they lost a job. He felt their pain, and that empathy gene was implanted in his daughter, who has waged a lifelong campaign to help the less fortunate in society.

For young Janet, the plight of the disadvantaged was something she saw close-up, in the people who came to her father's office. In a message to the Treasury staff after she was confirmed as secretary on January 26, 2021, Yellen explained why she had become an economist: "My father was a doctor in a working-class part of Brooklyn, and he was a child of the Depression. He had a visceral reaction to economic hardship, telling us about patients who lost their jobs or who couldn't pay. Those moments remain some of the clearest of my early life, and they are likely why, decades later, I still try to see my science—the science of economics—the way my father saw his: as a means to help people." Childhood friend Barbara Schwartz, who has known Yellen since kindergarten, attributed the Yellen family's compassion to a combination of a religious belief in leading a constructive and beneficial life, and the influence of the Bay Ridge community during the 1950s and early 1960s.

"Partially, it's probably the Jewish background where you have this belief in *Tikkun Olam*. Repair the world is the principle," said Schwartz, who carpooled to Hebrew school with Janet every Wednesday at Congregation Beth Elohim, also known as the Garfield Temple, a reform synagogue in Brooklyn. That concept stuck with them, even though Schwartz, who retired from a career in insurance and finance in 2008 and moved to Atlanta, was never particularly religious. Neither was Yellen, whose interest in being an observant Jew waned over the years, much like her father, who she said was raised as an orthodox Jew but rejected religion in adulthood.

Another childhood friend, Jim Brochu, recalled Julius Yellen as "a very kind and gentle man, very refined looking, very soft-spoken, a lovely guy. I remember his shingle said, 'Dr. J Yellen.'" Brochu, a lifelong New Yorker who became a successful stage actor, playwright, director, and author, said he became Janet's first boyfriend when the two were thirteen.

"They were an all-embracing family," said Brochu, whose own mother died when he was a toddler. "There was a warmth when you entered the Yellen home. There was always something on the stove. And you would get a tray of something immediately upon walking in. So, there was that caring that came from her parents that I certainly think she inherited as a very empathetic human being."

Rich Rubin was a grade school classmate whose father was out of work from time to time. Now a physician who lives in Portland, Oregon, Rubin remembered how sensitive the Yellen family was to the plight of the unemployed, and that sensitivity has remained a part of Yellen's character. "I think she understands that people could be out of work for reasons beyond their control," he said.

*❊* *❊* *❊*

IF YELLEN INHERITED COMPASSION FROM HER FATHER, SHE INherited many more traits from her mother that help explain the historic accomplishments marking her seven decades of life. Ruth Yellen taught her daughter to be superorganized and always prepared, value public service, observe social rules, settle for nothing less than perfection—and always make the most of opportunities that come to financially comfortable families. That meant eating regularly at fine restaurants, wearing fashionable clothes, and going on cruises to foreign destinations.

Her children and their friends from Bay Ridge all describe Ruth Yellen as a woman who was as kind and thoughtful as her husband but with a more forceful personality and the person who ran the family while her husband was treating patients.

Ruth traced her family back to the mid-1800s near Hamburg, Germany. Her father ran a bar in Jersey City near a ferry terminal where passengers were transported to and from Manhattan. He lost the bar after the ferry service was terminated and had to get a job as a postman. Although Ruth had a college degree, she chose to give up her teaching career to become a housewife and doctor's assistant when the children were born.

Julius's entire day was taken up by his practice. He'd get up in the morning and drive off in his Oldsmobile to make house calls. Then he would have office hours and make another round of calls after that. The family would always eat dinner together at the early supper hour of 4:45 p.m., so Julius could return to work for evening office hours.

The Yellens' life changed dramatically when John was around seven and Janet barely more than a toddler. Julius fell down the back stairs to his office and cracked his skull. He ended up blind in one eye and couldn't drive anymore. So, Ruth had to drive him twice a day on house calls and sit in the car reading a newspaper or book while her husband treated patients.

Ruth ran the family and also took over the family finances. At the time, Dr. Yellen was usually paid in cash—John remembered him carrying a wad of bills with a rubber band around it in his pocket. Ruth later told John that his father never kept detailed records of his payments so when it came time to pay his taxes, he estimated it. "She didn't get the sense that he was being devious, but he'd say, 'Oh, gee, I did a little bit better this year. So, I think I will say my income is this and I'll pay this much income tax.' When my mother found out, she was just terrified. So, she took it over and she did all the income taxes."

One of Ruth's passions was the stock market, which she discussed with a cousin, Peter, who had worked for IBM and was an investor. She had a handful of shares in companies such as Reynolds Tobacco and AT&T and would follow their prices religiously. Every evening after dinner, she would send John down to the corner to Hinsch's candy store to pick up the last edition of the *New York World-Telegram and The Sun*, which listed closing stock prices. "And then she'd sit in the living room on a green sofa with her feet up on a coffee table, and she'd have an envelope. On the back of an envelope, she'd write in her little, neat handwriting the stocks and the prices," he said. His sister attributed her own interest in finances and investing to her mother.

Ruth was highly organized. "In terms of how your brain works, I'm closer to my father and Janet has my mother's brain," John continued. "My mother had that same kind of potential as Janet." He remembered his mother was an obsessive-compulsive about keeping their home neat and organized. She covered the couches with slipcovers and changed the drapes twice a year. Not satisfied to stop there, she would go to Hinsch's and repeatedly try to persuade the owner to better organize his store, a frequent prodding he did not take well.

She was an avid reader and had a collection of books in the living room. W. Somerset Maugham and Oscar Wilde were among the authors who stood out in John's mind.

She was community-minded, serving on the school PTA, and as a den leader when John was a Cub Scout. After Julius became partially blind, she volunteered to produce books in Braille because she thought there wasn't enough quality literature for the sight-impaired to choose from. She bought a special machine that typed the pages with raised dots used to read by touch and produced entire books.

Another trait that stood out to her children and their friends was her insistence on following a strict dress code and always showing proper etiquette. "My mother was quite elegant. She cared a lot about how she looked and dressed," said her daughter. "She had her set of rules. If you went into Manhattan, you were supposed to wear white gloves; and you didn't wear white shoes after Labor Day. We went on a number of cruises, and you always had to look just right. My mother must have taken five trunks full of clothing for the four of us. I can still remember getting off the ship to clear customs in New York and seeing this gigantic set of luggage on the dock." Janet's friend Susan Grosart remembered Ruth was determined that her daughter was going to have a wonderful wardrobe as she prepared in the summer of 1963 to head off to Pembroke, the women's residential college at Brown University in Providence, Rhode Island. Ever since, Yellen has dressed well in high-quality, tailored outfits, whether teaching a class of college undergraduates or running the Federal Reserve, where she was known for her high-collared jackets purchased from the upscale women's boutique Nina McLemore in fashionable Chevy Chase, Maryland.

Food was very important to Ruth. The family always had complete dinners at home and ate at fine restaurants on many Sundays and on Wednesday evenings, when Julius took off from work. As a result, Yellen became a lifelong "foodie." She has eaten at some of the best restaurants in the world and is admired for her gourmet cooking. Virtually every friend remembered dining with her at a top restaurant or eating an amazing meal in her home served with a vintage wine. Some friends recalled the exact meal and wine decades later.

Perhaps the most important trait Ruth instilled in her daughter was the drive to be the best at whatever you do. It meant striving to be perfect, and that goal can produce a lot of anxiety if you worry about falling short. But for someone of Yellen's intellectual gifts, it gave her the self-confidence to achieve lofty goals and be undeterred by barriers erected against women in the male-dominated field she pursued. Janet Yellen faced such obstacles her entire life and overcame them without ever looking back or holding any griev-ances. Ruth expected her to plow ahead and win without complaint.

"Janet's mother was not subservient to her father at all," recalled Grosart. "Not that she was domineering. They were truly equal, doing different things, different personalities, but even though she didn't work outside the home, she wasn't the little wife waiting to put dinner on the table. And she was a role model for Janet, and that was true for a lot of us. My mom was a customs house broker. She had a career of her own. Most of us grew up in an era where women were not oppressed and were active in many differ-ent ways. You grow up with that attitude. You don't fall into that line, 'Oh, well, I'm a woman. I shouldn't do this.' It's more, 'I'm good at this. I should do this.' It's just part of who she was and where she is today."

Ruth "was very serious about school," Yellen said. "She did not tolerate deviations from perfection terribly well. If you got any-thing less than an A or an A+, you really had to account for why your grade was less than perfection. I still remember in my first year at Pembroke, when I took German and had to account for why I got a B, one of the few I'd received in college. I really had little interest in foreign languages. And, frankly, I felt a B was good enough. I remember her reaction: that's no kind of an answer to give me that you didn't care enough about it.

"So, this perfectionist thing, where I'm always prepared—and there's a lot of truth in that—it absolutely comes from my mother."

John Yellen had a similar description of their mother: a loving but superorganized and demanding person who insisted that the children achieve top grades through their college years. When he was an undergraduate and wrote letters home, Ruth would reply with letters that corrected his spelling and grammar, hectored him to study hard, and instructed him on how to spend money she sent him down to the penny. To this day, Janet Yellen, whether giving congressional testimony, chairing a meeting, or teaching a class, is the most prepared person in the room.

✣ ✣ ✣

HER MOTHER'S PUSH FOR PERFECTION AND YELLEN'S NATIVE intelligence guaranteed she would be a superlative student. A dozen classmates, many who have had little interaction with her for sixty years, remember her vividly as a brilliant student and overachiever with a broad range of interests that stretched from music, creative writing, travel, anthropology, psychology, and culture to rock-collecting, math, science, biology, and economics.

"Janet was just always the smartest person in the room, but she was also unassuming, humble, and gentle," said Mary Azzara Jacobson, a classmate at Fort Hamilton High School. They worked together on the school newspaper, *The Pilot*, Mary as reporter and Janet as editor in chief. Janet's humility, which virtually every friend and colleague noted, "is not put on. It is for real," said Susan Grosart.

Julius and Ruth Yellen could afford to send their children to private school but chose to send them to New York City's public schools. "The public schools were excellent, and there were some terrific teachers," Yellen recalled.

Janet went to P.S. 102, a five-minute walk from home. Even in grade school, it was clear to classmates that she had the drive to excel while always remaining modest. She didn't hesitate to answer questions in class and was no shrinking violet, but she didn't boast about her achievements. "She's brilliant. She's got this wonderful gift, but she's also a very down-to-earth human being," observed friend Barbara Schwartz. "The time that I remember most with Janet was just her being a really good friend, someone that I loved being around, I had fun with. She was very playful. She had a very good sense of humor. She still has those qualities."

From P.S. 102, the kids went to William McKinley Junior High School for seventh through ninth grades. The school system had just set up a selective program for gifted students to complete three grades in two years. Janet and Florence Capaldo Kimball were among the small group of students chosen for the accelerated curriculum at McKinley. "So, we were a close group at McKinley," Kimball said.

Grosart remembered cowriting a play with Janet in junior high about the Algerian War for independence from France and staging it for the other students. "We were cued into the national and international scene then," she said. "We shared the *New York Times* a lot of days. We were concerned about what was going on in the world."

At the same time, a daughter of a successful physician enjoyed experiences as a teenager that her less affluent friends, such as Susan, could only dream about: summer cruises to foreign ports ranging from South America to northern Europe.

In July 1960, just short of her fourteenth birthday, Janet and her family embarked on a month-long cruise from New York to Buenos Aires and back aboard the *S.S. Brazil*. It was there she met future actor/author Jim Brochu, who was the same age. "The cruise director had put together a mixer for the teenagers," Brochu recalled. "Janet was born three days before me—she's August 13th of '46 and I was August 16th of '46. I guess I was always attracted to older women. Joan Crawford was on the cruise, and we were at a mixer with her two children, which is how I got to know Joan Crawford." Artist Al Hirschfeld, famous for his caricatures of celebrities, also was on the cruise, along with his family. Those chance encounters eventually led Brochu to write a memoir, *Watching from the Wings*, published sixty years later, in 2020, about movie and theater stars he met over the years.

Jim and Janet became fast friends. They explored the ship with another thirteen-year-old from Queens, Carol Overfelder; did the limbo together; and dated briefly back home after discovering they were neighbors in Bay Ridge.

"Here we are in the middle of the ocean, and we found out we lived a block away from each other, so that was a connection right there," Brochu said. "We would hang out after we got home. I got to know her; I think I took her to a dance, too, but I know I had a little crush on her, and I gave her my class ring from school. She still has it. And she told me to my face that she wasn't giving it back," he added with a hearty laugh. Indeed, Yellen admitted she has kept the ring all those years.

"She was studious, serious, absolutely the smartest person, but fun," continued Brochu. "Here we were kids on the ship having conversations with adults. I don't think there were many thirteen-year-olds who could do that, but she certainly could." Brochu did not go to school with Janet; he was sent off to a military boarding school on Long Island, but they have remained in touch over the decades.

Carol Overfelder Kleinman remembered the cruise vividly. Only about thirty families made the entire voyage, including the Yellens, the Overfelders, and Jim and his father, and this group spent a lot of time together at cocktail parties and other social events. Carol had one distinct memory of running around the ship with Janet and Jim when they discovered a storage area that contained all the streamers that are thrown from the ship's deck at port departure celebrations. "I think we broke into it or just opened it and were so excited that we found all these goodies."

After they returned home, Jim took Carol to a Christmas dance, "but I learned he apparently was two-timing me because he took Janet out. And he never gave me a ring," she joked. Kleinman and

Yellen did not stay in touch but reconnected at Kleinman's initiative in 1997, after Yellen was named chair of the Council of Economic Advisers. They have stayed in contact mostly through email ever since and had dinner at the 1789 restaurant in Georgetown on November 2, 2017, just hours after President Trump announced he would not reappoint Yellen as Fed chair but would nominate Fed governor Jerome Powell instead to replace her. It was a somber evening as they tried to relax over fine food and wine, laughed about happy times in the past, and tried not to dwell on the deeply disappointing event that had transpired earlier that day.

❖ ❖ ❖

As she entered high school, Janet encountered the first of many social barriers that stood in the way of women. Students completing junior high school took a test, and those with high scores had the option of attending a special high school for bright students rather than their local high school. At the time, however, the two closest schools for gifted students—Peter Stuyvesant in Lower Manhattan and Brooklyn Tech—were open only to boys. Gifted girls like Janet could go to Hunter College High School for girls on the Upper East Side of Manhattan or Bronx Science, a co-ed school, but both were quite a distance away and entailed long commutes. Neither was a viable option for Janet, who decided along with her circle of girlfriends to attend "The Fort," as Fort Hamilton High was known. Built in 1941 along the shoreline, the school is an imposing structure with a classical Greek front and a watch tower that offers a panoramic view of the Verrazzano-Narrows Bridge, New York Harbor, Staten Island, New Jersey, the Statue of Liberty, and Lower Manhattan.

Yellen didn't apply to any of the high schools for gifted girls, nor did her friends. They were happy to attend Fort Hamilton

High, which had a strong academic reputation and a roster of good teachers. "Fort Hamilton was an excellent school," she said. As it turned out, Yellen thrived at The Fort, where she became the first illustrious graduate to be enshrined in the school's Hall of Fame thirty-three years after she departed.

She thrived there because, ironically, the gender bias in the school system that the bright girls of Bay Ridge encountered in the early 1960s proved to have an unexpected upside for them: the brightest kids at Fort Hamilton High were girls. They had no competition from the bright boys siphoned off for the special schools, so they dominated the honors classes and the attention of their teachers. They comprised 80 percent of the honor roll. They ran the school newspaper, *The Pilot*; the literary magazine, *The Anchor*; and the yearbook, *Tower*. "Maybe that's why the women in my class rose to all kinds of professional positions and had more opportunities in high school than they would have if all of these other bright male friends hadn't gone off to Stuyvesant and Brooklyn Tech," Yellen reflected. She became editor in chief of *The Pilot* in her senior year and wrote poems and short stories for *The Anchor*. Charles Saydah, a classmate, worked on the newspaper with Janet, became a journalist, and worked for years at *The Record* in Hackensack, New Jersey. "Janet and a lot of the other girls could have run with any of those guys who went to Stuyvesant and Brooklyn Tech," he said. "We knew that in junior high school. But they didn't because they couldn't."

Mary Jacobson said none of the girls felt gender repression "because there were no barriers to excelling. We did very well. I never remember feeling that I was going to be outshone by a boy other than in sports. But in terms of intellectual achievements and school leadership positions, there was no barrier or a sense that you couldn't shine."

In those areas, no one shone brighter than Janet. She was the top student in her class of six hundred. She received a perfect score on a Regents geometry exam. She studied geology on Saturday mornings at the American Museum of Natural History. She was in a science honors program at Columbia University. Her mother sent her to private speech lessons to get rid of the Brooklyn accent, though she still retained a trace of it through the years.

Janet and Susan Stover Grosart attended Sunday matinees of classical concerts for schoolchildren at Lincoln Center, courtesy of wealthy patrons of the arts. "Schools got tickets on a rotation basis, and when it came to our high school, nobody seemed to want to go. So, she and I would go, and it was fabulous. World-class concerts and musicians," Grosart said. During their junior year, the pair were selected for a weeklong series of lectures at the Rockefeller Institute during a school vacation period. "There was just a whole lot that went right over my head, but it was really fascinating to have the chance to hear world-class scientists talking about different things," she added.

The only academic part about school that freaked out Yellen were the pop quizzes an English teacher gave in tenth grade. "It drove Janet crazy, absolutely crazy because she works harder than anyone else to be totally prepared. But you couldn't prepare for them, and it used to drive her nuts," Grosart laughed. "Of course, she did well anyway."

It wasn't always nose to the grindstone. Grosart recalled that shortly before graduation, the two of them, "both really goody two-shoes," and a third classmate, who has since died, played hooky and went to Coney Island for the day. "We rode the Thunderbolt and the Cyclone, the rollercoasters there, over and over again. Then Janet said, 'Let's go try the Parachute Jump!' Now, I don't know if you know anything about the Parachute Jump. It looks like an erector set that's about to fall down. Somehow, she talked me into getting into this swing with her, and I've been afraid of heights ever since." The 250-foot-tall ride took seated riders to the top along guide wires and then released them in a swift fall as the parachute opened. The ride, which ended with a forceful bounce into a net, terrorized generations of Coney Island visitors. Built for the 1939 New York World's Fair, the Parachute Jump was discontinued, but the tower remains as a historic landmark.

Adele Corradengo Wilson saw the first inklings of Janet's astute analytical skills that flourished during her career as an economist: "In Mr. Davino's senior English class, we were discussing a poem about how a flower is not the same if you take it apart. And I remember Janet saying she thought that was really naive because you really need to examine things. And the more you examine them, the more you see in them and understand them." A decade later, Yellen used that reasoning in advising a PhD candidate at Harvard, encouraging him to look at more angles of his hypothesis. The result was a joint research paper they wrote that remains a trailblazer in the study of monopolies.

One of Janet's passions at the time was rock-collecting, a hobby sparked at age eight by her brother's interest in geology and by family visits to the American Museum of Natural History, which houses an impressive wing dedicated to minerals. She and John started buying samples in the museum shop. As their interest grew, her mother wrote to mining companies, such as Phelps Dodge Corporation in Arizona, and asked them to send them samples of minerals that they unearthed. "I can't imagine any company would do this now, but my recollection is that maybe five or six of them sent us minerals that became the core of our collection," Yellen said. "They were things that you wouldn't find in New York." Eventually her collection grew to two hundred specimens. During her junior year in high school, Janet became part of a citywide geology club. The students would meet at one another's homes and go on mineral-collecting trips to local quarries and trade rock samples. "It's a little bit like stamps. There's a system for cataloging minerals, and we would realize we're missing one and focus on how we could acquire it," Yellen explained. "There were stores in New York that sold minerals. Crocoite, found in Tasmania, was one mineral I wanted more than anything else. It has these spikes of orange crystals. I saved up my allowance for weeks and spotted a specimen in this mineral store. I bought it, and when I came home on the subway, I dropped it. It has this slender web of crystals and it just shattered. I kept all the pieces. It was a significant thing to me. I haven't done anything with it other than drag the rock collection around over the years." Another interest was creative writing. For a class assignment that required short poems, she wrote "Journey's End": *Chill winds of time blow strong, the tree is bent, the fruit grows with the red on the vine, a tree without leaves leaves no purpose. Life ebbs.* In a second poem, "Sands of Time," she wrote: *Secure, with wisdom gained through toil and tears, he'll stand with those who've left their footprints on the sands of time.*

For the literary magazine, she wrote a poem, "Soliloquy," about a person who is blind but uses other senses to enjoy each season of the year. It ends:

> *Though I see not*
> *The golden sun*
> *Nor stars at dusk*
> *Nor mountains draped*
> *In purple robes,*
> *I feel not sad.*
> *I pity those*
> *Who sight possess*

*But cannot see*
*As well as I.*

Janet wrote a short story for *The Anchor*, "Who Walks Alone," about a farm boy who desperately wanted to escape his depressing life and bleak future with his alcoholic father, and finally makes a run for it, hoping to catch up with a faint rainbow he sees in the distance. When Charles Saydah read it in school, he said, "I thought it was incredibly pretentious. It was really laid on thick, talking about bending birches, the comfort that the solitude of the forest gave him and stuff like that. It was affected. As an old man, I reread it. And you know, Janet's held up really well. I said, Jesus, there's a lot in there. She incorporated a lot of stuff and it's pretty good."

The school newspaper occupied much of her senior year, as she cranked out thoughtful editorials on a variety of topics under the guidance of *The Pilot*'s faculty adviser and an early mentor, Jacob Salovay. "He was a very instrumental teacher for us," said Mary Azzara Jacobson. "He had been head of the paper since shortly after the school opened in 1941. Like a number of teachers who had served in the war, he was two years in the Navy. He was married, had no children, and was dedicated to the school. Even though the school was only twenty years old, *The Pilot* had won the Columbia Scholastic award for the best newspaper twelve times. We were very proud of that, and we loved him."

Jacobson recalled Salovay inviting her, Janet, Charles, and other staff to his apartment for dinner with him and his wife. "We felt so special. I still remember these book-lined shelves. He was a unique person." Fifty years later, around the time Yellen was nominated for Federal Reserve chair, Jacobson arranged to meet her in New York before a speech to the Economic Club and handed her a copy of some published poems Salovay had written. Yellen would recite one of them during a commencement address she gave to the Fort Hamilton High School Class of 2021.

Janet's editorials revealed an early interest in foreign affairs and public policy, particularly economics. One noted that the school had two foreign exchange students, one from Syria, from where many students had relatives, and the other from Vietnam, which was only beginning to emerge in their awareness as a conflict zone. She wrote that the exchange program was valuable in furthering understanding between people from different areas of the world. "Since our generation will help guide tomorrow's world, it's of the utmost importance that we be familiar with different races, creeds, and governmental systems," she wrote. "Many of the participants in this program became leaders in their respective countries. The impression we leave with them is likely to remain in their minds for years to come, so we high schoolers had better show them good behavior."

Another editorial concerned a debate in New York about whether the city should start charging people who could afford the cost of tuition at some of the free colleges, such as Brooklyn College and Queens College, or whether to restrict enrollment to those who couldn't afford to pay. Janet's stance was that the colleges should start charging tuition for those who could pay because that is the only way to raise revenue to finance expanded enrollment. In fact, that ultimately did happen in New York.

Signs of her future interest in labor economics surfaced in an editorial entitled "The Last Term." She wrote about the importance of completing high school to be eligible for a well-paying job, concerned that the million students dropping out of high school would lack the skills needed for the job market.

And her respect for all workers, regardless of status, reveals itself in an editorial entitled "What Kind of Job?" It begins: "Two-thirds of the country's labor force are unhappy with their jobs. Will you become one of them?" It goes on to argue that each person should seek an occupation that suits the individual's specific talents and interests. "Success consists of enjoyment of the work in which one engages, and results from a feeling of pride in one's personal accomplishments. . . . An able mechanic need not consider medicine or law a *more honorable* profession." The editorial notes that universities are "overcrowded with students who would be far happier in vocational schools or on-the-job training." It ends by quoting John Gardner, then president of the Carnegie Foundation for the Advancement of Teaching, who became secretary of Health, Education, and Welfare for President Lyndon Johnson in 1965, that "an excellent plumber is infinitely more admirable than an incompetent philosopher. The society which scorns excellence in plumbing because plumbing is a humble activity and tolerates shoddiness in philosophy because it is an exalted activity, will have neither good plumbing nor good philosophy. Neither its pipes nor its theories will hold water."

❖ ❖ ❖

AS THEY LOOKED BACK ON THEIR HIGH SCHOOL YEARS TOgether, Yellen's female friends felt empowered to succeed despite the barriers that existed, thanks to their parents and teachers, and the good fortune to meet one another. "Our parents pretty much said, you can do or be anything you want to be," said Barbara Schwartz. "We were all going to college, and we weren't going to find husbands. We were going to get an education. That may have been the beginning of feminism and breaking glass ceilings. Of course, it didn't have that label at the time. It was 'You can do what you want to do.' And everybody in our social circle is a high achiever: at least two psychologists, a psychiatrist, a surgeon, someone who clerked for Chief Justice [Warren] Burger."

That may have been the exception for co-ed high schools at the time, said school friend Julie Cohn Lippmann, who retired as a clinical child psychologist and did interviewing for admissions to her alma mater, Cornell. Lippmann said she often heard young women applicants say they chose high-powered all-girls high schools "because it allowed them to have a greater voice and be free of the constraints of the boys overshadowing them."

In high school, where she was a reporter and humor columnist for *The Pilot*, Lippmann remembered, "I wrote some very sarcastic stuff about the different tracks for boys and girls. So clearly the ideas about feminism and achievement were out there, but not so much in our practical experience. I mean, we were pretty hefty achievers, although most of us went initially into the more classic women's professions, such as teachers and social workers. And then eventually a few went to medical school and many went on to greater achievements. But it wasn't the expectation back then."

Lippmann, who laughed that she—not Yellen—had been voted "most likely to succeed," was certain that her friend never pictured herself becoming a traditional wife of the 1960s or a stay-at-home mom. "Janet was taking these science courses, which was not the typical thing that most of us girls were doing. If we went into Manhattan on Saturday, we were probably going shopping at Ohrbach's department store, not taking those courses. So, she must've been generating feminist qualities, but I think it was really more an issue of achievement, a quest for learning, doing what she felt was right for herself and not being afraid to show her intelligence without a lot of concern for what the other members of the class might think."

Classmate Jackie Leo, who made journalism a career, summed up Yellen as someone who was "born a feminist without being a feminist," meaning a woman who never let anything stand in her way toward reaching her goals without making the issue a personal crusade or harboring a victim's sense of grievance or retribution.

"I think it's a fair assessment. I mean, I wasn't actively a feminist," Yellen said when asked about Leo's observation. Throughout her career, Yellen was always very interested in women's issues and usually agreed to participate in programs or events that advance women's rights. "But it's not like I'm sitting around thinking, I face a lot of barriers toward getting ahead. I'm being discriminated against because I'm a woman. I didn't feel that I just had to get married and have a family, and that if you graduated from college without having a Mrs. title, you were a failure in life. I had no such thought."

Joanne Lipman, the former *USA Today* editor in chief who has written about gender bias in the workplace, said Yellen's attitude about feminism is very much a reflection of her age. She grew up at a time before the feminist movement gained traction in the 1960s, when traditional families were the norm. The wife quit her job when she got married and then soon became pregnant. There was no expectation that women would have high-powered careers. Gender discrimination in employment was the norm and no one talked about it. "Women like her were thinking less about the barriers and more about the opportunities," said Lipman.

Over the years, though, Yellen had given much thought to the barriers and how to break them down. "I have had much more occasion to think about all the ways in which women are held back in their careers since I've gotten older and studied women in the workforce more and become more attuned to the problems of women in economics," she said. "I've experienced rising consciousness."

That growing awareness propelled Yellen toward a public-service career fighting for a better life for all, and particularly equal opportunities for women.

That was the spirit of Fort Hamilton High School. The theme of the yearbook, *Tower*, was "building" character and morals, a reference to the construction of the Verrazzano-Narrows Bridge, which she covered as a reporter for *The Pilot*. It was completed a year after her graduation in 1963.

The school motto, emblazoned on the wall in the entrance hall, is "Enter to grow in mind, body and spirit. Depart to serve better your God, your country and your fellow man."

Like the massive bridge going up within sight of the high school, Janet Yellen had a sturdy foundation and was ready to journey across to the wider world. Mindful of the school motto, if not its sexist wording, she set off to college to do just that.

# - 2 -

## AN ECONOMIST EMERGES

*"I found Harvard very difficult . . . a very
hostile environment, with so few women"*

HER STRONG ACADEMIC RECORD GUARANTEED THAT JANET
Yellen would get into a top college of her choice. She had ruled
out the all-female Seven Sisters schools, such as Smith and Mount
Holyoke in Massachusetts, because she wanted a co-ed environment. That made highly rated Radcliffe appealing. It was a college
for women but part of the Harvard University community; female
students took classes with Harvard professors and male students,
and they earned joint Harvard-Radcliffe undergraduate diplomas.

There was a hitch. "I would have been interested in going to
Radcliffe, but it required Latin and Greek, which I had never
taken, nor was I interested in taking," she recalled. Her brother
John took Latin, her mother knew Latin, but "I really had no interest. I wasn't eligible for Radcliffe, but I wanted to attend a good
school." Pembroke in Providence, Rhode Island, seemed like a
good alternative.

Pembroke was Brown University's residential college for women. Like Radcliffe, it had co-ed classes with the men at Brown. Yellen discovered the school while accompanying John on a tour of the Brown campus. "I was impressed by Brown's excellence—and it was an Ivy League school and probably the best place I could get into." She applied for early decision and got admitted. Yellen took an economics course as a freshman and liked it. She already was inclined to enter the field. "I think it goes back to my upbringing and my family and somehow the combination of the Depression, people being unemployed, my father's practice, maybe my mother's interest in the stock market and managing the family." She soon learned how wise policy planners could use their knowledge and economic tools to bring about greater prosperity, thus lifting the prospects of the down-on-their-luck patients Julius Yellen treated. Her commitment to empathy economics was born.

High school friend Susan Stover Grosart said she clearly remembered when they were college freshmen and met over Christmas vacation. "We were walking along the street, and she had taken her first economics course. And she proceeded to give me a long lecture on how wonderful the theory of economics is. She had fallen in love with the field right from the very beginning."

Yellen flirted with math as a major but said she became hooked on economics as a future career because of the influence of classmate Carol Schwartz, who was a couple years older. "We were really close friends at Pembroke and for many years after that. She was majoring in economics and our friendship probably reinforced my interest."

In many ways, Carol Schwartz and Janet Yellen had parallel careers: native New Yorkers with keen intellects, accomplished women who broke glass ceilings in the worlds of economics and finance, both champions of ordinary people.

A May 6, 1981, profile by the *New York Times* of then-married Carol Schwartz Greenwald described a woman born in the Bronx and raised in Long Island who graduated magna cum laude from Pembroke College and earned a master's degree in economics from Brown University. In 1967, she became an economist at the Federal Reserve Bank in New York, moved to the Federal Reserve Bank of Boston in 1968, and earned a PhD in economics from Columbia University in 1971. "During this time, she was already making her way through an old male bastion," the *Times* wrote. "The Fed president in Boston, Frank Morris, took her to a meeting of the Federal Reserve policymaking Open Market Committee in Washington, where she was repeatedly congratulated as the first woman ever to attend such sessions."

In 1973 Greenwald became the first female assistant vice president of the Fed office in Boston, where she was responsible for forecasting business conditions and advising the board on monetary policy. In 1975, Massachusetts governor Michael S. Dukakis appointed her commissioner of banking. During her four-year tenure there, "Mrs. Greenwald earned a reputation as an outspoken battler for consumer rights," the *Times* said. "She outraged banks by accusing them of 'red-lining' certain neighborhoods, within which they allegedly discriminated against blacks and women in granting mortgages."

In 1979 she became an assistant professor at Harvard Business School, and in 1980 was chosen to be the first president of the newly created National Consumer Cooperative Bank, created by Congress to serve economically depressed areas where business and personal loans were difficult to get.

While the two women certainly followed similar professional paths, their personalities and politics could not be more different. The *Times* noted the extreme reactions others had to Schwartz

Greenwald: "Behind what is described as an often-combative personality lies what friends say is a first-rate mind that has enabled the 37-year-old Mrs. Greenwald to lead the way for women into many parts of the American banking community. 'Generally speaking,' said one friend who asked not to be named, 'people who know her either can't stand her or think she's dynamite.'"

Yellen also once thought Greenwald was dynamite, but she no longer has anything to do with her only close friend from college because they veered off in very different political directions. Yellen remembered that when they were students, Carol was a very religious Jew who kept kosher. Over subsequent years, Greenwald became an avid pro-Israel activist and a conservative Republican who embraced Donald Trump's candidacy for president in 2016, cofounding the political group Jews Choose Trump. Yellen stayed in touch with Greenwald even then, and when Yellen was Fed chair the two women met for dinner. But Greenwald's rabid support for Trump became more than Yellen could tolerate. After a lunch during which Greenwald gushed about how wonderful Trump was, Yellen concluded she couldn't continue their fifty-year-long friendship. They stopped talking to one another. Greenwald, who later became a financial adviser in Chevy Chase, Maryland, flatly refused to talk about Yellen and their long friendship.

In addition to her focus on economics, Yellen became involved in student protests over Pembroke's antiquated social code, which barred the female students from leaving their dorms to spend a night with a man. The protest was one of many signs of an emerging feminism across the nation. Many of Yellen's classmates still lived the lives of women from the 1950s—they went to college to meet a man who would make a good living, got married right after graduation, and started a family. If they had careers, they postponed them.

But Yellen's freshman year was a seminal time for the women's movement. *The Feminine Mystique* by Betty Friedan had been published in 1963, as was Gloria Steinem's article about her time as an undercover Playboy Bunny. Doris Lessing's novel on budding feminism, *The Golden Notebook*, had been published the year before. Yellen grew interested in the movement in her junior and senior years and discussed it more intensively while pursuing her PhD at Yale. Her involvement in the protest over the social code was a first step.

"At the time, the women who went to Pembroke lived in separate dorms," she explained. "We had 'parietal rules.' You could sign up for weekends to visit your family, but you weren't allowed to sign out and stay with a guy. And they had rules for Sunday afternoons where you could have guys over to visit you in the dorm, but you had to have at least one foot on the floor. I remember somebody was suspended for breaking these rules, and there were protests that I was involved in, because this wasn't fair."

Phyllis Santry was one of the victims of the rules. A class ahead of Yellen, she was thrown out of school at the end of her junior year in 1965 for being upstairs in a fraternity house with a male student she was dating at the time. "When they throw you out, they don't say you're suspended. They say, you're out. Goodbye, leave," said Santry, who went on to become an urban planner. Her boyfriend had also been thrown out of school.

"When you look back at it, the punishment did not fit the crime," Santry said. "They threw me out of school for being on the second floor of a fraternity house. It was graduation week, and we weren't even having classes. This was an enormous punishment because it didn't matter what we were doing up there. They weren't checking up to see if we were drinking or doing drugs or anything. And this was the Vietnam era. Jerry [her boyfriend] lost his deferment status. He could have been drafted to go to Vietnam."

After spending a semester out of school, Santry was allowed to reenroll and graduate on time in 1966, thanks to credits she earned in summer school. "I know that the year after I graduated, women were allowed to live in apartments off campus. And I guess the university figured this is a little silly to have a rule that they can't go to their boyfriend's room in the dormitory, but they're allowed to have their own apartment off campus," she said. "So, I guess the rules changed after I left."

The protest Yellen joined was sparked by the September 20, 1966, suspension of a junior with an excellent academic record who failed to sign out of her dorm room to spend an evening with a boyfriend. A petition supporting the student was circulated, and fifty students took it to Dean Rosemary Pierrel's residence late that night. The dean, who apparently was asleep, invited a small group of protesters to her office the next day. They complained that the penalty was too harsh and only encouraged girls to lie about where they were spending the night, which could be a problem if the college needed to reach them in a real emergency.

Subsequent protests grew to as many as three hundred students. The student government association appointed committees to reexamine the social code, and Yellen served on one of the panels tasked with overhauling the rules. Eventually they were relaxed.

The strict rules may have existed at the time, Yellen observed, "because abortion was illegal, and this was still the era in which if you've gotten pregnant, that was it. You got married or your life was effectively over. And there were shotgun marriages." Three decades later, she wrote a paper entitled "An Analysis of Out-of-Wedlock Childbearing in the United States" with her husband, George Akerlof, and Michael Katz, a colleague at Berkeley's Haas Business School. The paper found that the legalization of abortion and increased availability of contraception led to a decrease in "shotgun" weddings and, consequently, an increase in out-of-wedlock first births.

Katz, who took an undergraduate course taught by Yellen at Harvard in 1976 and later became an economist, explained the conclusion. "What we observed in the data was consistent with the following conclusion: Because women have more control over whether or not they had children, were they to become pregnant, there would be more out-of-wedlock births because men would not feel socially pressured to marry the women."

Anti-abortion forces subsequently cited the paper to bolster their case, to Yellen's chagrin. "That wasn't our intention, but it was used in that way," she said. "Inventing the pill and then legalizing abortion have given women much more control over their own lives. They didn't have to be protected as much because they could use contraception: take the pill. All of that had a dramatic effect on women's treatment. It was less necessary for parents to protect their daughters from getting pregnant and ruining their lives."

In her senior year at Pembroke, Yellen attended a seminar taught by notable Yale economist James Tobin, who had served on President John F. Kennedy's Council of Economic Advisers and was a renowned Keynesian economist. Like Yellen, Tobin empathized with the less fortunate in society and became a leading advocate of British economist John Maynard Keynes's seminal theory during the Great Depression of the 1930s that governments must step in with big spending programs to bring deep downturns to an end. Tobin promoted the use of the government's spending and tax powers to provide subsidies and help the unemployed find jobs to put food on the table. "When Jim Tobin came to Brown and gave a talk, I was just blown away by him," Yellen said. He left a lifetime impression on her and would soon be mentoring her in New Haven, Connecticut.

* * *

As a summa cum laude graduate of Pembroke, Yellen knew she had her pick of top graduate schools, and applied widely, including to Stanford, Berkeley, Michigan, Harvard, and Yale—but not MIT despite its excellent reputation. Her professors at Brown had discouraged her from attending MIT because its economics focus was highly mathematical. She got into every school she applied to, and it came down to Harvard or Yale. Harvard was appealing because so many renowned economists taught there, and her brother John was a graduate student there at the time. His roommate, a graduate student in economics, described a school "that made me feel it was a cold and nasty place," bolstered by an impersonal acceptance letter she remembered as being brief and cool in tone. Harvard's letter, she recalled, said, "You've been admitted. Let us know your decision by such and such date." In contrast, Yale's acceptance letter was warm and encouraging. "We know you're interested in macro- and international economics," she recalled. "And we have this set of people we think will match your interests."

The biggest lure was Yale professor James Tobin. He was the 1955 winner of the John Bates Clark Medal, awarded to the top economist under age forty, and later the 1981 Nobel Prize. Tobin was known for research showing that government fiscal policy—spending and taxes—was a more effective tool for ensuring a healthy economy than were the Federal Reserve's changes in interest rates and the money supply, as promoted by advocates of "monetarism," led by Milton Friedman. And whereas the monetarists were mostly concerned about controlling inflation, even if that meant increasing unemployment to slow economic growth and consumer demand,

Tobin's main concern was finding ways to increase employment for those who needed jobs to survive.

Yellen cited a famous story from when President Kennedy named Tobin to his Council of Economic Advisers. "I'm afraid you've got the wrong guy. I'm an ivory tower economist," he told the president, and Kennedy replied, "That's the best kind. I'm an ivory tower president." Such an exchange between a US president and an economist enthralled her. When she attended the seminar he gave at Brown, "I thought this was economics the way it should be done. And I wanted to work with him."

She was dazzled by his service on the Council of Economic Advisers and realized that was a career goal she aspired to. "I thought about what I wanted to do with my life, and this was the highest economic policy position with the most distinguished people you had. I love that blend of economics and practice. I read his papers and I was very interested in Keynesian economics. I understood that he was among a handful of the most distinguished Keynesian macroeconomists. I got to know him better and became very close to him over the years." At Yale, he became a mentor who reinforced the empathy she had absorbed through her father. "He was a person with moral passions. Social justice was core to who he was," Yellen explained. "At a time when economics was getting very mathematical and people were doing a lot of theory papers with mathematical analysis, which Tobin himself was very adept at, but for him economics was about human beings and their welfare. He had a kind of moral clarity about him that really, really impressed me. I found it deeply moving."

Tobin remained Yellen's economic North Star until his death in 2002, when she delivered a moving tribute to his influence on her—and American society—at a memorial service on the Yale campus. "For more than thirty years Jim has been my hero. I have been proud to serve as a foot soldier in Tobin's battle for an economics grounded in common sense and for kinder, gentler public policies to alleviate poverty and the needless misery of excessive unemployment," she declared. "What impressed Yale graduate students, though, was not just the clarity of Jim's reasoning but also his intellectual integrity and moral passion.

"Jim's moral compass helped me keep my bearings during my own stint in Washington," she continued, explaining that when she was at the Fed, he often reminded her that allowing a little more inflation was worth the risk to push unemployment down to help the disadvantaged. "The world is a better place because of Jim Tobin," Yellen stated.

"Even more than Jim the economist I shall miss Jim the friend," Yellen concluded. "He was always there when I needed him, as he was for all those whose lives he touched. Jim lived, as he died, taking care of those he loved."

In an oral history she recorded for the Federal Reserve in 2012 to mark its upcoming centennial, Yellen again cited Tobin's influence on her career as a practitioner of empathy economics: "He felt that economists are obligated to respond to calls to serve in government and to apply the tools of their trade to help improve the human condition."

Gary Smith, an economics professor at Pomona College who was a PhD candidate and teaching assistant with Yellen, noted that both she and Tobin shared traits most unusual for economists—"generosity, empathy, and an unpretentious personality."

❖ ❖ ❖

AS MUCH AS SHE LOVED ECONOMICS AND ADMIRED TOBIN, Yellen also came to realize that she was training for a profession that was not welcoming to women, particularly at that time. She was one of the few female PhD candidates in her first year at Yale, and the economics professors were all men. It was yet another case of women being excluded or treated unfairly, as she had discovered before and would again throughout her career.

Yellen remembered one woman in the department, Susan Lepper. "She had a Yale PhD and never rose above instructor. That bothered me. She was being taken advantage of. Women were not well treated in the profession." Lepper died in 2019 at the age of eighty-four. Before her retirement, she had worked as an economist at the Office of Economic Policy in the Treasury Department, which Yellen would later head.

Susan Lepper wasn't the only mistreated woman at Yale, Yellen said. Some of the male professors had wives who were distinguished economists, but they couldn't get professorships because of nepotism rules and would have to settle for research jobs at institutes or write papers jointly with their husbands to get published. Sexist attitudes prevailed among the male faculty members and administrators who justified the paucity of women graduate students as their desire to drop out of school and get married.

Yellen, however, did not feel personally discriminated against. In contrast to Lepper, she was fortunate to have a mentor like Tobin, who was not sexist like so many other males in the department. He treated her respectfully and chose her to be the teaching assistant for the most important core classes in micro and macro theory. Though there were few women graduate students, she felt like the male students included her in their academic and social activities. She was in study groups with them, hung out with them, and dated some of them. "I didn't feel 'Oh, I'm in this totally overwhelmingly male environment where I can't manage,'" Yellen said. In fact, she managed extremely well. In addition to Tobin, she had another distinguished mentor, a young, first-year professor, Joseph Stiglitz, who would go on to precede her as chair of President Clinton's Council of Economic Advisers and share a Nobel Prize with her future husband. She was the top PhD candidate in her class, and, as

Tobin's teaching assistant, took such excellent detailed handwritten notes of the core economic courses he and another professor taught, that they were photocopied and circulated among future generations of Yalies who took economics. Today, those copious notes are part of the university's lore, allowing first-year students to focus on the lectures and not worry about note-taking.

Yellen still has a set of her notes. So does economist Heidi Hartmann—more than one hundred yellowing pages of twenty-six lectures in clear handwriting replete with complicated mathematical formulas and graphs. Hartmann, who received her PhD in economics from Yale two years after Yellen, founded the Institute for Women's Policy Research based in Washington, DC, in 1987, and is Distinguished Economist In-Residence for Gender and Economic Analysis at American University.

Hartmann, who saved many documents from her time at Yale, noted that there was tremendous upheaval in society at the time she and Yellen were at Yale. "The anti–Vietnam War movement was big. Women's liberation began. It was the tail end of the active civil rights movement, and there was a Black Panther trial near campus in New Haven. So, there was a lot going on politically." The trial involved members of the radical group charged with the 1969 murder of a nineteen-year-old fellow Black Panther suspected of being an FBI informant. The year 1969 also marked the first time women were admitted to Yale as undergraduates, a gender breakthrough that was occurring at all-male colleges across the country.

Hartmann, one of two women to receive a PhD in economics out of a class of about thirty the year she graduated, recalled participating in a protest over an all-male private eating and drinking club called Mory's, which was located off campus and served as a popular place for faculty meetings. "In a period when there weren't many women faculty, all of the departments were in the habit of having their business meetings at Mory's. The meeting rooms were upstairs above the little restaurant that was for men only, and women in those departments would literally have to go up the outside stairway that was like a fire escape." Hartmann said the women at the protest would form a gauntlet outside the club and shout at men entering the club, calling them sexists.

"I remember [instructor] Sue Lepper had to go up those out-side stairs to attend meetings of the economics department," Hartmann recounted. "The female graduate students were outraged, and we wrote a petition to the economics department urging them not to eat and have official functions there. About a dozen female graduate students from multiple class years signed that letter, including Janet." Hartmann said she later learned that only two faculty groups stopped holding business meetings at Mory's: the law school and the economics department. Eventually, Mory's opened its doors to women after being threatened with the loss of its state liquor license because of gender discrimination. The club remains in operation.

Yellen only vaguely remembered the Mory's protest because she was more focused at the time on pursuing a successful career. "I went into the job market as one of the top candidates in my year. I got a job at Harvard, and I was really well supported by Joe Stiglitz and Jim Tobin. They recommended me for top jobs. I didn't have any episodes in which I was saying to myself, 'I wanted this and I didn't get it because I am a woman, and I was discriminated against'; I mean, quite, quite the contrary."

During Yellen's final year at Yale, despite a legendary reputation for organization and superpreparedness, completing her PhD turned into a somewhat chaotic sprint to the finish. It turns out that for once, she did not mind the rules her mother drilled into her: she procrastinated and messed around during her final term.

Vivian Nash, who started graduate school at Yale in 1969, lived initially with roommates from hell on the third floor of a house.

She escaped them by "becoming a refugee" on the second floor of an apartment that Yellen had rented for herself. They hit it off and rented an apartment together for the 1970–1971 school year, when Yellen was completing her studies. Their close friendship has endured ever since.

Nash recalled Yellen as seeming very sophisticated because she was from New York City, and Nash was from the small town of Lexington, Massachusetts. But Yellen could also be "extremely silly," recalled Nash, a retired psychologist who lives in Boston. "She was really smart, and she didn't need to work much. There was a radio station in New Haven with a contest about a mystery phone booth. And Janet spent that year driving around New Haven in her Dodge Dart, following the clues, looking for the phone booth. But she never found it. It was very funny."

But then Yellen had to crash to finish her dissertation: "I really had procrastinated." Yellen recalled. "I was a fourth-year graduate student and decided to look for a job. But I don't know what I was thinking to have gone into the job market without having a solid paper written for my thesis. Then Harvard called me and asked if I'd come and do this seminar. And I just panicked. I didn't have a seminar, and I didn't have a paper, and I suddenly wondered what could I have been thinking? I said, 'I'm sorry, I can't come next week.' And they asked, 'Well, when can you come?' I pushed it off three weeks and basically did my paper over the next three weeks." Entitled "Employment Output and Capital Accumulation in an Open Economy," Yellen described it as "quite mathematical—a theoretical thesis about wages and employment in open economies and the way wages influence trade, capital accumulation, employment, and growth."

On to Harvard.

✳ ✳ ✳

By her own account, Yellen's six years at Harvard marked a disappointing time in her career. She was a popular and highly regarded teacher but failed to earn tenure. She wrote a number of strong research papers, but many of her peers did not consider them to be of the highest caliber that led to tenure and star status for professors. She made some friends there yet found the social atmosphere far less welcoming and inclusive than at Yale. It clearly was a trying time for her.

The seminar that Yellen had put together so hastily at Yale went well, and Harvard hired her as an assistant professor. Before accepting, she interviewed with the Federal Reserve for a staff economist position in the international division and was offered the job. Yellen decided Harvard was a better career move in 1971, but the Fed would lure her back in 1977.

Edwin "Ted" Truman, who taught at Yale when Yellen was earning her PhD and sat on her oral exam committee, remembered Yellen's job interview at the Fed in 1971. He was a staff economist in the international department, which he would later head. "She was probably the first person with a Yale PhD in ten or twenty years to get an offer from Harvard," Truman said, noting that the economics departments at Yale and MIT were ranked higher than Harvard's at the time. "The director of the division of international finance and his colleagues tried to recruit her, and she remained on the list of candidates. I was at the Fed and we remained in touch. When things did not work out at Harvard, she went back on the market and we made her an offer. This time she accepted."

There was good reason to think Yellen would not last long at Harvard. The position came with a caveat: don't plan to put roots down here. "When I first came," she recalled, "the dean at the time said, 'Think of this as an interesting six years in which you'll have a lot of freedom to do what you want, but don't think of it as the beginning of a life at Harvard. You'll go off and you'll get tenure someplace else.' The truth is almost no one at that time who was an assistant professor got tenure. So, I didn't expect to. It would have been very unusual. Most tenured people were hired from the outside."

That was Harvard's business model. Hire freshly minted PhDs, tops in their class, give them a heavy teaching load for about five years, work them hard, and then kick them out to become acclaimed economists at other universities. After the market test elsewhere, they might be invited back and offered tenure since they had proven themselves to be stars.

Yellen's son, Robby, agreed that Harvard could treat its young professors cruelly. "That's always been Harvard's attitude: 'You're lucky to hang around here for a few years as an assistant professor and then we'll kick you out. And if you win a Nobel Prize, we'll take you back.' I saw some of that treatment of assistant professors when I was there as a graduate student," he said. "There was an annual skit party that took place at Christmas. It's supposed to be a fun thing where the students make fun of the professors in a nice way and the professors made fun of themselves. I remember in particular one skit where a professor who was one of the more gentle people there mercilessly made fun of one of the assistant professors, and it was quite clear she wouldn't get tenure. It's not a great way to behave." The few assistant professors who received tenure without leaving first "had that quality of being one of the boys," Robby added.

Yellen taught mostly graduate students, enjoyed the job, and proved to be an excellent professor—always prepared, clear in her presentations, and almost always showing up in a different stylish outfit. She was so good that in 1976 she agreed to teach a macroeconomics course also open to undergraduates because the professors who had been assigned the class were weak. "For many years, the macro class was taught very badly, and so toward the end of my time there, someone came and pleaded with me to teach that course," she said.

One undergraduate who remembered her very well back then was Michael Katz, the same student who twenty years later would coauthor the paper on abortions and shotgun weddings with Yellen and her husband, George Akerlof, when they were all at Berkeley.

"She was pretty much the same as she is now—incredibly earnest and dedicated," said Katz, who received his PhD in economics from Oxford University and joined Yellen as a faculty member of Berkeley's Haas School of Business in 1987. "I was somewhat of an obnoxious student, and she would just calmly and professionally answer my questions. I saved my notes from class when I was an undergraduate with her. I looked back at them twenty-seven years later, and they were just incredibly clear. It's not that I am the greatest note-taker but that Janet is an extremely clear thinker and clear presenter. It stood out then as it still does now."

Katz also remembered Yellen for being accessible and unassuming at the time, a rare trait for a Harvard professor. "I was a sophomore in Harvard Yard, and I still remember standing out in front of the dorm. By coincidence she walked by, and I talked to her about some economics stuff and then asked a question about something based on the class. She answered with humor and it was a fun talk. I wasn't used to faculty members doing that."

Her classroom duties gave Yellen the opportunity to teach jointly with luminaries of the profession, such as the late Martin Feldstein, who served as chair of President Ronald Reagan's Council of Economic Advisers in the 1980s. She also instructed future stars, including Lawrence Summers, the future Treasury secretary and president of Harvard University, and Jeffrey Sachs, considered one of the world's leading experts on economic development. Like many other students, Summers, who took her course in the spring of 1976, remembered a young professor who was extremely accurate and precise in her approach.

Among the faculty members who got to know Yellen well is Benjamin Friedman, a leading political economy scholar who started teaching at Harvard in the fall of 1972, a year after she arrived. He had an office around the corner from hers. They often had lunch together and occasionally socialized outside the office. "Two things about Janet really stand out in my mind," said Friedman, one of the rare Harvard professors who received tenure without being forced to leave after a few years. "First was how much macroeconomics she knew. And second, was how extremely articulate she was not just explaining what we know about macroeconomics, but why we think what we know is true."

Although she found teaching rewarding, Yellen thought the social climate was "cold"—as her brother's friend had warned when she had considered going to Harvard for graduate school. Friedman acknowledged that faculty members often felt isolated because they were spread out with offices off of long corridors. "Yale's economics department, which I used to visit, was just much homier in its setup. Imagine a dozen of your friends taking over some old Victorian house and each of you took a room." Friedman also noted that Yale's economics department had a tradition where everyone would gather in a basement lounge each morning at 10:30 for a half hour of coffee and conversation. "It was great. Harvard never had anything like that. We still don't. So, if that's the environment in which somebody has spent four or five years as a graduate student, and then all of a sudden they come to Harvard, where the department is spread out and didn't have any of those social institutions, it would seem isolating. I can easily believe that having come from a very different environment at Yale, she might've been disappointed."

Political economy scholar Jerry Green, a young, single professor who was hired by Harvard in 1970, remembered socializing with Yellen at department gatherings and hanging out with her. "She was very nice, quiet, very thoughtful, and was always interested in people," said Green, who like Friedman, was among the rare assistant professors to earn tenure without having to go somewhere else first.

Green agreed that the social environment was less than embracing and that Yellen never found a mentor to guide her as Tobin had done at Yale. "I think Janet was pretty well treated, but she didn't have close relationships with the older people in her field of macroeconomics. There was a big age gap and that was hard," he recalled. Green found a mentor in economics and political theory, his specialty. "There was no comparable figure like that in macroeconomics. The macro people were—I wouldn't say they were standoffish—but they didn't regard it as their job to bring the next generation along. They were nice people, but there was no single person who was the guiding hand of the group."

The bigger problem was the male-dominated culture. Like at Yale, there were barely any female professors or students in the economics department, and the women often felt excluded academically and socially.

During Yellen's first years at Harvard, there were only two other women on the economics faculty, compared with seventy men. One was Gail Pierson, who joined the department in 1968, two years after the first female faculty member to be hired by the department. Pierson became friends with department economist Arthur Smithies, a native Australian who recruited rowers for Harvard and was considered the godfather of the rowing team. Pierson liked water sports; she swam and sailed at the University of Michigan, where she received her PhD, but all-male Harvard

College refused to let her use its pool because the swimmers practiced in the buff. She was offered the tiny pool at Radcliffe, the women's college, but found it "dingy and small." So, Smithies encouraged her to take up rowing.

Pierson took to the sport immediately and became an excellent rower on the Charles River. In 1969, she became the first woman to row a single scull in the annual Head of the Charles Regatta. She trained hard and became good enough to enter international races. In 1975, she was a member of the celebrated "Red Rose Crew," the eight-female-member rowing team that won the silver medal in the 1975 world championships in Nottingham, England. Pierson said it was the first time a US women's team won a medal in an international rowing competition.

Gail Pierson, now Gail Cromwell, found many male faculty members to be openly hostile toward the female professors as if they were not worthy as peers. "I mean, we were upsetting their world," she recalled. "The faculty club was strictly all men, and their attitude was, What were we doing there? This must be a mistake because this woman doesn't know what she's doing. I remember that very distinctly." At least, she found support from one male professor in the economics department who would buck her up and make her feel she belonged at Harvard.

As she thought about Gail, whose father also was a doctor, Yellen said, "I will always remember meeting her for the first time. Gail said, 'We should get together sometime. Why don't we go running in the stadium some morning?' And I'm like, 'What?' And she said, 'Oh, you know, I train by running up and down the benches of the stadium.' Well, I couldn't in my wildest imagination consider doing anything like that. So, we never really hit it off and didn't have much to do with one another." Years later, while living in Berkeley, Yellen took up mountain hiking and half-marathons, perhaps inspired by the athletic Pierson.

Certainly, Yellen left a lasting impression on Pierson, who departed Harvard at the end of the 1973–1974 term and joined the MIT faculty. Three years later, tragedy struck. Her husband, Seymour Cromwell, also a champion rower, died of pancreatic cancer. He was forty-three. Their only child, a daughter, was born six weeks after his death, and his widow retired from academia. The Louisiana native, who still has a thick Southern accent, now makes her home in tiny Temple, New Hampshire, population 1,400, where she is an avid gardener and active in local and state politics—putting her economics training to work by helping to manage the town's $1.3 million annual budget.

The emotional trauma of losing her husband while she was pregnant derailed her plans to become a world-class economist, yet Pierson found satisfaction in seeing Yellen achieve that goal: "She has certainly done a marvelous thing with her career. And I think as a woman, I can be very proud of her success."

❖ ❖ ❖

EMPATHY ECONOMICS HAS ALWAYS BEEN AT THE CORE OF THE research papers Yellen is proudest of during her academic career and in the policy positions she embraced as a public official: How best to reduce unemployment and raise wages? What is the solution to growing economic inequality? Where can women find the same employment opportunities and pay as men?

At Harvard, however, she found herself writing papers on topics that were of less interest to her, mainly to be able to work with one of the only other female professors there at the time, Rachel McCulloch, a close friend who later taught at Brandeis University and died in 2016. They wrote a number of papers together about issues such as international trade, factor mobility, capital movements, and technology transfers. Looking back on that time, Yellen concluded that she had been driven to coauthor all those papers with McCulloch to overcome the isolation she felt as one of only two female economics professors.

"I found Harvard very difficult," Yellen explained. "I had come to see more clearly that it was really a very hostile environment, with so few women. The guys hung out together, generated ideas together, and ended up writing papers together. They did things together and talked while they were doing it. For example, when ten guys decided they were going into Boston to have Chinese food on a Sunday afternoon, they didn't invite me. Rachel made a huge difference to my life. The papers we wrote weren't on the core things I was really interested in. So being the only two women made a big difference."

Yellen's male colleagues agreed that Harvard in the 1970s was a difficult place for women to thrive and speculated that a Black male professor would have an easier time being integrated into the department than any woman. "It was very sexist at the time," said Joseph Stiglitz. "I can easily believe that Janet did not have an easy time there," added William James "Jim" Adams, a University of Michigan economics professor who met Yellen when he was a PhD candidate at Harvard in 1973. "Back then, of course, there were very few women. I don't mean just faculty. There were no women graduate students," said Jerry Green. "I remember many years where there would be one woman out of a class of thirty people until maybe the 1980s. Back then it meant Janet, a young woman, would have to stand up and teach a graduate class of virtually all men. It's socially a weird situation."

Harvard did not offer a woman tenure in the economics department until 1990. Claudia Goldin, who holds that distinction, remembered reminiscing with Yellen about a blatantly sexist incident that involved the two of them during the 1975–1976 school year, when Goldin was a visiting professor on leave from Princeton University. Yellen, Goldin, and a male professor were on a committee conducting the oral exam for a female graduate student. The student gave good answers to the questions posed by Goldin and Yellen. Then the male professor asked an obtuse question that neither of the women examiners understood. Apparently, the student didn't either, but gamely gave the best response she could, Goldin and Yellen thought.

When the student left the room, the three examiners debated what grade to give her. Goldin and Yellen agreed she deserved a "very good." The male professor responded in a patronizing manner that both women recalled clearly—and bristled at—decades later: "Well, girls, it's a 'fair.'" Goldin and Yellen were furious. "Janet and I looked at each other," Goldin recounted. "It's one thing to negotiate. It's another thing to impose." They stood their ground, telling him that the student would get a "very good" by a vote of two to one. "That was the end of that," Goldin added.

❖ ❖ ❖

AMID THE COLD ENVIRONMENT, SOCIAL ISOLATION, SEXISM, and less-than-satisfying topics she collaborated on with Rachel McCulloch, Yellen had a notable success working on a trailblazing academic paper with then-PhD candidate Jim Adams, whose dissertation involved a lot of empirical research in Europe, where he had an unexpected encounter with Yellen.

At the end of the summer of 1972, Adams and his wife splurged on a night at an inn with a Michelin two-star restaurant in southwestern France. It was called the Cro-Magnon in Les Eyzies-de-Tayac in the Dordogne region, which was famous for the Lascaux Cave, where prehistoric drawings were discovered. Hence the name Cro-Magnon.

"We were at the pool waiting for dinner, and I was sitting with my legs in the water when I saw these two young women pushing the gate open and coming toward the swimming pool. And in the vanity of my youth, I can see that the two of them were looking at me. And sure enough, they come right up to me. And one says, 'You're Jim Adams, aren't you?' And this is more than a Dr. Livingstone moment because we had been in a very remote area of southern France, speaking only French. And to hear someone I did not know identify me by name in English was very surprising. It turned out to be Janet who knew me by name even though we had not met directly. She and her traveling companion were making a tour of very good restaurants in France. We chatted a little bit and promised we would look each other up when we got back to the department of economics."

Yellen and her Yale roommate, Vivian Nash, had been on an extended summer vacation, attempting to eat at all fifteen Michelin three-star restaurants in France. They occasionally settled for two-star restaurants like the one where they encountered Adams and his wife. "We went on a mostly eating tour of France," acknowledged Nash. "Janet really was a foodie, the first real foodie I knew." Another trait inherited from her mother.

Back in Cambridge, Yellen lived near the Adamses, and—as further proof that she was a devoted foodie—invited the couple to a dinner that he recalled more than four decades later. "She cooked that meal on her own and had one of the finest wines that I can remember," he said. "I can still tell you what it was. It was a 1960s vintage Château Cantenac Brown. Janet definitely made music in the kitchen."

On the academic front, Adams, whose focus was industrial organization, was at odds with his thesis adviser over the central concept of his research about economic power. "I tried a variety of ways to convince him, but he didn't want to listen to any of it. I'm feeling frustrated, a little bit angry, a little bit anxious because it's time to wrap up the thesis. And I come out of his office and who's there, but Janet. She gives me a cheery hello and asks how things are going. I told her that there is an important element in my thesis that my intuition tells me is true, but my adviser says it's got to go. She said, 'Well, you know, I'm a macroeconomist and I do international trade, as well. I'm not in your field, but I'd be happy to talk to you about it. And if I can be of any help, let me know.'

"So later in the week, we talked about this kernel of an idea I had, and she said, 'That's very interesting. Would you like to continue talking about it?' That was the birth of our paper, which ended up being by far the most important piece of work I ever have done and was something that she became well-known for also. It was called 'Commodity Bundling and the Burden of Monopoly' and was published in the *Quarterly Journal of Economics* in 1976."

Monopoly power is assumed to be bad for consumers because monopolists can reduce supply below the demand for a product in order to drive up the price. The paper Adams wrote with Yellen showed how a monopoly can also produce too much of a product when items are bundled together for sale as a unit. The result could be a price that would be lower than if the individual items were sold separately. That is good for consumers if they want the whole package, but not if they only want some of the items.

In the real world, items often are bundled as a way to sell less popular items along with highly coveted ones. One example would be an automobile with a package of options buyers are forced to purchase even if they only want a couple of the options. Another example is the exclusive sale of season tickets to college football games even though attendees only want to see a few of the games. The average ticket price is less than what a single ticket to the most popular game would cost, but it would be more than the cost of the least popular game if it were sold separately.

An example of a buyer being forced to pay for unwanted items bundled into one package is the hilarious scene from *Five Easy*

*Pieces* in which the Jack Nicholson character is told by a diner waitress that there are no substitutes to a set menu, and he couldn't have toast as a separate order. So, he asked for a chicken salad sandwich on toast but hold the mayonnaise, butter, lettuce, and chicken salad.

Harvard economist Jerry Green, who was associate editor of the *Quarterly Journal of Economics* at the time and advised the pair about the article, described it as groundbreaking because it demonstrated how retail operations often work in bundling goods, whether a washer and dryer or a computer with a service contract, and determined the optimal price for those combined items. "At the time people didn't realize that this was a big deal in industrial organization, but they wrote the very first paper in the field and the field has skyrocketed forty-five years later."

By the time Yellen became Treasury secretary in 2021, the article had been cited in subsequent academic papers more than 2,100 times. It is an impressive number that indicates the importance the paper has had as a foundation for subsequent research on the topic.

For Adams, working with Yellen made him a better scholar. "A lot of what I do is intuitive. For Janet, that intuition is only the beginning of the exercise, you have to work something out in its entirety and not just the original confirmation. You patiently work through a thing to explore lots of different facets. That's the scholarly side of what she does.

"Janet also taught me to approach things with a truly open mind about where it's going to lead. You don't just find what you're looking for, call it a day and publish. You go off in a variety of different places from the base to explore just how meaningful the result is. I wanted to declare victory, publish, and move on. And she said, 'No, no, wait. We need to explore this.' And it was in a lot of the exploration that she recommended that I think the most significant implication of that article came out."

In many respects, the paper reflected Yellen's gift for empathy by putting Adams and herself in the shoes of both the seller and the buyer to determine whether the price was appropriate for each.

Beyond her empathy, Adams was also impressed with Yellen's ability to explain complicated issues for a lay person and to be open-minded in examining an issue, traits she exhibited consistently in her public policy posts. "It is precisely because she's such a deep thinker that she is able to articulate things in a very clear sort of way in a profession where people seem to be more interested in being clever than being correct and displaying a certain alpha-male mentality and aggressiveness, where you make something so obfuscated that most people can't understand," Adams said.

"Secondly," he continued, "she truly is open-minded, and once she has convinced herself based on the power of her thought and exploration, she has the courage of her convictions. In terms of this overly narrow conception most economists have of what the vices of market power might be, once she explored thoroughly the theoretical framework on our behalf, she had the courage to go forward with the concept I started with. It was a complete role reversal for us in terms of gender stereotypes: She was systematic and dispassionate. I was impulsive and hot-blooded. The other thing that I would say is that Janet is not simply smart, but relative to many economists, she's also wise. There are many smart people who can flip economic models the way a good short-order chef can flip pancakes or burgers. But there are relatively few economists who are truly wise as well as being clearheaded. And that's a combination you don't often see."

Adams, who has spent time in administration as a dean, concluded with an observation about Yellen's ability to really listen to other people, a key component of empathy: "In my experience, the higher people rise in administration and leadership positions, the shorter their attention span gets as they listen to people. When you talk to them, you feel like you have to start running, and then you find you're stumbling over your words and ideas, and the person is losing interest because you can't say things fast enough that are novel and amusing. Janet is most remarkable in being exactly the same person I met fifty years ago. The great power, responsibilities, and leadership that she has had have not changed who she is as a person. And that's very unusual."

By all accounts, Yellen was an excellent and popular teacher, confirmed by one survey that found students in her class had the highest comprehension rating. Yet she knew that she would have to leave Harvard to pursue a career as an economist. The social environment for women was hardly inviting. Though she coauthored some notable papers, her research overall fell short of Harvard's elite standards for economics professors in both quantity and quality. She was not a prolific writer, compared to other young colleagues who were producing acclaimed papers on a regular basis. Her collaborations with Rachel McCulloch weren't on her main interests. Her forte was sharp analysis of existing problems rather than creative breakthroughs that led to novel discoveries. Even the commodity bundling paper Adams and she authored did not get her top rating.

"If you look at her research trajectory when she was here, she was working with Rachel McCulloch, and it's not obvious that that ever went anywhere," said Harvard economist Benjamin Friedman. "She published very little in that period," added another top Harvard economist who did not want to be identified in order to speak candidly. "She just wasn't terribly successful. I think her paper on commodity bundling was fine, but the kind of people who got tenure wrote ten papers like that. At that point in her life, you would not have expected her to have had remotely as distinguished and remarkable a career as she's had, but she came into her own later."

Andrew Rose, a longtime protégé of Yellen's at Berkeley who became dean of the business school at the National University of Singapore in 2019, conceded that her research did not measure up to that of colleagues: "At that time, other junior faculty at Harvard were producing superimportant stuff every week. And she just realized very quickly, it was just not going to work out for her."

Was it Yellen's distaste for writing? Did she lack that creative spark? Was she more interested in public policy as a tool for social good than spinning her wheels on ivory tower theoretical research and topics that only her colleagues favored? Was she, as some colleagues suspected, intimidated by the superlative work of her mentor, James Tobin, and did she feel she would never measure up to his work? An unnamed colleague, speaking frankly, said she once remarked that every paper Tobin wrote was such a jewel that neither she nor anybody else was likely to produce a paper that rose to his level. Or perhaps it was the social isolation of being a woman at alpha-male Harvard that hampered her research and injured her psyche. As Yale roommate Vivian Nash observed, "I think for academic success, you need to push the envelope and sort of carve out your space, your territory. And she probably didn't do that."

All of those factors surely coalesced to convince her in the fall of 1976 that this academic path was not going to work out, and she needed to set out in search of a new career track, disappointment in hand, destination uncertain.

Then she met George.

# - 3 -

# BERKELEY BOUND

*"Janet can disagree with you in the most agreeable way imaginable. She's honest and frank intellectually."*

LEAVING HARVARD BEHIND, YELLEN HAPPILY ACCEPTED A COVeted job at the Federal Reserve headquarters in Washington, DC. It was familiar terrain. Her interview at the Fed for a job in 1971 before deciding to head off to Cambridge, Massachusetts, made a favorable impression. She also worked there as a consultant in the summer of 1976 while contemplating her next career move. Her job as a staff economist in the international division in 1977 was a good place to land. The Fed had a reputation for employing only top people, and Yellen could put her academic training to work in the real world at arguably the world's most powerful institution for influencing the direction of the US economy, indeed the global economy.

Over the ensuing four decades, as an academic and public policy official, Yellen emerged as a leader of "new Keynesian" economics, founded as a counterweight to "trickle down" economics. The latter was a right-wing belief popularized during the Reagan years in the 1980s that tax cuts for the rich would filter down to everyone else and create broad-based prosperity. Not true. In fact, the rich got richer and the less affluent became poorer. Yellen's research helped demonstrate that government intervention is vital to produce fair economic outcomes.

Shortly after she was named Treasury secretary, economist Paul Krugman heralded her seminal contributions in his November 26, 2020, *New York Times* column. "In later work Yellen would show that labor market outcomes depend a lot not just on pure dollars-and-cents calculations, but also on perceptions of fairness," he wrote. "I can vouch from my own experience that this work had a huge impact on many young economists—basically giving them a license to be sensible. . . . She also never forgot that economics is about people, who aren't the emotionless, hyperrational calculating machines economists sometimes wish they were."

Yellen had no inkling when she first worked at the Fed that in future decades she would be putting her empathy economics to work as the head of the powerful organization.

The Federal Reserve Act of 1913, signed into law by President Woodrow Wilson, created a central bank system with twelve regional branches. Established in the wake of a 1907 bank panic, its goal was to replace the vicious boom-bust cycles and bank runs of the past with financial stability by serving as the lender of last resort. Over the decades, by moving interest rates up and down and managing the supply of money circulating in the economy, the Fed shaped the economy's pace of growth, the rate of inflation, and the level of unemployment—and not always successfully. Because the United States had the world's largest economy and the dollar was the currency most in demand by other countries, the Fed's actions rippled across the oceans to every other continent.

It was a good job, but a bad time in Yellen's life. Her father, a heavy smoker, had died in 1974 of heart disease, and three years later, in the spring of 1977, her mother suffered a heart attack while on a cruise. Ruth spent time in a physical rehabilitation hospital and then returned to the family's home in Brooklyn, where she lived alone. "My brother, his wife, and their baby went off to Africa on an archeological project while my mother was still in the rehab hospital, and they were really in a remote spot," she explained. "I was quite worried about my mother."

The first night she was there, Yellen heard her mother call in the middle of the night. She had suffered a stroke. With no one else able to care for her mother, Yellen was forced to take a leave of absence from work soon after starting at the Fed. Her mother was paralyzed on one side and hospitalized for months. When she was released, Yellen moved her into a nursing home. It was a highly stressful time for Yellen. Growing up, she remembered her mother making her promise never to put her in a nursing home. Now, she had not only gone against that pledge but was worried that the cost of the nursing home would rapidly deplete her mother's savings. "I was scared out of my mind about my responsibility to care for her and manage her finances. That was very stressful. I was basically by myself; I wasn't married, and this was a huge burden that made me quite unhappy."

Yellen found some solace in her work at the Fed. She met a lot of economists who shared her interests, and she was in a section that did research on trade and statistical analysis, which involved high-end academic content that appealed to her. "It was a place from which I could go back to academia if I wanted, but I was also interested in public policy and welcomed the opportunity to be able to become involved in it." But she didn't accomplish a lot because she was there only a year and a half, and for a third of that period, she was on leave to care for her mother.

Still, she had the opportunity to do research on a project concerning Special Drawing Rights, or SDRs, an arcane but vital instrument for helping countries in financial trouble. SDRs were created in 1969 by the International Monetary Fund (IMF), the global organization created after World War II to ensure a stable system of trade, financial transactions, and currency exchange rates. Wealthy nations would "donate" SDRs that needy nations could tap and exchange for hard currencies, such as dollars, German marks, Japanese yen, or, in later years, euros. Donor nations received interest on their SDR deposits with the IMF, and borrowing nations paid interest for tapping SDRs, so the net cost to the donors was negligible.

At the Fed, Yellen's main project had been to write a paper on how SDRs work, when you could justify an allocation and how they would impact the global economy. She wrote it for Henry Wallich, a German-born economist who was a member of the Fed's Board of Governors from 1974 to 1986. Before then, he had been a professor at Yale and taught a graduate class in monetary theory. Yellen enrolled in his class but then decided to wait and take it when Wallich went on leave and her mentor James Tobin taught the class. Yellen knew she would not share Wallich's conservative philosophy and rigid view of monetarism, namely that governments needed to control inflation at all cost—even at the risk of a recession and high unemployment. It was a belief based on his experience living through Germany's period of hyperinflation before World War II, which created economic chaos and led to Hitler's rise to power.

"Wallich thought that the long and short of Special Drawing Rights was that they are like global money and that creating more would cause inflation," Yellen said. She came to the opposite conclusion, that SDRs are a cost-effective and humanitarian way to aid countries in financial straits without sparking inflation. And Yellen took great satisfaction forty-four years later, on April 1, 2021, when she announced US support for a new IMF allocation of $650 billion in SDRs. One of her first acts as Treasury secretary, it was another indication of her empathy, this time for poor nations hit hardest financially by the COVID-19 pandemic. "I particularly savored the new allocation of Special Drawing Rights. It was a real accomplishment. There hadn't been an allocation for many years."

The size of the US contribution fell just within the level the Treasury is allowed to pledge without congressional approval, and that maneuver led to a heated exchange at a congressional hearing between Yellen and Republican senator John Kennedy of Louisiana, who claimed incorrectly that the move would cost American taxpayers $180 billion. Yellen countered that the interest the United States would have to pay to borrow the money and the interest it receives on the SDRs was basically a wash and is justified by the benefits of a strong global recovery that increases demand for US exports. Who would have thought that a televised hearing about SDRs would prove to be dramatic TV? Yellen made her point in her well-established manner: clearly and firmly but calmly and courteously, in the face of three minutes of hectoring and interruptions by an angry and animated Kennedy.

❖ ❖ ❖

IN ADDITION TO THE STRESS OVER HER MOTHER'S ILLNESS AND difficulty in dealing with Henry Wallich, Yellen had also been in some bad relationships with men. Economist Alicia Munnell, who worked for the Federal Reserve Bank of Boston at the time, recalled meeting Yellen in Washington and socializing with her occasionally. "I was divorced at the time and we were having this conversation about men and I remember it was like we were rolling our eyes and thinking they are a difficult group to live with," said Munnell, who twenty years later would be on the Council of Economic Advisers with Yellen. "It was clear that something had just not worked out."

"She didn't get tenure at Harvard, her father had died, her mother had a stroke, and Johnny was in Africa," added former Yale roommate Vivian Nash. "I mean, it was a terrible, terrible time, and she just seemed very beaten by it." But Yellen was fortunate to meet George Akerlof not long after her mother was settled in the nursing home, and she said, "we hit it off."

Akerlof was an economist on leave from the University of California, Berkeley, and working as a visiting researcher at the Fed in 1977. Six years Yellen's senior, he was also going through a rough patch. He had recently gotten divorced and was upset that he did not get a promotion to full professor at Berkeley. So, he took a leave to work at the central bank for a year and then accepted a professorship at the highly regarded London School of Economics. Fellow staff economist Donald Kohn, who eventually rose to Fed vice chair, remembered meeting George as he arrived in the office one day with a puppy that proceeded to pee on the floor. George sheepishly acknowledged that Kohn's recollection was accurate. "Well, people at Berkeley would do such things. It was common for people to bring their dogs to the office."

Akerlof first met Yellen at a farewell party for a Fed staff member. Subsequently, he attended a luncheon seminar by economist Jo Anna Gray. "We both arrived a little bit after the main group and sat at the extra table, where we met each other again. So, we owe that to Jo Anna," Yellen recalled. "We got together after that and we decided we liked each other, and on our first date we went to see a Russian movie at the Kennedy Center."

After a few more dates, they quickly decided to get married since they wanted to be together. Akerlof was going to the London School of Economics and Yellen also received an offer from the school.

As their wedding venue in the summer of 1978, they chose the posh Cosmos Club, housed in a Beaux Arts French-style mansion built at the turn of the twentieth century on a section of Massachusetts Avenue known as "Embassy Row." It was a well-known Washington "Gentleman's Club" founded in 1878 with the goal of advancing the knowledge of its three thousand members in science, literature, and art. "To be considered for membership in the Cosmos Club, an individual must be a person of 'distinction, character and sociability' who has done meritorious original work in science, literature, or the arts," the club explains on its website. Its roster included US presidents, Supreme Court justices, and Nobel Prize laureates—none of them women as of 1978. At that time, women were not allowed to be members or even use the main entrance without a member as an escort, which meant Yellen had to use a different entrance to attend her own wedding. It was a small door to the far left of the members' entrance, and it led into a tight, dimly lit corridor that ran beneath a flight of stairs. In 1988, twenty-five years after admitting its first Black member, the club finally opened its membership to women to avoid losing its DC liquor license for gender discrimination. As one longtime employee noted, "What's the club without alcohol."

Why the men-only Cosmos Club for the ceremony and reception? "We were sponsored by a woman who was a friend of my family, and we did not think about the restrictions on women at the club that still persisted at the time," Akerlof explained. "I think the reason we did not think about it was that we could not imagine that there would be—or that there were—such restrictions by the late 1970s."

Yellen wasn't pleased when she learned about the club rules. She also thought women were allowed to be members since the sponsor was a female judge whose late husband had been a member. Whatever the rules for membership, Yellen remembered that women weren't allowed to go through the front door because men lived in the club. "We discovered when we went to look at where the ceremonies would be that they ushered us into the kitchen, which was a little strange. We only later figured out what had gone on. But the space was rented. I didn't like it, yet making this a cause célèbre when we needed to find a place to get married in difficult times wasn't my top priority."

She was thirty-two, considered an advanced age for women to wed at the time. "Certainly, my mother would have been delighted to see me get married sooner, so I had pressure coming from that side," she said. "It really comes down to whether you met somebody you want to get married to. And the answer was I hadn't at that point. I wanted to continue my education to get a PhD. That was always important to me. When I gave a speech at the one hundredth anniversary of women's education at Brown, I looked into the archives the university maintains of graduates it interviews at every class reunion. Many described getting married right out of college; putting careers on hold; helping their husbands go through, say, medical school; and then they ended up getting divorced. The beginning of your career was after a divorce."

✤ ✤ ✤

GEORGE ARTHUR AKERLOF WAS BORN IN 1940 IN CONNECTI-cut. His father, Gösta, was a Lutheran who emigrated from Sweden as a young man and became a chemist. Akerlof's mother, Rosalie, was a descendant of German Jews, like Yellen's mother, and was a housewife who raised George and his three siblings. When Akerlof was a toddler, his family moved to Dayton, Ohio, where his father worked for the Monsanto Company during World War II, conducting research that led to the manufacture of detonators for the first atomic bombs. The family later lived in Pittsburgh, where Gösta worked as a chemistry professor at the University of Pittsburgh. The family moved in 1950 to Princeton, New Jersey, where Gösta held a series of high-level jobs at research laboratories that did work for the Navy, NASA, and private industry. He received a number of patents for inventing equipment used for chemical reactions.

Young Akerlof spent the remainder of his youth in Princeton, where he attended the preppy Princeton Day School and Lawrenceville School before heading off to Yale as an undergraduate. Akerlof became interested in economics at a much earlier age than did Yellen, grade school, in fact. "When I was in third grade the teacher asked what we wanted from Santa and I said, 'I'd like a factory.' 'Well, why a factory?' 'If you have a factory, you could buy whatever you want.' So, I think I was always an economist."

He decided to do his graduate work at MIT because it had attracted many giants of the economics profession at the time, including Paul Samuelson who won the Nobel Prize in 1970 and wrote the standard economics textbook used by students for decades. "MIT was a place that one would have wanted to go," he said, noting that most of the students who got prestigious fellowships went to MIT rather than to Harvard.

After receiving his PhD in 1966, Akerlof got a job at the economics department at Berkeley. That same year, he wrote a breakthrough paper about the economic impact of asymmetric information, "The Market for 'Lemons': Quality Uncertainty and the Market Mechanism." It was not about the fruit, but a low-quality product, such as a used car that is called "a lemon" when its defect is discovered following its purchase. Information is asymmetric, Akerlof showed, when the seller knows whether a car is a "lemon" but the buyer does not.

Akerlof's research showed that markets are distorted when the seller has more information about the quality of a product than the buyer, particularly an item such as a used car that might have a hidden defect. It explained why a wary buyer will pay much less for a car only a few months old than for a new car. His finding was a breakthrough because classical economics assumed sellers and buyers had the same information about a product and that would produce an efficient market. Akerlof pointed out that a buyer will pay more for a used car if the seller provided a warranty against it being a "lemon."

Akerlof completed the thirteen-page paper in his first year at Berkeley and submitted it in 1967 to the *American Economic Review*, which rejected it. He submitted it next to the *Journal of Political Economy*, which also rejected it. Then he was off to New Delhi, India, where he had planned to spend the 1967–1968 school year. He revised the paper while in India and sent it to the *Review of Economic Studies*, where it was rejected once again. The fourth time was the charm: the *Quarterly Journal of Economics* accepted it, and it was published in 1970. Berkeley rewarded his accomplishment by giving him tenure. He received a much greater reward for the paper thirty-one years later: the Nobel Prize in Economics, which he shared with A. Michael Spence of Stanford University and Joseph Stiglitz, Yellen's first-year Yale professor and later her predecessor as chief White House economist. The prize was awarded "for their analyses of markets with asymmetrical information."

In an essay he wrote that was published on the Nobel Prize's website, Akerlof said his paper about lemons "deals with a problem as old as markets themselves. It concerns how horse traders respond to the natural question: 'if he wants to sell that horse, do I really want to buy it?'" Such questioning, Akerlof noted, is fundamental to the market for horses and used cars, but it is also at least minimally present in every market transaction. It was the first theoretical paper on this topic and posed a major unanswered question: How does asymmetric information affect markets?

It would seem a rare instance in which a Nobel Prize–winning paper had initially been rejected so many times, yet in economics, it has happened frequently, according to a 1994 article in the *Journal of Economic Perspectives* by Joshua S. Gans and George B.

Shepherd. Entitled "How Are the Mighty Fallen: Rejected Classic Articles by Leading Economists," the authors listed numerous economic giants who faced rejection, including Nobel laureates James Tobin and Milton Friedman.

The article noted that Akerlof's "seminal contribution to the economics of information" had been labeled "a lemon" by three scholarly journals. The editor of the *American Economic Review* found his paper "interesting," but the journal "did not publish such trivial stuff," Akerlof told the article's authors. The *Journal of Political Economy* said in its rejection letter that "the paper was too general to be true. Thus, in the view of this referee my paper predicted too much," Akerlof said. The third rejection echoed the first, calling the paper "trivial." The quarterly that accepted the paper did so "with some degree of enthusiasm," Akerlof said.

The 1994 article continued: "The rejections discouraged Akerlof. 'I do think its early rocky reception did have an effect on my own work. It was not until 1973, when I spent six months on sabbatical in England, that I realized that quite a few people had read the paper and even liked it. I believe I would have done follow-up work on "The Market for 'Lemons'" sooner if I had not been made to feel lucky just to have it published at all. I must say I still feel very lucky that it was published.' Akerlof believes that journal editors refused the article both because they feared the introduction into economics of informational considerations and because they disliked the article's readable style . . . which did not reflect the usual solemnity of economic journals."

Twenty years after winning the Nobel Prize, Akerlof reflected on all the early rejections: "I think this is the way science in general works. If you're doing something that's outside the paradigm, you're not accepted by those people who are in the paradigm. It took something like one hundred years for astronomers to accept the fact discovered by Copernicus that the sun might be in the center of the universe and not the Earth. So, this is something that's quite common."

Bolstered by the publication of his article and tenure at Berkeley, Akerlof decided to take another one-year leave during the 1973–1974 school year to work in Washington as a staff economist for President Richard Nixon's Council of Economic Advisers, which was headed by Herbert Stein and included as a council member his Yale professor, William Fellner, who had been influential in his decision to become an economist.

Akerlof joined the Nixon administration as the Watergate scandal started to erupt. He always remembered the date of the break-in, June 17, since that is also his birthday. "I wasn't a supporter of Nixon, but I didn't see any reason why I shouldn't take the position. It was a job for an economist and the CEA [Council of Economic Advisers] hired me. I can't say that they liked everything that I did there," he said. "There was the oil embargo in 1973, and I was worried that the price of oil would go through the roof rather than be rationed. In that case, it would cause inflation, which would then lead to measures to cut that inflation and cause a lot of unemployment. So, I was in favor of rationing, but that was something that Herb Stein didn't agree with."

Back at Berkeley again as an associate professor, he became upset when the university would not promote him to full professor. He also had just gotten divorced, so in 1977 he headed back to Washington to work at the Fed and to meet the woman with whom he would spend the next five decades and counting.

❖ ❖ ❖

AFTER THEIR WHIRLWIND COURTSHIP AND MARRIAGE IN 1978, the couple headed off to the London School of Economics. They enjoyed living in England and teaching at the university, which attracted students from all over the world who would return home to serve as senior officials in their governments' finance ministries and central banks. Even so, living in the United Kingdom at the time was challenging. They happened to be there during the 1978–1979 "Winter of Discontent," a tumultuous period so named because of a series of crippling strikes and double-digit inflation that brought down the Labour Party government and installed Conservative Party rule under Prime Minister Margaret Thatcher.

The couple returned after their year in London to Berkeley. Akerlof was welcomed back to the university's economics department, and Yellen was offered a position teaching international business at the Haas School of Business.

What Yellen may not have known at the time was that she got a helping hand to land the job at Haas from Laura D'Andrea Tyson, an economics professor at Berkeley who went on to become President Bill Clinton's chair of the Council of Economic Advisers from 1993 to 1995 and director of the White House National Economic Council in 1995–1996. She was the first woman to hold both titles. Tyson was very impressed with Yellen's scholarly research on labor markets and her reputation as an outstanding macroeconomist who had been a protégé of James Tobin; she saw her as a real star for Berkeley. Tyson would be instrumental in advancing Yellen's career over the next twenty-five years, as well as being a good friend.

With positions in the economics department and Haas secured, Akerlof and Yellen spent the next fourteen years happily ensconced at Berkeley, where she mastered new material to teach business school students and emerged as one of the top professors at Haas. In 1982, she became only the second woman to receive tenure at the school where graduate students enrolled after having had experience working in the business world. As a result, she said, "they were practical, were interested in things they thought had some use or applicability, but didn't have a lot of interest in theory for its own sake. That forced me, year after year, to think hard about how my teaching applied to the real world and to make the connection between theory and real-world developments—to stay closely in touch with current events and to think about how these events related to economic theory."

Andrew Rose, whom Yellen hired to teach at Haas in 1986, spent thirty-three years teaching there before heading off to the National University of Singapore, where he became dean of the business school. He remembered Yellen much as her many Harvard colleagues had: as an extraordinarily well-prepared and conscientious professor who was focused on making sure her students understood the content. "We were teaching the same core macroeconomics course. She taught me how to teach the course," said Rose, who also teamed up with her as coauthor of the first five or so papers he produced at Haas. "She really took me under her wing and mentored me, but she still treated me as a colleague. So, she's been a very big, positive influence on my life. There is no doubt that Janet is genuinely a humble person, but she also knows how to play people very, very well. She really wants people to understand. If you ask her a question, she's going to answer it in tremendous detail, not use two words where fifty will suffice, but she's very sincere in trying to express her understanding of your problem and her solution to it. She realizes that if she answers you in tremendous detail and gives you four explanations, when one would have done it, you're not going to be asking her many questions because you don't want to hear all of the answers."

Not surprisingly—given Yellen's determination that students get a rock-solid comprehension of course material—she was named Teacher of the Year multiple times. "The tradition at Berkeley for a long time was when you won Teacher of the Year, a picture was taken of you and hung outside the Dean's office," Rose said. "When we moved buildings, those pictures came down. And for some reason, somebody gave me her picture, which I hung in my office until

I left Berkeley. And that became sort of a joke because it became a shrine, and there were offerings to the goddess when Janet was in Washington for the Clinton administration time from 1994 to 1999."

Longtime Haas colleague James Wilcox recalled that Yellen had developed a reputation for being a popular teacher with top ratings from the outset. "Most importantly, it was because of her clear explanations. She had a logical train of thought and was able to convey it," he said, "but I'm guessing the students also sensed that she was a nice person who treated them well." He also attributed her popularity to a good sense of humor she hides in public appearances: "She has this infectious, entertaining laugh and can take teasing well when academics make remarks to each other that are not very flattering. She was plenty happy when people were making fun of her. And she could also turn the tables on them, not with a sharp wit that had a bite to it but with a clever wit. I can still see her laughing to the point where she tried to wipe away the tears from laughing so much."

Michael Katz, Yellen's former Harvard student and subsequent colleague at Haas, cited her extreme preparation and organization as a business professor; traits she had obsessively followed at her mother's insistence: "It's a lot of work and a challenging job that she took seriously. I mean, she would throw herself into it completely. I still remember a time I'd seen her outside the business school, and she was walking along with a brown grocery bag filled with books because she was teaching a Harvard Business School case on Boeing and Airbus that were fighting about government subsidies, and she wanted to make sure she had enough background information for it. So, she'd gotten out fifteen books where most faculty members, including myself, might read a couple articles, and then sort of wing it. But when she does something, she takes it very seriously."

Her meticulously prepared lecture notes are also something of a legend at Haas, much like her notes of James Tobin's courses at

Yale. They always began, "My name is Janet Yellen," as if she might forget to introduce herself to new students. That's also how she began her message to Treasury Department staff upon being sworn in as secretary on January 26, 2021.

"That written introduction is a running joke with her friends," added Katz. "She always prepares to the nth degree. That's the thing about her. She's just so earnest and wants to be so prepared. Any of us would say, 'Look, obviously you don't have to write that out. You'll be fine if you don't pay that much attention to the detail.' She didn't have to get those fifteen books to teach about Boeing and Airbus, but she just wants to really do a good job."

Haas economics and finance professor Richard Lyons, who served as dean of the business school from 2008 to 2018, saw in Yellen someone who wanted her students to fall in love with economics the way she had. "It's like when somebody is thrilled by an idea, that's how you get them into your field," he said. "You can superficially toss a lot of stuff at them and they can memorize it and they can take an exam. But her view is, 'I want you to be thrilled by this stuff, really see into it.' That was always her modality in the classroom."

In describing her as a colleague, Lyons added: "We have a phrase at Berkeley that we use for admissions. That phrase is 'confidence without attitude.' And boy, if she doesn't personify that, I don't know who does. You can feel the competence in her presence, her capability. It's palpable. And at the same time, you could never describe her as arrogant or holier than thou or full of attitude. She's absolutely terrific that way. That's one of the things I associate with her most. Janet can disagree with you in the most agreeable way imaginable. She's honest and frank intellectually. She will never pull her punches if she disagrees with somebody. But she knows how to do it in a way that doesn't make people feel like they're being personally attacked. That ability to provide intellectual feedback in a way that is productive and well-received, that's an art. There are a lot of people who are not good at that. She really is."

Berkeley colleague David Teece, the international business specialist, remembered her empathy most: "I recall she and George had a house with a rental unit and a tenant who was an elderly person. They never talked about it as an economic relationship but as a person they cared about. Caring about society has always been a hallmark of hers. I wouldn't call it bleeding heart care. I would call it genuine empathy coupled with smart ways to think about how to improve the well-being of people. I run out of patience with people who have empathy but no plan of action for the problem at hand, who have bleeding hearts but don't have ways to connect in a helpful way. Janet has the intelligence to connect policies to the problem that have a positive impact with minimal collateral damage. That's how to think about a very smart empathetic person."

Clearly, Yellen had found a comfort level at Berkeley that she lacked at Harvard. It also was clear that she enjoyed teaching more than the research requirements of academia. "My sense from my mother is that writing papers was something that imperfectly suited her," said her son, Robby. "She's good at many aspects of it, but I don't think it was something she was exactly passionate about. I think teaching was something that really fit her very well. The way to think about it is that teaching is about practice and paper writing is something else. I think one of her real strengths is as a practitioner."

❖ ❖ ❖

HER PREFERENCE FOR TEACHING NOTWITHSTANDING, YELLEN did some notable research papers at Berkeley, including a much-cited 1984 article published in the *American Economic Review*, entitled "Efficiency Wage Models of Unemployment." It was a groundbreaking paper that found wage levels were not determined merely by the supply of labor and the demand for it, as classical economics assumed, but also by human considerations: a wage level that provided self-esteem for the worker, quality performance for the employer, and a bond of loyalty between both. That explained why employers paid higher wages even though there were unemployed people willing to work for less.

Akerlof credited his wife for inventing the term "efficiency wages" and producing an insight that is a bright example of her philosophy of "empathy economics": She found that employers do not necessarily want to hire workers at the lowest possible wage because they need workers who are loyal, hardworking, and efficient, and that requires them to pay. The higher wages create a bond between the employer and worker that leads to higher productivity for the business.

"This goes back to Janet having empathy," Akerlof explained. "This was thinking about what other people were thinking. Prior to this, it was about people who left their jobs or were fired from their jobs, and then they'd look for jobs. This says something more, that you're going to get a market equilibrium where the employer wants the loyalty of the worker and the worker actually wants to have the loyalty of the employer. And one way that's shown is by paying a higher wage than what they can just get where the supply of labor is equal to the demand for labor."

Thinking about the plight of the unemployed, their pain, their economic insecurity, and how they must feel, has been part of Yellen's makeup since her father treated so many down-on-their-luck patients. "Our major reason for going into economics is that we were worried about unemployment," said Akerlof. "It's a tremendous waste to have people who want a job and who are not able to find one. We're worried about unemployment for two reasons. One is about people who are unemployed for strictly economic reasons. Beyond that, people who think they should have a job lose their identity when they are unemployed. They feel as if they're not living up to who they should be. We both felt that human part. So, when you're talking about empathy, it's not just about people not having the money, it's also seeing what people are feeling. It's about self-esteem and the esteem of everybody else."

That approach marked a departure from traditional economic thinking, which looked at the problem of unemployment from financial considerations, not personal feelings. A spate of news articles about Yellen as she rose to high public positions often cited the inspiration for her theory of wage efficiency as the caregiver she and Akerlof hired at an above-market wage to ensure she paid special attention to their son, Robby, who was just shy of three years old when the paper was published. "That story is not true. It was the other way around. We had the theory already and then applied it when we hired her," Akerlof revealed.

For Robby, the paper reflects his parents'—and his—view of economics in broader terms than had been done in the past. "Relationships really matter, and one needs to think about what relationships look like," he said. "If you just think in crude contractual terms about employment, then you miss things. If paying people more than you have to creates a better relationship, that's worth it. That's how they think about the world, and I do, too. What's missing from a lot of economics is thinking deeply about relationships, about informal understandings and norms that exist between people."

Colleague Lyons considered the paper a breakthrough: "Efficiency wage theory has helped us understand why firms set wages a little higher than you might otherwise think. And then it sticks there with unemployment rising. That's just a wonderful example of failing markets left to their own devices, doing the best they can to generate unemployment. It's that kind of insight that on some level seems obvious, yet economists just didn't think that way for a long, long time."

Throughout the 1980s and into the mid-1990s, Yellen and Akerlof teamed up to write a number of papers that dived deeper into empathy economics—putting themselves in the shoes of the employed and unemployed to assess how their motivations and thought processes affected levels of unemployment. One such paper looked at labor turnover and how workers who hated their jobs would not leave them during periods of high unemployment, creating even higher barriers for those already unemployed.

On a very different topic, they published a paper in 1991 with protégé Andrew Rose to examine how the economic reunification of Germany the previous year would affect the German economy, including unemployment, the Deutsche Mark—the currency at the time—and various industries in East Germany that were not competitive with their West German counterparts. Titled "East Germany in from the Cold: The Economic Aftermath of Currency Union," it proved to be prescient.

"I think that is her best paper and also my best paper," said Akerlof. "I think we were the first to call exactly what the problems were of integrating East Germany into West Germany at a one-to-one exchange rate between the West German Deutsche Mark and the East Mark. That was an important paper because it identified for the German government exactly what the problems were that actually subsequently transpired. It says the only industry in East Germany that would be viable was going to be electricity production."

Yellen recalled that the paper predicted high, long-term unemployment for East Germans, who were accustomed to job security. "Our work attracted the attention of the German government at the time. We came up with a plan that we proposed for what Germany should do to deal with unemployment in Eastern Germany," she said. "Our plan was to have large wage subsidies, which would particularly support labor-intensive industries capable of creating jobs in the East. In 1992, [Chancellor] Helmut Kohl's chief economic adviser invited us to come to Germany to meet with Kohl . . . and discuss our reactions to ongoing developments. He arranged a tour for us that involved visiting factories and meeting with government officials and local businesspeople in East Germany. It was clear that unemployment was just terrible. It was going to be a long-lasting problem, as we had predicted in the paper."

Yellen also cowrote a paper with Rose that offered new insights into how trade imbalances affect currency exchange rates. He praised the papers she and Akerlof wrote together for questioning the rational behavior assumed by classical economic theory. Traditionalists contended that when people departed from rational choices, the variance was too small to matter. Yellen and Akerlof concluded that a series of small departures from rational choices add up to a big deal. "That was one genesis for what is now a huge area of economics called behavioral economics," explained Rose. "George was one of the first ones to take psychology and small deviations from rationality seriously."

Former Treasury secretary Lawrence Summers said the couple made a powerful team: "Janet and George were terrific complements to each other as scholars. Janet had a kind of disciplined precision and policy interest, and George had this very abstract creative way about him. So, they were very productive together on minimum wages, efficiency wage costs, and a variety of different things."

Akerlof remembered Summers fondly as an editor of one of their joint papers in 1988. "Larry was working for the Michael Dukakis presidential campaign at the time, and he made very good comments on that paper," Akerlof said. "We're still friends." It was a description that belied the on-again, off-again rivalry that pitted Summers against Yellen through the decades.

❖ ❖ ❖

FOR SOMEONE SO ORGANIZED AND FOCUSED ON TEACHING AND research, the birth of their only child in 1981 posed a new challenge for Yellen. "I remember it being hard, a real juggling act," she said. "But George was very involved in taking care of Robby, and he did at least half of whatever needed to be done, probably more. Childcare takes a lot of time, but academic jobs have a lot of flexibility. George was immensely helpful and we managed. Everything was fine."

Yellen never let work or motherhood interfere with her love to cook gourmet meals for guests. "I used to do Julia Child–type cooking," she said. "I enjoy cooking, and we used to have a lot of dinner parties. You know, life has changed so much. I haven't had somebody over for a real dinner in such a long time. We go out now with people to restaurants. People work. The world is becoming increasingly competitive, not just Washington, but academia, too. More people are struggling to get ahead, and life is harder. Back then, we took time off on weekends. We went to museums and did other family things with Robby and hung out with him. We worked plenty, but not every single second."

When Robby was very young, his parents belonged to a babysitting co-op with twenty couples who would babysit for one another and earn points they could redeem with another couple so they could go out to dinner and a movie. Later, they enrolled Robby in a school that stressed parental participation. "They definitely expected parents to go on school trips or volunteer to bake cookies or something else and sell homemade things at a fair," she recalled. "I was busy. I didn't want to go on the school trips. So, I accepted the assignment of baking for the school fair."

It was not a task she enjoyed, she confided to friends at the time. She had agreed reluctantly to bake a dozen zucchini loaves that the school fair would sell for $2 each. It took her a full day to buy the ingredients, prepare and bake the loaves, wrap them up, pack them up, and take them to the fair. The economist in her calculated that the ingredients alone cost nearly as much as the $24 total the loaves would raise for the school. It rankled her that the school would assume women had nothing better to do with their time than spend a day preparing baked goods that would raise such a paltry sum. Yellen's preference would have been to simply write a check for $200 as a donation to the school, but she completed her assignment dutifully if not happily. Gender bias expert Joanne Lipman saw Yellen's experience as the emergence of a tug-of-war between stay-at-home moms and working moms that became more prominent in the 1980s. "It became a culture war between the two," she said. "We're now in an era where whatever your choice is, it's your choice. But at the time, there was a real struggle. You could see it in the bake sales and PTA meetings that were always during the day."

❖ ❖ ❖

IN 1994, YELLEN GOT A CAREER-ALTERING PHONE CALL FROM Alan Blinder, a distinguished Princeton economist who at the time was a member of President Clinton's Council of Economic Advisers. Clinton was going to nominate Blinder to be vice chair of the Federal Reserve Board of Governors, and he called to find out if she was interested in joining him as a member of the Federal Reserve Board of Governors in Washington. She didn't hesitate in her answer:

"When Alan called me, George immediately said, 'This is something you've always wanted to do. Tell them you'll definitely do it if they offer it, and we'll figure out how to make it work.' That was really fantastic of him. I told Alan that if they wanted me to do it, it was a definite yes."

Yellen had never forgotten the allure of Washington when James Tobin talked about his work in the Kennedy White House. Now she had an opportunity to make her own mark in the nation's capital. "I wanted to be involved in macroeconomics policy at a high level, and I was very interested in monetary policy," she explained. "There really aren't that many jobs at the federal level that involve macro policymaking. There's the Fed, the CEA [Council of Economic Advisers], and the Treasury, and that's pretty much it. So, if that's your interest, this has got to be one of your dream jobs. And you know, it was for me. I knew it would be a wonderful opportunity. I just wanted to do it. I found writing papers a lonely struggle. While it's satisfying to get some done, it can be frustrating to write them. They often get rejected. You often rewrite them dozens of times before they end up seeing the light of day. There are a lot of frustrations involved in doing research, although there are also a lot of rewards." Months passed after Blinder first sounded her out for this "dream job," and she heard nothing. Then an invitation to interview for the position came while Yellen and her family were vacationing on the Hawaiian Island of Lanai and finding her proved difficult. "We were in an out-of-the-way spot, and this was before the days of email and easy communication," recalled Robby. "They were trying to contact her to offer her this job, and nobody could reach her because we were on this island. My father's administrative assistant managed to figure out how to get in touch with us. It was all rather dramatic at the time. They flew back early, and she was invited to meet [Treasury secretary] Lloyd Bentsen in Rancho Santa Fe, California. They went down there to meet him and he interviewed her for the job. It was her first taste of high-level politics."

The career change would have a big impact on the entire family. "Life changed a lot for us when we moved to Washington," said Robby. "She had this existence as a professor writing papers with my father, and this became an important break in my mother's life."

And there was an additional benefit beyond leaving academic papers behind, she remembered. No more baking zucchini breads. She would send Robby to a private school that didn't expect parents to do anything but pay the bill.

## - 4 -

# FINDING HER WAY AT THE FED

*"I know a lot about very little, but she can cover
the whole gamut of economics"*

JANET YELLEN GOT HER DREAM JOB AS ONE OF SEVEN MEMBERS
of the Board of Governors of the Federal Reserve thanks at least
in part to her gender, an admission she made readily. "Clinton was
committed to diversity, and my guess is that they were definitely
looking for a woman," she said. "There were two vacancies, and
I think they did not want both to go to white males. So, my guess
is that I was a beneficiary of affirmative action. They were really
trying to identify women and minorities who could do these jobs."

Yellen had many backers within the administration: Laura
D'Andrea Tyson, the chair of the White House Council of Eco-
nomic Advisers who had lobbied to get her a faculty position at
Berkeley's Haas School of Business. Yale mentor Joseph Stiglitz was
a member of the council, and former Harvard student Lawrence
Summers was a top Treasury Department official.

Laura Tyson recalled pushing to put Yellen in the post, not because she was a woman but because of her strong credentials as an economist. "As soon as that Fed job came up, I thought, 'Yes, we should do this,'" Tyson said, though she agreed that others involved in the selection were concerned with increasing diversity at the Fed. It was a great career move, as far as Yellen was concerned, because moving from the abstract world of academia to the real world of public policy was exciting: "All the government jobs I have had involve formulating policy about real problems, working with people who are trying to make the best possible decision but in finite time. Unlike research papers, it's not something that will typically hang over one's head for years on end. I find it very satisfying to be in jobs where you encounter lots of new problems and where both theory and evidence are relevant in deciding what to do. I enjoy working on problems with people who are trading ideas, bringing all possible resources to bear, discussing alternatives, making decisions, then moving on to other pressing issues."

On April 22, 1994, President Clinton nominated Alan Blinder and Yellen to the Fed, the first Democratic additions to the Republican-dominated board since 1980. Yellen described herself to reporters as a "non-ideological pragmatist," according to a *Los Angeles Times* article.

At her confirmation hearing before the Senate Banking Committee three months later, Yellen was dutifully circumspect about her policy proclivities, as she echoed the standard views of Fed officials about the need for the central bank to keep inflation in check. "She warned against tolerating inflation so as to achieve short-term reductions in unemployment, saying that inflation would inflict long-run harm to the economy," the *New York Times* reported on July 23, 1994.

Yet the true Yellen could not be totally constrained and her compassion for the less fortunate leaked out, as the *Times* noted: "Ms.

Yellen, 47, startled some in the audience when she emphasized the needs of average folks. 'What the Fed should be pursuing is the economic welfare of working people, of all Americans,' she said. The central bank has more commonly been known for its links and sympathies with Wall Street and big commercial banks."

The full Senate confirmed Yellen to a fourteen-year term as a Fed governor, 94–6. She joined another woman already on the Board of Governors. Susan Phillips, an associate economics professor and administrator at the University of Iowa, was appointed to the board in 1991 by the first President Bush. She was also a trailblazer: the first woman to head a US financial regulatory agency as chair of the Commodity Futures Trading Commission (CFTC) in 1983. The CFTC was established in 1974 to oversee futures and options trading, which originally involved mostly agricultural products. But it grew exponentially over the years to include exotic derivatives, the kind that led to the 2007–2009 financial crisis that Yellen and her colleagues at the Fed would have to combat.

Being a Fed governor "really suited my mother and her talents," said Robby Akerlof. "Washington's very male-dominated atmosphere is similar to the one she faced in academia, but her set of political skills are better suited to Washington. One of her real talents is that she can make a very convincing argument, yet she's self-effacing and doesn't overwhelm you with her ego. She wins people over very much with the power of her arguments and manages to inspire a lot of loyalty among people. It has served her extremely well and she got into her wheelhouse when she went to Washington."

After twenty-three years working in academia, Yellen also managed the transition to government work in Washington smoothly, not only because she was primed for the change, but also because the job requirements as a member of the Fed Board in some respects had much in common with being a professor. The day was highly structured with meetings, the workday was not grueling—absent an economic crisis—and governors could spend much of their time doing research on the state of the economy so they could decide what policy course the Fed should take. They would examine the latest economic statistics prepared by the Fed staff and other government agencies, read academic studies on the latest economic trends, and meet with a variety of people representing business and consumer groups to collect anecdotal evidence of what was going on in the economy. They also would give speeches on the state of the economy, much like classroom lectures. For some governors, the work was somewhat isolating: they worked alone in their offices, often ate lunch by themselves, and had time to think deeply about the economy when they weren't busy dealing with bank supervision issues and administrative chores. Yellen was unique as a junior member of the board in that she was interested in being briefed on the latest trends by Fed economists, something they normally only did for the chair of the board.

The comparison to academia had its limits. Unlike professors, Fed governors wielded tremendous power, possibly more than any unelected position in Washington. Indeed, the entire Federal Reserve System is among the most powerful and least understood institutions in government. School civics classes teach students about how Congress, the presidency, and the judicial system work, but the Fed gets scant, if any, attention, even though its actions influence everyday life—the cost of consumer goods, home mortgage and car loan rates, interest on deposits, the job market and wages, home and stock prices, even the value of the dollar compared to other currencies, which influences export and import prices and the cost of overseas travel.

The Fed accomplishes this in a powerful, but indirect, manner by setting the interest rate that banks charge one another for overnight loans they keep on deposit at the Federal Reserve. These funds are the banks' "reserves." The interbank interest rate for these loans is called the "federal funds" rate—commonly referred to as the "fed funds" rate. The Fed determines what this overnight loan rate should be to meet its monetary policy goals, and that rate, along with expectations about how the Fed might move it in the future, influences all other interest rates, from short-term loans to thirty-year mortgages. Stock and bond prices are also heavily influenced by Fed rate moves. When the Fed cuts rates, all forms of business and consumer loans become less expensive and stock prices go up, as bonds that now carry lower interest become a less attractive investment alternative and as economic growth prospects improve. The foreign exchange value of the dollar also tends to fall, making exports less expensive for foreigners and imports more expensive for US consumers. When the Fed raises rates, lending becomes more costly, stock prices usually fall, bond yields rise, growth of profits is expected to slow, and the exchange rate of the dollar rises because investments in US bonds now offer higher returns.

What causes inflation? There are many reasons, but a main one is when consumer and business demand is greater than the supply of goods and services that can reliably be provided over time. Strong demand prompts businesses to hire and expand capacity. That's fine so long as businesses have some extra capacity to expand production and hire people with the right skills looking for jobs. When the demand runs into supply constraints at businesses and in the labor market, the excess demand prompts an increase in wages and prices. Then the price increases can build on themselves because people begin to expect them and raise wages and prices in anticipation of future increases or to make up lost ground if prices have outrun wages or squeezed profits. If it's not careful, the Fed can encourage such a price spiral by keeping interest rates too low, triggering excess borrowing and spending.

The increase in the inflation rate during the COVID-19 pandemic is an example of demand exceeding supply, not because of an overheated economy, but because of a series of bottlenecks in manufacturing and shipping. That has been exacerbated by a labor shortage caused by people shunning the lowest-paid jobs or leaving the labor market because of health concerns or the lack of affordable childcare. The Fed assumed inflation would subside once supply bottlenecks ended and the labor market returned to traditional patterns. But high inflation could persist if the prospect of rising prices becomes engrained in consumers' expectations.

When the Fed wants to stimulate a weak economy and reduce unemployment, it adopts an "accommodative" policy. That means it keeps interest rates low or reduces them—which is called monetary "easing"—to spur more lending and greater economic activity. Conversely, if the Fed is worried about a too-hot economy in which demand outstrips supply and increases the prospect of higher inflation, it adopts a "restrictive" policy. It increases interest rates—monetary "tightening"—and maintains them at a relatively high level to keep economic growth more in line with sustainable supply. The Fed began raising rates in 2022 to prevent higher inflation from becoming engrained in the economy.

The last four decades have seen extremes in both directions. In 1980, the Fed boosted the federal funds rate to a record 20 percent to combat double-digit inflation triggered by excessively easy monetary policy over the prior fifteen years and exacerbated by a crippling oil shortage. The result was the worst economic downturn since the Great Depression of the 1930s, as unemployment neared 11 percent by 1982. Inflation was defeated, but it took several years and severe pain for millions of Americans. Still, the greater stability in prices set the stage for several decades of nearly uninterrupted growth. In the early 1980s, the Fed focused on controlling the supply of money circulating in the economy. But it no longer does so because the money supply proved to be an unreliable way of managing inflation.

Three decades later, in response to the financial crisis of 2007–2009, the Fed slashed its interest rate to zero, started buying US Treasury bonds directly to pump trillions of dollars into the economy and lower mortgage and other interest rates, scrapped banks' reserve requirements, and began paying interest to banks on their deposits with the Fed. These extraordinary moves allowed the economy to recover and resume growing over the following decade, albeit more slowly than expected or desirable. But the economy fell off a cliff again when the COVID-19 pandemic forced a historic shutdown of economic activity in the spring of 2020. The Fed came to the rescue again with more bond-buying and zero interest rates. The Fed's success in reviving a critically ill economy twice in recent times shows how much it has learned about monetary policy since the Great Depression, when it did not ease policy aggressively and raised interest rates partway through the recovery—just the opposite of the easy money medicine the sick patient desperately needed at the time. If the Fed erred during the pandemic, it was the opposite of the past: it had provided too much stimulus that ignited inflation, a problem the central bank was forced to combat in 2022.

When Congress created the Fed, the system represented a compromise among public and private interests and between advocates for central vs. regional control—and it gave the new agency considerable independence from short-term political pressures. That's come in handy as the Fed has focused on its "dual mandate" of promoting full employment and achieving price stability, objectives mandated by Congress in 1978. In particular, the Fed can pursue unpopular interest rate hikes to combat inflation without being required to respond to pressure from the president or lawmakers, whose main concern is low interest rates and a booming economy in time for election years. The president names the Fed Board chair and six other governors, and Congress confirms them; but once installed, they cannot be fired by the elected politicians for their policy decisions. They can only be removed for "cause," which means malfeasance in office, such as accepting a bribe.

The governors who run the Fed—a collection of economists and people from business and finance—are appointed for a single fourteen-year term, though few stay that long. In rare cases, governors have served longer than fourteen years by first completing a departed board member's unexpired term and then winning reappointment to a full term. The chair of the board is nominated by the president for a four-year term; there is no limit on how many terms the chair serves so long as his or her tenure as a governor hasn't expired.

Interest rates are determined by the Fed governors and the presidents of twelve Federal Reserve Banks that represent US geographic regions. These Federal Reserve districts were created more than a century ago based upon their economic activity at that time. They are located in Atlanta, Boston, Chicago, Cleveland, Dallas, Kansas City, Minneapolis, New York, Philadelphia, Richmond, San Francisco, and St. Louis. Each president is chosen by the regional bank's board of directors, which is composed of bankers, businesspeople, and community representatives. The regional bank presidents must also be approved by the Fed's Board of Governors. Each regional bank's responsibilities include overseeing financial institutions in its area, providing loans to banks when needed to keep the financial system healthy, clearing checks, circulating currency, and enforcing federal consumer protection and fair lending laws.

The Fed governors and bank presidents meet eight times a year to determine interest rate policies. When they assemble, they comprise the Federal Open Market Committee (FOMC). It is so named because the committee influences interest rates by buying or selling

Treasury securities on the "open market," an operation carried out by the Federal Reserve Bank of New York. Only twelve of the nineteen committee members get to vote on monetary policy issues: the seven members of the Board of Governors; the president of the New York Fed; and four of the remaining eleven regional bank presidents, who rotate as voting participants every year.

They meet in a modern-day temple: a four-story headquarters building shaped like the letter H along Constitution Avenue and looking out at the National Mall. The white Georgian marble façade is in a classicist style stripped of ornamentation other than a sculpture of an eagle perched atop a ledge several floors above the main entrance. Designed by Paul Philippe Cret, the building cost $3.5 million to construct during the Depression and was dedicated by President Franklin D. Roosevelt in 1937. In 1982, it was named the Marriner S. Eccles Federal Reserve Board Building after the chairman appointed by FDR, who was in many respects the architect of the modern Fed, advising Roosevelt on its reorganization in 1935 and running it for more than a decade.

The interior is just as imposing as the exterior. One ascends to the boardroom, where the Board of Governors and FOMC meet, via a two-story atrium with dual staircases and a skylight etched with the outline of an eagle. The atrium floor is marble. The steps, walls, and columns of the atrium are of travertine marble from Italy. The ornate iron work on the stair rails was crafted by a Philadelphia artisan, Samuel Yellin. The fixtures were designed by Sidney Waugh from the Steuben Glass Company in Corning, New York. Oddly, he etched the signs of the zodiac on the glass rims of the fixtures, giving the impression to visitors entering the building that the Fed is guided by the stars in steering the nation's economy. No one at the Fed knows why he chose that design.

The FOMC convenes in an expansive two-story boardroom, fifty-six feet by thirty-two feet, and sits around a Honduran mahogany table that measures twenty-seven feet by eleven feet at its widest point, with a three-piece black granite insert. It is the fourth table to be used by board members. The original is in the building's library. Above the Honduran mahogany table hangs a 750-pound chandelier designed to resemble one from the Château de Malmaison, the retreat used by Napoleon and Josephine.

Initially, the FOMC made its interest decisions in secret to preserve flexibility and reduce political influence over its actions, but in recent decades it has become increasingly transparent. In 1994, it began releasing statements of its actions at the conclusion of its meetings. That same year, it began releasing transcripts of meetings with a five-year lag. In 2004, it moved up the release of summarized minutes of its meetings from six weeks to three weeks after they occurred. In 2011, the Fed chair started to hold news conferences, and the FOMC agreed to issue increasingly detailed forecasts by members on their outlook for the economy and interest rates. All of this was done to help financial markets price stocks and bonds based on realistic projections of what the Fed might be doing in the months and years ahead. Even with all this transparency, Fed officials are usually circumspect in their remarks, using "Fedspeak," or coded and often obscure language, to avoid misleading the markets about future intentions that frequently shift as the economy changes.

Although the Fed chair holds only one vote on the twelve-member FOMC, he or she is by far the most dominant force in guiding policy, because the chair leads the FOMC and sets the agenda for the meetings. In addition, the chair is the public face of the institution and held most accountable to Congress. The Fed operates best on broad consensus, and the chair works hard to craft unity that avoids dissents on interest rate decisions. Most of the time, the FOMC vote is unanimous. The chair also strives to maintain independence from the political branches of government so as to be seen acting in the best interests of the country, not the president who appointed the chair. That is why the Fed rarely changes interest rates in the months leading up to a presidential election, lest the move be seen as helping or hurting one of the candidates. It is also why Fed chairs usually keep comments on other aspects of economic policy to very general terms so they won't be seen as an endorsement or criticism of a president's agenda.

Fed chiefs are not immune to political pressure, however, particularly when they rachet up interest rates to curb inflation—or take away the "punch bowl just as the party gets going." That metaphor is credited to William McChesney Martin, who ran the Fed from 1951 through 1970, the longest tenure by a chair. In one memorable example, Chair Arthur Burns, under intense lobbying from President Nixon, pumped up the economy prior to Nixon's reelection campaign in 1972, moves Burns defended on economic grounds but which led to a burst of inflation a year later. And in the lead-up to the 2020 election, President Donald Trump openly and repeatedly attacked Fed chair Jerome Powell for not cutting interest rates to zero. The Fed subsequently reduced rates, but not to zero, as the president was advocating, citing as its reason a weakness in the economy—not Trump's tantrums.

Fifteen years before Yellen joined the Fed, President Jimmy Carter appointed as chair economist Paul Volcker, who had the unenviable task of taming an inflation rate that topped 13 percent in 1979. The 6-foot-7, cigar-chomping Volcker led the Fed on an unprecedented course of high interest rates that triggered a deep recession. That did the job. Volcker was hailed as the inflation slayer, and President Ronald Reagan rewarded him in 1983 with another term, even though Volcker was a Democrat and Reagan a Republican. Four years later, Reagan turned to fellow Republican Alan Greenspan, a wily political animal who knew how to play power brokers from both parties.

In his early years, Greenspan played saxophone in a jazz band, memorized baseball statistics, and became a disciple of Ayn Rand and her philosophy of objectivism. It puts self-interest in pursuit of happiness above all else—the opposite of Yellen's embrace of empathy. Beginning in the 1950s, Greenspan ran a highly successful consulting firm and advised Republican politicians. In 1991, President George H. W. Bush reluctantly reappointed Greenspan to another term even though the president complained that the Fed chief was cutting interest rates too slowly and had caused a mild recession in 1990–1991. In fact, the Fed had slashed rates from more than 8 percent at the start of 1990 to 3 percent by September 1992. But it didn't help Bush. He lost reelection that fall to Bill Clinton.

Satisfied with a 3 percent interest rate, the Fed sat on its hands well into the winter of 1994. This was the world Janet Yellen would join later that summer. She was the most junior member of the Board of Governors, but she would quickly have an outsized influence on the nation's central bank—and the US economy.

✣ ✣ ✣

IN FEBRUARY 1994, GREENSPAN'S FED RAISED INTEREST RATES for the first time since 1989, an unexpected move that shocked an unprepared bond market and triggered a mass sell-off. The reason: bond prices in the resale market fall when interest rates rise so that the buyer can get the same percentage return as on a newly issued bond. Consider a thirty-year $100,000 bond paying 4 percent a year, or $4,000. If a new $100,000 bond carries a 5 percent interest rate, the 4 percent bond will sell for only $80,000 so that the $4,000 annual interest payment now equals 5 percent.

When Yellen attended her first FOMC meeting on August 16, 1994, the committee already had boosted the fed funds rate four times, from 3 percent to 4.25 percent. The "Greenbook," the report on the economic forecast and recommended policy actions prepared by the Fed staff for FOMC meetings, had said the fed funds rate needed to increase another full percentage point to keep the economy on an even keel without overheating. Most of the debate focused on how big an increase to adopt.

Greenspan welcomed Yellen to the meeting at the start, then surveyed committee members for their opinions. Yellen was among the last to speak. She argued for a very small increase in interest rates so unemployment could decline further "without risking significantly a pickup in inflation," according to the official transcript. Greenspan argued for a one-half percentage point boost in interest rates, from 4.25 percent to 4.75 percent—double the quarter-point increase the FOMC normally approved when it was raising rates. He said a larger increase then might make future increases unnecessary. Greenspan surveyed the committee for reactions. When he finally came to Yellen, she consented. The vote was 12–0.

Yellen soon aligned herself with the new vice chair, Alan Blinder, since they were the first Democrats on the FOMC since the Carter years. "Alan and I were very close in part because we were Clinton appointees," she explained. "Alan knew Clinton because he'd been at CEA and worked on the '92 campaign. At the time, Clinton was raising taxes and cutting budget deficits, and I suspect that the last thing he wanted to see was interest rates go up. We got there at a time when the economy was improving very rapidly following Clinton's big budget deficit-reduction package in '93." The two Clinton appointees decided that the Fed could raise rates to keep inflation in check without slowing the economy's momentum.

"So, we arrive in '94 and Alan and I voted to raise interest rates, which was something that Clinton most likely wasn't really happy about," Yellen explained. "We were in a situation where an honest read of the economy just seemed to call for tightening monetary policy. And we knew we had a president who had appointed us and who would probably be very unenthusiastic about what we were doing. The Fed is independent and, as a governor, your job is to make the best judgment, based on the evidence. And, of course, we know what happened in the nineties, which is the economy went on a tear. It boomed and unemployment fell to the lowest levels we'd seen in thirty years without any increase in inflation.

"Alan and I thought raising rates was the right thing to do, but we also worried about an overreaction. You can do too much and can kill the economy. It's a delicate matter. We were worrying that Greenspan was being too aggressive. So, we were supportive, but also we were concerned that we were part of something that might kill the economy. Just the fact that we'd been appointed by a president who was tightening fiscal policy and looking to the Fed to compensate by keeping the economy on track and growing gave me a feeling of extra responsibility. No one ever leaned on me about it."

Blinder, who took over as vice chair seven weeks before Yellen came on board, laughed that it had been so long since a Democrat had joined the Fed Board of Governors—fourteen years—that "I used to joke that I felt like a kidney transplant." With Yellen's arrival, he said, "we were consistently a small minority group on all manner of bank regulatory and supervisory matters, things that get no attention in the financial press."

Unlike the free-market Reaganites on the board, Yellen and Blinder believed in closer federal oversight of the banking industry to protect consumers from abuses. "There wasn't much dispute in those early days on monetary policy," Blinder recalled. "As the two liberals—as the conservatives who comprised most of the FOMC called us then—we thought interest rates needed to go up. So, there was not a lot of conflict about that until at the end of that tightening cycle. By November '94 through February '95, both of us were feeling uneasy about how far and fast the Fed had come on interest rates. There was some substantial disagreement between us and

Greenspan over monetary policy at the end of that tightening cycle, but not for most of the others on the FOMC."

At Yellen's second FOMC meeting in September 1994, Greenspan recommended that the group keep the fed funds rate at 4.75 percent, but he warned that growing economic momentum and upward pressure on prices—inflation was running at 3 percent—would likely require a sizable boost in interest rates at the committee's next meeting in November. The FOMC backed him with just one dissension from the president of the Federal Reserve Bank of Richmond, J. Alfred Broaddus, who favored an immediate rate hike.

The November FOMC meeting sparked a debate over the staff's recommendation that interest rates would have to jump 1.5 percentage points to 6.25 percent to slow a rapidly growing economy and engineer a "soft landing"—Fedspeak for an economic slowdown that restrains inflation without causing a recession, known as a "hard landing." Greenspan proposed going halfway immediately with a three-quarters of a percent boost.

The two "liberals" argued that the staff proposal was overkill and failed to consider the long lag period from when interest rates go up to when the economy slows. Yellen warned that the Fed could cause a recession in 1996 by going too far, but also acknowledged that without "some further tightening, I think there would be an unacceptable risk that inflation would accelerate." She said she preferred a half-percent increase but could live with three-quarters of a percent rise. Blinder used the analogy of cranking up the thermostat in a cold hotel room and then waking up at 2:30 in the morning in a sweat. The classic mistake of monetary policy, he argued, "is overdoing it . . . impatience in waiting for the lagged effects of what already has been done." At the end of the meeting, Greenspan had prevailed with a unanimous vote. The Fed had now boosted rates from 3 percent to 5.5 percent in less than a year, and it wasn't done.

At its December meeting, the FOMC kept rates unchanged, as it acknowledged the lag highlighted by Yellen and Blinder five weeks earlier. On February 1, Greenspan pushed for another rate boost to 6 percent—double the rate when the FOMC met barely a year before. Yellen expressed concerns that such a move increased the odds of a recession, as did Blinder, who revived his analogy of the impatient hotel guest turning the thermostat too far. In the end, however, both reluctantly went along with Greenspan. They acknowledged his observation that the financial markets were expecting a half-point rate boost and might crash—along with the dollar—if the Fed disappointed. Once again, Greenspan got a unanimous vote. It would be the last time the Fed raised rates for more than four years.

The day before that vote, the FOMC debated whether the Fed should adopt an explicit inflation target that it would make public and use to guide policy. Greenspan tapped Richmond Fed president Broaddus, an anti-inflation "hawk," to argue in favor of such a target, and Yellen, a leading "dove" on the issue, to argue against. Broaddus stressed that a clear target would help the Fed foster a better economic performance. "I am convinced," Broaddus said, "that it could help improve and increase our contribution to the nation's economic welfare." Yellen countered with her signature empathetic argument, that the Fed had to be flexible in allowing higher inflation to avoid a recession, higher unemployment, and the human suffering that would result:

"To me, a wise and humane policy is occasionally to let inflation rise even when inflation is running above target," she argued. Ensuring that inflation always stayed below the Fed's target—even when temporary shocks such as oil price hikes occurred—would require so big an increase in interest rates that a major economic downturn with high unemployment would be the result. It was a trade-off Yellen found unacceptable. "The extreme proposal—that we need to counter shocks with a pure inflation target—is to me draconian."

She also raised the argument that the Fed's credibility would be on the line because the FOMC would not stick to an inflation target if that meant crashing the economy: "Who would be prepared to believe that the FOMC is single-mindedly going to pursue an inflation target regardless of real economic performance? So, that means that the targets are going to be perceived as a hoax. They are not going to be any more believable than I would be if I told my child that I was going to cut off his hand if he put it in the candy drawer."

The subsequent debate revealed the full committee was split right down the middle. Greenspan tabled the proposal.

Looking back at that period, Blinder said he and Yellen huddled together almost every day as the two doves surrounded by hawks. Their close working relationship in itself was unusual. "Governors don't pal around with each other very much," Blinder explained. "One of the reasons is because of the Sunshine Act [which restricted private meetings of policymakers]. Anytime three of us were in the same room together, we used to make a joke that somebody had to leave before we got arrested. That discouraged much in the way of social time with your fellow governors. But Janet and I were kind of like a committee of two. We didn't know each other that well before, but after a few months, the two of us were fast friends and we have been ever since."

"The Fed is inherently a conservative organization. It is, after all, a central bank," he continued. "As the first Democrat to go there in fourteen years, I was also the first member of the board to allow the AFL-CIO [American Federation of Labor and Congress of Industrial Organizations] in the building. Wow. But I thought we're a central bank for all the people, and we should hear from them. That was not the preexisting view in the house."

Blinder noted that a big divide separated him and Yellen from the rest of the board over a key role of the Fed beyond setting interest rates: supervising and regulating banks to make sure they remain solvent and avoid reckless financial transactions. "Greenspan said he would have just been happy to get rid of bank supervision. I really believe in it, not that we would try to tie banks up in knots, but a number of questions would come up about concentration, bank mergers, expansion of bank powers into new spheres. Consumer protection was a big one where left-right perspectives differ much more than on monetary policy. There were any number of board votes at that time on regulatory issues that went 5 to 2."

Yellen's brother John remembered her expressing concern about a change in banking rules that would allow them to engage in activities that would boost their profits but might put at risk the funds of small savers and investors. "I think she was probably thinking about my mother, this woman who gets the newspaper every night and writes stock prices on the back of an envelope. You're not talking about a fortune, but whether to sell ten shares of this and buy ten shares of that. This ordinary housewife kind of person was probably on her mind when I heard her talking about how unfair this rule would be for someone like that."

Yellen did not know a lot about regulation, Blinder said, "so she absorbed things really quickly and smartly, and was not afraid to stick her neck out where she thought her neck should be stuck out. But she was cautious about what she said. Almost everyone came into FOMC meeting with a script and read it to be careful about what they said. Janet was like that. Greenspan would just talk and I would talk from notes, but Janet wanted to measure her words and not say things that when the transcript was published, five years later, she would say, 'Oh, I wish I never said that.' She was hyperprepared. When she became Fed chair and had to hold these press conferences that she inherited from [predecessor] Ben Bernanke, she hated them. The amount of effort it took her to prepare for them was enormous. I used to tell her, 'Janet, you could do a third of that preparation. You know the stuff better than anybody else.' But that didn't matter. Her way is to do three times as much preparation as she needs."

On monetary policy, Yellen and Blinder had an unlikely ally in Fed governor Lawrence Lindsey, a conservative Republican economist appointed to the board by President George H. W. Bush in 1991. Known for having a good sense of humor and being a maverick on economic policy, Lindsey grew very fond of Yellen and stayed in touch after he went to work for President George W. Bush as chief economic adviser.

"Janet, Alan, and I were of like minds quite a bit," he said in explaining their informal coalition to exert greater leverage over Greenspan. "The chairman was all powerful. So, it was really more incumbent upon us to work together to try and shape policy, and I think we had an influence. It wasn't really us doves against those hawks. It was that we all hang together or we all hang separately and become ineffectual in terms of influence."

Lindsey added that he admired Yellen's transparency. "I don't think she was ever deceptive in where she was coming from. I've known her a long time, and I have always had a candid conversation with her about our disagreements. It's very hard to debate in Washington today, but back in the nineties, people could actually have an honest conversation. It was a different era."

❖ ❖ ❖

YELLEN'S PARTNERSHIP WITH BLINDER ON THE FED DID NOT last long. Blinder, a loyal Democrat and 1992 campaign adviser, was hoping Clinton would name him to replace Greenspan in 1996. After all, it was an election year, and Greenspan had a long record as a partisan Republican before joining the Fed. Their rivalry broke into the open as a result of several speculative news stories about who would head the Fed when Greenspan's term expired, and that led to tension between the two men. Greenspan had improved his own chances for reappointment by winning universal plaudits for slowing inflation without throwing the economy in a ditch. After the string of sizable rate hikes throughout 1994 and into early 1995, Greenspan reversed course, engineering rate cuts in 1995 and early 1996. A consummate politician, Greenspan also had forged a close working relationship with then Treasury secretary Robert Rubin, a trusted Clinton confidant on economic matters.

Financial markets all but demanded that Clinton keep Greenspan, and he did not disappoint. Once it became clear to Blinder that he was not going to get the job, he resigned from the Fed. His last day was January 31, 1996. Three weeks later, Clinton officially nominated Greenspan to chair the Fed for another four years. Yellen's friendship with Blinder may have created distance between her and Greenspan. But when Blinder left, she became close to Greenspan, which allowed her to have more influence over interest rate policies than a relatively new governor ordinarily would have.

Greenspan, who retired in 2006 after nearly nineteen years as Fed chair, grew fond of Yellen as a colleague on the Board of Governors. He later told friends that he admired her training as an academic, which he was not, and depended on her to keep him abreast of the latest economic studies. One confidant said Greenspan often "was up to his ears in work and didn't have time to read all the latest studies. So, he trusted her to summarize them for him because he had tremendous respect for her intellect."

By 1996, Greenspan convinced himself that inflation was less of a threat than he had previously thought. The reason was a belief, based largely on intuition, that a sluggish economic rebound following the 1990–1991 recession, with its anemic pace of job creation, made workers perpetually "insecure" and willing to forgo wage increases in return for greater job security. Workers obviously preferred pay increases that were higher than inflation to improve their standard of living but often settled for cost-of-living increases that kept their current standard of living intact. If worried about losing a job, however, they would be more willing to go without a pay increase or accept a small one. Weak wage growth meant less inflationary pressure. This was a significant hypothesis for the Fed because, if true, the FOMC could relax interest rates more than under the conventional models it was using.

Greenspan's problem was that he was having trouble convincing the FOMC that he was right, in part because he could not produce a credible economic model to prove his hypothesis. Later in his nineteen-year reign as chair, Greenspan was revered by Wall Street and Fed colleagues for his deft leadership that led at that time to the longest economic expansion since World War II. Presidents of both parties felt they had no choice but to reappoint him, and *Washington Post* journalist Bob Woodward even dubbed him "Maestro" in his 2000 book of the same name that chronicled Greenspan's orchestration of the central bank. In the mid-1990s, Greenspan was still regarded as a mere mortal, and most members of the FOMC were skeptics about his "insecure worker" hypothesis. But he had a valuable resource in Yellen, who would help him make his case to keep interest rates where they were: from a peak of 6 percent in early 1995 to 5.25 percent in January 1996.

At the time, "inflation had been coming down and there were a lot of people around the FOMC table who were very worried that it was going to pick up again and the Fed should be tightening monetary policy," Yellen recalled. "But Greenspan had this instinct that this is a different thing. This isn't inflationary. He said the labor market changed in ways that made unions and workers much less aggressive about bargaining and wages. Firms weren't experiencing cost pressures and profit margins were good. He just didn't see any of the pressures that would lead to inflation."

During the spring and summer of 1996, many FOMC members were prodding Greenspan to raise interest rates right away because the Fed doesn't like to boost them close to Election Day, lest it be accused of trying to influence a presidential election. But he was a strong-willed individual who was determined to act based on his own mindset. "Greenspan has his own idiosyncratic framework—one that differs from that embraced by most economists these days," Yellen continued. "He would talk to people in the committee about why he thought it wasn't necessary to raise rates when we weren't in an inflationary environment. And the people were kind of rolling their eyes. I think he may have felt that he was in danger of losing control of the committee. Some staff economists who reported to Greenspan also thought he was making a huge mistake. It was the staff and most of the committee against Greenspan, with Greenspan struggling to keep control of the situation and not raise rates."

Yellen rescued Greenspan from his tight spot by writing a cogent and thoughtful memo interpreting what was happening in the labor market and why inflationary pressures weren't increasing. "I gave it to Greenspan and said, 'This is how I look at what you're discussing.' I think he really appreciated my memo as a contribution. He even distributed it to the entire committee. I don't think he felt he had much support from the staff. That left him scrambling entirely on his own to explain his reasoning to a committee, and also a staff, that are in disagreement. So, in that period, I formed more of an alliance with Greenspan."

Yellen kept a copy of the twelve-page memo, dated June 10, 1996, and titled "Job Insecurity, the Natural Rate of Unemployment, and the Phillips Curve." It outlined a theory that explained Greenspan's hypothesis: worker insecurity caused by a technological boom that was eliminating jobs kept wages and prices from rising even when unemployment was very low and would have increased inflation in prior times.

The memo, laden with equations and references to various economic models, cited evidence of a decline in wages that "is consistent with a statement made by Alan Greenspan in various speeches—that increased job insecurity should result in a willingness on the part of workers to accept a cut in real wages for a time, but not indefinitely." She concluded that job insecurity appeared to limit worker turnover, as employees choose to keep the jobs they have, even without pay increases, rather than risk looking for work elsewhere. And the lack of turnover means fewer new workers to train, which bolsters company productivity—and, thus, profits.

The memo concluded by noting that reports on local economic conditions from the Fed's regional banks found a surprising lack of workers leaving jobs, an unusual development when the labor market is so tight, another sign that Greenspan's instincts were correct: "The absence of any barking from this particular dog strikes me as mild evidence that something has changed."

Former Fed vice chair Donald Kohn, who was a senior staffer at the time, remembered Yellen's memo as being instrumental in helping explain the FOMC's puzzlement about an economy that was growing strongly but generating less inflation and slower wage growth than expected. "Greenspan had a hypothesis that the recession created 'worker insecurity' and, as a consequence, there was less cost pressure and less inflation pressure," he recalled. "We didn't need to tighten policy quite so much, and Greenspan did some surveys to measure this 'worker insecurity.' But Janet took his insights and wrote down a model that embedded his insights in a broader labor market macro model and gave it to Greenspan. He was really impressed and very grateful that someone was taking him seriously and showing how you would work this out in a mathematical model. After that, they had a good relationship, from my staff perspective. He had a lot of respect for her."

With Yellen's help, Greenspan's "worker insecurity" argument prevailed, and the FOMC kept interest rates unchanged for the rest of 1996.

* * *

In mid-1996, Yellen and Greenspan found themselves on opposite sides of a crucial debate about inflation. He wanted the Fed to commit to zero inflation as its ultimate goal. Yellen, always empathetic toward all the workers who would lose their jobs if the central bank pursued that goal, had argued that a little bit of inflation is an equitable trade-off to prevent mass layoffs. Yellen won the day and, in so doing, left a marker that guided the Fed for a generation.

At an FOMC meeting on July 2, Greenspan revived an inconclusive debate from late 1994 about whether the Fed should adopt an inflation target, something Yellen had opposed at the time. Now, he put a different question to the committee members: If we are going to be guided by an inflation target, what is the definition of "price stability"? Yellen was first out of the gate with a carefully prepared argument that it should be defined as 2 percent inflation. Her first point was that the Fed needed a small inflation cushion to prevent a dangerous deflationary spiral, which occurs when prices fall and proves difficult to reverse. Keeping inflation slightly above zero would allow the Fed maneuvering room to avoid such a dire situation.

Her second argument was that zero inflation would necessitate that wage increases also average zero, which meant that for every worker that got a pay raise, one would have to get a pay cut. Once again, she was worried about the impact on low-income workers struggling to pay the rent and feed their families. Yellen said that allowing a little inflation would be more than offset by the social benefit of higher employment and wages. Targeting 2 percent inflation would still be an improvement over the current 3 percent inflation rate.

Then she put Greenspan on the spot. "Mr. Chairman, will you define 'price stability' for me?" He replied, "Price stability is that state in which expected changes in the general price level do not effectively alter business or household decisions." She still didn't let him off the hook. "Could you please put a number on that?" she persisted to laughter around the table. "I would say the number is zero, if inflation is properly measured," he answered.

Greenspan then went around the room asking committee members how they would define "price stability," and a consensus quickly formed around Yellen's definition. It was a rare rebuke of Greenspan, yet he took it well, acknowledging that the inflation target would now be 2 percent.

On July 3, as the group assembled again to wrap up its two-day meeting, Greenspan began by reminding everyone "how very important it is for all of us to recognize the highly confidential nature of what we talk about at an FOMC meeting." He then added a stern warning: "The discussion we had yesterday was exceptionally interesting and important. I will tell you that if the 2 percent inflation figure gets out of this room, it is going to create more problems for us than I think any of you might anticipate. I beseech you all, especially those of you who have not heard this speech before—and there are a number in this room who have not—to realize that it is very damaging to this institution when anybody conveys information from inside the System concerning what members of this group are thinking or what the FOMC is likely to do. You are all free to indicate what you think the economy is doing. . . . What you do not have the right to do is to talk for the Committee."

The committee members remained tight-lipped, and the Fed did not hint until more than a decade later that it was following a 2 percent inflation target. Finally, on January 25, 2012, Fed chair Ben Bernanke formally set an explicit inflation target. It was 2 percent.

Economist Laurence Meyer, who had just joined the Board of Governors a week before that July 1996 FOMC meeting, recalled it as both his first and most interesting committee meeting during the six years he served in the post. "This one was just captivating," he said. "Janet came in and really had articulated a view of what price stability meant. That was the beginning of a 2 percent goal, and the chair said, 'Do not tell anybody we talked about this, or there'll be hell to pay.' That was an amazing period during which the staff did a lot of studies and most people on the outside thought the objective was 1.5 to 2 percent. But it's amazing that the committee didn't adopt a quantitative objective of 2 percent for such a long time after that."

Donald Kohn said Greenspan at the time did not want a specific inflation number that might tie his hands. "He was very concerned," Kohn said. "I don't think he was necessarily opposed to something around 2 percent. After all, inflation was running around 3 percent at the time. He had this definition of price stability: when inflation is low enough that households and businesses don't have to pay any attention to it in their decision-making. He just didn't want to be specific at all. He saw it as a constraint and thought there would be political repercussions. That's why he said it would be a horrible thing if it ever got out."

Robby Akerlof credited a paper that his father wrote with economists George Perry and Bill Dickens for providing his mother with the ammunition she needed to make her persuasive argument. "They wrote two papers on a rationale for having more inflation," he explained. "The basic idea was that having a little bit of inflation is a way of giving a wage cut to people without having to reduce their salary in nominal terms. That's a beneficial feature of having a little bit of inflation because it can help you to have a higher employment rate. Those papers were an attempt to formalize this argument, and I believe my mother produced something internal at the Fed beyond those papers that would have helped to codify this, as well."

By September of 1996, Yellen found herself at odds with Greenspan on a different issue. He had come to believe intuitively that a productivity boom was underway because of the rapid growth of the internet and soaring business spending on computers. It was another reason why the economy was becoming more efficient, and thus able to grow faster with less unemployment than previously thought, without sparking higher inflation. Greenspan felt hampered in making his case, however, because official government statistics did not show a productivity boom. He argued the measurements were flawed and underestimated the real productivity of workers in a burgeoning internet age.

The impact of the productivity boom Greenspan highlighted set off a vigorous debate among economists around the country, with some supporting Greenspan's view and others pooh-poohing it. Neither Yellen nor Laurence Meyer, who quickly became a like-minded friend of hers on the board, bought the productivity argument. They felt interest rates needed to be nudged up to keep inflation in check. So, in advance of the September 24 FOMC meeting, the pair went to Greenspan and urged him to recommend that the committee tighten rates. As Meyer later wrote in his 2004 memoir, *A Term at the Fed*, "We both said that we would not be able to support the Chairman much longer if he didn't recommend a move. It was not an ultimatum, but it was a message that our patience was running out." They left without any commitment from Greenspan.

At the meeting, Greenspan argued for standing pat, and cited his productivity hypothesis to explain why rising wages were not spilling over into price increases. Left unsaid, though clearly on his mind, was the fact that the presidential election was just weeks away, and the Fed shouldn't intrude with any move that would help or hurt President Clinton or Republican nominee Bob Dole. Meyer and Yellen were skeptical of the productivity argument but reluctantly went along with Greenspan's recommendation, even though Yellen had just characterized the economy as "operating in an inflationary danger zone." The vote was 11–1, with one bank president favoring a rate increase. "Later, I understand that the Chairman referred to me as 'politically tone-deaf,'" Meyer wrote in his memoir. "For the sake of the Fed's independence, I was quite happy to be politically tone-deaf. And I'm also pleased that the Chairman, in contrast, was politically savvy."

Greenspan ultimately proved to be right about productivity. The economy grew for ten straight years, from 1991 to 2001, the longest expansion in history at the time, without worrisome inflation. It ended in March 2001, a year after the dot.com bubble burst. Greenspan had worried years earlier about inflated stock prices for internet companies leading to a crash. He was right about that, too.

Meyer served with Yellen on the Fed for only eight months before she went on to a new job, but they became good friends during that short time, and she left an indelible impression: "There's an order where people sit around Fed meetings, and I was sitting next to Janet. And when you have the go-arounds, you raise your hand and the secretary puts you on the list for when you're going to talk. And if Janet went first, there was nothing left for me to say. I would tell her, 'Come on. I've got to go before you the next time.' She's an amazing scholar and a generalist. You don't find these too much anymore. I know a lot about very little, but she can cover the whole gamut of economics. She had this incredible clarity and ability to present in ways that everybody understood and had the total respect of everybody on the board and the FOMC. I love

Janet. I would say everybody loves Janet. She's the nicest person in the world."

Yellen left the Fed in February 1997 to become chair of President Clinton's Council of Economic Advisers. "I remember having a conversation with her about that," Meyer said. "She had been offered this by the president. She really loved being at the Fed and said she would like to stay, but you can't say 'no' to the president."

# - 5 -

# CLINTON'S GOOD OL' BOYS CLUB

*"I guess we made the short list"*

Janet Yellen was settling in comfortably as a Federal Reserve governor and making an impact after a little more than two years in the job. Then in late 1996, an offer came from the Clinton White House to chair the Council of Economic Advisers, one of many senior jobs that had to be filled following Clinton's reelection and the formation of a second-term administration. She wasn't the first choice.

Clinton's top economic advisers, particularly deputy Treasury secretary Lawrence Summers, were delighted when CEA chair Joseph Stiglitz, considered by some to be a volatile personality, decided to leave and become chief economist at the World Bank. Stiglitz, Summers, and Gene Sperling, the newly named director of the National Economic Council (NEC), were high in brain power but frequently clashed over policy differences. Several colleagues recall a lot of shouting matches. Conflict was common because the National Economic Council was a new White House office created by Clinton to coordinate economic policy. In fulfilling that mission, the NEC often poached in areas the CEA considered its territory.

Alan Blinder seemed to be a natural choice to head the three-member CEA, which usually recruits top-notch university professors willing to take a leave for one or two years. Blinder had been a member of the council during Clinton's first term and had been vice chair of the Fed before returning to Princeton in early 1996, when it became clear he would not replace Alan Greenspan as chair of the central bank. Incoming White House chief of staff Erskine Bowles called Blinder and offered him the job. To Bowles's surprise, Blinder turned him down, saying he could not work in an administration where he knew he would be in continual conflict with Lawrence Summers. Bowles would not take no for an answer and persuaded Blinder to come to Washington to meet face-to-face with Clinton.

It's next to impossible to say "no" to the president of the United States, but Blinder mustered the courage to do just that. He explained that it would not be in Clinton's interest to have a CEA chair butting heads with Summers, who, Blinder noted, had the disruptive habit of arguing about every policy issue just to be contrary and win the debate. Blinder thanked the president for offering him the job but said he just could not accept it.

Other officials involved in finding a new CEA chair said Blinder might have taken the job under conditions that gave him more authority over policy than was acceptable to the White House, so the search for a candidate resumed. "People looked around for someone they knew," said a former senior administration official. "There was a desire to have somebody people were comfortable with rather than to bring somebody completely new from the outside. Everyone thought Yellen was a first-rate macroeconomist. The two driving forces in that appointment were [Treasury secretary] Robert Rubin, who was captain of the economics team, and Erskine Bowles."

In contrast to her response when offered the Fed job, Yellen did not jump at the chance to join the Clinton White House. She loved working at the Fed, felt she was doing interesting and important work there, and wasn't sure she would fit in the highly political environment at the White House. On top of that, Republicans had won control of Congress in the 1994 elections and were on an anti-government kick to eliminate federal agencies and offices after spending four decades as the minority party. Among those high on its list was the CEA, which Republican lawmakers considered a waste of money, even though its budget was tiny. It had survived with the help of prominent Republican and Democratic economists. They lobbied aggressively on behalf of the office as an indispensable in-house think tank that provides, in the CEA's own words, "objective economic advice" to the president based on analysis of research, empirical evidence, and the best data available. Departing chair Stiglitz; Berkeley colleague Laura Tyson, who was leaving as director of the National Economic Council; and CEA chief of staff Michele Jolin all joined in an effort to persuade Yellen to take the job.

"She was happy where she was at the Fed," recalled a friend who worked in the White House at the time. "She was thinking, 'Where should I be? What's the right role I should play to influence the policy process?' So, at first, she said, 'I want to be helpful, of course, but I'd really rather not. I'm happy where I am.' Honestly, I think she wants to make a difference, and I can see her and George together at their dinner table figuring this stuff out and she says, 'I'll play my role wherever is best. I'm not looking for the trappings or prestige of the job.' The quality of the job was always her focus."

While teaching at Harvard, Yellen had a chance to work at the Council of Economic Advisers as a staff economist. One of her Yale professors, William Fellner, who also taught her husband,

George, was a member of the CEA and invited her to lunch with Alan Greenspan, who chaired the council from 1974 to 1977. They took her to the White House mess, and Greenspan said he wanted someone to build a forecasting model. "I would have been open to going to the CEA to get more involved in policy," she said, but not to work on an in-house forecasting model. So, she stayed at Harvard.

Robby Akerlof, who was fifteen at the time his mother was considering chairing the CEA, recalled the family discussing the pros and cons of the job: the influence on policy vs. the rough-and-tumble politics. "Our perspective was that this is just an incredible thing to be asked to do. It was outside of any expectations of what could possibly happen," he said. "The problem was that the politics in the White House are very different from the politics at the Fed. I think she really knew how to navigate the Fed, which has these well-defined rules about how everything operates. That goes back to her mother's influence. She knows how to work within a system with rules and really do things well. Jumping into the White House as someone who was kind of at the margin gave her pause. I mean, the CEA chair is often someone who doesn't get a lot of respect in the White House."

As Yellen vacillated, Lawrence Summers came over to her house, and they talked for a long time about the job and whether it was something she could and should do. "He was very nice about it and discussed it with me in a lot of detail," she said. "I was thinking that I had just been at the Fed long enough to understand how the place worked. My influence was increasing over time, and I felt like I'm finally making a contribution; I knew the lay of the land; my relationship with Greenspan had improved; I was sympathetic with what he was trying to accomplish and thought I was being helpful. I was happy. And I knew that the CEA job involved having to know absolutely everything. I didn't feel I knew absolutely everything. I knew there were enormous holes in my knowledge relative to a job that required advising the president on everything. That concerned me."

The chance to influence presidential policy won out. Shortly before Christmas 1996, Yellen said "yes," and Clinton nominated her as the eighteenth chair of the council, just four months after it marked the fiftieth anniversary of its creation. Former Yale roommate Vivian Nash went to Washington to watch Clinton introduce Yellen and other new cabinet members at a news conference. Yellen had been standing next to departing Labor secretary Robert Reich, who, like her, was barely five feet tall in shoes. "Janet told me later that Reich had whispered to her, 'I guess we made the short list,'" Nash said. "She thought it was so funny."

At her confirmation hearing before the Senate Banking Committee on February 5, 1997, Chairman Alfonse D'Amato, a New York Republican, joked at the outset, "I've just indicated to the nominee, Janet, what great affection and devotion she must have for the president, as well as this nation, to give up this magnificent, incredible position you already have, the fourteen-year term on the Federal Reserve Board, to undertake this position," which could come to an abrupt end at the will of the president. Senator Barbara Boxer, a California Democrat, who introduced the nominee to the committee, called Yellen "the perfect candidate" and noted her life-long goal as an empathy economist to "raise the standard of living for everyone."

In her opening statement, Yellen observed that the economy was in "very good health," and the "misery index," the sum of the inflation and unemployment rates, was the lowest since 1968. Highlighting her signature issue of inequality, she said, "We need to reverse the disturbing trend that emerged in the 1970s toward widening of the gap in earnings between those at the upper end of the wage distribution and those at the bottom."

Even so, she hardly came across as a left-wing do-gooder. Rather, she described herself as a "non-ideological pragmatist," and then backed that up during the hearing by supporting Clinton's push to balance the federal budget. Yet, she opposed a Republican-backed proposal for a balanced-budget constitutional amendment as being too inflexible in times of economic distress.

She also came out in favor of changing the inflation calculation for determining annual cost-of-living adjustments in Social Security benefits, even though it would mean smaller yearly increases for seniors. It was a change Democrats found abhorrent but was embraced by many Republicans as a sensible budget-reduction move. Putting her economic beliefs above her partisan loyalty, Yellen conceded that most members of her profession believed the consumer price index overstated the actual increase in the cost of living. The powerful senior citizen lobby raised hell over the proposal, and the change was never made.

In another surprising admission in response to Republican questioning, Yellen said she favored unwinding the 1933 Glass-Steagall Banking Act. It barred commercial banks from also becoming stock and bond brokers, because Congress saw reckless banking practices as a cause of the 1929 stock market crash that ushered in the Great Depression. In later years, Congress chipped away at the wall separating bank lending and financial trading until Glass-Steagall was all but dead in the 1990s. She said she was not philosophically opposed to letting banks get back into long-barred investment activities, but Congress should move slowly on that front to make sure banks did not plunge headlong back into foolish financial activities that would put their solvency at risk once again.

Yellen's go-slow advice was ignored. Aided by support from the Clinton administration and under intense pressure from the powerful financial industry, Congress voted overwhelmingly in November 1999 to repeal the last vestiges of Glass-Steagall—and allowed history to repeat itself. Just eight years after that vote, reckless banking practices triggered a financial crash that ushered in the Great Recession of 2007–2009.

Yellen's performance before the committee sold even the Republicans, who were impressed with her clear, thoughtful, and honest responses. She was confirmed by the full Senate unanimously, and on February 18, 1997, she officially took charge of the CEA.

The two other members of the council at the time were Alicia Munnell, the former Boston Fed and Treasury Department economist who had first met Yellen in Washington in 1977, and Jeffrey Frankel, who knew Yellen from his teaching days at Berkeley. Munnell, who had joined the council when Stiglitz ran it, figured the arrival of a new chair meant she should leave. "I said, 'Welcome. I think this is a sign for me to go.' And she was so nice. She said, 'I don't know this job. Please stay, just stay for some period of time.' And so, I did, and it was wonderful and a pleasure to be around her," Munnell recalled. "We worked, went to meetings together, gossiped and laughed and growled because [National Economic Council director] Gene Sperling was keeping us until all hours of the night, and I wanted to get the hell out of there. We had a great working and personal relationship."

"She's unique as someone who has accomplished so much and has had so much recognition and yet is just a normal human being," Munnell continued. "I remember sometime during July 1997, I'd had the worst day ever; everything that could've gone wrong, went wrong. And she looked at me and said, 'Let's go have a martini.' So, we went to this fancy restaurant, sat in the bar area, and drank a martini. It was the most wonderful martini I think I've ever had. And have you ever heard her laugh? It's a belly laugh. It's the best laugh." Munnell left the council on August 1, 1997, to become a professor at Boston College and director of its Center for Retirement Research.

Jeffrey Frankel, who had worked as a staff economist for the council in the 1980s, returned as one of the three members two months after Yellen took charge. He recalled that they were at a disadvantage from the outset because a group of economic policy heavies was well entrenched. "The CEA was not as influential as it otherwise would be because we were latecomers," he explained. "You had Bob Rubin and Larry Summers at Treasury and Gene Sperling at the NEC. They had been working loyally and extremely effectively for Clinton for some years by the time we got there. They had a much longer-term relationship with Clinton and had been doing a great job. They had this view that economic policy was their baby and didn't want other agencies to play. They had a real advantage."

George Akerlof echoed that observation: "Treasury had Bob Rubin and Larry Summers, who are extremely good at argumentation, and they're rather dominant people. They tended to be very powerful in carrying the day. So, when somebody new comes in and arrives on the scene, it's very hard to get your views across." George stressed, however, that in Summers's case, his drive to dominate is based on a conviction that his position is correct, and he never sees an intellectual argument as a personal battle. "Larry is such a good economist, that you always have to listen to his arguments," he said. "So, I think throughout the Clinton administration, Janet and Larry were really quite good friends. I remember him coming later to Berkeley, and Janet gave an introduction for him that was just utterly wonderful." Who knew at the time, that Yellen and her former student would become rivals twenty-five years later when President Barack Obama had to fill one of government's most powerful jobs: head of the Federal Reserve?

They may have been lifelong friends, but Summers—along with Rubin—still kept Yellen and her team out of the loop on the Asian, Russian, and Latin American financial crises that had erupted during her tenure at CEA, even though they considered her to be an excellent economist and manager of the council. And a friendship with Summers had its limits. "I remember when she took the job in the Clinton cabinet, she said her biggest fear was that Larry Summers was going to say something bad about her to the media because he's very critical and he doesn't watch his mouth," said friend Vivian Nash.

Yellen acknowledged that she never really felt like a White House insider with a lot of sway. "It was Clinton's second term. A lot of people had been there since day one, and a ton of what we were doing began in the postelection transition," she said. "Somebody new who came along would find relationships had formed and people had their chains of influence. They already had decided on the priorities with an agenda mapped out."

Despite a lack of influence on the crises of the day, Yellen found other aspects of the job appealing, particularly the opportunity to brief Clinton on economic issues. After all, she was skilled at playing the role of the professor who made everything so clear to the students, and Clinton was a very bright student. "He was very astute about policy," she confirmed. "I thought he was extremely intelligent."

New York Federal Reserve Bank president John Williams, who worked with Yellen when she became head of the Federal Reserve Bank of San Francisco in 2004, remembered meeting her in Washington in the late 1990s, when she was CEA chair and he was on loan from the Fed in Washington to serve as a council economist for a year. "She was choosing the person when I applied for the position, and we chatted about the role," recalled Williams, who later succeeded her as San Francisco Fed president. "What really struck me is just how enthusiastic she was about working at the CEA, the kind of issues the group was engaged in. It's like an economics policy think tank.

"One of the things she did with President Clinton at the time was the weekly economic briefing, which originally was presented in person by the chair and then later became a written document.

It's sent to the president and the secretary of Treasury, and other key cabinet officials. I ended up getting very involved in writing those weekly economic briefings. She's a really great educator and teacher and thinks hard about how to convey ideas and simplify things to their core. That was a skill obviously required when communicating with the president of the United States, one of the busiest people in the world. But President Clinton was intellectually very curious. She made that point: he's a president who is interested in ideas, especially those that affect real people and jobs. She was so excited about this role as a translator of complicated ideas about economic policy in words that nonexperts can understand."

That task helped Yellen adapt to the confines of her new job after serving as an influential member of the Fed Board of Governors. "I was amazed that she made the transition as easily as she did," said Berkeley colleague Andrew Rose. "When you are a governor, you have well-defined tasks that they split up, and the FOMC only meets every seven or eight weeks. But the council is every day. You've got to be able to roll with the punches and figure out how to allocate your scarce resources. She did that surprisingly well, because the council is the opposite of an academic job in the sense that you have to be spontaneous, you have to prioritize, you can't do everything. Politics is much more important." Indeed, while frustrated by limited influence in pushing more empathetic economic policies blocked by both the centrist Democrats in the White House and Republicans in Congress, Yellen learned some valuable lessons about rough-and-tumble Washington politics that would guide her in subsequent jobs.

❖ ❖ ❖

SCANT INFLUENCE ON POLICY WAS NOT THE ONLY DISADVANtage Yellen faced in her new job. Another was a familiar obstacle: gender bias. Numerous women and men who worked in the Clinton administration said it was not easy to survive, much less thrive, in what many of them described as a "good ol' boys" culture. Several were only willing to describe the work environment in candid terms by remaining anonymous.

"It's just harder to operate in an all-boys club. And my sense is that's what the Clinton administration was," said one female White House official who worked with Yellen at the time. "She's not a good old boy. She is what she is. I think Clinton respected her a lot, and took her very seriously, but the administration was really an old boys' kind of environment. I would say she held her own there, but I don't think the president viewed her as a pal."

A high-ranking member of the Clinton administration concurred: "There was a group of men given to behavior that was a bit more locker room than would be acceptable today. And I suspect if you were a male, like me, who was outside of it, it probably affected you less than if you were a woman who was outside of it." The official said some women in the administration unfairly blamed gender discrimination for their performance failings, but he conceded that the Clinton years were not populated by a bunch of well-behaved "nerds" who treated everyone with respect and tolerance. "I think there is probably some tendency for people who have other disappointments to project them onto these kinds of gender issues," the official said. "But at the same time, it was not a nerdy culture. Let me put it that way."

Another male colleague remembered overhearing a conversation Yellen and other women working at the CEA had. "They were complaining about how the boys from Treasury sat down at a meeting and were into sports, and Janet and other women were just standing there listening," he said. "And they felt excluded because they were women."

Daniel Tarullo, an assistant to the president for international economic policy when Yellen headed the CEA, cited the contrast between hyperactive males and women who had to exercise self-control at meetings. "One thing I remember observing at the time was the patience that Janet and Laura [Tyson] had in not getting agitated the way lots of guys would both get agitated and get away with getting agitated in meetings," said Tarullo, who later became a Fed governor and colleague of Yellen's there from 2009 to 2017. "I recall thinking at the time, 'Is who they are a byproduct of the fact that they have to be more conscious about controlling what they say, what they do than a guy would be?' It's not the hardest thing to believe because in every White House there are a lot of type A personalities, there's a lot of forcefulness in the way people are trying to get things done, a lot of elbows can be thrown. And if you take an environment like that and add to it an element of gender-specific bias, that can certainly make for an uncomfortable situation."

Laura Tyson said she did not have major problems dealing with the men in the Clinton White House because she had high-level positions that they respected. Still, she saw plenty of evidence of sexism, particularly the way First Lady Hillary Clinton and her health care task force were treated. The president had chosen his wife to head the panel with the goal of producing a plan for universal health care. "My colleagues—I'm referring to the people who headed all the agencies—treated the health care task force as, 'That's just a spouse thing,'" Tyson recalled. "Are you kidding me? She's a serious person. She's done all this work on this. She actually is one of the smartest people around. You can't think of this as, 'Well, she's just a spouse.' This was so wrong."

As she thought more about that period, Tyson recalled another example of gender discrimination: being excluded from meetings she believed she should have been invited to attend. "I finally went to a deputy to the president with my chief of staff and was told, 'What happens around here is men come in all the time and insist on going to meetings, and then they get in. You need to insist on going, and then you'll get in.' Isn't that interesting that that stands out in my mind," Tyson said. She then recalled attending an economic summit meeting in Naples and didn't have a seat at the main table: "I had a seat at the side table, and then somebody said, 'No, Laura needs to be there. Put her there.' I didn't insist on being at the main table. But the point is that I was not initially assigned to it."

Such treatment of women, Tyson added, was not unique to the upper echelons of the Clinton White House. That was common practice in all administrations, all government agencies, everywhere in the private sector in the 1990s. "It was that way then, and it's gotten better over time," she explained. "I think having women in these positions helped move the process forward. I guess what I'm saying is I would not characterize it as a Clinton White House problem. I'd characterize it as a broader problem. It's true for any administration. And it's gotten better because administrations care more about gender appointments. You move the process along by appointing women to positions of power, and then the women move the process along. And then sometimes women have to recognize that they need to do what male colleagues do and say, 'I need to be at this meeting I wasn't invited to.'"

American University president Sylvia Mathews Burwell, who held a variety of senior staff jobs in the White House and Treasury Department back then, pointed out that President Clinton had named more women to senior positions than any prior administration, and the women created a support group for one another like a chain pulling women into more senior roles. Burwell said she did not feel intimidated by the behavior of the alpha males, in large measure because she worked for Robert Rubin and knew he wasn't going to treat her in a sexist manner. "It wasn't something I spent a lot of time on or focused on," Burwell said. "What I do think is true, though, is that women took care of each other."

Yellen has never been comfortable publicly discussing the atmosphere within the White House. She admired the fact that Clinton appointed so many women and people of color to senior jobs but often told friends that it operated like a boy's locker room, forcing women to become close allies for support. She and Environmental Protection Agency (EPA) administrator Carol Browner became fast friends on a personal level, and Browner would confide how terribly she felt she was treated by the men in the White House when they would rudely shoot down her proposals. During Clinton's first term, they forced environmental issues to take a back seat to the president's push for health care reform. In his second term, Browner pushed for more stringent air quality standards and was lambasted by Clinton's economic advisers for pushing a regulatory change that would produce only a small social benefit at a very high cost to industry. Even Yellen disagreed with the justification of the move on economic grounds, though she and Browner always dealt with one another respectfully. Browner ultimately prevailed when Vice President Al Gore, the administration's biggest supporter of better environmental protection, weighed in on her behalf.

Several other women in the White House recalled meetings where the men ignored their ideas or interrupted them. So, they made a pact beforehand to voice support for one another's proposals to make one another more visible and heard during policy discussions.

That is a common tactic women use in all business settings because the White House is hardly the only place where male dominance is so prevalent, said gender discrimination expert Joanne Lipman. She said she encounters descriptions of the same scenario every time she speaks to women's groups: "You're in a meeting, a woman says something and it's crickets. It's like nobody heard her. Then two minutes later, some guy raises his hand and says exactly what she just said. And everybody looks at him and they're like, 'Hey Bob, great idea.' And the woman thinks, 'Oh, it must be just me. I'm not speaking articulately enough. I'm not speaking up enough.' But it's not her. It's because the men in the room are literally not hearing her."

"So, one of the strategies I give them is called 'amplification,' which applies to any underrepresented person, a woman or minority," Lipman said. "Before the meeting, you say, 'If you're going to speak, I'm going to echo what you said and give you credit for it by name. So that people know that it's your idea.' There's another very common problem for women and there's been a ton of research on this, as well. Women are interrupted three times more frequently than men are. Research at Northwestern University found that even at the Supreme Court, female justices are interrupted three times more frequently than male justices."

Laura Tyson saw a silver lining in the difficulty women have in being heard in male-dominated environments: they become better team players and are better at forging a consensus than men. "A lot of the gender research suggests this, and I do think it's true for me and for Janet, too, which is the team-player aspect of the job that is valued in the White House," she said. "Maybe because over time it was harder for them to have been heard, they are more likely to hear every voice and they're more likely to listen. They're more likely to say, 'Let's work together.' So, there's a team player kind of openness and that's important." Tyson said her own reputation for teamwork as Clinton's first chair of the Council of Economic Advisers was a reason she was named director of the White House National Economic Council when Robert Rubin left the post to become Treasury secretary. The key function of the NEC director is to coordinate policy among numerous agencies.

Working in the White House is unique in that it is difficult for men as well as women, said Joseph Stiglitz. "In my experience, it's always a rough-and-tumble environment, and getting your views heard is never easy, especially if you're an economist who is using analytic rather than political arguments," he pointed out. "That's not the language that most people in the White House speak. They are much more into the politics of everything."

"But I certainly can envision if you put on top of that always-present difficulty just a little layer of sexism, life in the White House will be very difficult and probably make working there even worse," Stiglitz continued. "There were a couple people in the Clinton administration who used very rough language. They were infamous for their profanities and [Clinton political adviser] Rahm Emanuel was off the charts. But that's part of the rough-and-tumble of White House politics. Actually, I think it was remarkable how well most of the people got along."

That's not how many women at CEA remember it. They recall Emanuel having an outsized ego, and he has readily admitted to sprinkling every sentence with what he called "the f-bomb." They found Summers difficult to deal with and encountered constant tension with National Economic Council director Gene Sperling, a lawyer by training. Several former colleagues said Sperling was so persistent in prevailing on a policy issue, he would wear down his opponents. "You literally had to make sure you had a good night's sleep before you tangled with Gene," laughed one male colleague who held a senior position in the White House at the time.

"I think Gene didn't have the kind of nuance you need to deal with a strong, centered, and experienced woman like Janet who was disagreeing with him," said one of Yellen's female confidantes at the CEA. "She wanted to be helpful and have good policy. Gene didn't take her contributions in the sense that this will make it all better. He would complain, 'Janet can't be saying, blah, blah, blah.' Janet recognized he has unique political communication skills when it comes to explaining policy. CEA liked to stay in their nonpolitical lane and do their good work but sometimes we got drawn into these political processes. He wasn't able to see where Janet could help him be better."

Another female colleague who wished to remain unidentified agreed Sperling was a challenge because of his reputation for being relentless. "It's how he works, which is all the time," the female staffer said. "It's his approach to the job. He's not a particularly difficult personality. It's just that Gene is like a dog with a bone."

As for Summers, "Janet handled Larry exquisitely and effectively," her CEA confidante explained. "He didn't get under her skin in ways that he did with Joseph Stiglitz and Alan Blinder when they were at the CEA. He drove them to distraction. They were just so annoyed by him all the time because of his arrogance, inability to work with other people, and insistence on debating everything. Larry just made them crazy.

"I feel that Janet's approach was, 'I have dealt with this my whole life. That's what these men are like.' And she has this unique style, which is collaborative at her core. She's 100 percent focused on getting to the best answer on policy and informing it in the best possible way, even though she ran up against a White House climate that was a tough boys' environment. So, she was able to work with Larry and they got along. I think he deeply respected her and that always came through. At the same time, for Larry, people are just disposable, so when an alliance with Janet wasn't necessary, he would happily just move on to the next thing and leave her out."

A woman who worked for Clinton's National Economic Council said of Summers: "Larry has a very combative intellectual style. That's not unusual in the economics profession. That kind of interaction was encouraged and valued in the White House, and Larry was just very successful at it. Research and surveys show that women generally have not fared well in those environments, which are based on the idea that somehow the truth comes out of confrontation. It's just not a very comfortable environment for a lot of women. But in Larry's case I would not personalize it. It is just his style."

"There is a competitive dynamic around the president, which I've certainly seen in more than one administration," continued the woman, who held a senior economic position in the Obama administration. "People want to stand out and get the president's ear. And sometimes that gets conflated with policy differences. So, the dynamics are tricky. Clinton's chief of staff was not good at picking up on that to make sure you have a truly inclusive environment. Rather, he compounded it by allowing a lot of elbow-jockeying behavior."

Another woman keenly aware of the sexism that prevailed in the Clinton White House is Rebecca "Becky" Blank, who joined the CEA in 1997, when Alicia Munnell left for Boston College. Blank, who was a dean at the University of Michigan before her government service, worked as an economist in the first Bush administration. Following her service on the CEA with Yellen, she returned to academia. She then came back to Washington to work for President Barack Obama in the Commerce Department, where she rose to deputy secretary and acting secretary. She became chancellor of the University of Wisconsin–Madison in 2013 and president of Northwestern University in the summer of 2022—the first woman to hold that position.

Blank found all three administrations to be difficult, male-dominated environments for women, particularly economists. "The Obama administration wasn't that much different [from the Clinton administration]," she recalled. "The first Bush administration was a real boys' club. Remember, only 10 percent of economists are women. It's just the nature of the work. Whenever you're in the White House, there are a lot of sharp elbows. Everybody is out to protect their domain, to gain face time with the president, to get recognition. It's a really tough environment, a very political environment. I didn't think Janet always negotiated that fully."

Blank, who has stayed in touch with Yellen and had lunch with her a number of times over the years, continued: "My impression is she got a lot better at the politics during her years in San Francisco [as president of the Federal Reserve Bank from 2004 to 2010] and then at the Fed in Washington. The CEA was not an environment she'd been in before. What you have to do in those environments is have them need you, have a job where they need to involve you, need your advice, need you to bring something to the table. Janet brought that." Indeed, while Yellen struggled with little success to advance her own agenda to make the economy work better for the less advantaged, she played a valuable role in providing solid economic justification for policies that were priorities for the White House, such as the benefits of free trade.

Blank said women like herself and Yellen learn to develop a strong sense of self-worth and a thick skin to thrive in such macho cultures. "If you let this bother you, you wouldn't have become an economist. You wouldn't have been in these jobs. You have to be a reasonably self-confident person who knows that when you speak, you're going to say something that is worthwhile, and they've got to listen to you because otherwise you'll never open your mouth in that environment. Janet was very good at that. She knew what she knew. She never hesitated to speak up when it was her area of expertise. And she had something to bring to the table."

"Economics is a particularly tough profession," Blank continued. "It's not just male-dominated in terms of numbers of men, it's male-dominated in terms of patterns of behavior, more so than some of the other social sciences. I've heard descriptions of economic seminars where the women get interrupted fifteen times in the first five minutes. It's the nature of economics. The modal cultural behavior is very male aggressive. And if you aren't willing to be out there with sharp elbows, jump in and shout right back, you won't survive.

"You have to be confident, and you can't put up with guff. You've got to be one of the boys. I know there are plenty of women who don't survive well in that environment. It's not what they're comfortable with. And if you can't let a bunch of stuff roll off your back, you're going to feel insulted and angry all the time.

"One of the ways that you negotiate this as a woman is to have a much higher IQ than most of the guys you're dealing with. I think that's true of Janet. She's just smart as the coin of the realm in any field. People would learn that pretty quickly, and that makes up for a lot of other things. And when you're actually at the top of an organization, you don't have all of the little microaggressions."

Blank then explained why much of the male domination in her field stems from the influence of eighteenth-century economist Adam Smith, whose seminal work, *The Wealth of Nations*, became the basis of modern classical economics with its focus on how efficient free markets, competition, and rational self-interest lead to prosperity:

"My theory about this is the way in which the profession has evolved with this very individualistic view of how the world works based on everyone's self-interest. We each pursue only our own self-interest. We don't care anything about community. We don't care about each other and you end up with a perfect equilibrium. Now that's a model that is almost never really used in the profession, but it is at the base of what you've learned in Econ 101. And that's a very male view of the world. There's no community, there's no family that has a role here. Institutions have no role, power has no role. It's all sort of economic self-interest. This type of model attracts certain types of people, and that then creates a certain culture."

Blank expounded on this belief in an essay, "What Should Mainstream Economists Learn from Feminist Theory," for the book *Beyond Economic Man: Feminist Theory and Economics*, edited by Marianne Ferber and Julie Nelson.

"In far too many cases, economists generalize about household and individual behavior from studies based on male behavior," she wrote. "There is substantial evidence that in many situations, women face different constraints than men. In the standard economic model, this means that they will make different choices and face different outcomes. It is crucial that we understand the differences in the constraints that affect women's behavior if we want to claim to understand economic behavior in general." Toward that end, she said feminist scholars should produce models that show how individuals' interconnectedness with families and within communities produce new insights about economic behavior. She also noted that the standard economic model not only falls short of explaining the behavior of many women, but it also does not adequately explain the motivations of "many low-income men, nonwhite men and women, and many nonassimilated immigrants."

As she summed up her argument, she wrote, "In introductory undergraduate microeconomics courses I have the sense that the following scenario is frequent: out of a class of one hundred students, ninety-nine will listen to the lectures and think to themselves, 'Although interesting, this is sort of crazy; nobody really thinks this way.' Those students do what they must to pass the course and forget it soon afterwards. But the one remaining person in that class lights up. This is almost always a male. He realizes this model describes the way that he thinks and acts. To that person, the economic model *is* intuitively obvious. It is that one person who is most likely to become an economist. Small wonder then that fifteen years later, sitting around the lunch table with a group of other similar selectively chosen economists, everyone believes that the standard economic model indeed describes how most people think about the world. It's certainly the way most people who choose to study economics think about the world."

Twenty-eight years after the essay was published, Blank said, "I realize that's old, but these issues haven't changed very much, I fear."

She was right about that. As recently as January 2018, the annual meeting of economists in Philadelphia included a panel discussion about gender bias throughout the profession. "Paper after paper presented at the American Economic Association panel showed a pattern of gender discrimination, beginning with barriers women face in choosing to study economics and extending through the life cycle of their careers, including securing job opportunities, writing research papers, gaining access to top publications, and earning proper credit for published work," according to a *New York Times* article on the gathering.

"Economics departments have gradually increased their share of female faculty members over the past 20 years. But only one in five tenure-track economics professors is a woman, according to the American Economic Association's Committee on the Status of Women in the Economics Profession," the article continued. "In many parts of the profession, gender progress stagnated over the last decade. About one in three new economics doctoral students was a woman in 2016, and fewer than one in three assistant professors were women. In both of those cases, the share of women was essentially unchanged from 2006.

"But the barriers women face in this long male-dominated field extend well beyond online harassment. Women must be significantly clearer writers than men to have their work accepted to major economic journals, according to a paper titled, 'Publishing While Female,' that Erin Hengel, a University of Liverpool economist, reported at the conference. They must also wait longer to have their papers published in journals.

"The bias creeps into the most popular introductory economics textbooks, which refer to men four times as often as they do women.

Ninety percent of the economists cited in those textbooks are men, Betsey Stevenson, a University of Michigan economist, told the panel on gender issues in economics, based on a paper she is about to complete. When women are mentioned in textbook examples, they are more likely to be shopping or cleaning than running a company or making public policy."

❖ ❖ ❖

YOU WOULD THINK THAT BETWEEN THE GOOD OL' BOY CULTURE of the Clinton White House and the aggressive male personality drawn to the economics profession, Yellen and her female colleagues had all they could do to exert their influence at the CEA. But things got even worse for them beginning January 18, 1998. That was the day the Monica Lewinsky scandal broke into the open. Lewinsky was a White House intern who had sex with President Clinton in the White House. He initially denied having an affair with her, but the preponderance of evidence to the contrary was overwhelming, and he finally admitted the truth.

In the early days of the scandal, when Clinton was still in denial mode, he tried to enlist the support of women in the administration to defend him. He had invited cabinet members to the White House and insisted that he had not had an affair. He then expected everyone—particularly female officials—to go before the news media gathered outside the West Wing and publicly defend him. Yellen didn't have to worry about doing that since her office was next door to the White House, and she could use a side exit and avoid the throng of reporters.

Yellen initially believed Clinton's denial about having sex with Lewinsky. Even so, friends said she was bothered by the White House ploy to marshal support for the president. "She was suspicious of what they were doing," recalled a female colleague. "It left a bad taste and a feeling that a lot of the women shared of, frankly, being used. It was pretty stunning to think they expected the women to be trotted out. Some did. Some stood in front of the White House and vouched for the president."

Robby Akerlof remembered his mother talking about that meeting and how there were two ways to exit the White House, a side door that led directly to the adjacent Old Executive Office Building and the West Wing front door, where reporters and TV cameras were assembled. "They were encouraged to go out and talk to the press after this meeting," he said. "She told me how [Secretary of State] Madeleine Albright seemed in particular to be pushed out there. Clearly, they were very much looking for female validators of Clinton at this period. So, I think she was a little bit encouraged to go out there with Madeleine Albright. She definitely didn't want to go out and be one of those validators.

"Looking back on the later Clinton years, there was a lot that was disappointing for her both policy-wise and personally. There wasn't that promise that was there initially, such as trying to get health care reform done," Robby Akerlof said.

Colleagues said Yellen tried to compartmentalize the scandal, since she had to provide Clinton his weekly economic briefing, sometimes in person. "That was her forum with the president, and she also attended every budget meeting with him," the female White House staffer related. "It was a distracting time, for sure. The Lewinsky stuff was pretty much occupying the senior staff's time, even as the White House tried to operate normally and the economy remained strong."

Another female colleague of Yellen's at the time recalled how the scandal hung over the White House. "Things got a little slower at the council at that point because the whole White House was focused on survival, and they weren't really moving a lot of policy forward," she said. "We wrote white papers on topics we thought were important and were setting our own agenda a little more than would normally happen. Janet and I would go out to lunch together at least once a week for about a six-month period and look at each other and say, 'Are you going to resign? What do you think about this?' We were both appalled at his behavior, in part because of what this meant in terms of women.

"One of the hardest decisions ethically to make was do I stay at the council working for someone whose behavior towards women I thought was terrible. On the other hand, if I had left—and certainly much more if Janet had left—the council would have suffered. If we walked out on it, the council would be cast into the outer darkness by the White House politicos. There were really important issues that we were working on. You came to do a job and we stayed to do the job. But I will say we had some long conversations about the ethics of this and under what circumstance would you leave and when wouldn't you."

Yellen chose to stick it out. The Lewinsky scandal dragged on for more than a year, leading to Clinton's impeachment by the Republican-controlled House of Representatives in late 1998. In February 1999, he was acquitted, when the Senate failed to muster the two-thirds vote required for removal from office.

When he was finally in the clear, Clinton invited all of the cabinet members and senior staff to the residence on the second floor of the White House to express his contrition. Yellen was among those in attendance and found it memorable: "It's not often that you're sitting in the president's house and he's apologizing for his behavior and for what he had put everybody working for him through. He's saying, 'I'm really sorry. I know I disappointed you. I know my behavior is not something to be proud of.'"

After Clinton addressed the group, they were offered a chance to speak. Yellen said she chose not to but others opened up. "A lot of people quoted scripture and basically said the equivalent of, 'You've done wrong, but you are a good person doing good work, and God loves you and will forgive you.' Most people were very supportive, but there were a few people who were more critical. I remember [Health and Human Services secretary] Donna Shalala saying the equivalent of you've really disappointed us. This was a reckless and thoughtless way to behave. It's a failure of moral leadership. I remember sitting there and agreeing—that it was utterly reckless and that it endangered what we wanted to accomplish. But I didn't feel like I wanted to say that." And she certainly did not want to give him a pass and say we understand that boys will be boys and we forgive you.

Yellen thought it was an extraordinary moment—a president apologizing and being comforted or chastised. It was such an emotional and personal meeting that she thought it should remain confidential. And yet, by the time she returned to her office, the wire services already had a full accounting of what people had said. So much for respecting confidences.

※ ※ ※

AS DIFFICULT AS SHE FOUND THE WHITE HOUSE ENVIRONMENT, Yellen was determined to stay focused as much as possible on having an impact on important policies, which is why she took the job in the first place. During her nearly thirty-month tenure, she oversaw two annual reports to the president and played at least a minor role in shaping dozens of policies. A White House summary of those years showed her involvement in talks on social security, private pension reforms, the North American Free Trade Agreement (NAFTA) and other trade issues, childcare, telecommunications, competition in the electric power market, and a proposed settlement with the tobacco industry. She became involved in a study on how to promote the social and economic well-being of racial and ethnic minorities, participated in discussions about financial markets and banking, and traveled with Clinton to China and Japan.

In June 1998, the council issued a report titled "Explaining Trends in the Gender Wage Gap," which concluded that the gap between women's and men's wages had narrowed substantially since the signing of the Equal Pay Act in 1963, but that a significant wage gap remained. Women made sixty cents for every one dollar earned by men in 1963. It grew to about seventy-seven cents when the report was written and topped eighty cents by 2020. On other issues, Yellen testified before Congress on the economic impact of mergers and helped formulate policy on consumer privacy and natural disaster insurance.

Her research in these areas helped reinforce Yellen's belief that government needed to intervene to help level the economic playing field. She saw the importance of regulation to end discrimination against minorities seeking bank loans, subsidies to help low-income parents afford childcare so they could work, and improved safety nets for workers who lost their jobs when their companies moved operations overseas.

Yellen also played an important role in shaping the president's annual budget at a time when Clinton was aiming to balance the federal ledgers for the first time in thirty years. One of her principal assignments as chief White House economist was to put together the economic outlook, which had a huge impact on spending and revenue estimates. In consultation with the Treasury secretary and budget director, she had to produce a credible forecast of economic growth, unemployment, and inflation. The process often became contentious when Joseph Stiglitz headed the CEA because of his personality and views that were too far to the left to suit other Clinton advisers, colleagues recalled. Yellen, by contrast, brought centrist views, competence, and calm to the task.

"The assumptions about unemployment or productivity can create vast swings in what your deficits are going to be," said American University president Sylvia Burwell, who worked at the Treasury

Department at the time. "It's important that you get the actual numbers right. That process was run by Janet. I can remember she made sure everyone got heard, but she wasn't afraid to express her own voice. She is really smart, secure in who she is, and a good listener. And Janet is like Goldilocks. You know, not too hot, not too cold, but just right," added Burwell, who served as director of the Office of Management and Budget (OMB) and secretary of Health and Human Services for President Obama. "She was no drama, but she was strong and she had a point of view, which she expressed. She understood the role and knew how to get the work done. Her ego is not too small and it's not too large. She had confidence to deal with Larry Summers and everybody else, but she wasn't trying to lord over people with her economic knowledge or anything like that. She was respected, not feared. And she got more done in the long run because of it.

"That's why I think she's the Goldilocks of economic policy, of politics, and of management. Look at all the jobs she's had and done extremely well. It's because she listens, she treats everyone with respect, her ego is just right, and she is secure in who she is. She's not confrontational in any way, but strong. That's the thing that I think is so unique about Janet. She has empathy but also has that strength. Nobody thinks Janet's a pushover."

Daniel Tarullo, the White House international economic adviser at the time, recalled a White House budget meeting he attended with Yellen in 1997, shortly after she joined the council. "The fiscal picture was not looking great, and some in the administration were beginning to think about quite significant cuts, including to social programs," he related. "We were in a White House conference room that didn't fit many people. It was already dark when the meeting ended, and Janet and I walked out of the West Wing lobby together, and we're walking back to our offices next door in the old EOB [Executive Office Building]. She turned to me with just this look of pain and concern on her face and said, 'Do we really want to be a part of making these kinds of cuts?' The reason I remember that is because it is a classic Janet attribute, which is her forthrightness about things. It wasn't just a political issue for her to navigate. It came down to the substance of what the impact would be on people. Fortunately, it didn't ever come down to making the cuts, but it's funny sometimes how these things stick in your mind, that little conversation with Janet walking across that parking lot."

Yellen's biggest impact during her time on the CEA was on climate change policy, she and her colleagues agree. In December 1997, the Kyoto Protocol was adopted, and it committed nations to coming up with plans to limit greenhouse gases. It was enormously controversial in Congress. Not only were there more global warming skeptics at the time, but even those who believed that human activity was increasing global temperatures worried about the huge economic cost of a government mandate to curb the use of fossil fuels and other causes of harmful emissions. In a preemptive strike, the Senate passed a resolution on a 95–0 vote in July 1997, opposing ratification of any climate treaty that would "mandate new commitments to limit or reduce greenhouse gas emissions" or would "result in serious harm to the economy of the United States."

Yellen had the unenviable task of making the economic case for combatting global warming. And as was her habit, she threw herself into the job, finding ways the United States could reduce emissions at little or no cost to the economy, and then trying to sell them to a skeptical Congress and American public. She testified numerous times before Congress on ways to achieve the Kyoto Protocol targets efficiently, such as through international trading of emissions permits. This was a system in which those countries or companies with emissions below the targets could sell their spare allowances to those who exceeded the levels so that when averaged out, everyone met the targets. She and the council also worked with a number of developing countries to identify ways they could cut their emissions.

"I felt I had an important role in dealing with climate change, so that became a big piece of what we were doing," Yellen said as she looked back at that period. "It was something the White House really needed me to do. I think I made some contributions. Was I hugely influential? No. But I played a positive role." An added benefit was that Lawrence Summers wasn't involved in the climate issue because he was preoccupied dealing with an Asian financial crisis that had erupted at the time, so Yellen wouldn't have to worry about butting heads with him on policy decisions.

Colleagues said Yellen typically understates her accomplishments. "I've worked with a lot of smart people, and Janet was among the smartest," Rebecca Blank said of their time together on the CEA. "We'd talk about a problem and then she'd sit down for a minute and say, 'Well, it looks like this.' And she described it in a clearly defined model form that went to the essence of what it was. I've never seen anyone who can translate a discussion into an economic model that captures the main point as fast and as well as she could. And she would pull information together from across the fields of economics in looking at a particular problem. She'd say, 'There's this main piece of research over here that says that. What do you think about this? And then there's this over here, you know.' It made her just a wonderful person to work with."

Tarullo said Yellen's work on climate change advanced the ball noticeably. "She was saying we really need to do something to mitigate emissions now," he recalled. "That was in contrast with a lot of economists who were worried about the impact of carbon emissions but were thinking in terms of what we could do to mitigate the effects twenty or thirty years from now. That was one thing that stood out."

Despite her research and arguments, Yellen encountered enormous resistance in Congress to do anything about the problem. "She would go up to the Congress and give testimony regarding why we should be doing something about global warming, yet they weren't listening to this at all," recalled George Akerlof. "Now global warming has occurred much faster than I think we were expecting, and it seems much more urgent at the moment. At that time, it seemed that there was enough time to postpone doing anything."

CEA colleague Jeffrey Frankel recalled the big political concern at the time was that complying with the Kyoto Protocol commitments would impose too high an economic cost. "After the president signed it, there was this overwhelming demand from various committees in the House and Senate for Janet in particular to testify about it because they wanted to know [if it would] be economically ruinous," he said. "We had this set of arguments that said, no, it would not be economically ruinous if we do it in the right way, including getting the participation of developing countries, and other reasons we thought they might accept, such as including market mechanisms like tradable permits and fungibility across different greenhouse gases, not just carbon dioxide. We said that if we do all these things, it won't be that expensive."

Initially, Yellen felt very nervous about testifying because she wasn't sure she could honestly say the economic costs would be relatively low. It didn't help that the Republicans in charge of Congress were mistrustful of the CEA's work and were watching very closely to see if they could prove political bias in its various policy positions, an effort that stemmed from the earlier failed effort to eliminate funding for the agency. Council staffers felt they were being harassed by congressional Republicans who were demanding all kinds of internal documents. That raised the stakes for Yellen who threw her entire team into a mammoth effort to ensure that the economic analysis was correct. Once she meticulously worked through the numbers, she became comfortable with her conclusion that combatting global warming would not entail great cost. She made the case repeatedly.

On March 4, 1998, she testified before the House Commerce Committee on the economic costs of the Kyoto Protocol. Her nine thousand–word opening remarks read like a thoughtful Professor Yellen lecture—clear, well-organized, comprehensive, and persuasive to those who had an open mind on the issue. She explained that the cost of doing nothing to combat global warming would be substantial in the form of agricultural industry losses, higher energy consumption for air conditioning, and increased health care costs due to pollution and damage from more frequent natural disasters. She laid out the administration's proposals to increase research and development into new technology for reducing greenhouse gases and reforms in electricity production to reduce costs to consumers. She promised that efforts to reduce pollution would be flexible, market-based, and efficient. "We do not anticipate any significant aggregate employment effect if we achieve the conditions we have discussed," she said. "The effects on energy prices . . . will occur only ten to fourteen years in the future." She concluded that "the economic impact of the protocol will be modest under the conditions we have identified."

It was a compelling analysis, but it fell on deaf ears in Congress. Even so, Yellen never gave up on the issue. Twenty-two years later as Treasury secretary, she announced an unprecedented campaign by her department to curb global warming under the coordination of the first "Treasury Climate Hub" in agency history. It is run by a "climate counselor" whose responsibilities include financing projects that reduce greenhouse gases and looking for ways to use tax policy to encourage reductions in harmful emissions. "Climate change requires economy-wide investments by industry and government as well as actions to measure and mitigate climate-related risks to households, businesses, and our financial sector," Yellen said on April 19, 2021, in announcing the initiative as a top department priority. "Finance and financial incentives will play a crucial role in addressing the climate crisis at home and abroad and in providing capital for opportunities . . . that strengthen our economy."

At an international summit on climate change in Venice on July 11, 2021, Yellen recalled her 1998 testimony. "I told Congress to think of Kyoto as a form of insurance for our planet. Wouldn't even a significant investment in transitioning our economies away from carbon be worth it if it saved priceless coastal cities like Venice? If it helped ensure that we kept the world livable? And, if we addressed climate change intelligently, the benefits would far outweigh the costs.

"In the end, we all know the outcome of that prior effort. Fast forward to today, I am happy to report that the landscape has changed in the United States. President Biden has committed to reduce US emissions from 2005 levels by at least 50 percent by 2030, and we're seeing a new consensus around a plan to achieve a significant portion of that reduction."

Michele Jolin, Yellen's chief of staff at the CEA who remained a close adviser over the years, said Treasury's climate initiative and Yellen's continued activism show just how deep her commitment is to the issue. "When you fast forward to today, this gives you the depth of how long she's been working on this issue—since the nineties," she explained. "Her experience on these issues is so deep that it makes so much sense to me that they're doing all this stuff at Treasury. It's something she's been working on for a long time." Had Congress listened to Yellen in 1998 and curbed energy consumption, Russia might not have earned enormous oil export revenue to finance its attack on Ukraine twenty-four years later.

❖ ❖ ❖

ONE OF THE MOST MISGUIDED POLICY DECISIONS OF THE CLINton presidency occurred while Yellen was at the CEA: the administration's failure to regulate the burgeoning field of financial derivatives. Blame it on poor judgment, fears of taking on a powerful financial industry, and rampant sexism by a group of male decision-makers who had dismissed alarms raised by a female colleague. Yellen passively went along with them. Less than a decade later, it led to economic calamity.

A derivative is a financial contract between two parties whose gain or loss is "derived" from an underlying reference rate, index, or asset that fluctuates in value, such as stocks, bonds, commodities, currencies, interest rates, and market indexes. These contracts, often a form of speculation or hedging, were being traded increasingly by financial institutions and other corporations as private—or "over-the-counter" (OTC)—transactions. As such, they lacked government oversight as occurred when traded on regulated exchanges despite the risk that a big player in a transaction might suffer enormous losses or default if there were an unexpected sharp change in the underlying asset, since many of the big bets were highly leveraged—made using borrowed money. And that could cause a chain reaction, leading to disruption of the financial system. In fact, by the mid-1990s, several major derivative deals went south, triggering hundreds of millions of dollars in losses, lawsuits, and claims of fraud.

As these over-the-counter trades proliferated, they began to gnaw at Brooksley Born, chair of the Commodity Futures Trading Commission (CFTC). She became convinced that derivative activity needed to be regulated before a financial catastrophe was triggered by big and risky bets that soured. These trades had already caused market disruptions in recent years, so in 1998, the CFTC proposed regulating derivatives. Other top government regulators—Treasury secretary Robert Rubin, Fed chairman Alan

Greenspan, and Securities and Exchange Commission chairman Arthur Levitt—squashed the proposal. They said Born's agency had no jurisdiction over derivatives and that the lucrative market would simply move overseas if it thought federal oversight was coming.

Yellen was only peripherally involved in the issue. "I didn't have much of a role in this. But I did observe what went on," Yellen recalled. What she observed was shameful mistreatment of Born by her male colleagues, who were ranting about her continuously. Yellen agreed with the men's argument that what Born proposed was dangerous and irresponsible, but she thought that did not justify their sexist attacks on her. The proposal went nowhere, as the financial industry, Congress, and the Clinton administration all weighed in to condemn it. To make sure the issue didn't resurface, Clinton, in one of his last acts as president, signed the Commodity Futures Modernization Act, which formally took away the jurisdiction the CFTC had claimed over OTC derivatives. It, in effect, made clear that there should be no regulation of the industry.

In December 2007, seven years after Clinton signed the act into law, the very kinds of derivatives Born had wanted to regulate, including credit default swaps (CDSs), led to a financial meltdown and housing crisis that produced the worst downturn since the 1930s; as the stock market crashed, millions of people lost homes in foreclosures when housing prices collapsed, and unemployment soared. Some victims bore financial scars a decade later. In a 2009 interview with the *New York Times Magazine*, Clinton said he regretted not trying to regulate derivatives, although Congress would not have gone along.

In 2010, a chastened Congress that was now in Democratic control passed a set of tight federal regulations over the derivatives market and other financial activities that represented the most stringent oversight adopted since the Great Depression. The Dodd-Frank Wall

Street Reform and Consumer Protection Act, named for Representative Barney Frank, D-MA, and Senator Christopher Dodd, D-CT, and signed by President Obama, carried out what Born had proposed to do in 1998. The new law revived government regulation of the financial industry, which had lobbied successfully to chip away at restrictions imposed by Congress in the Glass-Steagall Act passed seventy-five years earlier to prevent another 1929-style stock market crash. As proof that history repeats itself, bank regulators began reversing some of the Dodd-Frank rules at the behest of the powerful financial industry just a few years after the law was enacted.

Looking back on that episode, Yellen told friends that much of the pushback against Born was gender bias toward a woman the male regulators considered pushy. Their attitude was that she had no business taking on the issue. Who the hell does she think she is? Little woman, know your place. Within a decade, when derivative trades contributed to a financial meltdown, Yellen came around to the view that Born had been right all along. Until then, however, Yellen had sat on her hands while watching Born get her butt kicked.

Yellen's only saving grace was that she never publicly condemned Born's proposal as had the male regulators, something Born greatly appreciated. "I felt that compared with many of the people who I was interacting with in office, she was a compassionate economist," Born said of Yellen's subsequent career as she reflected twenty-three years later on the controversy that had engulfed her. "She cared about people. She cared about employment. She cared about wages, she even oversaw research on the impact of gender on wages. I also did not think that she gave in to pressure from lobbyists the way I thought many regulators did. And I didn't think she believed in the self-regulation of markets and market participants. I think she knew that government action could alter human behavior in ways that would prove beneficial to society as a whole. She was an advocate for that."

Yellen had an opportunity to make amends to Born in person when she was back at the Federal Reserve as vice chair more than a decade after the controversy died down. Yellen ran into Born at the checkout line of the Georgetown Safeway on Wisconsin Avenue and told Born that she had long wanted to apologize for not doing more to support her on derivatives regulation. She said she felt terrible for not defending Born from all the personal attacks. Born responded that she felt enormously grateful that Yellen was the only one of the top economic policymakers at the time who did not denounce her either publicly or in person, and that she had great respect for her.

A short time later, Yellen was invited to speak at a dinner honoring Born that was hosted by the National Women's Law Center, a women's rights advocacy group Born helped create. "Brooksley Born turned out to be 100% right and I consider her a hero," Yellen said in a tribute that deeply touched the former CFTC chair.

Watching Born's persecution drilled two lessons into Yellen she would remember in her future government posts. First, financial markets left to pursue profit at all costs without strict federal oversight inevitably lead to economic disaster and pain for average working Americans. Second, don't let male colleagues bully you into backing away from the policy path you know is correct.

❖ ❖ ❖

BY THE SUMMER OF 1999, YELLEN KNEW IT WAS TIME TO LEAVE the whirlpool of White House politics and unfulfilled policy goals for the more serene waters of academic life back in Berkeley. The Haas School of Business had generously given her a five-year leave of absence, an unusually long stretch, and it would soon be up. Robby would be heading off to Yale University as an undergraduate in the fall, and the White House was getting into campaign mode for the 2000 presidential election, which meant there would not be much in the way of serious policy issues for her to handle.

Serving as CEA chair proved to be an interesting experience for Yellen, despite the lack of influence and the challenges she faced in the highly political environment that envelops the White House. After all, how many people get to be in a room with the president of the United States when he is apologizing for having an affair with a White House intern and then lying about it. Things like that never happened at the Fed. Even with her misgivings about trading in a Fed job she really enjoyed for a stint at the CEA, she valued learning how the White House operates. It would come in handy two decades later when she went to work for a different president. Yellen returned to her less polarized, less demanding, and less stressful academic world in August 1999. "It was hard for her to play that political game in many ways, but I think she did the best she could," son Robby said. "It was a rough two and a half years and I think that was the most she could take. They planned for a long time to return to Berkeley."

And that's just what Yellen and her husband did.

# - 6 -

# A RESPITE AND THEN A CRISIS

*"And virtually nothing happened. I mean, it was really pathetic."*

AFTER HER TUMULTUOUS TIME IN WASHINGTON, YELLEN'S return to Berkeley seemed like a true reprieve. "I enjoyed getting back to teaching. I had a richer blend of outside activities," she recalled. Her focus was on teaching rather than research. The years spent working on public policy at the Fed and the White House made the transition back to research-oriented academia hard. And while she found writing difficult, Yellen coauthored a book with former Fed colleague Alan Blinder.

*The Fabulous Decade: Macroeconomic Lessons from the 1990s* was published in 2001. Until the 2000 dot.com bust led to a recession that same year, the American economy had grown for ten consecutive years, the longest expansion in US history at the time. As a result, the federal government ran a budget surplus from 1998 through 2001, something it had last achieved in 1969 and not since. "This had been a very successful decade for the economy, and we were trying to identify the ultimate causes of that success," she explained. "Part of the message was that monetary and fiscal policy had been very well executed. There also had been some elements of luck, such as falling costs for semiconductors and information technology, for example, that enabled the economy to perform exceptionally well."

Though a successful decade for the US economy in aggregate, the 1990s saw a continued expansion of the gap between the haves and have-nots as a result of Clinton's free-trade policies, budget-balancing push, and centrist social policies. The stock market rewarded companies that laid off American workers and moved plants overseas, and his welfare and criminal reform initiatives had a negative impact on the poor. The growing inequality concerned Yellen, yet she was not in a position to advance her empathy economic agenda until she was back at the Fed in 2004.

Good luck and good policy came together for Yellen and her husband later in 2001 as well, in the early morning of October 10, to be precise. The home phone rang, Akerlof picked it up and Yellen listened. The caller was a friend of his in Stockholm. He was on the Nobel selection committee and informed Akerlof that he had just won the prize in economic sciences. He would share the award and the $1 million that accompanied it with Yellen's Yale mentor, friend, and former colleague Joseph Stiglitz, who was teaching at Columbia, and A. Michael Spence of Stanford University. The prize cited "their analyses of markets with asymmetric information," whereby "actors on one side of the market have much better information than those on the other."

It was the ultimate vindication for Akerlof's paper on "lemons" in the car market that had been rejected three times before being published in 1970. The Nobel citation said, "George Akerlof demonstrated how a market where sellers have more information than buyers about product quality can contract into an adverse selection of low-quality products. He also pointed out that informational problems are commonplace and important. Akerlof's pioneering contribution thus showed how asymmetric information of borrowers and lenders may explain skyrocketing borrowing rates on local Third World markets; but it also dealt with the difficulties for the elderly to find individual medical insurance and with labor-market discrimination of minorities."

"Oh, it was really wonderful," Yellen recalled when the phone rang that autumn morning. "George had been rumored as a likely winner, and his name routinely appeared on lists of potential winners. So, I can't say it came as an utter shock when he won, but nevertheless in the moment, it was a shock. His friend said, 'You've won the prize!' Then suddenly all hell broke loose, and the phones were ringing off the hook as it became public. It was extremely exciting."

The couple was engulfed in good wishes from friends, Berkeley held a celebratory event, and Akerlof was inundated with interview requests. "George was asked repeatedly to explain what 'lemons' was about," said Yellen, who knew her husband was not the most articulate speaker when it came to explaining complex theories. Yellen, who is known for simplifying arcane issues for a lay audience, would sit there thinking he needed an easier explanation. "At first he had trouble reducing it to a sound bite," she said. "But it was all good. A lot of people were happy for him and celebrating his career. There were a lot of parties."

Over the next two months, Yellen took a break from her teaching assignments to become George's travel agent and scheduler. She made arrangements for a group of ten to fly to Stockholm for the ceremony: her brother and sister-in-law, George's brother and sister-in-law, and some friends. The traveling party needed formal clothes for three nights of events that included meetings with Sweden's king and queen. Yellen and Akerlof spent about $20,000 for the group's travel and formal wear. That year's banquet marked the

one hundredth anniversary of the Nobel prizes, and Yellen was enthralled by the gathering that included many past Nobel laureates.

By tradition, Nobel acceptance speeches are supposed to be
short and light. And Akerlof came through using the occasion for
a pithy explanation of asymmetric information that occurs where
buyers and sellers have different information. That allows con art-
ists he called "tricksters" to take advantage of gullible buyers—"the
other side":

"It has been present since the dawn of trade," he explained. "In
this century it's present when people buy a car and in the past when
they bought a horse. The horse trader would bring a sad old nag
to market and put a live eel down her throat to make her frisky. A
high-strung stallion would be given a bucket of beer to make him
mellow. On one side of the market are the tricksters. The other side
avoids the tricksters. In the extreme, markets can totally collapse
because of tricksters. And the good may lose out as well as the
bad. And so, it is difficult for the individual elderly to buy medical
insurance, because those willing to pay high premia are presumed
to be sick. And so, it is difficult for young people to attain credit
to pursue their ideas, because the true will be mixed with the false.
This is the stuff that markets are made of: How to sort the good
from the bad. In exploring such problems economists have gained
an understanding of what is needed to make markets work. We understand a pivotal piece of the puzzle why some countries are poor
while others are rich. And we can work for the cure of the poverty
that causes hunger, disease, and lives spent more in misery than in
self-fulfillment for much of the globe."

The trip had a special significance for Akerlof because he is a
son of Sweden. Before his father immigrated to the United States,
he had served in the Swedish military and was briefly stationed as
one of the guards outside the king's palace. Akerlof still had relatives living in a country town in northern Sweden where his father

grew up, and he and his entourage visited them in chauffeured limousines. As a Nobel laureate, he was greeted as a celebrity by the local mayor.

❖ ❖ ❖

AFTER THE EXCITEMENT OVER GEORGE'S NOBEL PRIZE DIED down, Yellen resumed life as a tenured and esteemed member of the Haas School of Business faculty. The less demanding pace gave her both time and energy to host dinner parties for which she would whip up memorable gourmet meals. She also became an avid hiker and runner.

Running and hiking turned into quite an adventure for her—not always a pleasant one. She had gotten to know Sheila O'Rourke, a senior university attorney who was very athletic and talked her into signing up for a marathon program to get into shape. Yellen had never done much in the way of exercise but managed to get in shape to complete a half-marathon (13.1 miles) in New Orleans, ignoring the pain of shin splints.

Then her friend prodded Yellen to go on an annual summer backpacking trip in the High Sierras near Yosemite National Park. It involved rugged hikes at altitudes as high as thirteen thousand feet. The trip left her in the best physical condition of her life. So, she was eager to go again the next summer. It did not go well. During one hike, she tripped and fell, breaking her wrist. An off-duty park ranger tied her arm in a sling, and she had to ride down the mountain on a mule for eight hours while writhing in pain to get medical help. Once her wrist healed, she was game enough to go on a third hiking trip the following summer—and complete a second half-marathon in New Orleans. She loved the physical activity. "Then, the financial crisis came along and I stopped working out as much," she said. "I got to be in worse physical shape. And I was very worried about everything that was going on."

In 2004, good timing and good luck would merge to catapult her back into public service and on a path toward historic accomplishments. Robert Parry decided to retire as president of the Federal Reserve Bank of San Francisco. By coincidence, the person overseeing the search for a successor was one of Yellen's former students at Harvard, Roger Ferguson. At the time he was vice chair of the Federal Reserve Board in Washington, and immediately thought of her as an ideal candidate for the job.

Laura Tyson, by then dean of the London Business School, was also approached about the job but didn't find the offer appealing and suggested Yellen. "She was," Tyson said, "doing an outstanding job teaching and was an outstanding macroeconomist who could do this job."

Fed colleagues in Washington also thought Yellen, fifty-eight at the time, would be perfect for the post. The regional bank's search committee contacted her, and she found the prospect of returning to the Fed appealing. When the committee offered her the job, she immediately accepted. On June 14, 2004, Yellen became the eleventh president of the Federal Reserve Bank of San Francisco, the first woman to hold that post. She was not the first female president in the Federal Reserve System, however. That distinction belongs to Karen Horn, who became president of the Federal Reserve Bank of Cleveland in 1982.

"That was a very good move for her," said son Robby. "It came along kind of serendipitously after she had a nice, quiet period, which in a way was useful. She had a period to rest and recharge. When this job came along, she was definitely interested because it's tough going from being a policy person back into academia, and she is more bent toward being a practitioner."

❖ ❖ ❖

BEING A PRESIDENT OF A FEDERAL RESERVE BANK HAD LOTS OF advantages over being a Fed governor in Washington. For one thing, Yellen did not have to relocate again. She could commute from Berkeley across San Francisco Bay to the bank in downtown San Francisco. There were also multiple perks she did not get as a Fed governor. Bank presidents are not fully government jobs, as are governors, but something in between public and private sector posts. So, she started out with an annual salary of $300,000, roughly double what she would have been earning as a member of the Federal Reserve Board of Governors. The retirement benefits were also better. The compensation was not out of line when you consider that Yellen's region was the largest in the Federal Reserve System, accounting for a fifth of the US population and income and more than one-third of the land mass: Alaska, Arizona, California, Hawaii, Idaho, Nevada, Oregon, Utah, and Washington—plus American Samoa, Guam, and the Commonwealth of the Northern Mariana Islands.

Yellen used her people skills to spend a lot of time in community outreach, whether at a Lions Club or Chamber of Commerce meeting. That involved a lot of travel, since the states in her region ranged from the Mexican border to Alaska and from Utah to Hawaii. "She was great at it," said David Tang, a lawyer who was vice chair of the Federal Reserve Bank of San Francisco's board of directors and a member of the search committee that selected Yellen. "Very personable, very open, and explaining very difficult economic topics in a way that people could really grasp." Many of her trips were to disadvantaged neighborhoods and rural groups that normally did not receive visits from a Fed bank president.

Tang described a memorable trip he made with Yellen. One of the bank board members was the head of a native Alaskan corporation that operated a large Alaskan mining operation in the

Arctic Circle. "The board member invited us to visit this mine. It was fantastic because it's way out there, far from any kind of urban center, and gave us a sense of how people there were generating economic output. She was in the great outdoors in hiking boots and the only means of transportation were all-terrain vehicles. And so here she is riding in the trailer. We had terrific talks with a lot of the community leaders there. Seeing her in that context—out in the woods hale and hearty—was just great. That's her. She's resilient. She's tough. She's a woman for all seasons."

The position required Yellen to focus on management skills for the first time in her career. The closest she had been to a manager previously was as chair of the Council of Economic Advisers, which had a staff of a few dozen people. The San Francisco Fed had two thousand employees, many of them assigned to processing checks. Just months after she became bank president, however, Congress had approved electronic check clearing, which eliminated the need for employees to feed paper checks into machines, sort them, pack them into bundles, and ship them all over the country to the banks from where they had been issued.

As a result, one of the first duties of the economist who devoted her career to helping people find well-paying jobs was to lay off hundreds of bank employees. "The last thing I ever wanted to be involved in was laying people off, but what I found was they were really nice," she recalled. "They all saw exactly what was happening, and they understood that it was inevitable that they were going to be laid off. Some of them said, 'Don't worry so much about us. We'll be able to get on. I've wanted to do X for a long time and I never did it.' It kind of surprised me."

Yellen swiftly made changes to the senior staff, including the research director; moves that created ill will among those she replaced with her favorites. Her team included John Williams, who had met Yellen while spending a year working for her at the Council of Economic Advisers, and Mary Daly, a staff economist. Both were protégées who thrived under Yellen's leadership and later succeeded her as president of the bank. In 2018, Williams went on to head the New York Fed, the second-most powerful job in the system after the Fed chair, and Daly replaced him in San Francisco.

Yellen got to know Daly well when she asked the younger woman to organize a committee to rethink benefit programs for all twelve reserve banks. Yellen and the other bank presidents met regularly to discuss system-wide policies other than monetary affairs, and she was assigned to oversee revised retirement, thrift, and health care programs for employees. Yellen was very pleased with the result.

"I asked Mary to run this whole operation about our benefit plans, and she got to know people throughout the system," Yellen said. "Mary did a great job with that. So, we started working real closely together. I thought very highly of her."

Yellen's encouragement meant the world to Daly, a high school dropout from a broken family who got her life together with the help of mentors like Yellen. Her rise to president of a reserve bank is a success story worthy of a Horatio Alger rags-to-riches novel.

"I have traveled a very crooked path," explained Daly. "That's why I think Janet has been so helpful in my career by giving me confidence and showing interest in what I did. I didn't graduate from high school. My family had big disruptions that many families have, and the whole family blew up, and we all scattered around with different people when I was fifteen. I dropped out of high school, and then I ultimately got fortunate when I was seventeen and found a mentor named Betsy Bain, who saw something in me and said I should get a GED [graduate equivalency degree] because I wanted to be a bus driver or something that had union wages.

"I did that and then Betsy nudged me to take just one semester of college, which she paid $216 for so I could go to the University of Missouri–St. Louis. I did pretty well, and she says, 'Well, if you've gotten that, you could go ahead and get a four-year degree.' So, I did, and then I got a PhD in economics. Now I'm the president of the San Francisco Fed. And it's just been this journey where different people have guided me. Janet would be in that lineage of people who materially changed the course of my life because they took a special interest in me."

"Janet has the scarcest skill of being able to combine a sharp analytical mind with a big heart and humanity," Daly continued. "It's not an everyday occurrence that somebody has those two skills so well-developed. And she did one of the most remarkable, important things that any professional person has ever done for me. I had worked on a speech with her, and it didn't go well. It was the first one I'd ever done, and I wanted to write the best speech that anybody had ever given. But this was not a success, so I'm just mortified and disappointed in myself. I felt like the world will come to an end. I traveled with her to the speech and had a lasting feeling that I had disappointed her, and I felt it was because I hadn't graduated from high school. I never talked to her about this, but I knew she could tell how I was feeling, and she never said anything to me.

"So, a year later we're in New York for a giant conference I had organized, and it was a huge success. Afterwards, she said, 'Why don't you drive with me to the airport.' So, we get in the car and she tells the driver, 'I'd like you to take this other way.' What she did was take us past her childhood home in Brooklyn. When we got there, she said, 'I lived down there,' and then started telling me about her dad and her mom and her childhood, and how they hadn't come from silver-spoon backgrounds, and how her father would do pro bono work. Then something really important to me happened. As if she knows where I have been and what I have been through in life, she turns and says, 'So, I'm not that different than you.' I mean, talk about leveling me in the world and giving me an opportunity to feel like I belonged in this professional setting here with Janet Yellen, this famous person. She tells me she's not that different than me. It was a remarkable gift. That's her magic."

In recalling that drive through Bay Ridge, Yellen said, "I was trying to convey to her that I came from a pretty ordinary background. I mean we were comfortable enough, but we didn't have a fancy house or upbringing."

The two women also shared some lighter moments at the San Francisco Fed. Daly related one humorous incident two years after Yellen had arrived: "She and I are basically the same height—just under five feet—although gravity is not on her side. She thinks she's taller than me, and I don't think so. And she said, 'We're going to have a height-off.' So, she goes into her private bathroom in front of the mirror. And she says, 'You take your shoes off. I'm taking my shoes off.' I have kind of spiky hair, and she says, 'You've got to smash your hair down because I don't want it to be a false sense of height.' So, I smashed my hair down, and she made John Judd, the research director, call it. Can you imagine how mortifying this must be for him? He says, 'I'm sorry, Janet, but Mary's taller.' And I felt so bad for him. This poor research director had to tell Janet that I was taller than her. It was so funny. I still laugh about it and tease her about it, explaining that gravity's not on her side because she's older than me. I'm four-eleven-and-a-half and she's shorter than me. I rounded up to five feet on my driver's license to give myself that half inch."

❖ ❖ ❖

Soon after replacing Robert Parry as president of the San Francisco Fed, Yellen brought about significant changes in the culture of the bank. During his eighteen-year tenure, Parry, who was previously chief economist at the bank holding company Security Pacific Corp., brought a formal, hierarchical structure to the organization. "Bob is a lovely person but he had a very rigid structure," said one bank official who did not want to be identified. "He didn't have a lot of interactions with support people, just those at the top. And with everybody else, he smiled at but didn't really engage. When Janet arrived, it was as if the Red Sea had parted. We all could do what we were trained to do and thrive at doing it."

John Williams, who succeeded Yellen as president of the Federal Reserve Bank of San Francisco, said her friendliness and down-to-earth manner won over everyone at the bank, from senior managers to security personnel. Initially, employees at the bank felt intimidated when she was announced as the new bank president, he said. "Her resume was so extraordinary—Fed governor, renowned academic professor, chair of the Council of Economic Advisers. Most people were just in awe and nervous about someone who is obviously on a different intellectual level yet she would talk at bank events about herself; her hobbies; what she did in her spare time, such as doing a half-marathon and going on hiking trips. Everyone thought she was amazing in her accomplishments, but just a regular person who would eat lunch in the cafeteria often and talk to employees. That won over people pretty effectively."

"Janet would talk to everybody," Mary Daly agreed. "She would talk to you in the elevator. She was very conversational with the security personnel, with the cafeteria personnel, with anybody basically. And as a consequence, for those folks in particular, she's still beloved. If she walks into the bank, a sea will surround her because she has such a tremendous reputation of just being a people's person."

In fact, that's exactly what happened when Yellen returned to San Francisco several years later as Fed chair to hold a town hall meeting with employees at the bank. It turned into a spontaneous tribute to her. "They were just so warm. It was like a lovefest," she recalled. "They were just lavishing affection in my direction, particularly young women who seemed very much motivated by me and my success. If you're normal and friendly, it turns out it actually counts for a lot in the effectiveness of an organization."

Yellen's affable personality, combined with her academic rigor and ability to vastly expand the circle of people she would consult, was nothing short of transformational to veteran staffers. "She's not about breaking things that exist and trying to rebuild them," said the anonymous bank official. "But she brought in this gracious intellectual curiosity and asked us questions. It was so stark from the Bob Parry regime, where we had rigidly prepared briefings that we practiced and then presented. It was all scripted, there was very limited cross talk, and it would be done just between Bob and a couple of the principals. It was a very formal process.

"Then Janet comes in, and she doesn't actually care at all about the formality. She wants to run it like an academic seminar," the official explained. She encouraged everyone to participate in policy debates and exchange ideas in a conversational manner. "It was just a sea change. It was so remarkable and changed how we did things from then on. Janet can foster that debate chiefly because she is a good listener and very curious. She was eager to hear what people had to say. She asks these questions with a gentle Janet way. She's nonthreatening in her appearance and in her demeanor, so she can ask those questions and can create dialogue."

Yellen used her training as an academic and experience as a Fed governor to turn the bank's research department into a high-powered think tank that produced real-time reports on economic trends—particularly her specialty, the labor market—that she could use to support her views when she attended the Federal Open Market Committee meetings in Washington to review the Fed's interest rate policies. Previously, the research department depended on academic studies, which can have a long lag time between when data are gathered and the studies are published. That is not helpful for making real-time monetary policy. She pushed researchers to plug current data into academic models to better explain the latest trends. That approach allowed Yellen to come to FOMC meetings well armed with current evidence—her trademark for preparation.

Yellen's arrival at the San Francisco Fed made people raise their game, recalled Williams. "She knew more about the topic than you, and you have to add value, bring some new perspectives. She really set high expectations for people by coming into briefings really prepared asking, 'How far are you willing to go with these arguments? How convinced are you? I'm not convinced by that.' She really homed in but in a very nice way, asking for the best arguments and noting when we weren't so certain and needed to think far more about something. That whole experience was like a postdoctorate. I learned so much from her about how to do things, to get all the information and different perspectives, and then come to a very clear and strong conclusion. The one thing about Janet is she listens to everybody, and, at the end of the day, she comes out with a view. It's not wishy-washy."

Yellen agreed with Williams's description of her interaction at meetings. "It's how I get the most out of policy meetings: thinking through issues, hearing people debate different points of views, asking hard questions, asking them to do analysis that will be helpful," she said.

Her predecessor, Robert Parry, prepared for FOMC meetings in Washington by insisting that the staff produce a detailed economic forecast, even though the Fed staff at headquarters would do that with greater skill. The San Francisco staff hated doing their own forecast, and Yellen considered it a waste of time. Instead, she asked her staff to take the Washington economists' forecast and evaluate its pros and cons as if they were attending an academic conference. "I said, 'Look, I want you to do that and come and tell me about it.' They loved that," Yellen said. She held larger meetings; encouraged broad debate; and boosted morale among her economists, who often used the debates as a springboard to writing research papers. "That's more my style of interacting with people with whom I work, and I think that's been true throughout my career."

The staff responded so positively to Yellen's embracing style at meetings that when she left in 2010 to become vice chair of the Federal Reserve Board of Governors, the regional bank formally named the scene of their discussions the Janet L. Yellen Conference Room.

Another change Yellen brought to the bank presidency was a focus on ways to help those left out of economic prosperity, an issue that has always consumed her even though it had never been front and center for the Fed. "Questions of income inequality, of course, are not part of the Federal Reserve's dual mandate from Congress, which is to foster price stability and to promote maximum sustainable employment," she said in a November 6, 2006, speech. "Nonetheless, this has been an interest of mine for a long time. . . . Much of my interest in macro policy has been founded on the belief that it can and should improve the lives of the broad range of our nation's people."

Yellen then talked about how a lack of education and training in the current age of technological transformation, combined with the loss of low-skilled jobs in an era of globalization, were at the root of the problem, and that American society would benefit from greater investments in education and the social safety net. "There are signs that rising inequality is intensifying resistance to globalization, impairing social cohesion, and could, ultimately, undermine American democracy," she added prophetically, as if anticipating Donald Trump's election as president a decade later and his antidemocratic tendencies. "Inequality has risen to the point that it seems to me worthwhile for the US to seriously consider taking the risk of making our economy more rewarding for more of the people."

As a practical step to address inequality, Yellen made the San Francisco bank's community development program more prominent. The program implements the Federal Reserve's mission to promote economic growth and financial stability for low- and moderate-income communities. The aim is to ensure that banks are making loans to small businesses and individuals in these neighborhoods to encourage affordable housing, neighborhood revitalization, thriving businesses, and increased employment. The Fed was required to focus on this problem under the Community Reinvestment Act (CRA) of 1977, which was enacted to combat discrimination in lending. Even so, community development was a backwater for many Federal Reserve banks.

Not for Yellen, long focused on championing the needs of those left out of a growing economy. She revitalized community development efforts in San Francisco—and later did the same at Fed headquarters in Washington when she became chair in 2014. She gave the issue so much prominence that on November 30, 2018, after she had returned to private life, the Fed Board announced the creation of the Janet L. Yellen Award for Excellence in Community Development, which would be given annually to an outstanding employee in the program. "During her tenure as chair of the Federal Reserve, Janet Yellen elevated the importance of economic and financial inclusion as well as the community development function," her successor as Fed chair, Jerome "Jay" Powell, said. "She often reminded us that an inclusive economy is a vibrant economy. It is a legacy that my colleagues and I are honored to carry forward."

Focusing on community development proved to be valuable to Yellen as San Francisco president for reasons that went beyond helping lower-income people. From 2004 to 2007, it provided early intelligence on an emerging housing crisis that would soon explode across the nation.

The housing crash was caused by a combination of factors: soaring house prices, relaxed lending requirements for "subprime" mortgages, repackaging of these higher-risk mortgages into investments that carried higher interest rates than US government bonds, and the huge growth of exotic derivatives. There was the credit default swap (CDS), a derivative that allows an investor to "swap," or offset, a credit risk with another investor as a hedge against a default on the loan. There was the "collateralized debt obligation" (CDO), another derivative comprising a variety of loans and other assets whose value serves as collateral for the promised repayment. These were peddled by investment banks and were considered safe because of rising real estate prices, approval by ratings agencies that determined the risks, and the smug assumption by investors that they could safely hedge their bets with collateral and the knowledge that residential real estate would only keep rising.

Then it all unwound. House prices crashed, homeowners defaulted on loans, and all the "safe" exotic investments bought with borrowed money collapsed in value, ushering in the Great Recession from December 2007 to June 2009—so named because it was the worst economic downturn since the Great Depression.

A senior Fed official said the community development program that Yellen had elevated offered a window into the coming housing crisis because many of the subprime mortgage borrowers were lower-income residents of California, where housing prices soared higher than in other parts of the country. "I think it was helpful for Janet to have the vantage point that she did going into the crisis," said the official. "If we didn't have our community development footprint in order to implement the Community Reinvestment Act, we would be missing a really important line of sight into what was going on among a segment of the population. Janet was attentive to the community development part of the portfolio and getting to know some of those issues in her district. So, as the crisis started to heat up, that was really important to her insights at the time."

She might have seen the crisis coming before many of her Fed colleagues, but much like her mea culpa for being passive during the 1998 dispute over regulating derivatives, Yellen admitted that she did not fully understand what was going on and felt powerless to prevent the looming crash. It was another painful lesson about the consequences of trusting the markets to self-regulate against excess. As the housing crisis turned into a deep national downturn, Yellen would stay focused on remedies for low-income Americans, who always suffer the most when the economy slumps. She also would vow to be a vigilant regulator in the future, convinced that only the government—not private interests—can be trusted to maintain financial stability.

※ ※ ※

THE GREAT RECESSION WAS THE RESULT OF PRIVATE GREED, weak government regulation, and the public's herd mentality. Once a party gets started—in this case, rising house prices—everyone assumes it will never end, so they keep celebrating even when the hosts show them to the door. Signs had abounded that the housing bubble was about to burst, but buyers and lenders still jumped in, convinced they could still profit. And government regulators, as often was the case, did too little too late.

As powerful as the Fed is, as a risk manager, it has sharply curtailed authority. It can supervise commercial banks and bank holding companies. But investment banks are overseen by the Securities and Exchange Commission (SEC), thrifts are regulated by the Office of Thrift Supervision (OTS), and state-chartered banks that do not join the Federal Reserve System are regulated by the Federal Deposit Insurance Corporation (FDIC). Mortgage lenders are regulated by state and federal consumer protection agencies. That patchwork of regulation put the Fed at a disadvantage in anticipating the housing crisis because most of the risky deals were handled by financial institutions that were not under the Fed's watchful eye.

To the extent that she could improve supervision of lending practices when she arrived at the San Francisco Fed, Yellen shook up her bank's supervision section. She brought in people from other regional banks with reputations for being strong regulators and promoted others already working in San Francisco. The larger problem is that Fed supervision in general was not a priority during the Alan Greenspan era because he was an advocate of letting a free market regulate itself.

Politicians in Washington were also on an anti-regulatory kick. In 1999, President Clinton had signed into law the Gramm-Leach-Bliley Act, which formally put an end to Glass-Steagall Act protections against financial excess and allowed investment banks to operate virtually free of regulation. So, even if it wanted to, the Fed couldn't oversee investment banks that were subsidiaries of commercial banks that the Fed did regulate. "The SEC had the authority over the investment bank, and the Fed was supposed to defer to the SEC even though it had authority over the parent company," said a former senior Fed official. "So, you had no visibility into the investment banks. I'll tell you, in 2008, when the investment banks were in trouble, working with the SEC was very difficult. Goldman Sachs, Morgan Stanley, Merrill Lynch, Bear Stearns were not bank holding companies. They were just investment banks. The Fed had no authority over them at all. And the SEC was not really a rigorous supervisor."

Before Bear Stearns collapsed in 2008 and was bought in an emergency fire sale by JPMorgan Chase, the former Fed official continued, "we had conversations with the SEC and we said, 'These guys are in trouble. They are going to fail. You need to do some something, make them bolster their capital liquidity.' And all we got back from the SEC was, 'Well, the data they submitted last night showed they had plenty of liquidity.' Then later that night, the chief risk officer for Bear said, 'We can't open tomorrow morning. We don't have enough capital.' And the SEC was shocked even though we'd been calling them for a week telling them there was a problem. Maybe the Fed wasn't as good a supervisor as it could have been, but the SEC certainly wasn't."

Yellen recalled that in her first week in the job in 2004 she was briefed about what was happening in the real estate markets from staff in the supervision office. She did not have a role in supervising banks as president; that was a role reserved for the supervision office and the Fed in Washington. The Federal Reserve Act charges the Board of Governors in Washington with responsibility for bank supervision, and local supervisors report to counterparts at headquarters, not to the regional bank president. The reason is to make sure often cozy relationships between a local bank's management and the regional president do not influence judgments about the bank's financial solvency. While she kept her hands off of direct supervision, Yellen met regularly with top officials of the major banks in her region, such as Wells Fargo and Tokyo Mitsubishi. Through those contacts, she would get a general picture of economic trends.

"My supervisory people had a risk evaluation unit trying to understand what they should be worried about in banks," Yellen said. "They were very worried about the housing and commercial real estate markets. Banks were making loans on easy terms at a very rapid rate for land development and construction. The banks seemed like they were taking on significant risks. They warned that this was a very bad and worrisome set of developments and that we didn't have the tools to deal with it." That was certainly the case. Yet even in mid-2005, Yellen and other Fed officials failed to foresee the collapse in housing prices that would begin in the summer of 2006. Nationally, they fell more than 25 percent until starting to recover six years later; California suffered an even bigger drop—more than one-third of home values were wiped out, on average. The effect on homeowners, mortgage companies, and other financial institutions that bet big on steadily rising house prices was devastating for them and the rest of the global economy.

That did not seem to be a likely scenario to Yellen and other members of the Federal Open Market Committee when they met for a two-day meeting on June 29–30, 2005. They spent the first morning assessing the unusually rapid rise in house prices but concluded that it did not pose an imminent risk to the wider economy. Instead, the committee was more focused on the threat of inflation and voted to raise interest rates a quarter percent. The Fed had been boosting the rate at virtually every meeting that year and the next by that same quarter point, sending the federal funds rate from 1 percent in mid-2003 to 5.25 percent in mid-2006, when falling house prices forced the committee to reverse course and start cutting rates.

At the June 29–30, 2005, discussion, Yellen cited reports about lax lending for deals that her directors at the San Francisco Fed called "stupid," a description that drew laughter from the others. She agreed with the rest of the committee on the need to nudge up interest rates another quarter point to keep inflation in check but warned that rates shouldn't go much higher or it would trigger a downturn.

Reflecting back on the coming crisis in 2005, Yellen said her supervisors in San Francisco were lobbying their counterparts in Washington to step up regulation of banks. She recalled the FOMC discussion about housing in mid-2005 but noted that it was a problem for the Fed regulators and Board of Governors to address, not regional bank presidents who serve on the FOMC to set interest rates but don't have a role in determining policy for regulating banks. "It wasn't just a question of monetary policy. It was a question of lending practices, supervision of banks, capital requirements, and what to do about growing concentrations of commercial real estate loans," she said. "And virtually nothing happened. I mean, it was really pathetic. The bank regulators did almost nothing." In 2010, when she rejoined the Board of Governors in Washington, Yellen became a zealous advocate for tighter bank supervision, having recognized the price the country pays when it trusts banks to do the prudent thing.

"When things are going really well, the bankers don't want anyone to touch their very profitable business," Yellen said. "So, they lobbied against having higher capital requirements. The bank regulators in Washington tried to put out tougher restrictions on what banks can do and to tighten capital requirements, but after intense lobbying, they published some supervisory guidance on commercial real estate that said if you have a high concentration of risky commercial real estate loans, you should be careful to manage the risks more carefully than normal. This 'guidance' had no teeth. I thought it was hardly worth the paper it was printed on."

Yellen knew of course that Greenspan had an anti-regulation mindset so she didn't talk to him about the need for more supervision of financial institutions, but she did go to some Board of Governors' meetings on supervision to argue that more needed to be done. "It seemed really clear this was going to end up being a problem," she said. "There was nothing subtle about this. My banking supervisor told me that if you look at the banking history of the United States, banks often fail because of commercial real estate. It's a classic thing. This is what most waves of bank failure have been about. And all of the signs that supervisors should be trained to look at were flashing red. What was happening with leverage in the system was harder to see with the derivatives and the CDOs [collateralized debt obligations]."

Even if these risky transactions weren't so opaque, Yellen's regulators were hobbled by the fact that they lacked supervision authority over the financial institutions in her district that were most in trouble, including Washington Mutual and IndyMac. They were overseen by the Office of Thrift Supervision. "We had to extend discount window loans to these banks in their final days, and by the time we got to late 2006 and 2007, it was pretty clear we were going to have a financial crisis," she said.

Washington Mutual, known as WaMu, was a savings and loan bank that had 43,000 employees, 2,200 branch offices in fifteen states, and $188 billion in deposits at the end of 2007. In 2008 it became the largest failed bank in US history, brought down by home loans that went sour. IndyMac Bank was the largest savings and loan association in the Los Angeles area and the seventh-largest mortgage originator in the United States. It represented the fourth-largest bank failure when it collapsed in 2008. Like WaMu, it imprudently had made too many risky home loans.

Perhaps the most notorious financial institution in Yellen's district was Countrywide Financial Corp., which grew to become the nation's largest mortgage company under the leadership of Angelo Mozilo, the poster child for the greed and recklessness behind the financial meltdown.

In 1969, Mozilo and a partner founded Countrywide Credit Industries in New York and later moved their headquarters to California. In 1997, Countrywide spun off Countrywide Mortgage Investment as an independent company called IndyMac Bank. Countrywide soon became a leading nonbank national mortgage company. Mozilo initially spurned subprime mortgages as too risky, but as his company lost business to competitors, Countrywide started approving subprime loans in the 2000s. By 2004, it was the nation's largest home mortgage lender with more than $200 billion in assets, and the company branched out into other financial services.

When the housing market collapsed, Countrywide plummeted with it. In November 2006, as its value was sinking, Countrywide changed its charter from that of a bank holding company overseen by Federal Reserve regulators to a thrift, presumably believing the Office of Thrift Supervision would be a more lenient overseer. Two years later, in 2008, the ailing company was bought by Bank of America. Mozilo, who received an estimated $500 million in compensation in the 2000s before the crash, was accused of duping borrowers into costly mortgages with unfavorable terms, but he was never charged with a crime. In 2010, he reached a settlement with the Securities and Exchange Commission over securities fraud and insider trading charges. Under terms of the settlement, Mozilo did not have to admit to any wrongdoing.

Yellen remembered distastefully dealing with Mozilo and Countrywide until the change of charters. "We supervised Countrywide, which was a bank holding company based in California," she said. "I used to meet with Angelo Mozilo routinely. He was aggressive and struck me as overconfident," said Yellen, who found Mozilo to be a most unpleasant person to deal with. "As I began to better understand what was going on in the loan business and the kinds of loans that were being made and Countrywide's role in it, I found it a very scary proposition to see what was happening. We were concerned with Countrywide's rapid growth and the weaknesses in their risk controls. That led us to crack down in terms of our supervision. They didn't like what we were doing so they went charter shopping and changed charters."

Given all the financial problems occurring around her, Yellen's normally shrewd analytical skills failed her, and she did not connect the dots that created a picture of an emerging disaster for the wider economy. "I really wasn't focused on some of the developments that resulted in the worst and most damaging aspects of the crisis," she admitted. "I saw what was happening in housing and how it would likely affect many banks, and yes, there were many failures of smaller banks. I spent a lot of time dealing with one after the next in areas that we supervised. But I did not see the broader problems in the financial system that were connected to derivatives with CDSs [credit default swaps], with all the leverage at the investment banks. That was the heart of the crisis, but I did not see it unfolding. No one in the Fed really understood it until it was blowing up."

Yellen realized that there was no broad financial stability program in place to determine the health of the entire financial system. Regulations at the time were focused on the solvency of individual banks, not the big picture and the risk of a nationwide financial crisis. Investment banks on Wall Street were making more loans and creating a bevy of exotic instruments but were outside the purview of Fed regulators. The Securities and Exchange Commission oversaw them but was far more laissez-faire in using its regulatory authority. Even Countrywide escaped Fed oversight except for a very small bank it had acquired. "Our sole focus under the law was the safety and soundness of the depository institutions that we supervised," Yellen complained. "We weren't allowed to peer directly into the mortgage company subsidiaries."

Yellen finally recognized the scope of the crisis on August 9, 2007. That is when France's biggest bank, BNP Paribas, announced it was freezing $2.2 billion worth of funds because the growing US subprime mortgage defaults had unleashed a panicky scramble by investors for cash. Meanwhile, Countrywide's bank was trying to secure an emergency loan from the Fed to funnel it into the mortgage company, but the Federal Reserve Act prohibits such loans to help a troubled parent, and the Fed Board of Governors resisted intense lobbying for the loan. "The whole financial system was blowing up," Yellen said. "At the end of the day, to rescue the entire system, the Fed basically had to pour out loans to financial institutions and bolster bank capital to stop the system from collapsing. It was like we had a nuclear bomb going off."

Why were financial regulators so slow to see the coming explosion? "The Fed was set up in 1913 after the banking panic of 1907 to be a lender of last resort, which is a very critical function in the financial crisis," Yellen explained. "It's like saying you train to be a fireman, but you didn't train to do fire prevention. In spite of the fact that periodically you were called on to extinguish a fire, nobody ever assigned you to have a unit to try to spot fire risks. That's how the system worked. There was no regulator that had the job of trying to assess the riskiness of the system as a whole."

When Ben Bernanke replaced Greenspan as Fed chair in February 2006, he sensed a coming crisis. A renowned Princeton scholar on the Great Depression who was chosen by President George W. Bush, Bernanke had served as a Fed governor before taking over as chair four years later. "Bernanke, to his credit, saw this hole and knew other central banks were doing much more on the financial stability front," Yellen said. "He assigned a small crew of people to work on financial stability and prepare periodic reports. He saw that this was a missing link and he tried to get it filled, but the people didn't have sufficient time and very quickly everything blew up."

# - 7 -

# PUTTING OUT THE FINANCIAL FIRE

*"In the run-up to Halloween, we have had a witch's brew of news"*

ALTHOUGH JANET YELLEN HAD LIMITED AUTHORITY AS A RE-
gional bank president to deal with the lax lending standards that
triggered the housing crisis, she certainly could play an important
role in rescuing the US economy as a member of the interest rate–
setting Federal Open Market Committee. Transcripts of those meetings illuminated her insights and influence. They also highlighted
her concerns dating back to childhood about how the latest economic collapse—when belatedly recognized—would affect average
Americans threatened with the loss of their jobs and homes, and
steps the nation's central bank could take to ease their suffering.

As has been a lifetime custom, she came to the eight FOMC
meetings a year with clear, well-prepared analyses of economic
conditions in both her region and the nation. Transcripts of the
meetings reveal how she would pepper her remarks with humor as
she described with colorful detail and insights the state of various
economic sectors, the labor market, wages, and inflation. She also

gave sharp tutorials on issues such as how to properly measure inflation and productivity, and often led the way in discussions about how the FOMC could improve its communications with the markets to provide more transparency and guidance on its future plans.

At her first FOMC meeting as president of the San Francisco Fed on June 29, 2004, Chair Alan Greenspan welcomed back his former colleague after a seven-year absence. Later in the meeting, he recognized Yellen to make her economic presentation. "President Yellen?" he said tentatively, then added to the group's laughter, "It took me a while to figure out how to address you!"

Yellen's return to the FOMC was greeted warmly by committee members. Donald Kohn, a Fed governor at the time, was impressed with how well prepared she always was. She read her presentations from a notebook and was so cogent that he would stop doodling or thinking about what he was going to say and listen to her. She often used her research group at the San Francisco Fed to shed new light on some issue that was facing the FOMC, so everybody listened to her, even the committee hawks.

During the run-up to the housing collapse that appeared all but inevitable by the summer of 2007, Yellen expressed growing concerns about the sustainability of the boom in commercial real estate initially, and then worried more about residential housing, as both sectors were fueled by easy credit and soaring prices. Yet she failed to see that the country was sitting on a ticking financial time bomb that would soon explode, causing the entire economy and financial system to nearly crater. Then again, neither did any of her colleagues on the rate-setting Federal Open Market Committee. Instead, from her first FOMC meeting as San Francisco president and well into 2007, the main concern Yellen and other committee members shared was the need to make sure the Fed was keeping inflation in check.

After a brief and shallow recession in 2001, the economy had started expanding at a healthy clip, but the federal funds rate had been reduced in June 2003 to just 1 percent, a level that allowed for cheap lending by banks, from mortgages to car loans. The committee thought that was too low a rate for a growing economy. So, starting at that June 29, 2004, session, when she had returned to the FOMC, the committee raised rates in quarter-point increments at nearly every meeting until it reached 5.25 percent in mid-2006, where it stayed until the housing crisis was in full fury in September 2007. Yellen was not a voting member at her initial meeting but voiced no objection to the 2004 rate hike, which made sense at the time since there wasn't the slightest hint of the housing crisis to come four years later. In years when she had a vote, she never dissented against a rate increase, although at times she cautioned that the committee needed to analyze data carefully before its next bump-up in rates to ensure it wasn't being too aggressive.

In hindsight, Fed officials admit they should have seen the crisis coming, particularly since they had devoted an entire FOMC session on June 29–30, 2005, to the run-up in housing prices and the potential consequences for the national economy if prices slumped 20 percent. The economists doing the briefings had mistakenly concluded that the most likely outcome would be a 2001-style downturn: short and shallow. "It was going to be kind of like the 2000 dot.com bust. There would be a mild recession," Kohn recalled. "We didn't see the financial fragilities that were building up in the economy, unfortunately."

At the start of 2006, Yellen was now a voting member of the FOMC, and she began to express growing concerns about rising house prices and the spillover effect. At Greenspan's final meeting as chair on January 31, after more than eighteen years at the helm, Yellen expressed concern "that the economy faces some pretty big downside risks, especially having to do with the interrelated issues of possible overvaluations in housing markets." Nevertheless, she was largely optimistic in her forecast: "I would say that the overall outlook is quite positive." Then taking note of the fact that Greenspan was an avid tennis player, she added, "Needless to say, it's fitting for Chairman Greenspan to leave office with the economy in such solid shape. And if I might torture a simile, I would say, Mr. Chairman, that the situation you're handing off to your successor is a lot like a tennis racquet with a gigantic sweet spot." The room erupted in laughter.

By the time the June 28–29, 2006, FOMC meeting took place, now with Ben Bernanke installed as chair, Yellen was growing worried about supporting a continued boost in interest rates to keep inflation in check at a time when housing prices had started to slump. She said the committee should consider forgoing a quarter-point increase in interest rates until it could better determine the magnitude of the weakness in the housing market. "I see a lot of uncertainty right now," she said. Yellen voted, nonetheless, for the rate boost, calling it a "close call." Little did she or the rest of the FOMC know that it would be their last increase for more than a decade—or that they would be slashing the rate to zero in a little more than two years as the economy became unglued.

At the next meeting, on August 8, 2006, Yellen fretted more about the housing sector. "The recent falloff in housing activity and the deceleration in house prices have been faster than expected. A large homebuilder in our District summarized the views of many of our contacts when he recently commented that 'the housing market has not yet popped, but a hissing sound is now clearly audible.' He pointed to rapidly rising cancellations as a particularly ominous sign. I will be watching the incoming data closely for signs as to whether the housing slowdown remains orderly as hoped or takes a steeper downward slide, posing a greater risk to the economy." Though she still had some lingering worries about inflation and saw a good case for raising rates again, she agreed the committee could finally pause because inflation expectations were contained and the financial markets were not expecting another rate boost.

At the September 20, 2006, FOMC meeting, the clouds over housing grew darker. "The speed of the falloff in housing activity and the deceleration in house prices continue to surprise us . . . and it seems a good bet that things will get worse before they get better," she said. "A major homebuilder who is on one of our boards tells us that home inventory has gone through the roof, so to speak. He literally said that," she said to laughter. "With the share of unsold homes topping 80 percent in some of the new subdivisions around Phoenix and Las Vegas, he has labeled these the new ghost towns of the West." Despite her grim report, other committee members shrugged it off, assuming either that it was just a regional problem or that the market would soon right itself since the economy as a whole seemed to be in solid shape. They were still more worried about inflation.

Indeed, later that fall and into early 2007, Yellen became more optimistic about the outlook as the housing downturn slowed and the economy hurtled through barriers to continued growth. "After a precipitous fall, home sales appear to have leveled off," she observed on December 12, 2006. As a nonvoting member of the FOMC at the January 30–31, 2007, meeting, she said her best-guess forecast was a "soft landing"—a slowing economy that avoids a recession—accompanied by moderating inflation.

She stuck to that forecast in the spring even while acknowledging greater risks to the economy, as financial markets were swooning with greater frequency amid the burgeoning housing crisis. "I view the conditions for growth going forward as being reasonably solid," she said at the June 27–28, 2007, meeting. "In terms of risks to the outlook for growth, I still feel the presence of a six hundred–pound gorilla in the room, and that is the housing sector.

The risk for further significant deterioration in the housing market, with house prices falling and mortgage delinquencies rising further, causes me appreciable angst. Indeed, the repercussions of falling house prices are already playing out in some areas where past price rises were especially rapid and subprime lending soared."

Yellen cited Sacramento in her own district as a bright example of a metropolitan area where delinquencies on subprime mortgages were rising sharply. Adding to her worries, her husband, George, remembered, was a trip she made to Idaho to visit a real estate development. "Janet came back home and was quite shocked at the fact that they had developed all this real estate and none of it was selling," he said.

Yellen's optimism about the economy had turned on a dime by the time the FOMC met again on August 7, 2007, just months before a string of home loan defaults and a swooning stock market triggered the start of a full-fledged housing crisis in December 2007. "The market for mortgage-backed securities is now highly illiquid, and there are indications that credit problems are spilling beyond the subprime sector," she said. "Subprime" referred to risky loans foolish banks made to people with poor credit ratings because the banks figured they could always foreclose on the borrowers and count on rising home prices to recover their loans when they sold the houses. They never considered that prices would plummet below the outstanding mortgage balance. "It thus seems likely that lending standards will tighten for a broader class of borrowers in the mortgage market," Yellen continued. "The drop in equity prices and rising rates on most risky corporate debt are further negatives for growth. . . . So, I think it likely that the fed funds rate will need to fall appreciably over the next few years."

Two days later, her worst fears were confirmed when subprime mortgage defaults prompted France's BNP Paribas bank to freeze its funds in the face of investors' desperate dash for cash. That was the day she changed her forecast from there *might be* a crisis to there *was* one. That's when the ticking time bomb went off.

Financial markets went into a near panic, as everyone who borrowed heavily to make housing bets that had soured searched desperately for funds to pay off their debts. But no one who had spare cash was in a mood to extend credit. Defaults and bankruptcies loomed like falling dominoes. It was time for the Fed to step forward in the role it was originally created to play: lender of last resort. Indeed, it truly was the last resort for many troubled financial institutions.

Fed chair Bernanke, who knew well how the central bank worsened the Great Depression seventy years earlier by tightening credit prematurely, was determined not to make the same mistake this time. On August 10, 2007, he called for a rare emergency conference call with FOMC members to inform them that credit markets were freezing up and the Fed would be issuing a message that it would be available as an emergency source of loans in hopes of calming the financial system. "The Federal Reserve is providing liquidity to facilitate the orderly functioning of financial markets," the statement said, ending with, "As always, the discount window [low-interest loans reserved for banks in dire need] is available as a source of funding."

The announcement did not have the desired effect, and six days later, on August 16, Bernanke held another conference call. "I think we're also seeing a certain amount of panic, a certain amount of markets seizing up, with good credits not being able to be financed, and a good deal of concern that there is a potential for some downward spiral in the markets that could threaten or harm the economy," he said. The FOMC agreed that the Fed should make clear to the markets that it would help bolster the housing market by accepting home mortgages and related assets as collateral for emergency loans.

When the FOMC held its next regularly scheduled meeting, on September 18, it voted to cut its federal funds rate from 5.25 percent to 4.75 percent. Yellen, who had enthusiastically backed the steps Bernanke was taking, warned that "our contacts located at the epicenter—those, for example, in the private equity and mortgage markets—report utter devastation. . . . I think a fifty-basis point cut right away is appropriate."

At the subsequent meeting on October 30–31, the FOMC cut rates another quarter point, and Yellen felt the worst of the crisis may have passed. Meanwhile, regional bank presidents on the committee with hawkish views began objecting to Bernanke's approach. They did not see a threat to the economy that justified a rate cut that could reignite inflation. Most went along with the majority grudgingly, but Thomas Hoenig, longtime president of the Federal Reserve Bank of Kansas City, dissented.

Yellen believed such hawkish views were detached from reality. Financial conditions were worsening, and the Fed rate cut and reassuring words had not eased the credit crunch banks were facing. Widespread concerns about the condition of many financial institutions made investors afraid to lend, particularly for more than very short terms, such as overnight loans. When the Fed increased lending available through its emergency "discount window," many banks were reluctant to borrow because it would be seen—erroneously—as a sign of their financial distress.

On December 12, the Fed, which traditionally provided troubled banks overnight loans at a fixed interest rate, announced it was establishing a Term Auction Facility (TAF). It allowed banks that were largely healthy but in need of short-term cash infusions to bid on interest rates auction-style for twenty-eight-day loans and still keep their reputations for financial soundness intact. It was the first of many unprecedented programs Bernanke and his staff devised to deal with the financial crisis over the next few years by using creative interpretations of their legal authority. Critics challenged his unorthodox moves, but Yellen had his back the entire time, recognizing that emergency times required emergency responses. Once again, as mentor James Tobin had taught her back at Yale, the government should use all the powerful tools available to it—and even create new ones—to restore the economy to health as soon as possible to alleviate the suffering of the millions afflicted by the downturn.

At the FOMC's December 11 meeting, the day before the TAF program was announced, Yellen sounded a pessimistic note about the economic outlook, as the committee agreed to cut interest rates another quarter point. "The possibilities of a credit crunch developing and of the economy slipping into a recession seem all too real," she said. "I am particularly concerned that we may now be seeing the first signs of spillovers from the housing and financial sectors to the broader economy. . . . I fear that we are in danger of sliding into a credit crunch."

In January 2008, as economic conditions grew more dire, Bernanke held two conference calls with the FOMC. On January 9, he polled members on whether the times required an extraordinary action: slashing interest rates before waiting until the committee's regularly scheduled meeting at the end of the month. The consensus was to wait until the planned January 29–30 session.

But Bernanke couldn't wait that long, as financial markets continued to slump, he held another conference call on January 21, to propose an immediate and sizable rate cut: three-quarters of a percent. "I was reluctant to call this meeting, both because of the [Martin Luther King] holiday and because the Committee did express a preference on January 9 for not moving between regularly scheduled meetings, and I accepted that judgment on January 9," he began. "However, I think there are times when events are just moving too fast for us to wait for the regular meeting. I know it is only a week away, but seven trading days is a long time in financial markets. . . . Global stock markets have been falling very sharply, both in Asia and in Europe."

"In some sense, it was a lucky break that today was a holiday because in the middle of the day we got a very good read on what the markets are doing tomorrow, and so we can get ahead of things as opposed to being forced, after a couple of disastrous days, to respond," Bernanke continued. "Again, I don't know if this would help, but I think that indicating that the Fed is on top of the situation and that we are proposing to address economic and credit risks aggressively would help. . . . I think we have to take a meaningful action—something that will have an important effect. Therefore, I am proposing a cut of 75 basis points. I recognize that this is a very large change."

Yellen, although not a voting member in 2008, strongly endorsed the proposal, and the committee approved it with just one dissent. When the regular meeting was held eight days later, the FOMC cut rates another half percent. President of the Federal Reserve Bank of Dallas, Richard Fisher, one of a quartet of inflation hawks on the committee, dissented because he did not think the situation was that dire. He foolishly worried that the Fed would uncork inflation with its dramatic moves to reduce interest rates.

As the economy spiraled into a deadly plunge dragged down by financial chaos, Bernanke held another conference call on March 10 to inform the committee that the Fed was creating a new emergency lending program, a Term Securities Lending Facility (TSLF), that would lend up to $200 billion of Treasury securities for twenty-eight days—rather than overnight, as in the existing program—and that it would accept troubled residential mortgage–backed securities as collateral even though they were risky assets that triggered the financial meltdown. The aim was "to foster the functioning of financial markets," the Fed said in announcing the program. "The purpose of this facility," Bernanke explained to the committee members, "is to help alleviate the rapidly escalating pressures evident in term-collateral funding markets."

Hawks on the FOMC saw the move as reckless and pushing the Fed into uncharted territory from which it could not retreat. "I can see the criticism of almost lending blind, taking substandard collateral," complained Dallas Fed president Fisher. "I think we should view opening up this sort of expansive interpretation of the act as a relatively irreversible step because it will be next to impossible to put this interpretation back in the bottle," chimed in Richmond Fed president Jeffrey Lacker. "I respectfully oppose this Term Securities Lending Facility."

In fact, Bernanke did not need the FOMC's approval to create the program, although he preferred to know the committee supported him. Donald Kohn, who had been promoted to vice chair of the Fed Board in 2006, noted that it was not an easy decision, but he supported it as essential. "We are broadening the collateral. We're expanding securities lending. We're lengthening terms. We're being more aggressive in the term funding markets. We're holding auctions. This is an extension of what we've been doing all along in response to this crisis, and this is just the next step," he said. "I think we can step back when markets improve, but it is a precedent. There are moral hazards. There are risks. There are reputational risks. I agree with all of those things, and as Chairman Bernanke can tell you, I was resistant to this idea when it was raised a little while ago. But I have changed my mind. . . . The first and most important of them is the downward spiral that we're in. . . . The markets just aren't operating."

Kohn's reference to "moral hazard" is the concept that lenders and borrowers will continue to take on irresponsible risks if they know they'll be bailed out and won't have to pay the consequences for their risky actions. It has long been a quandary for central bankers, who often would let small financial companies fail but rush to aid large ones considered "too large to fail" because they would drag the global financial system down with them.

Although Yellen was keenly aware of the moral hazard argument, she again signaled her unwavering endorsement for the extraordinary steps Bernanke was taking to avert another depression like the one he studied so extensively as a scholar. "I strongly support the proposed Term Securities Lending Facility. I certainly agree that we face a situation in which systemic risk is large, and it's escalating very quickly. A dangerous dynamic has set in," she said. "I think financial stability is truly at stake here, and although there are financial and reputational risks in pursuing this approach, it is a creative and well-targeted approach, and it is worth taking these risks to try to arrest the downward spiral in market conditions. . . . I am not 100 percent convinced that this is going to work, but I definitely think it is a good idea to move ahead and to do so quickly."

The new program had been established against the backdrop of a new crisis on Wall Street. Bear Stearns, one of the nation's largest investment firms, was in deep trouble because of its heavy investment in mortgage-backed securities that plunged in value. On March 14, the company concluded it did not have enough capital on hand to open. Two days later, to prevent a total collapse of the firm, JPMorgan Chase—at the urging of the Fed—announced it would purchase the once-proud investment company for $236 million, a paltry $2 a share. A year before, Bear Stearns's stock was trading at $170 a share. In return for agreeing to buy the investment house, Chase was able to secure a $30 billion loan from the Fed.

Two days after watching Bear Stearns's near-catastrophe resolved, the FOMC voted on March 18 to slash interest rates by another three-quarters of a percent. Fisher voted no, and was joined by Charles Plosser, president of the Philadelphia Fed. "A number of contacts have provided comments reinforcing the view that a significant credit crunch is under way," Yellen said in supporting the rate cut. "In one example, the CEO of a bank in my District reports that several of the nation's largest mortgage lenders have suspended withdrawals from open home equity lines out of concern that borrowers could now owe more than their homes are worth. As a final anecdote, a banker in my District who lends to wineries noted that high-end boutique producers face a distinctly softening market for their products, although sales of cheap wine are soaring." That provided the tense committee members some needed gallows humor.

The Fed cut rates another quarter point at its April 29–30 meeting, lowering the fed funds rate to 2 percent, down from 5.25 percent just ten months earlier. Fisher and Plosser again dissented. At the next meeting, on June 24–25, the FOMC made no change in rates, but Fisher dissented, saying he thought rates should rise. Yellen, who had vacillated for more than a year between hopeful and fearful, was now feeling more positive. "I think the economy has shown resilience so far, and that's reassuring, but I don't think it's assured for the future. The aggressive policy actions that we have put in place since January are actually working to cushion the blow, and that's part of the reason that we haven't seen a greater unraveling so far."

On July 24, Bernanke held a conference call to inform the FOMC that the Fed wanted to extend its emergency lending programs beyond September, when they were set to expire. In one of the few instances when she was less than enthusiastically supportive, Yellen said many banks in her district would be borrowing funds even though they were on the brink of insolvency and would be unlikely to repay the Fed. She explained that her supervisors did not have the resources to determine the health of all the banks in her district. "So, it does give me qualms about the proposal," she added. In response, Bernanke showed he had her back this time, praising the job her regulators were doing. "President Yellen, San Francisco did a really good job in a difficult situation," he said. "We were following that very carefully."

The Fed kept interest rates unchanged at its August 5 meeting, where Yellen said she saw growing financial risks "but no recession." She would later learn that the economy, in fact, had entered into a deep recession the prior December, a fact that underscored the limits of economic forecasts during chaotic financial times, even for a shrewd analyst like her. All economists had to deal with a cloudy crystal ball because the statistics they would assess to determine the future lagged the present day by weeks or months.

Everything grew darker on September 15, 2008, when Lehman Brothers, the nation's fourth-largest investment bank, filed for bankruptcy. Unlike Bear Stearns, it lacked the assets needed as collateral for emergency loans or the interest of a buyer willing to absorb it. Bernanke and Treasury secretary Henry Paulson concluded that there was no way to save the company given its extremely weak condition compared to other brokerage firms. Financial markets went into free fall, and credit markets froze up as panic ruled the day.

"I certainly remember that weekend when they were making a call about what to do about Lehman," son Robby said. "I remember my mother called me and said, 'I just found out that they're not going to be able to bail out Lehman.' And I think both of us were really distraught about that because of the fallout."

When the FOMC met the following day, Yellen offered evidence of a plunge in high-end consumption, a sure sign of financial distress: "East Bay plastic surgeons and dentists note that patients are deferring elective procedures. Reservations are no longer necessary at many high-end restaurants. And the Silicon Valley Country Club, with a $250,000 entrance fee and seven-to-eight-year waiting list, has seen the number of would-be new members shrink to a mere thirteen."

As the financial crisis deepened, and Bernanke worried that the wheels of the financial system were coming off, he convened a conference call on September 29 to tell the committee that the US Treasury Department was creating a $700 billion Troubled Asset Relief Program (TARP), which would purchase troubled companies' assets and stocks to stabilize the system and mitigate foreclosures.

On October 7, he convened another conference call to propose that the Fed and the central banks of Canada, Europe, Sweden, Switzerland, and the United Kingdom jointly announce a half-point cut in interest rates the following day. "We're having a lot of meetings off the regular cycle. I think it's just a sign of the extraordinary times that we're currently living through," he began. The staff then explained that markets were continuing to drop despite the announcement of Treasury's TARP initiative. Yellen's support was full-throated: "In my opinion, a larger action could easily be justified and is ultimately likely to prove necessary. We're witnessing a complete breakdown in the functioning of credit markets." The hawks on the committee were skeptical but went along, and the vote was unanimous.

At the regular October 28–29 meeting, the Fed cut rates another half point. "In the run-up to Halloween, we have had a witch's brew of news. Sorry," Yellen deadpanned as everyone cracked up. "The downward trajectory of economic data has been hair-raising— with employment, consumer sentiment, spending and orders for capital goods, and homebuilding all contracting—and conditions in financial and credit markets have taken a ghastly turn for the worse. It is becoming abundantly clear that we are in the midst of a serious global meltdown." She finally was forecasting a recession. "Given the seriousness of the situation, I believe that we should put as much stimulus into the system as we can," she argued. "We need to do much more, and the sooner, the better. One might argue against such a policy move in favor of a wait-and-see approach to better gauge if the recent flurry of policy initiatives will turn things around. In normal times, I would have some sympathy for this argument, but these are about as far from normal times as we can get. We are in the midst of a global economic and financial free fall, and the confidence of households, businesses, and investors is in shambles."

In a rare agreement, Dallas Fed president Fisher said with humor, "I will conclude with actually once again agreeing with President Yellen, as I think I have done twice in history. . . . I think it's very important that we have all hands on deck, that we have a unanimous decision."

At its final meeting of 2008, on December 15–16, the FOMC voted to slash the fed funds rate from 1 percent to zero. Remarkably, the rate would remain at zero for seven years until December 17, 2015, when the committee raised the rate by a quarter point at the suggestion of a new Fed chair: Janet Yellen.

During the 2008 meeting, Yellen warned that the Fed's biggest worry at the time was not inflation, but deflation, a risk that would haunt the central bank throughout the financial crisis. Unlike inflation, deflation is much harder to stem, as was seen during the Great Depression. Once people become convinced that prices are actually falling, they postpone purchases, figuring they can pay less in the future. In a self-fulfilling prophesy, prices continue to fall for lack of demand. It is a vicious cycle that is exceedingly difficult to reverse, and one the Fed wanted to avoid at all costs.

Once interest rates were at zero, the best method the Fed found to stimulate the economy and guard against deflation was to pump huge amounts of money into the financial system. This became known as "quantitative easing" (QE). At the start of 2008, the

Fed held about $800 billion of medium-term Treasury notes it had purchased from banks. Starting in November and through March 2009, the Fed bought about $1 trillion worth of mortgage-backed securities, bank debt, and Treasury notes, which provided banks huge sums of cash to make loans and stimulate the economy. By June 2010, it held $2.1 trillion of various forms of debt. Further purchases were halted as the economy started to improve, but resumed in August 2010, when the Fed decided the economy was growing too slowly. In a short period of time, the Fed's assets—known as its "balance sheet"—had nearly tripled.

On January 16, 2009, Bernanke held a conference call to discuss a topic Yellen knew well from her time as a Fed governor: her debate with Alan Greenspan fourteen years earlier on whether to set an inflation target at zero or 2 percent. "First of all, obviously, we have talked about this issue many times before. I think in 1995, President Yellen was involved in a debate or a discussion on this topic, so it is an oldie but goodie," Bernanke said. "In the current situation, there are some circumstances that might make an explicit numerical objective more attractive."

Yellen responded that there was a good reason to adopt an explicit inflation target. "There is growing concern that the Fed is printing money with abandon to stimulate the economy, and the combination of trillion-dollar deficits and trillions of dollars of money creation can have only one outcome in the long run, which is high inflation that debases the currency. Now, I think this reasoning is completely misguided, but it is out there, and I think we need to consider it because it is dangerous for our credibility as an institution. So, I also think we have to say that we are not willing to tolerate very high inflation." The issue was tabled, and it wasn't until 2012 that Bernanke finally announced an explicit inflation goal of 2 percent—seventeen years after Yellen had first proposed it because of her conviction that a little more inflation was an economically sound and compassionate trade-off to produce a little less unemployment for those struggling to make ends meet.

After another bleak economic winter, the Fed started to see green shoots of growth in the spring of 2009. "It is a welcome relief to say for the first time in recent memory that the economic data since our last meeting have not been uniformly disappointing," Yellen said at the April 28–29 FOMC meeting. "Overall, financial conditions have improved, and I have seen no indication that a dangerous deflationary dynamic has thus far taken hold. These are encouraging signs, but we should be careful not to overreact to developments that may yet prove to be will-o'-the-wisps."

By the June 23–24 meeting, Yellen was more confident the recession was at an end: "On the bright side, overall financial conditions have certainly improved since we last met. That bodes well for recovery. It's encouraging that so many banks have been able to raise private capital, and in many respects market stress has subsided. The bottom line for me is that we likely will need to maintain the current stance of policy for a very long time to get back to full employment, and my main concern is that markets will anticipate and we may be tempted to withdraw our accommodation too soon, thereby aborting the recovery." She recalled how the Fed had prematurely tightened policy in 1937, and the economy plunged back into a depression.

At the August 11–12 meeting, with an expansion clearly underway, Yellen argued for more monetary stimulus to keep the economy on an upward trajectory. "Winston Churchill once remarked that nothing in life is so exhilarating as to be shot at without result," she said, provoking laughs. "Well, exhilaration may be an exaggeration, but I am at least hugely relieved that our financial system appears to have survived a near-death experience. And I am optimistic that you will not be the Chairman who presided over the second Great Depression." Although the worst is over, she continued, "I foresee a slow recovery over the next several years with stubbornly high unemployment and very low price inflation, not the sharp rebound that typically follows deep recessions." While favoring more stimulus at the time, she said it is vital for the Fed "to emphasize and defend our independence, to express confidence in our ability to tighten monetary conditions when the right time comes, and to stress our determination to maintain price stability."

In November, the FOMC voted to gradually slow the pace of its debt purchases. Yellen agreed but warned of a "persistently weak labor market and stagnating wage income," and again raised the prospect of a "dangerous deflationary situation" if the Fed repeats its past mistake by raising interest rates too soon.

At its final meeting of 2009, on December 15–16, the FOMC agreed to allow most of its emergency lending programs to expire on February 1, 2010. Yellen went along, but her philosophy of empathy kicked into high gear, and she emphasized her worries about high unemployment. At every FOMC meeting throughout 2010, she reiterated her concerns about stubbornly high unemployment and premature moves to raise interest rates that could trigger deflation. The unemployment rate had peaked at 10 percent in the fall of 2009, double the rate before the recession hit, and was still above 9 percent in late 2010.

Bernanke knew of Yellen and George Akerlof as major figures in "new Keynesian economics," which argued for continued, extensive government intervention after recessions because the market was too inefficient to return to health on its own. Bernanke recalled that Yellen had significant influence on the FOMC by virtue of her sharp analysis. "I was very impressed by her," he said. "At the Fed, the chair sets the agenda and leads the decision-making. The Board vice chair and the president of the Reserve Bank of New York also have lots of influence, much of it behind the scenes. Other FOMC members gain influence over policy decisions in large part by the quality of their commentary at the meetings and the respect that people have for their intellectual contributions. Janet was always extremely well-prepared. When she spoke, everyone listened very carefully."

"This is not a criticism because it's part of what they're supposed to do, but at FOMC meetings a lot of the presidents would spend their allotted time riffing on their general impressions of conditions in their district, talking about what various business leaders had told them about the state of the economy in their part of the country," Bernanke continued. "Janet did that too, but for the most part she relied on her skills as a macroeconomist. Her presentations, which she usually read from prepared notes, were always very careful. She often advanced new thoughts and ideas. She was one of the most influential people on the FOMC, because she supplemented the anecdotes with theoretical and empirical insights that shed light on the bigger picture."

"Once the crisis had begun in the fall of 2007 and going on in 2008, she was certainly more pessimistic than most on the committee about the effects of financial stress on the real economy," the former Fed chair recalled. "She argued early on that the breakdown of the credit system was going to slow the recovery and, of course, she was right."

Bernanke valued Yellen as a key ally and leader of the FOMC doves who helped him counter the group of hawks opposed to the Fed's aggressive steps to cope with the financial crisis, and then pushed for pulling back early. "She resisted the hawks very strongly," he said. "And while Janet didn't pound the table for new initiatives, she certainly pushed back hard against that hawkish perspective and was again very influential."

One of the more "hawkish" Fed governors during the crisis agreed that Yellen was very supportive of Bernanke but was not one of the crisis decision-makers. That role was filled by Bernanke; President George W. Bush's Treasury secretary, Henry Paulson; and his successor, Timothy Geithner, who took charge in 2009, when Barack Obama became president. This official, who did not want to be identified, downplayed Yellen's early warnings of a housing bubble as low-key observations rather than alarmist: "If she thought that the housing bubble was at risk, in her role she could have done something about it. I would hardly call her a clairvoyant or particularly interested in housing risks at the time."

Geithner, who was president of the New York Fed before becoming Treasury secretary, remembered Yellen as "a wise, steady, thoughtful voice" at FOMC meetings. "As the storm was building, clouds were darkening and things fell apart, she was, from my perspective, on the right side of all those things we had to do," he said. "A lot of that stuff was pretty divisive on the FOMC. There were a few people who were pretty much against most of the escalation we did. In hindsight, I think she looks like she was on the right side of history. I'm sure everybody was uneasy about many of the things we had to do, but I thought she was very smart and wise on most things."

"One thing about central banks is that they are full of people who are like generals in wars. The echoes of past inflation mistakes dominate everything for many central bankers," Geithner continued. "They view the risk of high inflation as the overwhelmingly predominant threat. She had a much more balanced view and recognized that it was a much more complicated calculation." Geithner added that central bankers always worry about encouraging "moral hazards"—bailing out financial players who keep making foolish bets because there are no consequences for their recklessness. But Yellen was not doctrinaire on the subject and would weigh the need for a bailout based on the fallout for the overall economy and average people if the Fed refused to come to the aid of a major financial institution. "She was refreshingly liberated from a lot of dominant beliefs in central banks that sometimes get in the way of pragmatic, good judgments," he said.

Mary Daly, Yellen's protégé and current president of the San Francisco Fed, noted that throughout the crisis, Yellen never abandoned her empathy for the unemployed and other individuals damaged by the fallout, not just the impact on the financial system. "She has all of the heart of caring about people," Daly said. "She's able to pull apart how much scarring there will be in the labor market, how much scarring there will be in household balance sheets because they've got this colossal housing market crash that's injured their solvency. And then she thinks about how long it will take for them to get back to full fruition and consume and spend again in the ways they're accustomed to. That's the part about Janet that often gets overlooked. It's actually the very core of who she is, what she believes in, and how she studies economic problems."

As Yellen reflected on her role on the FOMC during the crisis, she became animated talking about the hawks she had had to contend with, including one she considered a fool. She continued: "I remember him saying after Bear Stearns collapsed, 'Everybody knows what's coming, and nothing much can happen from here on because everybody sees what the problems are, and the markets will take care of it and price everything.'" She thought, Buddy, you're smoking something.

Yellen acknowledged that the FOMC was not directly involved in a lot of the emergency programs that Bernanke and his staff were setting up, but "I was always supportive of him. He sometimes had fights on his hands, but they didn't come from me. I think I was always somebody he could count on to be supportive and help him influence other people to go along. He often would look to me to talk first and say something to get a discussion going in a way that would be constructive from his point of view. So, we were intellectual allies from day one."

Yellen recalled how Fed officials and other regulators in Washington worked around the clock to deal with the crisis. Often a financial institution would notify them on a Friday that it was failing, and they would work all weekend to find a solution before the markets opened on Monday. She was personally involved in one marathon weekend helping Wells Fargo, based in her region, acquire a large bank that was failing. "I guess in some ways I wish I had done more to prevent the crisis," she continued. "I feel like I did something, but maybe I could have done more. Maybe I should have pushed harder to raise capital requirements for community banks. I certainly recognized that the quality of loans had deteriorated enormously, that there could be huge losses if housing prices fell. I spent a lot of time thinking about that, looking at it, telling people about it. But I neither understood nor saw the thing that really caused the financial crisis—the leverage outside the banking system and the role of derivatives. That's something I couldn't have done anything about. And neither did anybody else understand until it happened."

When regulators conducted postmortems on the crisis, they found numerous failures. They included a lack of authority to supervise Wall Street firms and lax oversight in cases where regulators had oversight powers. Like Yellen, regulators failed to comprehend the complex kinds of risky investments being created and traded.

One example was Citicorp, one of the world's largest banks, which was taking on enormous risks investing hundreds of billions of dollars in investments about which regulators were unaware. One example was a "structured investment vehicle—or SIV. It was a nonbank financial institution Citicorp established to borrow short-term money at a low interest rate and invest it in products that produced a higher return. If the investments failed, the SIV would be unable to repay its loan.

"When things blew up, everybody was asking questions like, 'What's a SIV?' Nobody at first knew," Yellen conceded. "There was also complete ignorance about Lehman, Bear Stearns, and other stand-alone investment banks. But the risks at Fed-supervised firms like Citi I think we should have known more about."

Clearly, the crisis weighed on her and prompted her to wish she had done more to regulate derivatives earlier in her career.

※ ※ ※

WHEN YELLEN FIRST INTERVIEWED FOR THE SAN FRANCISCO Fed job, search committee member David Tang suspected that someone of her abilities and experience would be lured back to a senior position in Washington. So, he put it to her directly. "Her response was that she had spent enough time in Washington and enjoyed very much coming back to the Bay area," he recalled. "Her husband was teaching at Berkeley at the time. They were living up in the Berkeley Hills, going for hikes and all of that. And she said this job here was just wonderful, and this is what she wanted to do. I asked the question, not because I didn't think she was fully committed, it's just that it was obvious that she had all of the credentials for government service and that she would be a top candidate for any of the economic roles that would be available."

Tang's instincts were right on. After six years as president of the San Francisco Fed, Yellen would be returning to Washington. The seeds for that move may well have been planted in the spring of 2008, although Yellen surely didn't know that at the time.

Barack Obama, the junior senator from Illinois, was competing for the Democratic nomination for president, and as the financial crisis deepened with the near collapse of Bear Stearns, Obama wanted to give a speech on the need to rein in Wall Street excesses with new financial regulations. At the time, Congress was debating the Dodd-Frank bill to tighten federal regulation of the financial industry, and Obama planned to endorse that approach. First, however, he needed to get up to speed on the crisis. At the time, there was a lot of confusion about what was going on with the fire sale of Bear Stearns, so his economic advisers arranged for him to get telephone briefings from Timothy Geithner, then president of the New York Fed, and Yellen.

"So, he talked to them, and Geithner was, I guess I would describe as kind of close to the vest. He wasn't really explaining what was happening," recalled one adviser. "And Janet Yellen, who was always kind of a rock star teacher and a brilliant academic, explained all of what the Fed did and here's what we were afraid of. She walked him through it. When it was done, Senator Obama turned to me and said, 'Wow, who is that? Who is Janet Yellen? That was amazing. She was great.' There was some connection in that moment between Obama and Yellen, which later on maybe predisposed him to like her and her insights."

On March 27, 2008, Obama gave a memorable speech at Cooper Union in downtown Manhattan about the crisis. "Under Republican and Democratic administrations, we've failed to guard against practices that all too often rewarded financial manipulation instead of productivity and sound business practice," he declared. "We let the special interests put their thumbs on the economic scales. The result has been a distorted market that creates bubbles instead of steady, sustainable growth; a market that favors Wall Street over Main Street but ends up hurting both."

Obama blamed powerful lobbying by the financial industry, with its generous campaign contributions to politicians in Washington, for weak federal oversight that allowed unfettered and reckless activities by the industry. It would often devastate the economy and then get generous bailouts from Congress when financial institutions got into trouble. "If we can extend a hand to banks on Wall Street when they get into trouble, we can extend a hand to Americans who are struggling, often through no fault of their own," he declared.

It was a speech that Yellen could have given. After Obama was elected president, he tapped Geithner to be his Treasury secretary. But he didn't forget about Janet Yellen. Two years after her memorable briefing, President Obama would call her back to Washington at the urging of his economic advisers—just as David Tang had predicted.

President Barack Obama nominates Janet Yellen to be chair of the Federal Reserve Board on October 9, 2013. (credit: Getty Images/Chip Somodevilla)

Federal Reserve governor Daniel Tarullo swears in Janet Yellen as Federal Reserve chair on February 3, 2014. (credit: Federal Reserve Board)

Newly installed Fed chair Janet Yellen meets with other members of the Board of Governors on February 18, 2014. (credit: Getty Images/Andrew Harrer/Bloomberg)

Fed chair Janet Yellen presides over a meeting of the Federal Open Market Committee on March 4, 2016. (credit: Federal Reserve Board)

Fed chair Janet Yellen gives a farewell speech to the central bank's staff on February 1, 2018. (credit: Federal Reserve Board)

Fed chair Janet Yellen marks the central bank's one hundredth anniversary with former chairs Alan Greenspan, Ben Bernanke, and Paul Volcker on May 1, 2014. (credit: Federal Reserve Board)

Fed chair Janet Yellen testifies before the House Financial Services Committee on July 12, 2017. (credit: Getty Images/Jim Watson/AFP)

Traders at the New York Stock Exchange react to Fed chair Janet Yellen's announcement of an interest rate increase on June 14, 2017. (credit: Getty Images/ Drew Angerer)

Janet Yellen poses with former Fed chair Ben Bernanke at an unveiling of her official Fed portrait on October 1, 2019. It will hang with those of other Federal Reserve chairs. (credit: Janet Yellen)

Janet Yellen is the lone woman walking with President Bill Clinton and his team of advisers in 1998. (credit: Stephen Crowley/*New York Times*)

Treasury secretary Janet Yellen holds a virtual meeting with Black Chambers of Commerce on February 5, 2021, to promote passage of the American Rescue Plan. (credit: Getty Images/ Nicholas Kamm/AFP)

Fed chair Janet Yellen talks with students at the Manufacturing and Technology Center of Cuyahoga Community College in Cleveland, Ohio, on September 26, 2017. (credit: Getty Images/Ty Wright/Bloomberg)

Fed chair Janet Yellen poses for a selfie at a European Central Bank conference in Frankfurt, Germany, on November 14, 2017. (credit: Getty Images/Alex Kraus/ Bloomberg)

Vice President Kamala Harris swears in Janet Yellen as Treasury secretary on January 26, 2021. (credit: Getty Images/Drew Angerer)

Janet Yellen (second row, left) poses with President Joe Biden and his cabinet on April 3, 2021. (credit: The White House)

Treasury secretary Janet Yellen discusses financial risks of climate change at the COP26 Summit in Glasgow, Scotland, on November 3, 2021. (credit: Getty Images/ Christopher Furlong)

Janet Yellen talks to a park ranger after she broke her wrist in a fall while hiking in the Sierra Nevada mountains in northern California in 2005. (credit: Sheila O'Rourke)

Janet Yellen and husband, George Akerlof, celebrate son Robby's high school graduation in 1999. (credit: John Yellen)

Janet Yellen poses with her husband, George Akerlof, on October 10, 2001, in Berkeley, California, after he was named the winner of the Nobel Prize in Economics. (credit: Getty Images/Monica Davey/AFP)

# - 8 -

# CLIMBING THE FED LADDER

*"The next financial crisis will be something completely different"*

WHEN FED BOARD OF GOVERNORS VICE CHAIR DONALD KOHN decided to retire in the spring of 2010, Janet Yellen immediately surfaced as the consensus candidate among President Obama's top economic advisers. National Economic Council director Lawrence Summers; Treasury secretary Timothy Geithner; and Christina Romer, chair of the Council of Economic Advisers, all knew Yellen well and were high on her based on both her skill set and her personality.

Geithner, who had left his job as New York Fed president the year before, was tasked with putting together a list of candidates to replace Kohn. "The choice was obvious," he said. "It was easy, obvious, and sensible to choose Janet." Kohn agreed: "My recollection is that there was a very strong consensus among the decision-makers that she would be the most obvious and best choice to replace me. She was highly respected as an economist and liked as a person. She had the experience on the Board of Governors. She had experience at the reserve bank, so she was part of the FOMC. She was completely geared up. It would be a seamless transfer."

Christina Romer was a close friend of Yellen's from when they both taught at Berkeley, and she was among the group of relatives and friends invited to travel to Sweden when George Akerlof received his Nobel award. Romer called Yellen to sound her out. Rahm Emanuel, the White House chief of staff, called to offer the job and Yellen accepted.

The new job came with a financial penalty, however. Yellen was the highest paid person in the Federal Reserve System, making about $400,000. The vice chair made less than half that, but money wasn't an issue since Akerlof could retire at full salary and had been offered a visiting scholar position in Washington. Son Robby was off teaching in England. So, the move back to the nation's capital made sense. Yellen and Akerlof kept their Berkeley home and rented one in Washington, assuming they would be there only a few years. Neither suspected at the time that it would be a permanent move.

John Williams was surprised Yellen would give up her job at the San Francisco Fed, which he would inherit. She had influence, respect, good pay, and a pleasant personal life. When he questioned her about that, she responded, "This is where I'm needed. The president is asking me to play an important role in an important time, and it's hard to say 'no' when you're being asked to do something important and you're being trusted to do that.'"

Robby, who received his PhD from Harvard and became an economist and academic like his parents, said his mother's decision set her on a historic course as an economic policymaker, though that was not foremost in her mind at the time. "We might've had a word about her eventually becoming Fed chair, but her reaction was, 'Of course not.' She just didn't think such a thing would happen," he said. "That's her personality. I don't think she ever sought any of these jobs. These are things that happened to her, and maybe that's a good way to go into them."

On April 29, 2010, President Obama announced his nominations to fill three vacancies on the Fed Board of Governors: Yellen for vice chair, and MIT economist Peter Diamond and lawyer Sarah Bloom Raskin, Maryland's top financial regulator, for governors. "The depth of experience these individuals bring in economic and monetary policy, financial regulation, and consumer protection will make them tremendous assets at the Fed," Obama said.

At the time of the trio's nomination, Democrats controlled the Senate but lacked the sixty votes needed to prevent Republicans from blocking their confirmation, which was a possibility because many GOP senators were angry over the Fed's extraordinary steps to boost the economy. They complained that some programs stretched the limits of the Fed's authority and that the enormous amount of money the central bank was pumping into the financial system risked igniting inflation.

At their confirmation hearing on July 15, Senator Dianne Feinstein, D-CA, introduced Yellen as someone who "has the depth of knowledge and experience required to make the important decisions that could possibly have a strong positive and profound impact on our economy."

Senator Richard Shelby, R-AL, one of the Fed's fiercest critics, complained that in managing the financial crisis, Bernanke and his colleagues were "overly opaque and not receptive to providing information to Congress or the public." He continued: "The Fed often seems more interested in seeking additional power and authority, even though it failed to use its current authorities in the run-up to the crisis, a lot of us believe. Ironically, despite its recent failures, the Fed could soon be rewarded with expanded authorities and powers under the Dodd-Frank bill. With that in mind, I would want to hear what lessons have been learned, and how the nominees intend to use those lessons as members of the board."

In her opening remarks, Yellen repeated the theme that characterized her long career as an economist: the impact on Main Street, not Wall Street. "We have learned a harsh lesson about the dire consequences a financial crisis has for ordinary Americans in the form of lost jobs, lost homes, lost wealth, and lost businesses. And those of us charged with overseeing the financial system should always keep this human cost in mind." Yellen also stressed the importance of an independent Fed that is not beholden to prevailing political winds in Congress. "When central banks are independent, economies perform better, inflation is lower and more stable, and long-term interest rates are lower and less volatile," she said. "I should stress, though, that independence brings with it both responsibility and accountability. . . . That means the Fed must explain its actions, outlook, and strategy and provide the information necessary for Congress and the public to understand and evaluate its policy decisions."

When Shelby questioned her about lax regulation that contributed to the recent financial meltdown, Yellen said it was inadequate for years: "We have learned in hindsight it was very hard for all of the regulators involved to take away the punch bowl in a timely way." She said a key lesson was the need to impose more stringent capital requirements on banks.

Asked a similar question by Senator Bob Corker, R-TN, Yellen admitted that regulators failed to grasp how badly mortgage underwriting standards had declined, and the growing risks from the complex securitization schemes traders had created. "I wish we had focused more on the systemic risk," she conceded.

On September 29, both Yellen and Raskin were confirmed by the Senate unanimously. Diamond was not so fortunate. His nomination was blocked by Republicans, who said he lacked experience and was a big-government Keynesian. Diamond went on to win the Nobel

Prize later that year, and Obama nominated him to the Fed Board two more times, but he finally withdrew in June 2011, when it was clear he would not win confirmation. The Republicans wanted to make an example of one of the three nominees but were reluctant to target either woman when the GOP already suffered a gender gap among female voters. "Shelby was out to get the Obama administration, and Peter was just the unlucky person that they decided to take it out on," Yellen recalled a decade later. In March 2022, Raskin, nominated by President Biden to rejoin the Fed Board of Governors, met the same fate as Diamond. She withdrew because too many senators opposed her, in part because she saw climate change as a key factor in regulating banks' financial stability. Even Yellen thought Raskin's views were outside the mainstream on that issue and privately argued against her nomination. Yellen also thought Raskin had been a weak member of the Fed Board of Governors when they served together. The White House foolishly ignored her counsel.

Yellen officially became vice chair on October 4, 2010, the second woman to hold that post. The first female vice chair was another trailblazing economist, Alice Rivlin, who served from 1996 to 1999. Rivlin previously had been the founding director of the Congressional Budget Office and subsequently the first female director of the White House Office of Management and Budget.

Yellen quickly gained clout in her new job. "She was a very good vice chair," said Bernanke, who became a distinguished fellow in residence at the Brookings Institution think tank in Washington after leaving the Fed. "She wasn't too happy with a few of the senior staff and pushed for some changes, which I was happy to let her take the lead on. One key aspect of the vice chair's job is to oversee the committee assignments of Board members and make sure that things are working properly, and she took that responsibility very seriously."

Daniel Tarullo, Yellen's former Clinton White House colleague who became a Fed governor in 2009, recalled that when she joined the board a year after he did, she shook up the way the staff produced economic reports for the Board of Governors. "Janet really paid a lot of attention to encouraging a diversity of analyses and views that exist within the Fed staff to make sure the different ways of looking at things were brought to the board," he said. "The cultural norm was that the staff would get together, wrestle things to the ground, and have disagreements with each other. But when they did their Monday briefing to the board, there was a single staff view. She knew there was lots going on underneath that and that the board would profit from seeing those internal disagreements. It was something to be valued, not suppressed. And over the course of her few years as vice chair, the richness of the analysis to which we were exposed increased substantially. It was something that Ben thought was a good idea, too."

❖ ❖ ❖

EVEN AS THE EFFECTS OF THE HOUSING COLLAPSE EBBED, YELlen spent her early months back in Washington engaging in postmortems on the causes of the financial crisis and helping the Fed implement new safeguards contained in Dodd-Frank. The new law, the biggest overhaul of financial regulation since the 1930s Glass-Steagall Act, imposed a set of tough rules and new consumer protections with the aim of preventing future financial crises.

The law contained provisions for all the reforms Yellen had called for while at the San Francisco Fed. It limited commercial banks from investing in risky speculative activities such as hedge funds. It created a Consumer Financial Protection Bureau to regulate mortgages, student loans, and credit cards. It required banks to increase their capital requirements—the percentage of their assets held in low-risk forms such as cash and bonds. It authorized the Fed to regulate large financial institutions that weren't traditional banks. It established rules for "stress tests" of banks begun two years earlier by the Fed to determine whether the largest banks had adequate capital during a severe downturn. And it authorized the Securities and Exchange Commission (SEC) and Commodity Futures Trading Commission (CFTC) to regulate over-the-counter derivatives—enacting Brooksley Born's proposal twelve years after it first created a firestorm.

Barely two weeks on the job, Yellen gave a speech on October 11 to the National Association for Business Economics in Denver, where she explained how financial regulators were determined to learn from their past mistakes. "A first-order priority must be to engineer a stronger, more robust system of financial regulation and supervision—one capable of identifying and managing excesses before they lead to crises," she said. "It is now clear that our system of regulation and supervision was fatally flawed."

"It's important to be realistic about the challenges that lie ahead," she continued. "By its nature, policy designed to manage systemic risk fights dangers that may never lead to crises. We may sometimes be like the boy who cried, 'Wolf!'—and the villagers may not be pleased about being roused from their beds. . . . Will future regulators and monetary policymakers be accused of bursting 10 of the past 2 asset bubbles? These dangers are real. But the events we've recently lived through make it clear that we have no choice but to embark on this road. We've all been asked, 'Didn't you see this mortgage disaster coming? Why didn't you do anything about it?' Our task now is to implement intelligent policies to contain future bubbles and credit binges, and to make sure that those that do occur inflict a lot less damage on the economy. Next time I hope we can say, 'We did see it coming, and we did something about it.'"

A month later, Yellen was interviewed for ninety minutes by the staff of the National Crisis Inquiry Commission, which was created by Congress to determine the causes of the housing crash and propose ways to prevent a recurrence. Yellen readily admitted her errors. "I don't think I was terribly worried [about a housing crash], but my supervisory staff sometime in 2004 was certainly starting to worry. . . . I can't say the concerns reached the level— with the benefit of hindsight—that they should have." By 2005, "I personally was worried about a bubble in the housing market, and I was raising concerns about national economic instability," she said. Yellen added that while she saw a need for tougher regulation, she knew that was the province of the Fed in Washington, not her bank in San Francisco.

"For my own part, I did not see or appreciate what the risks were with mortgage banking, ratings, SIVs [structured investment vehicles], securitization until it happened," she continued in a long mea culpa. "I thought, like the 2000 dot.com bubble, the economy could handle it with Fed support. Did I anticipate a massive meltdown? I wish I had, but I didn't. We made assumptions that were wrong. We didn't ask what ratings agencies were doing. We weren't thinking about financial stability." She added that it was stunning to learn that many large institutions were unaware of risks they were taking on and that she found it very difficult to work with regulators from the Office of Thrift Supervision, who lacked a spirit of collegiality and cooperation with the San Francisco Fed's regulators, as Yellen's staff sought to rein in risky mortgage practices by Countrywide.

"The next financial crisis will be something completely different—and will we have the ability to spot it? This is really hard," she concluded. "I think we are really motivated to do better and make sure it doesn't happen again." One commission staffer observed that Yellen had been far more honest about her shortcomings and mistakes than other financial officials who testified before the group.

In her new role as vice chair, Yellen assumed the responsibilities traditionally assigned to the Number Two, including overseeing the reserve banks and ensuring the check-processing and payment system ran smoothly. In addition, she was busy implementing the new regulatory requirements in the Dodd-Frank law passed by Congress. She made sure that banks had enough capital to weather another crisis and looked broadly at the financial system to determine where it might be vulnerable.

When Bernanke became chair in 2006, he recognized that no one was in charge of making sure the overall financial system was stable, but before he could address that shortcoming, the housing crisis exploded. After that, he made it a priority to create a separate Fed division charged solely with monitoring the financial system for cracks that could cause another crisis. The first director of the Fed's Division of Financial Stability was staff economist Nellie Liang who worked with Yellen to come up with more stringent rules for bank supervision. Their collaboration continued over the years, and in July 2021, the Senate confirmed Liang as Yellen's Treasury undersecretary for domestic finance.

Yellen's efforts to remain vigilant about bank financial problems, however, were impeded by an unlikely source, her friend and like-minded monetary policy colleague, Daniel Tarullo. He was the Fed governor in charge of banking supervision and regulation and did not like to share what he knew with other board members, including Bernanke and Yellen. "Dan was incredibly capable. He may be the most influential nonchair governor of the Fed ever," said one former Fed governor. "He completely shook up the regulatory side, largely to the good. He's an enormously talented operator, but a difficult personality. He had this bureaucratic instinct of wanting to keep information to himself. Bernanke was an enabler of this. He had an implicit deal with Dan: 'You're in charge of the whole regulatory thing. It's your domain.' So, Dan wouldn't share information with others. Janet was extremely frustrated with this, as I think she absolutely rightly should have been."

The former governor continued: "She would say to me, 'My nightmare is some investment bank is going to blow up, and the first time I'm going to find out about it is going to be in the newspaper and we'll be called to testify, and Dan will not let us know about it.' She made various attempts to push him to share more information, but he just wouldn't, and I think that led to a very tense relationship."

Tarullo was more cooperative in sharing regulatory information with Yellen when she became chair in 2014, and she was pleased with his performance. They worked well together and remained friends in subsequent years.

❖ ❖ ❖

IN ADDITION TO ENSURING THAT THE FED'S NEW POWERS TO oversee broad financial stability were operational, Yellen left an enduring legacy as vice chair in another important area: Fed transparency, guiding the central bank toward greater openness to the public about monetary decisions with so much impact on the lives of all Americans. It was an issue she had long championed when she first joined the Fed in 1994.

For most of its history, the Fed was secretive about its deliberations and actions, forcing the markets to figure out its interest rate policies by observing how the New York Fed traded US Treasury securities to raise or lower rates. Starting after the FOMC meeting on February 4, 1994, shortly before Yellen joined the Board of Governors, the Fed issued a statement indicating what it had done. Initially, the statement was vague, but in subsequent years it became more detailed about the state of the economy, the action the FOMC had taken, the reasons for its action, and its forecast for future interest rate moves. To make the Fed even more transparent, a communications subcommittee headed by Yellen recommended in March 2011 that the Fed chair begin conducting quarterly news conferences in the afternoon after the conclusion of each two-day FOMC meeting. The aim was to clarify the Fed's written statement and allow markets to digest the news while they were still open. And so, on April 27, 2011, Ben Bernanke held the first news conference in the Fed's ninety-eight-year history.

Another important change Yellen championed are forecasts about what the economy would be like in the long run to give financial markets as much advance notice as possible about the Fed's long-range thinking to avoid surprises that could roil them. "In particular, we had a long-run forecast for inflation, which everybody essentially said was 2 percent, although we were not at the point where we wanted to publicly adopt a numerical inflation objective," Yellen said.

The 2 percent target that Yellen had advocated seventeen years earlier was finally announced by Bernanke at a January 25, 2012, news conference. The Fed also began releasing quarterly summaries of FOMC members' projections for economic growth, the unemployment rate, inflation, and their view of appropriate interest rates. "Issuing the projections of our policy rate—the fed funds target— was very controversial," Yellen said. "Some people on the committee thought it was a bad idea to introduce that in our statements."

Yellen persevered and won near-unanimous support for that change by arguing that showing the range of outlooks by FOMC members would better inform markets about the Fed's thinking and lead to calmer responses to interest rate moves.

"I believe that our formal consideration of this statement today marks a truly momentous occasion in the history of the FOMC," Yellen said, according to the January 25, 2012, transcript of the committee's debate over releasing the economic projections. It was not hyperbole. Central banks had long hidden behind a veil of secrecy, and the overdue moves toward transparency by the world's most powerful central bank could only make businesses and consumers better informed about economic conditions and make the Fed more accountable to the public.

Jeffrey Lacker, president of the Federal Reserve Bank of Richmond at the time, recalled that getting the FOMC members to agree on their new communications policy was difficult because of concern about how to deal with "maximum employment," part of the Fed's dual mandate. Many worried that by specifying a numerical inflation target, they would feel pressure to define maximum employment in numerical terms. Yet while the Fed's tools could control inflation, they couldn't have the same impact on the labor market. A century of conducting monetary policy provided the Fed with plenty of evidence that inflation eventually ebbs when the central bank slows the economy. But employment does not always increase as much as expected when the Fed boosts economic growth. In fact, the expansion that began after a shallow recession in the early 1990s was dubbed the "Jobless Recovery."

Although she spent most of her time as head of communications policy, pushing for more openness by the Fed, several instances in which confidential Fed discussions leaked out prompted Yellen to push for guidelines that would restrict FOMC members' discussions with outsiders. The concerns dated back to 2007, when the *Wall Street Journal* began publishing detailed accounts of ostensibly confidential Fed deliberations. But it wasn't the financial press that worried Fed officials as much as a lucrative niche business: newsletters sold to financial institutions with tips on what the Fed was likely to do in the near future.

Fed officials met regularly with the newsletter writers to exchange views off-the-record, and they enjoyed the talks because the visitors were knowledgeable and thoughtful. The officials usually were careful not to share any confidential information, and many were circumspect in offering opinions about future Fed moves. Still there was always the risk of unintentional leaks or careless remarks that could tarnish reputations. "The mildest thing somebody might do is go tell a bunch of clients, 'Well, when I was talking to Janet

Yellen last week, blah, blah, blah,' and then maybe they don't even repeat anything that you said, and they don't pretend to be giving insightful information. They're just name-dropping," Yellen explained. "That's not good. It means I'm seeing well-connected people on Wall Street and in Washington, aiding their businesses in ways that are a bit unseemly."

In some cases, off-the-record conversations proved to be damaging to the Fed's integrity, as financial institutions picked up confidential information about FOMC meetings before the release of detailed minutes published three weeks later. That was enough time to trade on the still unreleased information. "Our reputations were getting burned," Yellen recalled. It was her job to come up with a new policy to restrict these meetings and sanction Fed officials who violated the new rules, but many colleagues chafed at the restrictions because they enjoyed the conversations. Finally, she won acceptance of a new policy for interviews: "You should never say anything privately that you haven't said publicly, and you shouldn't be alone in these conversations. You should have somebody from the Fed press office with you taking notes."

Despite that policy, there were two embarrassing leaks in the fall of 2012 that shook the Fed deeply. First an article published in the *Wall Street Journal* on September 28 appeared to disclose nonpublic FOMC discussions from June, August, and September meetings, including monetary policy options. On October 3, a more troubling leak appeared in an article sent to clients of Medley Global Advisors, which produced one of the private newsletters that had prompted the Fed's communications restrictions. This article made predictions about what might be disclosed the next day when the FOMC minutes were released about its plans to resume bond purchases and raise interest rates in the future. The *Journal* story prompted Bernanke to issue a reprimand and reminder of the Fed's disclosure policy. The second resulted in a formal investigation that would eventually last five years and include the FBI and Justice Department. "This led to many years of terrible problems," Yellen said.

Members of the FOMC were grilled by Fed investigators and their phone records were reviewed, but the source of the leak was never found, and the matter seemed to be over following a stern lecture from Bernanke to the committee about the need to protect confidential information. However, a whistleblower who thought he knew the identity of the leaker and was unhappy with the Fed's inconclusive internal investigation prompted Congress to get involved. "The whistleblower gave information to congressional committees that then went after the Fed," Yellen said. "It was all in the newspapers, and it became a significant problem that I had to deal with during my term as chair."

The whistleblower's accusation that someone inside the Fed was the leaker prompted an intense Fed investigation that brought in the FBI, the Securities and Exchange Commission, and the Commodities Futures Trading Commission to see if insider trading had occurred.

It turned out that the whistleblower had erred. The identity of the true leaker was revealed on April 4, 2017: Jeffrey Lacker, who had been president of the Richmond Fed since 2004 and was the longest-serving member of the FOMC. He abruptly resigned, saying he broke the Fed's rules when he spoke with a financial analyst about confidential deliberations in 2012. His admission that he had failed to disclose the conversation even when questioned by investigators five years earlier came after he had been assured that he would not be charged with a crime. Lacker said the reporter, Regina Schleiger, had mentioned information she had obtained elsewhere, and he had failed to say that he could not comment. After her report was published, he said, he realized that "my failure to decline comment on the information could have been taken by the analyst, in the context of the conversation, as an acknowledgment or confirmation of the information." He added, "I deeply regret the role I may have played."

According to knowledgeable Fed insiders, Lacker was sacked by his board of directors for being the leaker, intentional or not, but was allowed to resign to save face. The Justice Department took an interest in the case in hopes of cracking down on all the people who profited from courting government officials to obtain confidential information they could sell to Wall Street traders. But no one went to jail because there was no evidence that Lacker benefited financially, and the newsletter claimed it was a news outlet protected by the First Amendment.

"This particular case was about loose lips," Yellen said. "This was not an insider selling information to make a profit. It was somebody who was indiscreet." Even so, it was grounds for dismissal, given the sensitive nature of the Fed's private deliberations. Lacker declined to discuss the matter.

In the fall of 2021, the Fed became ensnared in another ethics scandal when the presidents of the Federal Reserve Banks of Boston and Dallas announced their retirement following disclosures that they had been trading investments even while participating in Fed interest rate decisions. It was later disclosed that both Fed chair Jerome Powell and vice chair Richard Clarida had traded stocks in 2020 during periods of sensitive deliberation by the Fed, though there was no indication Powell had profited from his stock sale. But Clarida resigned on January 14, 2021, two weeks earlier than he had planned to leave the Fed, after filing an updated 2020 financial disclosure that showed questionable stock trades in advance of a Fed statement reassuring the markets. The timing of the trades suggested he may have benefited financially. The embarrassing episode involving the senior officials prompted the Fed to move quickly to tighten its ethics rules. Under its new policy, top officials will only be allowed to own mutual funds, not individual stocks, and trades of those funds will be limited to specified periods.

❖ ❖ ❖

WHEN THE FEDERAL OPEN MARKET COMMITTEE MET DURING the postcrisis years while Yellen was vice chair, the members' focus was not on interest rates—which were set at zero for the long term—but on the Fed's controversial quantitative easing (QE) program that it began in 2008 to spur economic growth and keep interest rates very low. It accomplished that by pumping huge quantities of money into the financial system through its purchase of longer-term government bonds and other securities from financial institutions. The Fed purchases increased overall demand for those securities, which had the intended effect of keeping interest rates on them low. As the economy still struggled to expand and unemployment remained high, the Fed resorted to this unconventional approach since it couldn't cut interest rates any lower. In late 2010, more than a year after the Great Recession ended, Yellen remarked at a committee meeting that recent economic data "reinforced my view that the path to recovery will involve a long, slow slog. I expect unemployment to remain elevated for years to come."

Most of the debate at the FOMC meetings was over how long to continue the monthly purchases, when to gradually reduce them—"taper" them in Fedspeak—when to end them completely, and how far in advance to inform the markets of any changes in the program. In November 2010, two years after the Fed purchased more than $1.7 trillion in securities, the FOMC decided to buy an additional $600 billion through the following June to keep long-term interest rates from rising. In 2012, as the unemployment rate hovered around 8 percent, the Fed launched a third quantitative easing program that called for open-ended purchases of $85 billion in securities a month—$40 billion more each month than it had been buying. After that, as the economy continued its slow path toward improvement, Yellen favored continuing the unorthodox stimulus program so long as unemployment remained stubbornly high. At the same time, she spent hours trying to figure out the best timing for the FOMC to signal to jittery markets when these extraordinary purchases would finally slow and then come to an end.

Always one to lighten up meetings with humor and colorful analogies, Yellen offered this explanation at an April 26–27, 2011, FOMC meeting of the challenge of announcing an end to its bond-buying spree, much to the amusement of her colleagues:

"Imagine that our Committee is the flight crew of a Boeing 747. We need to land at night at a nearly deserted airport, but we discover that the air traffic controller has fallen asleep on the job. The good news is we have a brilliant and highly experienced pilot and all of us trust him to accomplish a safe landing. Nonetheless, we have to keep in mind a few key facts. First, the instrument panel of a Boeing 747 has lots of dials and instruments. There is no unique right way to adjust them during the approach. Second, the cockpit is crowded, and the crew needs to work together harmoniously to execute a successful landing. And third, the passengers are all listening on the intercom system—and may be prone to panic. Our communications need to be clear, simple, and reassuring."

In August 2011, the committee decided to announce that sluggish growth would allow it to keep interest rates at zero "at least through mid-2013," a level of specificity that replaced "for an extended period." At the next meeting in September, the FOMC announced its plan to buy $400 billion Treasury securities with longer maturity dates than those it had been purchasing. On December 13, the committee marked the third anniversary of its historic move to lower interest rates to zero. That prompted Yellen to lament about a "lost decade" of high unemployment and the economic damage it has inflicted on average Americans. "As we engage in our usual festivities this month, we might also keep in mind the devastating economic circumstances that continue to confront so many people around the country," she said. "The longer this situation persists, the more likely it is that individuals who are unable to obtain work will be permanently scarred—a development that is not only tragic for them and their families but will also lower the potential of our economy." That gloomy outlook persisted into early 2012, as the Fed extended its projection for zero interest until late 2014.

At the March 2012 meeting, Governor Betsy Duke joked that her new forecast of the housing market was based on a lunch conversation with Yellen, who said she thought it was more advantageous to buy a house than continue renting one. Duke said Yellen told her that she was considering making an increased offer on a house because someone had put in a higher bid. Other committee members joked that Yellen must be worried about interest rates going up, and they now had a "Yellen index" to measure the strength of the housing market.

At the April 2012 meeting, Yellen provided her colleagues an update: "At the previous FOMC meeting, my esteemed colleague, Governor Duke, noted that I was facing a key housing decision. My family needs to vacate the townhouse that we have been renting for the past 18 months. And, as Governor Duke described, it looked in March like we might well become homeowners here in D.C., perhaps suggestive of a broader trend of renters starting to come back into the housing market. Now, I realize that all of you have been waiting with bated breath to hear the outcome of our decision-making process, so I would like to finally bring to an end that suspense by letting you know that we decided not to buy. Instead, we will be moving to another rental unit a mile or so away."

As other committee members joked that the market would tank on the news, she continued: "Needless to say, I hope that you won't interpret my family's decision as conveying any sort of broader significance about the housing market or the national economy. Rather, if there is any useful lesson from our experience, it is simply to underscore the difficulties of predicting idiosyncratic events, and the importance of not jumping the gun in interpreting any single piece of news."

In September 2012 with no improvement in the outlook, the FOMC announced its expanded quantitative easing program and predicted interest rates would remain at zero through mid-2015. At the next meeting in October, Yellen argued that the committee should specifically link any change in plans to specific economic targets: when unemployment falls to 6.5 percent or inflation rises to 2.5 percent. That's precisely what the committee did when it met in December. Its statement said the committee expects to keep interest rates at zero "at least as long as the unemployment rate remains above 6-1/2 percent, and inflation between one and two years ahead is projected to be no more than a half percentage point above the Committee's 2 percent longer-run goal." At the time, unemployment was averaging nearly 8 percent, and inflation was running below 2 percent.

In 2013, the Fed's continuance of its massive quantitative easing program began to draw growing opposition from FOMC members worried that the superlow interest rates propped up by the bond-buying might be causing a new bubble in the housing and stock markets. Jeremy Stein, a Harvard economist who joined the Board of Governors in May 2012, worried that the open-ended program was out of control and could lead to financial chaos in the markets when it finally ended. "The train is moving down the track," Stein warned at the FOMC meeting in March. "I don't want to slam on the brakes necessarily. I don't want to let it pick up speed, either, because that only makes your problem harder the next time around." He said the markets would react negatively if the Fed surprised them by beginning to slow bond purchases right away, so he said the Fed should begin acting three months later.

Yellen countered that she did not see the program posing a threat to financial stability and defended it as essential to give the sluggish economy more oomph. But Stein had won over two governors to support his concerns: Jerome "Jay" Powell and Betsy Duke. Powell was new to the board, having joined with Stein in May 2012. Despite their internal opposition, the trio reluctantly went along with a Fed announcement in May that it would not only continue the QE purchases but would expand them if the outlook deteriorated.

Then, on May 22, the market turmoil the FOMC feared when it came time to taper the program occurred. In an appearance before the Joint Economic Committee of Congress, Bernanke said the Fed could begin paring back its bond purchases "in the next few meetings." On top of that, minutes from the April 30–May 1 meeting released later that day revealed division among Fed officials over when to begin tapering its quantitative easing. The mixed messages led to confusion in the markets and produced the famously named "taper tantrum": stock and bond prices plummeted. Fortunately, the swoon was short-lived.

At his June 19 news conference following the FOMC meeting, Bernanke said the Fed might begin tapering asset purchases later in the year and end it completely by the middle of 2014. This time, the market reaction was more restrained.

At that June meeting, Yellen argued that the bond-buying should continue because a sustained economic recovery could still be disrupted. To make her case, she used another metaphor that became a running joke at subsequent meetings: her cross-country journey.

"Imagine that we're on a road trip from San Francisco to New York," she told her colleagues. "We'd anticipated pretty arduous driving conditions across the Sierra, so right about now we thought we'd be on the outskirts of Salt Lake City. Instead, we've made it all the way to Denver. It is great we have made such progress. Now it's entirely possible, and I'm optimistic, that our velocity on the remainder of the trip will match what we've achieved so far. But it's really quite premature to conclude that, and it's still quite a long way to the Mississippi River, let alone to the Lincoln Tunnel. Is this the right moment to ease up on the gas pedal? I don't think so."

At the next FOMC meeting in July, Yellen picked up where she left off the month before: "Some of you may recall that before our June meeting I embarked on a road trip from San Francisco to New York. I reported reaching Denver in a surprisingly short time, and while fearful of getting stuck there, I expressed my hope that progress would continue with a similarly rapid pace. Now, I'm sure you must be eager for an update. So let me say that I considered the June employment report sufficiently encouraging that after its release, I had anticipated that I'd be pulling into Kansas City just about now, where I planned to pay a surprise visit to Fed President Esther George. Unfortunately, incoming data since then has brought home the reality that the slog across Kansas may well take a considerable time."

As the group laughed, Betsy Duke chimed in that no one should be surprised about the slow car trip because "I've seen her car." In fact, it was a twenty-one-year-old vehicle, a 1992 Acura Legend that Yellen had purchased before coming to Washington in 1994. "It was a great car. It never had one single solitary thing wrong with it," she explained. "I loved this car, it was in perfectly good condition, and I never got rid of it."

Throughout the summer of 2013, financial markets remained unsettled about when the Fed would curtail its quantitative easing (QE) program, and the FOMC vacillated as economic data showed a mixed picture of economic health. At its September 18 meeting, the committee voted to continue its bond-buying to the surprise of Wall Street, which thought the Fed would begin tapering purchases. The FOMC was on the verge of doing that but held off because of worries about a shaky economy and the possibility of a federal government shutdown on October 1 over a budget dispute in Congress. In fact, a shutdown occurred that lasted seventeen days.

Finally, at its December 17–18, 2013, meeting, the FOMC voted to pare down its bond purchases by $10 billion a month beginning in January as a result of an improving economy.

The governors who had pushed to end the purchases became known as the "Three Amigos." Stein, Powell, and Duke frustrated Bernanke by coordinating their positions and coming to meetings with demands that the Fed provide a cost-benefit analysis of the QE program and set out conditions for when it's going to end, and pressuring him to pull back from new purchases. It was a huge problem for Bernanke; he fretted that potential dissents by three key colleagues on the Board of Governors would suggest a major policy rift that would unnerve financial markets. "This put a huge amount of pressure on Bernanke, and he responded in a way that was slightly awkward," Yellen said in explaining one factor that had provoked the "taper tantrum" in the spring of 2013. "Bernanke began discussing the taper at a time when the data were a little shaky, and people were somewhat worried about the economy. What he said was quite close to what market participants said that they expected. But the fact that he said it on a day when the dominant concern was about downside risks to the outlook didn't go over well. There was a huge reaction. Concern over potential dissents probably played a role in the timing." In truth, the "taper tantrum" didn't really amount to very much, but sometimes when and the way a Fed chair says something can set off financial shock waves. It was a momentary disaster that Yellen blamed in part on the "Three Amigos" who were constantly threatening to dissent.

Yellen had high regard for Stein's intelligence and knowledge about financial stability, but his unyielding crusade to end the bond purchases early created tremendous tension and division on the Board of Governors.

Stein, who returned to Harvard in May 2014, after spending just two years on the Fed Board of Governors, spoke highly of Yellen despite their policy differences. "I'm a huge admirer of hers. I like her a lot personally," he said. "She was obviously a real force as vice chair, a very aggressive and effective proponent of QE3 [the third round of quantitative easing]."

"I was a bit more of a QE skeptic," he continued. "So, we debated that fairly vigorously on a few occasions. I went along, I supported what we did, but I was more concerned about the risk side of the equation and more cautious. Jay Powell, Betsy Duke, and I were pushing to taper earlier than Janet and some of the others wanted to. I think history is probably pretty kind to her perspective because it ended up being helpful—I don't know how helpful—and in the years since a lot of the risks that I was concerned about didn't really manifest in a serious way.

"The thing that I recall very well is we were sitting in her office, we're having this debate and at some point I was saying, 'Well, I think there're some costs and some benefits.' And she looked at me and replied, 'Are you saying we should just go oars up? Should we just stop?' And I said, 'Well, I guess under some circumstances, yeah, maybe.' And she just thought I was a little nuts. And I think maybe she understood something about central banking that I didn't at the time, that you'd just never say you're out of ammunition. I think her view is certainly mainstream and I have a lot of respect for it."

Powell believed he was right in questioning whether the Fed had an exit plan and a rule for when it would halt its bond purchases. He didn't oppose the program on principle. Rather, he worried that

Bernanke had failed to make clear the appropriate rule for when to end the purchases, which were adding up to more than $1 trillion a year. Powell discussed his concerns with Bernanke between FOMC meetings and got the assurance he was seeking that the Fed chair had a clear target in mind for ending the bond purchases. That satisfied him.

During the summer of 2013, the debate over quantitative easing was not the only Fed controversy to grab Yellen's attention. Stories in the news media were speculating on who would replace Bernanke, who had signaled that he did not want to serve another term when his current one expired in February 2014. Eight grueling years running the central bank during the worst crisis since the Great Depression were enough for him. The stories mentioned two front-runners for the job: Janet Yellen and her former student and colleague, Lawrence Summers.

Little did Yellen suspect at the time that a ferocious political battle over Bernanke's successor was about to erupt—and she would find herself right in the middle of it.

# - 9 -

# REACHING THE TOP RUNG

*"A keen understanding about how markets and the economy work"*

ALTHOUGH FED OFFICIALS WERE LARGELY FOCUSED ON THEIR efforts to nurse a critically ill economy back to health in the fall of 2012, they could not ignore a political development that surfaced just two weeks before President Obama was elected to a second term. In a column on October 22 of that year, *New York Times* columnist Andrew Ross Sorkin reported that Fed chair Ben Bernanke "has told close friends that even if Mr. Obama wins, he probably will not stand for re-election" when his four-year term ended in early 2014. That meant the guessing game over Obama's choice of a successor to the powerful post had officially begun.

By March of 2013, Janet Yellen had emerged in speculative news stories as a likely successor given her long experience on the Fed, including as the current Number Two. In June 2013, a Reuters story cited five potential candidates: Yellen; former Treasury secretary Lawrence Summers; former Fed vice chair Roger Ferguson; Treasury secretary Timothy Geithner, who was stepping down

245

from his cabinet job; and Donald Kohn, Yellen's predecessor as vice chair. Similar news stories noted that Yellen would be the first woman, and Ferguson the first Black, to head the central bank.

That summer, the speculation focused on Yellen and Summers as the top contenders. A July 28, 2013, story in *USA Today* said a group of economists surveyed by the newspaper predicted that Obama would choose Yellen over Summers, the latter described as "a veteran Washington insider."

What *USA Today* and other news media did not know was that Obama had already made his choice four years earlier, and it was Lawrence Summers. It was a decision few outside Obama's small circle of advisers knew at the time, and it was only publicly acknowledged by Obama when he published the first volume of his presidential memoirs, *A Promised Land*, in 2020. After his election in 2008, with the economy on the verge of cratering, Obama said he wanted "Larry to help figure out what the hell to do (and not to do). . . . I had to sell Larry on serving not as Treasury secretary but rather as director of the National Economic Council (NEC), which, despite being the White House's top economic job, was considered less prestigious. The director's traditional function was to coordinate the economic policy-making process and act as a diplomatic broker between various agencies, which didn't exactly play to Larry's strengths."

Then Obama revealed the secret quid pro quo: "I told Larry I needed him, his country needed him. . . . My earnestness may have had some influence on his thinking though the promise (at chief of staff Rahm Emanuel's suggestion) to make Larry the next chair of the Federal Reserve no doubt helped to get him to 'yes' as well."

Despite his intellectual brilliance and impressive knowledge of economics, Summers was an odd choice to run the Fed, a job that requires finesse and people skills to get a large group of accomplished equals—at least when it came to voting—to go along with the wishes of the chair. Summers's arrogance and brutal honesty were precisely the kinds of traits that would provoke a rebellion among the members of the Federal Open Market Committee. Yet Obama was prepared to put him in charge of the Fed even though he captured Summers's personal liabilities brilliantly—if charitably—in his memoir: "As I got to know him, I'd come to believe that Larry's difficulties in playing well with others had less to do with malice and more to do with obliviousness. For Larry, qualities like tact and restraint just cluttered the mind. He himself seemed impervious to hurt feelings or the usual insecurities, and he would express appreciation (accompanied by mild surprise) when anyone effectively challenged him or thought of something he'd missed. His lack of interest in standard human niceties extended to his appearance, which was routinely disheveled."

A former senior Fed official said he sat in many meetings with Summers and watched him bully other participants with his intellectual abilities. "I've seen him do it to men," he said, "I've seen him do it to women, including Yellen. If you only saw that you would think that's a man-woman thing. But my view is he's not afraid to be an asshole to anybody. He's an equal opportunity asshole. But if you're sitting in a room and you see him do that to a woman, it may be more uncomfortable than if you see him do that to a guy."

A second former senior official at the Fed offered a very similar description of Summers's modus operandi: "Larry goes into his high school and college debate mode. That's just the way he's wired. Larry has a hard time recognizing the potential that other economists in his space could be right. And much like a debater-type person, he blows minor quibbles out of proportion. It's Larry's desire to make sure that he is perceived as the dominant economic thinker at the moment."

Summers demonstrated his relentless and tactless manner during a stormy presidency of Harvard University from 2001 to 2006.

First, he clashed with noted Black scholar Cornel West over West's political activism and alleged easy grading, prompting West to leave the school. Then in 2005, at a conference on why women were underrepresented in math and engineering at top research universities, Summers played down gender discrimination as a factor and suggested one reason was that women with young children might be unwilling to work as many hours as men. Then he provoked outrage among many women in attendance by citing research that suggested men may have a higher innate aptitude for math and science than women. By 2006, as the controversy refused to die, Summers resigned as Harvard president.

As a member of the Obama administration three years later, Summers assumed he would serve as NEC director for a year and then become Fed chair in early 2010, when Bernanke's initial term was up. But the worsening financial crisis scotched that. "I certainly heard during the transition in late 2008 that Larry Summers would be named as the next Fed chair," said Daniel Tarullo, who joined the Fed Board of Governors at the start of Obama's presidency. "But I remember thinking at the time that if Bernanke does a good job in the next year, that's going to be difficult to pull off because why would you want to do the proverbial changing of horses in midstream?" Tarullo was right. Obama reappointed Bernanke, and Summers left the administration in early 2011, presumably as Fed chief-in-waiting.

Amid all the speculation about Bernanke's successor in the summer of 2013, the White House leaked word that Summers was Obama's choice. The president's decision appeared to be based on both his promise to give Summers the job and the belief shared by top aides that Summers would be best able to handle a new financial crisis because he handled several during his time as Treasury secretary in the Clinton administration.

Almost immediately in response to the leaks, a vociferous anti-Summers campaign emerged, led by Senate Democrats, a broad cross section of economists, and women's groups that had condemned Summers for his sexist remarks while Harvard president. The arguments against him were many: his arrogance and patronizing manner, economic views that were to the right of most Democrats, and his opposition as Treasury secretary to tougher regulation of the financial industry in the late 1990s—a position many critics blamed for the 2007–2009 crisis.

Some of the stiffest opposition came from Democratic women in the Senate, including Elizabeth Warren of Massachusetts, a leading advocate of tighter financial regulation, and Barbara Boxer of California, who had been a supporter of Yellen dating back to her first appointment to the Fed in 1994. A female political strategist with numerous contacts in the Senate recalled senators worrying that Summers's nomination was a fait accompli, "but the women on the Hill were saying, 'No way, no way.'"

"So, Larry reached out to Elizabeth Warren and said, 'Do you want to come to my house in Truro [on Cape Cod]?' And she's in Boston and so insulted," said the strategist. "Larry thought that would be like a nice thing to invite her to his house and she was saying, 'No, if you want to talk to me, you come to see me.' It was this huge insult, and you can imagine how he would be clueless about that. The women in the Senate were tired of being talked down to by him during the financial crises. That's how he talked to them, like they were idiots, and I think that became very personal for them."

Neither Warren nor Summers was willing to discuss that incident or any other details about his effort to become Fed chair.

Women weren't the only senators who felt talked down to by Summers. Senator Sherrod Brown of Ohio had been on the receiving end of Summers's treatment and didn't like it one bit. He had once asked at a hearing about ways to protect manufacturing jobs, a big concern in his state, and Summers proceeded to lecture him as if he were a dunce, explaining that Brown was advocating industrial policy, something free-market economists reject as unsound. Many members of Congress had similar experiences with Summers's arrogance, and they didn't forget. And they certainly weren't going to support his bid to become Fed chair.

Brown certainly didn't. He drafted a letter of support for Yellen as Fed chair, managed to get twenty out of fifty-five Senate Democrats to sign it and sent it to the White House on July 25, 2013. The "Dear Mr. President" letter didn't mention Summers. Instead, it extolled Yellen as "the best person for this job." It cited her experience in conducting monetary policy, her communications skills, her empathy with Americans out of work, and "her independence, intellectual rigor and willingness to challenge conventional wisdom regarding [financial] deregulation"—an obvious dig at Summers's opposition to more stringent financial oversight. "Simply put, Governor Yellen would be an excellent choice to serve as the next Chairman of the Board of Governors," the letter concluded.

Brown drafted the letter "because he feared Summers's appointment would happen as part of the old boys club and he needed to escalate the issue," explained a Senate staffer involved in the effort. "He dictated the letter, it went to the Senate floor and got support that went beyond our wildest dreams."

Others weighed in as well. Heidi Hartmann, Yellen's former PhD colleague at Yale who later founded the Institute for Women's Policy Research in Washington, DC, drafted a letter in support of Yellen along with economist Joyce Jacobsen, dean of Social Sciences at Wesleyan University. They enlisted eight hundred prominent economists to sign the letter, and sent it to Obama shortly after Labor Day.

The letter cited Yellen's "superb" qualifications, independent thinking, and concern to combat unemployment. To avoid being seen as overtly political, the letter did not mention Lawrence Summers. But in a veiled dig at his difficult personality, it said, "There is less and less room in modern public policymaking, especially at the FRB [Federal Reserve Board], for a single leader to dominate discussion. Modern policymaking, in a world filled with uncertainties and complexities, must proceed through cooperation and consensus, led by effective leaders. Dr. Yellen has demonstrated the ability to hear all points of view and then act effectively."

The anti-Summers campaign was relentless. On September 6, 2013, about the same time that Hartmann was circulating her letter, Yellen's former mentor and friend, Joseph Stiglitz, penned an op-ed on her behalf that appeared in the *New York Times*. Unlike Hartmann, Stiglitz unleashed a withering attack on Summers, his bitter intellectual foe from their time together in the Clinton White House. "His great 'achievement' as secretary of the Treasury, from 1999 to 2001, was passage of the law that ensured that derivatives would not be regulated—a decision that helped blow up the financial markets," Stiglitz wrote. "Mr. Summers encouraged countries . . . to allow capital to flow in and out without restrictions—indeed insisted that they do so—against the advice of the White House Council of Economic Advisers (which I led from 1995 to 1997), and this more than anything else led to the Asian financial crisis. Few policies or actions have greater culpability for that Asian crisis and the global financial crisis of 2008 than the deregulatory policies that Mr. Summers advocated."

"Brilliance is not the only determinant of performance. Values, judgment and personality matter, too," Stiglitz's column concluded. "The choices have seldom been so stark, the stakes so large. No wonder that the choice of the Fed leader has stirred such emotion. Ms. Yellen has a truly impressive record in each of the jobs she has undertaken. The country has before it one candidate who played a pivotal role in creating the economic problems that we confront today, and another candidate of enormous stature, experience and judgment."

By then, Summers's chances of becoming Fed chair were plummeting to zero. Senator Jeff Merkley of Oregon, one of the Democrats who had signed Brown's letter promoting Yellen, recalled having reservations about Summers dating back to the start of the Obama administration in early 2009 because of Summers's aggressive dismantling of the Glass-Steagall Act that had barred banks from getting involved in hedge funds and other risky investments. "It was a very wrong-headed effort that bowed to the power of the big banks and set up our economy for exactly the types of problems that led to the 2008–2009 recession," Merkley said.

Merkley also opposed Summers because of his support for the Troubled Asset Relief Program (TARP), which was created to bail out financial institutions but not homeowners facing foreclosure. Merkley had written a letter of complaint about that to the White House on January 14, 2009: "The financial institutions responsible for the abuses that fueled the crisis have already received $350 billion with more to come. We should spend 20 cents on the dollar to address the root causes of the problem and help families whose homes are at risk." Summers responded with a letter saying the administration favored a $50 billion to $100 billion program to address the foreclosure crisis. "Quite frankly," Merkley continued, "what the administration did was based on the best thing for banks, not the best thing for homeowners. So, I felt that was a big betrayal."

Throw in Summers's brash personality and controversial comments about women's aptitude deficit in math and science, and Merkley decided that he would oppose Summers if Obama went ahead and nominated him for Fed chair. "I really thought Yellen was by far the better candidate for the job," he said. On September 10, while attending a hearing before the Senate Banking Committee, which would have to approve any Fed nominee, Merkley turned to another committee member, Elizabeth Warren, and asked if she planned to vote for Summers, and she said no. Then he leaned over and asked Sherrod Brown, who also said no. Ditto when he asked Jon Tester of Montana and Heidi Heitkamp of North Dakota. "I said, 'Are you kidding me? There's five of us sitting here who are not going to vote for him. And the Obama administration doesn't know this. We have to let them know. We need to do a group call and explain why we feel he's inappropriate and doesn't have the votes in the Banking Committee,'" Merkley said. "And my colleagues turned to me and said, 'No, let's not do a group call. You make that call.'"

So, on Friday, September 13, while attending the Pendleton Round-Up, an annual rodeo in Oregon, Merkley called White House chief of staff Denis McDonough and got his assistant on the phone. Merkley said he had some urgent information to relay. But the assistant said McDonough was unavailable, didn't have time to call back, and Merkley should say what's on his mind. The senator responded that Summers didn't have the votes in the Banking Committee.

McDonough, who returned to government in 2021 as President Joe Biden's secretary of Veterans Affairs, never called back. But later that day, he ran into Merkley at a briefing for senators on Obamacare. "I come out of that briefing and Denis confronts me in the hallway and starts screaming at me about betraying President Obama," Merkley recalled. "And I said, 'I called you to warn the administration didn't have the votes because it would have been incredibly embarrassing for President Obama to go through with the nomination and not have this piece of information. And you didn't even have the courtesy to call me back after I left an urgent message. I wanted to give you the details in case you wanted to lobby the members of the Banking Committee.'"

Merkley continued: "And he says to me, 'Oh, oh, I called you back. I called you back.' And I said, 'Okay, well, how about this? I have a device in my pocket that records every phone call coming in. And I'll bet you ten thousand dollars right now that your phone number is not on my phone. You're going to take that back.' And that was basically the end of the conversation. But it was a very strange situation for me to be in because, of course, I supported the Obama administration. But I did not think Larry Summers was the right person. And I did think Janet Yellen was the right person."

As the controversy raged over the summer, Yellen refused to get involved personally, telling supporters that it would be improper to campaign for a job that is supposed to be independent of partisan politics. "She did nothing at all to lobby for the job," said son Robby. "There was a period of six months or more where her name was put out in the newspapers as the lead person for the job. Everyone expected her to get the job, and the White House wasn't seeming to do anything to dispel those stories. We figured that this might happen, but we were not in any way fanning the flames. I don't think she ever sort of felt entitled to the job, so we were totally passive about that and then through the whole episode when Larry's name surfaced."

"We sat back and watched and were amazed by all this stuff that was playing out," Robby added. "It seemed damaging to Obama because of accusations that he was not someone who treated women well. We're fans of Obama, so we were distressed to see this happening. And then we were friends with Larry, so there was that complicating factor."

Jerome Powell, still a Fed governor at the time, bucked Yellen up when it appeared she would be passed over for the top job. He sensed that she felt Summers was going to get the post because

Obama had promised to name him. Powell told her she would be a terrific chair given all her nearly forty years of experience at the Fed, from a staff economist to vice chair, not to mention her distinguished academic record and time as head of the Council of Economic Advisers. He told her that no one had ever been more qualified for the job.

On Sunday, September 15, 2013, just two days after Merkley's call to McDonough's office, the White House announced that Summers was withdrawing his name as a candidate for Fed chair. "I have reluctantly concluded that any possible confirmation process for me would be acrimonious and would not serve the interests of the Federal Reserve, the administration or ultimately, the interests of the nation's ongoing economic recovery," Summers said in a written admission of defeat. Obama, who had been furious about the rejection of his candidate, heaped praise on Summers. "Larry was a critical member of my team as we faced down the worst economic crisis since the Great Depression, and it was in no small part because of his expertise, wisdom and leadership that we wrestled the economy back to growth and made the kind of progress we are seeing today," Obama said.

"The president really wanted to nominate Larry but ultimately came to the conclusion that he couldn't get Larry confirmed," said a senior adviser at the time. "As he was coming to that judgment, his team was telling him it would be costly, painful, hard, and maybe ultimately damaging to Larry to persist. As the president was coming to that judgment that it wouldn't work, he saw Yellen as a totally natural alternative. She was not as divisive, of course, and she came with a lot of credibility, experience, and no meaningful confirmation risk."

The senior adviser, who has good relations with both Summers and Yellen, felt Summers was unfairly treated by his own party. "The left decided Larry was too conservative. And they pinned the financial crisis on Larry because he had been partly responsible for what happened with leaving derivatives markets largely unregulated," he continued. "Regulating derivatives was a complicated debate, and there's no credible argument that the administration's deregulation policies were particularly relevant to what happened in the financial crisis. But that's the view of a large part of the left. They were worried about derivatives and risk-taking by banks and unfairly put it on Larry. And I think part of it is that Larry is a principled person who says what he believes and doesn't shape his views based on how popular you are going to be. He offended a lot on the left in the debates over those things. So, a lot of the Democrats made it clear to the White House that they would not support him."

Soon after deciding reluctantly to jettison Summers, Obama contacted his White House chief economist, Christina Romer, for an evaluation of Yellen, her longtime friend and Berkeley colleague. Romer talked Yellen up, and a satisfied Obama called to offer her the job. "He said the nice things you'd say to a person whom you're offering the job to," Yellen recalled. "I think he told me that Larry had withdrawn and he'd like me to do it. I said I was very honored by the offer and would do it." This was one of the few occasions when Yellen didn't say she would think about it for a while. "When the president of the United States calls you, what person says, 'I'll get back to you?'" Yellen asked with a chuckle.

On October 9, less than a month after Summers bowed out, Obama summoned Ben Bernanke and Janet Yellen along with their families to the White House to announce her nomination as Bernanke's successor. The thirteen-minute ceremony took place in the State Dining Room, where Obama stood at a lectern in front of a marble fireplace. An 1869 portrait of a pensive Abraham Lincoln pondering with his hand on his chin hung on the wall above them. Bernanke was to his left and Yellen stood to his right. After extolling Bernanke's leadership in rescuing the US economy from near collapse, the president turned to Yellen. "She's a proven leader and she's tough—not just because she's from Brooklyn," Obama quipped as the room erupted in laughter. "Janet is exceptionally well-qualified for this role."

Obama continued to praise Yellen as if she were his first choice to lead the central bank. "Janet is renowned for her good judgment. . . . She doesn't have a crystal ball, but what she does have is a keen understanding about how markets and the economy work—not just in theory but also in the real world. And she calls it like she sees it." Then, as if he was channeling Summers's weakness, Obama said, "Janet also knows how to build consensus. She listens to competing views and brings people together around a common goal." He also spoke of her lifelong commitment as an economist to increasing employment and said, "America's workers and their families will have a champion in Janet Yellen."

Obama noted the historical significance of his choice—the first woman to head the Fed in its one hundred–year history—and thanked Yellen for "not only your example and your excellence, but also being a role model for a lot of folks out there." He concluded by joking about her reputation for preparation and hard work, along with her fellow economist husband and economist son: "I've been told their idea of a great family vacation is the beach—with a suitcase full of economics books. But this is a family affair. We thank George and Robert for their support as Janet begins this journey."

Yellen responded with a pledge to use the Fed's powerful tools to help all Americans, especially those in need. "Too many Americans still can't find a job and worry how they'll pay their bills and provide for their families. The Federal Reserve can help if it does its job effectively," she said. "We can help ensure that everyone has the opportunity to work hard and build a better life. We can ensure that inflation remains in check and doesn't undermine the benefits of a growing economy. We can, and must, safeguard the financial system." She also noted the importance of forging consensus, another nod to Summers's Achilles' heel. The Fed's greatest strength "rests in its capacity to approach important decisions with expertise and objectivity, to vigorously debate diverse views and then to unite behind its response." She concluded: "Mr. President, thank you for giving me this opportunity to continue serving the Federal Reserve and carrying out its important work on behalf of the American people."

After Obama nominated Yellen, Summers sent her an email congratulating her on the post he had long coveted. An economist whose empathy was her calling card had bested one who had zero capacity for empathy.

At her confirmation hearing before the Senate Banking Committee on November 14, Yellen noted that the economy had improved significantly since the Great Recession, but unemployment was still too high at 7.3 percent and inflation too low at less than 2 percent. She said the Fed was using its monetary policy tools to promote a more robust recovery that would ultimately allow the Fed to reduce its reliance on the extraordinary bond purchases that had created such a big feud within the central bank and stoked opposition among congressional Republicans.

Yellen also spoke of her efforts over the years to make the Fed's actions more open and promised to continue along that path as chair. Then she turned to the crisis that had revealed flaws in the financial system and the government's ability to deal with them. "The Federal Reserve and our fellow regulators have made considerable progress in addressing those weaknesses," she said. "Banks are stronger today, regulatory gaps are being closed, and the financial system is more stable and more resilient . . . but here, too, important work lies ahead. I am committed to using the Fed's supervisory and regulatory role to reduce the threat of another financial crisis. Our country has come a long way since the dark days of the financial crisis, but we have farther to go."

On November 21, the Senate Banking Committee approved Yellen's nomination by a 14–8 vote, a far more partisan outcome than the unanimous Senate support she received when confirmed as vice chair three years earlier. Three of the committee's ten Republicans supported her and just one of twelve Democrats opposed her—Joe Manchin of West Virginia, a party maverick then and now. Manchin said at the time that he opposed her continued support for the controversial bond-buying program, the same complaint voiced by Republicans who opposed her nomination.

On January 6, 2014, the full Senate confirmed Yellen as Fed chair by a vote of 56–26. All forty-five Democrats voting that day supported her, along with eleven Republicans. She might have won over more Republicans who had acknowledged that they approved of her overall performance at the Fed, but they were furious about many Obama policies at the time—not just over what they considered the Fed's extravagant bond-buying program and overzealous regulation of financial institutions.

❖ ❖ ❖

THE COMPETITION WITH SUMMERS FOR FED CHAIR WAS A PAINful episode in Yellen's life. She was aware of all the buzz that she was the lead candidate, and while she did not feel entitled to the job, she was offended when it appeared that Obama had decided to name Summers without even giving her serious consideration. Yellen had confided to friends that she was convinced Summers had orchestrated a nasty campaign against her by spreading word that she lacked the gravitas, intelligence, and experience to handle a financial crisis. She resented his efforts to undermine her as underhanded, but said nothing. Yellen told friends she thought he had a weak track record when it came to managing after financial crises, as Stiglitz had claimed in his op-ed. He had embraced the Commodity Futures Trading Act of 2000, a misguided law that barred regulation of over-the-counter derivatives. It was his way of fending off Brooksley Born's campaign to regulate derivatives and, in the process, contributed to the subsequent financial crash.

Summers's hand was seen in a July 19, 2013, column in the *Washington Post* by Ezra Klein that carried the headline "The Subtle, Sexist Whispering Campaign Against Janet Yellen." Citing sources that included White House officials, Klein wrote that they "said she lacks 'toughness,' she's short on 'gravitas,' too 'soft-spoken' or 'passive.' Some mused that she is not as aggressively brilliant or intellectually probing as other candidates."

Yellen also felt that Summers had shown appalling judgment as president of Harvard when he questioned women's aptitude in math and science. She was offended by his remarks and considered them insensitive at a time when there was a big push to increase the representation of women in top jobs at the Fed and corporate America.

Yellen understood from her many years at the Fed that it's not a place where Summers's method of intellectually bullying people succeeds. Rather, the FOMC is a committee of strong-willed individuals who need to be guided toward a consensus by making them feel like they are making a positive contribution and that they want to cooperate in coming to an agreement as a group. Trying to force them into a policy position will only anger them. They need to be treated gently and with respect, hardly Summers's forte. Yellen appreciated that Heidi Hartmann and her friends got women involved to lobby on her behalf. They were able to tap into the disdain so many felt toward Summers and turned the competition for Fed chair into a battle between a strong, competent woman and an arrogant sexist male. It became a political drama that attracted attention even from those who normally don't follow the Fed.

Former senator Barbara Boxer of California, who retired in 2017 and later became a lobbyist for a Washington firm, also saw the nomination battle in gender terms, as she recalled helping boost Yellen's career, beginning with her first nomination to the Fed in 1994.

"Here was a brilliant woman with incredible stamina, focus, and confidence to go to the very top of her profession," Boxer said. "The reason I felt that way is that I was an economics major at Brooklyn College in the 1960s . . . one of only two or three women. She went to college a few years after I did, and I know that she faced a very skeptical majority because not many people thought women should do anything other than become a nurse or a teacher in those years. Therefore, I knew she had what it takes to break the glass ceiling in the field of economics. I also felt that she has a heart and understands the struggles of the middle class and would fight for them with policies that would help them. I remember organizing the women of Congress to back her when she got started in the early years under Bill Clinton. I believe that was very helpful because she faced stiff competition from prominent men in her field, including Lawrence Summers."

Although Yellen and Summers did not talk to each other at the time the battle over the next Fed chair was raging, they had spoken many times since, both during her tenure as Fed chair and more recently in her job as Treasury secretary. Yellen respected Summers's intellectual abilities and valued his advice, though she was none too pleased when he became the most prominent Democratic critic of the Biden administration's big spending plans in 2021 as being inflationary.

Summers had persistently warned in numerous columns and television interviews that a one-year $1.9 trillion relief program enacted in the spring of 2021, at a time when the Fed was adding its own stimulus with massive amounts of money pumped into the banking system, was unleashing a new bout of high inflation. "Excessive inflation and a sense that it was not being controlled helped elect Richard Nixon and Ronald Reagan, and risks bringing Donald Trump back to power," Summers wrote in a November 16, 2021, column in the *Washington Post* that urged the Fed and Biden to stop calling the problem transitory. "While an overheating economy is a relatively good problem to have compared to a pandemic or a financial crisis, it will metastasize and threaten prosperity and public trust unless clearly acknowledged and addressed." The column appeared in the wake of a government report that the consumer price index had risen 6.2 percent during the twelve months through October 2021, the highest rate in thirty-one years.

Privately, Yellen agreed with Summers that too much government money was flowing into the economy too quickly. That is why she had questioned whether the $1.9 trillion relief plan should be scaled back by a third early in 2021 before deciding to embrace it as is. She worried that so much money in the pockets of consumers and businesses would drive up prices at a time when the pandemic had caused shortages of goods in unprecedentedly high demand, but she also feared too meager a stimulus might be worse. Yellen and Summers were not worried about another $3 trillion-plus in spending Congress had been debating in the fall of 2021 to improve the nation's infrastructure, bolster the social safety net, and combat global warming because that money would be spread out over ten years and was offset by tax increases. Yet unlike Summers, Yellen remained convinced that the spurt of high inflation in 2021 would subside in 2022 if the COVID-19 pandemic subsided, ending supply bottlenecks and labor shortages that were driving consumer prices higher. She feared that Summers's very public attacks and warnings of long-term inflationary woes only undermined Biden's badly needed social agenda and jeopardized his presidency. Her fears came true in early 2022, as Biden's public approval ratings dropped and his multitrillion dollar social agenda languished in Congress.

* * *

AT BERNANKE'S LAST MONETARY POLICY MEETING, HELD JANUARY 28–29, 2014, his fellow members of the Federal Open Market Committee went through the pro forma motion of electing him FOMC chair, as is the custom at the start of a new year, and then elected Yellen to replace him after he officially departed on January 31. The members also used the occasion to salute Bernanke for his courageous and audacious leadership during the financial crisis. "I, too, Mr. Chairman, want to express my gratitude for all of your contributions to the Federal Reserve and to the nation and say what an honor it has been to serve with you," Yellen chimed in. "And I want to mention that the thought of filling your large shoes is a daunting challenge."

In its final act under Bernanke, the committee voted to taper its bond purchases by an additional $10 billion a month to $65 billion. It would be one more step toward normalcy and a welcome gift as Yellen prepared to take charge the following week.

Turning to another subject, the committee talked about expanding the chair's press conferences from four to eight a year—one after each meeting. The reason: the markets and news media had come to see a pattern in which the FOMC would only change policy when there was a scheduled news conference to explain its action, and that effectively tied the committee's hands from making any moves at the other four meetings. Looking at Yellen, Dallas Fed president Richard Fisher said, "If I recall correctly, it was Artemas Ward who said he loved his brother so much that he volunteered him to go to war in his place. We love you so much, Madam Chair," he said, using a title never uttered before in the

Fed's long history, "that we gladly volunteer you to give press conferences, if you're willing, at the end of each of our sessions." Yellen, however, was not willing despite her long advocacy for transparency. The reason why would become apparent in the early months of her tenure.

On February 3, 2014, as Bernanke officially departed, Janet Louise Yellen took the oath of office as the fifteenth head of the Federal Reserve System. The oath that all senior federal employees take, with the exception of the president of the United States, was administered by her longtime colleague, Governor Daniel Tarullo, in the massive boardroom. They stood before the grand marble fireplace with the Fed's symbol, a giant eagle, peering down on them. Husband George and other Fed Board members and staff attended the brief ceremony. Yellen, who was sixty-seven and had thought just a few years ago that she would be retiring at this stage in her life, did not give a speech after her swearing-in. Instead, she merely smiled broadly as the room broke into sustained applause.

A month later, on March 5, Yellen took the oath again administered by Daniel Tarullo. This was a more formal ceremonial swearing-in with invited guests that was held in the cavernous atrium. On this occasion she spoke briefly, pledging to use the Fed's vast powers to help improve the lives of everyone. "The tools we deploy, to guide the financial system and influence our vast economy can seem far removed from the lives and concerns of average Americans," she said. "And yet the decisions we make affect the welfare and shape the future of every American. I promise to never forget the individual lives, experiences and challenges that lie behind the statistics we use to gauge the health of the economy. The unemployment rate represents millions of individuals who are eager to work but struggling to provide for themselves and their families. When we make progress toward our goals, each job that

is created lifts this burden for someone who is better equipped to
be a good parent, to build a stronger community, and to contribute
to a more prosperous nation.

"Let me close by offering my heartfelt thanks for the many messages I have received since my nomination from individuals around
the country who have written to wish me well and offer their support. I pledge to do my very best to meet the challenges that lie
ahead."

It was another historic accomplishment for Janet Yellen. She
understood what she had achieved, though less on a personal
level than when she witnessed the reaction to her becoming the
first woman to head the most powerful central bank in the world,
including the goodwill messages she noted in her swearing-in remarks. "It had significance to an enormous number of people who
felt inspired to see a woman break that glass ceiling," she later said
of her feelings at the time. "It's partly because the outside world
regarded this as a major achievement for women that it ended up
having such significance to me. From my point of view, I've been
part of the Fed for a very long time. I knew people in the Fed well.
I felt very comfortable. I knew the difference between what you
do as chair and vice chair is not enormous. And I felt comfortable
because I understood what the job of chair would involve."

At the time, Yellen had not given much thought to her historic
accomplishment—the first woman to head the Fed. Yet it was hard
to ignore. "When I saw what the external reaction was, which was
huge, it said to me, 'I need to think carefully about how I handle
the issues concerning women in the world and in the profession,
and diversity more generally.'" Doing that was a challenge because
Yellen had never seen herself as a barrier breaker, even though she
had done just that so many times in her career. "Janet cares a great
deal about the position of women in economics, but she doesn't see
herself as the Joan of Arc of the profession who is breaking glass

ceilings," said friend and former Fed vice chair Roger Ferguson. "I think it speaks volumes to her that no one ever once said, 'Well, she got that job because she's a woman.' She got the job because she's always been capable of doing the job, and the person selected happened to be a woman. That's a very different way of looking at the world."

As she reflected on her nomination as Fed chair, Yellen talked about her insecurities that explain why she remained so passive during the rivalry for the job she had been thrust into with Summers. "You know, I tend not to run for things. I'm always apprehensive about my ability to do what's required," she said. "And I'm often conflicted by some sense that I may not be up to the job. But if somebody really asks me to do it and says they need me to do it, I tend to say, 'yes.' But I don't put myself out there and say, 'Oh, yeah, I'm going to go after that.'"

That reflection led to her feelings about being asked to take on a whole new set of challenges as secretary of the Treasury: "The same thing was true with this job that I'm in now. I did not run for it. I wouldn't have even thought I could do this job, but then, when they said they needed me to do it, I said I'd give it a shot." Privately, she would have been content if Biden hadn't asked her to serve. She wouldn't have had the stress, responsibilities, long hours, and steep learning curve that come with being Treasury secretary.

Joanne Lipman, the former *Wall Street Journal* and *USA Today* editor who has written about gender discrimination in the workplace, said the Summers vs. Yellen drama is a classic example of how men and women of her generation tend to pursue workplace advancement: Summers aggressively lobbied for the Fed chair, while Yellen passively sat back. "Women grew up acculturated to being pursued. The man asks you on a date; the man asks you to marry him, and it is unseemly for the woman to go out and ask for things herself," Lipman explained. "And it seems immodest to put yourself out there. That has been a cultural issue around women for hundreds of years. You wait to be asked, you don't raise your hand for anything. So, everything she did was so in line with what the culture tells you about a woman." The man, meanwhile, is waving his hand frantically in the air whether he is qualified or not.

There even is a name for that behavior pattern among women. The "Tiara Syndrome" was coined in 2005 by Carol Frohlinger and Deborah Kolb, founders of Negotiating Women, Inc., an organization that offers training and consulting to professional women. It describes how many women, when it comes to salary and raise negotiations and promotions, keep their head down, deliver excellent work, and hope that the right people will notice—and place a tiara on their head.

That rarely happens in the workplace, but Yellen was that rare exception. Though she failed to win tenure at Harvard, subsequently she kept getting the tiara placed on her head without going after her jobs as a Fed governor; chief White House economist; San Francisco Fed president; Fed vice chair; Fed chair; and, most recently, Treasury secretary. Little wonder she never saw herself as a woman victimized by workplace discrimination. As Yellen has often observed, her gender never seemed to hold her back; she never encountered obstacles in her path she couldn't overcome. That made it difficult for her to appreciate her unique accomplishments.

Even so, it was impossible for Yellen to ignore the sound of a ceiling cracking when she took charge of the Fed. "She has made every young woman across America realize that there's no position in the economic universe that a woman isn't suited to fill and to fill more competently than any man who has ever filled the same position," observed Senator Jeff Merkley, the Democrat from Oregon.

Equally notable was how low-key Yellen was about her achievements. She was always modest, never coming across as ambitious—

or pushy—as a misogynist would describe an accomplished female. Open ambition was one reason so many people disliked Hillary Clinton despite her historic achievement: the first woman to be nominated by a major party for president.

For Yellen, becoming Fed chair created a new kind of pressure. Doing a good job no longer was enough. She now had become a role model under constant watch. "This was the first time that people really talked about my mother as a glass ceiling–breaking person," said Robby. "I don't think it's something that she spent a lot of time talking about or was forced to think about as an issue she was going to have to address until then. It became an issue she had to wrestle with. She doesn't make a point of overemphasizing that herself. It's not a major part of how she talks about herself."

Over the next four years, Yellen could not avoid thinking about her new status and the mark she would be making for history now that she had become—so much to her surprise—a widely admired trailblazer.

# - 10 -

## MADAM CHAIR'S REIGN

*"She made it look easy. There were no major crack-ups."*

AFTER JANET YELLEN TOOK CHARGE OF THE FEDERAL RESERVE System in early 2014, her first Federal Open Market Committee session began with what passes for levity among the policy-setting central bankers and ended with a train wreck.

At their March 18–19 FOMC meeting, Dallas Fed president Richard Fisher sought to break up the serious business before the group. "To commemorate this being your first formal meeting, I wore the special 'Janet Yellen' tie, which shows the donkeys, who are the Democrats, and the elephants, who are the Republicans, just butting heads, and you flying in—I think it's on the wings of a dove—and spreading money around the system," he joked, as the room erupted in laughter. "Perhaps if it had you herding cats it might have been a better analogy for this meeting, but anyway, it's in your honor that I wear this tie." Indeed, herding cats was an apt analogy for Yellen to forge a consensus among her colleagues. One potential problem had been largely resolved for her. She could

269

continue to "taper" monthly bond purchases without perturbing the financial markets because predecessor Ben Bernanke had begun that process. Still, she had other tricky issues to deal with. An immediate one was the need to inform the financial markets that the Fed would keep its interest rates at zero, where they had been since December 2008, even if unemployment fell below 6.5 percent, the level the Fed had previously signaled might trigger a rate increase. The jobless rate had fallen to 6.6 percent in March 2014, a big improvement from 10.6 percent in 2010. Still, Yellen had no intention of raising interest rates until the unemployment rate fell a lot more.

To make sure everyone was on board, she held a conference call on March 4—two weeks before the next regularly scheduled FOMC meeting—to discuss how best to communicate the Fed's intention to keep its overnight lending rate at zero for the foreseeable future.

When the group met at Fed headquarters, all nineteen members of the committee had a chance to give their analysis of the state of the economy, as was the custom at FOMC meetings. Some speakers were long-winded, and it took superhuman concentration to listen to all the presentations, many of them repetitive. As the saying goes, "Everything has already been said, but not everyone has said it." That is why the meetings lasted for hours. As the session wrapped up, the group agreed to reduce its bond purchases by another $10 billion a month to $55 billion and change its guidance to make clear that the fed funds rate would remain indefinitely at zero even after unemployment fell below 6.5 percent.

After a smooth meeting, Yellen concluded by thanking everyone for reaching a consensus so efficiently. "I appreciate all of the time you were willing to take in sorting this out so that today didn't turn into a train wreck," she said. "There's one more opportunity for a train wreck, which I will try to avoid," she added, referring to her first news conference as chair that she would be holding shortly.

"Good luck," Fisher said. "I will do my best, that's all I can say," Yellen replied. "It will be a learning experience. Thank you all for your input and cooperation."

It proved to be a learning experience, indeed. And it turned into the train wreck that she had hoped to avoid.

Fed chairs had traditionally been opaque in their economic forecasts so that the central bank would not be forced into a policy move merely to confirm market expectations and avoid a nasty reaction. Alan Greenspan was a master at obfuscation. His speeches or congressional testimony often led Fed reporters to write contradictory stories about the Fed's next interest rate move. "The members of the Board of Governors and the Reserve Bank presidents foresee an implicit strengthening of activity after the current rebalancing is over, although the central tendency of their individual forecasts for real GDP still shows a substantial slowdown, on balance, for the year as a whole," he said at a Senate hearing in 2001, leaving everyone scratching their heads as to what he meant. Bernanke and Yellen were less enamored with "Fedspeak," preferring greater transparency. Bernanke paid a price when he provoked the market's famous "taper tantrum," and Yellen was also about to learn a painful lesson from being too clear.

Yellen handled the initial questioning from the assembled reporters smoothly. About forty minutes into the hour-long news conference, Ann Saphir of Reuters asked, "To be clear . . . once you do wind down the bond-buying program, could you tell us how long of a gap we might expect before the rate hikes do begin?" Yellen responded by violating the cardinal rule of Fedspeak: never be specific; always maximize your flexibility to alter direction as economic conditions change. "So, the language that we use in the statement is 'considerable' period. So, I—you know, this is the kind of term—it's hard to define," she began and later wished she had concluded. "But, you know, it probably means something on the order of around six months or that type of thing. But, you know, it depends. What the statement is saying is, it depends what conditions are like."

Yikes. Even though she conditioned everything with caveats, all the markets heard was "six months," which was a lot sooner than they had been expecting the Fed to start raising rates. Stock and bond prices immediately plummeted, and Fed watchers questioned whether Yellen had what it took to lead the central bank. The *Financial Times* said she "stumbled" at her rookie news conference. Others called it a "gaffe" and a "blunder."

The market damage quickly passed. Stock and bond prices recovered later in the day once traders took the time to read Yellen's comments more carefully and realized she was not signaling any change in policy. But the damage to Yellen's self-confidence persisted for years.

Fed governor Daniel Tarullo recalled watching the news conference at his desk, and when it was over, Yellen walked into his office. "She had this distressed look on her face, and she said, 'I'm so sorry. I had a misstep here,' and she worried that it would be an issue for us," he said. "I told her that newly installed people in very high positions have to adjust to the increased weight on whatever you say." He explained to her that if she said the same thing as vice chair, it would be the fifth paragraph of an AP story but now it will be on the front page of the *Wall Street Journal*. "I said, 'You know, it's just not that big a deal.' But what struck me was that she felt bad about it and wanted to tell people that she knew it was a misstep. I think it reflected her sense of responsibility to everybody else, which just underscored her collegiality."

Looking back at the episode more than seven years later, Yellen still blamed herself, not the markets or financial press for misinterpreting her remarks. "The truth is, I said something that I really hadn't intended," she said. "When the statement uses words like 'considerable time,' you're really not supposed to define exactly what the words mean. The intention is to leave it at that. But the reporters kept pushing me and pushing me, and being new to it I screwed up. I eventually said, 'Well, look, you wouldn't use a term like that, unless you meant at least six months.' Somehow it came out as six months. And it was certainly never intended to be six months, but I should never have said anything of that sort. There was a mess over it. It undermined my self-confidence that I made such a bad mistake." In fairness, it was a minor mistake that had no impact on Fed policy or the markets beyond a few hours of roiling prices. Yet a woman who carried the burden of perfection drilled into her by a demanding mother struggled to shake it off. Colleagues recall her apologizing for her error virtually every day for the next six months, even as they tried to reassure her that it was a trivial matter. "Everyone kept telling her, 'You don't have to apologize. You did great. Don't worry about it. It was the tiniest mistake ever,'" recalled a colleague on the Board of Governors. "Yet, she just kept kicking herself for it. That certainly is Janet holding herself to that high standard."

So, how could a seasoned Fed official who always went to such great lengths to be prepared, organized, disciplined, and cautious make such a careless slip of the tongue? Yellen revealed that the cause was a severe case of the flu from which she was still recovering. The weekend before the FOMC meeting, she was running a temperature of more than 104 and nearly went to the hospital. She had to prepare for the FOMC meeting and her first press conference and was in terrible shape. The Sunday before, she called the president of the Federal Reserve Bank of New York, William Dudley, who served as her deputy of the FOMC, and said she wasn't sure she would be well enough to run the meeting, and he might have to step in for her. Dudley, a colleague and friend for decades going back to their days together at Berkeley, worried that it would look very bad for him to sub for Yellen at her first meeting as chair. He feared the news media would create a story line that the first female head of the Fed was too old and frail to do the job. He was relieved when she recovered sufficiently to run the meeting.

"Eventually my temperature came down to the point where I felt I had to give it a shot," Yellen said. "But I really didn't do the kind of preparation I needed to. I felt quite sick throughout the two days of the meeting." The woman who spent a lifetime being prepared hadn't put in the marathon work over the weekend that she had planned for—going over the agenda for the FOMC meeting with intense scrutiny and preparing for every conceivable question she might be asked at the news conference.

After that experience, Yellen spared no effort to be prepared for future press conferences. She set aside three days and made her staff grill her in practice sessions on every conceivable topic and then critique her responses. They spent so much time prepping her that other routine work got delayed. She never made another gaffe. But she also had no intention of holding more than four news conferences a year, even though members of the FOMC kept pressing for holding eight—one after each meeting so they had more flexibility to raise or lower interest rates. Their rationale for the change was that the markets had come to assume the Fed would only alter policy at meetings when the chair could explain the move at a subsequent news conference. As a result, committee members worried that a policy change at a meeting without a scheduled news conference might surprise the markets, causing an ugly reaction.

At the September 16–17, 2014, FOMC, the president of the Federal Reserve Bank of St. Louis, James Bullard, pushed anew for a news conference after every meeting, but Yellen rebuffed him. She raised the matter herself at the March 17–18 meeting, and rejected it, saying it would require too much preparation for her and her staff. Though a longtime champion of Fed transparency, she never relented on the issue, and the Fed did not start holding news conferences after every FOMC meeting until January 2019—under her successor, Powell. "Being the big preparer I was, I wanted to be quite cautious about not getting myself into something I could easily come to regret," she later explained.

✣ ✣ ✣

PREPARING FOR FOMC MEETINGS WAS ANOTHER TASK TO WHICH Yellen devoted immense energy. Not surprisingly, she overhauled the system Bernanke had in place to draw in more staffers to prepare documents for the members and to seek a consensus on policy decisions before each meeting. Traditionally, three policy statements are proposed for the committee to consider for release after they meet: the "A" option is dovish, "C" is hawkish, and "B" is the moderate consensus statement almost always adopted.

Bernanke operated as a one-man show, personally drafting each version of the statement the committee would issue with the help of one senior aide. Yellen thought this process was risky. "If anything happened to him, there was not another soul to take over," she said. "If you think of business continuity, which I have had to do in places like the San Francisco Fed, you're always asking the question, 'If a person in charge is hit by a bus, what happens?' Is there somebody else who knows what's going on? Can they figure it out and do it? And the truth is that in the Bernanke era, it would have been a disaster. If he had been hit by a bus, there was nobody else who actually understood enough to run monetary policy."

Yellen cited an instance when Bernanke's top assistant, William English, had to take sick leave for a lengthy period for surgery, and Bernanke had to shoulder all the work himself. He had to do everything because nobody else knew what to do to help. "Ben didn't design that regime. I guess it had been that way for a long time," she said. "But it sometimes created problems when there were last-minute changes, such as a change in the statement."

She recalled one chaotic meeting in 2012: "Ben wanted to do something, and he suggested a new policy approach but found on the Monday before the meeting that no one on the board was supportive. He had to reconfigure what to do. The market dropped sharply that afternoon. He rewrote the statement on the fly and didn't have time to tell the committee beforehand of his change in plans. When the board members walked into the meeting, Ben essentially said, 'I've changed my mind.' We were running against the clock. The statement had to be issued, and people had their heads in their hands, saying, 'You're forcing me to vote yes or no. I haven't had time to think about it.'" It was a mess. Yellen believed the infamous "taper tantrum" occurred in part because of a similar last-minute statement by Bernanke that hadn't been thought through carefully. When she took charge, Yellen was determined not to run the committee that way.

Bernanke operated that way because he felt it was essential to keep the Fed's policy intentions confidential and didn't trust too many staff members to know what was going on. If, for example, there were ten documents to be distributed at a meeting, staffers' involvement would be limited to just the one they were preparing. It was all a need-to-know set of restrictions. "Very few people on the Fed staff had a complete picture or understanding of what was happening in monetary policy and what the key considerations were," Yellen explained. "I decided that was dangerous. We just could not go on doing things like that."

Yellen overhauled the process. She involved more staffers in writing draft FOMC statements and began preparing for the meetings much earlier. Her goal was to anticipate how the committee would vote so she could develop a consensus position even before the group met, essentially making the actual vote pro forma. Yellen would hold thirty-minute conversations with each member of the FOMC the Thursday and Friday before the meeting, and then circulate a second draft of a proposed consensus statement that better reflected their comments. She solicited concerns they had that needed to be aired. "I didn't want any surprises at the meeting. I wanted things worked out beforehand," she said. "We might change a semicolon or insert a word, but we wouldn't do anything major. We weren't going to rewrite the statement at the meeting. To do so entailed significant risks."

As part of her preparations, Yellen brought in a large group of staffers at both Washington headquarters and the New York Fed. She scheduled regular meetings of the Board of Governors to prepare for FOMC meetings since the seven-member board voted at all the rate-setting meetings, while voting among the regional bank presidents rotated. The groups would discuss comments by participants in redrafting statements, and if three people were inclined to dissent, the board and staff would discuss how to change the statement to meet the concerns so they could reduce the number of dissents. Those were sensitive discussions that Bernanke and his predecessors would never have let staff know about, but Yellen did. "I very much changed the process, and I believe that it continues under Powell. I never had a problem with leaks," she said.

Yellen's meticulous preparations resulted in orderly and efficient meetings but did not eliminate dissents. "It's all right to have dissents. There are people who feel strongly about things," she said. "I tried to satisfy concerns as best I could, but sometimes a disagreement is too big to satisfy your concern, and you would feel obliged to dissent. I didn't want to be surprised, and I didn't try to dissuade people from dissenting."

Indeed, there were occasional dissents—as many as three at one meeting—as FOMC members objected either because the Fed under Yellen had raised rates or failed to do so. Every Fed chair seeks a broad consensus but has encountered dissenters among the twelve voting members, a February 2017 study by the St. Louis Federal Reserve Bank documented. Going back to 1936, it found dissents ranged from an average zero per meeting under Thomas McCabe from April 1948 to March 1951 to 1.42 under G. William Miller's brief but tumultuous tenure from March 1978 to August 1979, when inflation took off. Yellen's dissent rate through December 2016 was 0.78 per meeting, a tad higher than that for Bernanke or Alan Greenspan, but nothing unusual.

Former Richmond Fed president Jeffrey Lacker, a frequent dissenting "hawk," recalled how Yellen was very diligent about calling before FOMC meetings. "Her assistant would call on Wednesday and set up a time for Thursday or Friday to talk," he said. "She had a point of view but tried hard to portray what she was advocating as being consistent with my principles and my perspective on monetary policy. I got the sense she did that with everyone she talked to. You had to kind of unpack what she said a little bit, but she was not deceptive at all. I mean, she was very candid about her point of view, and they were fruitful, substantive exchanges. I found myself having to prepare a day earlier for the task of hashing out a policy view. So, by Friday afternoon I started to feel as if I had to have thought it through a little more and spent more time on it before Janet called because she was going to grill me about where I was coming from. That was good for the committee and our deliberations, but I don't remember instances of having my mind changed by her specifically."

Former governor Daniel Tarullo remembered Bernanke would set the tone for a meeting by coming up with an idea that would form the basis of a discussion. "When Janet was chair, she would provide a direction for thought, but the elaboration of the policy tended to be a little bit more of a collective effort," he said. "Reserve Bank presidents and governors were not going to take easily to a passive role where they were told, 'Here's where we're headed unless you have the strongest of objections.'"

"Janet is very comfortable talking with people, and she does it very well," Tarullo continued. "She doesn't just sit there saying, 'Well, what do you want to do?' She would have a dialogue when someone had an inclination to say, 'Well, wait, what about this? The unemployment rate has been going down, but the number of people who are still not back in the labor force suggests something else.' She would engage them. So, I think people on the board felt that they really had an impact on the formulation of policy, but once she knew where she wanted to go, she did lead the committee. It wasn't like she was just waiting for a consensus to emerge. I couldn't imagine her delaying something or letting herself get knocked off center of what she thought was the right thing to do. As a result, there was an awful lot of good will towards her on the FOMC."

Powell was impressed with how Yellen used her intelligence and exhaustive research to find a way forward on her own. And once she settled on a position, she would defend it strongly—unlike Powell, who, as chair would test his conclusion by sounding out colleagues for their opinions.

Yellen also earned the good will of the professional staff, because she involved them more in the decision-making process and challenged them to perform at a high level. "She was more outgoing by nature than Ben and had more regular meetings with division directors," recalled a current senior staffer. "She knew the consumer affairs side of the Fed better than Ben and had kept up with the noneconomic divisions because she had overseen some of them either as a governor or as vice chair. That meant a lot to them because at the Fed, if you're not in the economics divisions—research and statistics, international, monetary affairs, and financial stability—you sometimes feel a little bit like an afterthought.

That was not the case when Janet was chair. She had invested a lot of time in some of those other divisions because she had played an oversight role for their divisions, and she kept that up as chair."

Yellen's obsessive attention to preparation, organization, and detail surfaced in other ways. One aide remembered that when they were going on a trip, Yellen suggested they arrive at National Airport three hours early and eat lunch there. "That's why she never missed a flight," the aide said. "I can't say that about a lot of other important people I worked with. She is the single most prepared person I have ever known. She is remarkable in the amount of time, attention, and effort she puts into making sure that meetings are productive because she has read the materials ahead of time and comes up with questions ahead of time. She's just very responsible in the way she approaches all of this. It's really remarkable."

Yellen often wrote a good chunk of her speeches. She had help from a professional speechwriter and an entire research division, but she would rewrite her speeches to make them more accessible to audiences that weren't filled with trained economists. "She takes her speeches very seriously," said the aide. "She would substantially rewrite the drafts she got from the speechwriter. She started working on them—this will not surprise you—very early, six weeks ahead of an event, and in some cases even longer because she recognized this was a medium that she felt comfortable with. She put herself under a lot of stress working on those speeches, but I think she recognized that this is an important way to communicate. And she had very high standards for how she wanted to do that. So, the speeches were stressful, but they showed me the value she placed on the written word and the importance of expressing herself really clearly and carefully."

A former senior Fed official and longtime friend noted that Yellen's obsession with organization sometimes caused her angst when another Fed official or staffer raised an issue at the last minute that disrupted her carefully laid plans. "The only time I've seen her in a bad situation is where everything has already been sort of determined. And then someone lobs in something at the end that upsets the apple cart," the official said. "In those situations, her frustration would show because she'd sort of set this up pretty carefully. And then all of a sudden, it's not quite going as smoothly as she had expected."

One such example was a last-minute challenge to her carefully formulated plan to begin reducing the Fed's enormous cache of bonds it had purchased for years to prop up the economy. The new proposal proved to be more workable. Despite the personal discomfort, she went along with the change after recognizing it was a sounder plan. "That showed she can be flexible when faced with something that is better," the official recounted. "I was really impressed by that because it went against her tendency to be very careful, thorough, and prudent. But this proposal *was* prudent. It was just that the best idea came up late in the game."

"She doesn't do anything half-assed," the official continued. "I mean, everything is done to an extremely high degree of competency and a high degree of thoroughness, which I think is very good for someone who's the head of the central bank because messing up has huge consequences."

Based on the economic record during her four-year stewardship—a growing economy with stable inflation and falling unemployment—it was difficult to accuse Yellen of messing up. She had not helped every person looking for work find a job or closed the yawning inequality gap, but her father's struggling patients would surely salute her efforts to make the lives of their descendants better than before she took the helm of the central bank.

❖ ❖ ❖

As the economy continued to expand in the wake of the Great Recession, Yellen knew that the Fed would have to start raising interest rates on her watch. The fed funds rate had been zero since the end of 2008, and she was keenly aware that inflation and asset bubbles would eventually build up and menace the progress already made if not restrained. The problem was that economic forecasts were unreliable in projecting just how soon and quickly inflation would pick up, and Yellen did not want to raise rates prematurely at the expense of slower job growth. It was a delicate dance. She always leaned toward tolerating a little more inflation to produce a little less unemployment. But as Fed chair, she certainly didn't want to rattle markets by appearing too tolerant of inflation.

Yellen calculated that she would have to pull the trigger sometime in the next year or two. To ensure markets had plenty of advance notice and wouldn't throw another tantrum, she meticulously laid the groundwork at FOMC meetings for raising interest rates twenty months before they were actually boosted—a triggering date she referred to as "normalization" and "liftoff." Having caused a brief market swoon with her "around six months" slip of the tongue at her March news conference, Yellen was determined to avoid a repeat. It was on her mind at every FOMC meeting.

When the committee met April 29–30, 2014, Yellen told the group, "If the recovery proceeds broadly as we expect, we will likely begin to raise interest rates sometime next year. I believe it is important that we communicate our normalization plans to the public well before that time." She repeated that goal at the next gathering on June 17–18: "As we resume our discussion today, let me remind everyone that we have set a goal of clearly articulating to the public our normalization strategy and framework at the time of the September meeting. This is an important deadline because I consider it essential for us to define concretely and communicate our plans well before the first steps in normalizing policy become appropriate." Meanwhile, the FOMC continued to taper its bond purchases with the goal of ending them later in the year.

At the July 29–30 meeting, Yellen continued making the point, "I believe we are on track to roll out our revised policy normalization principles and strategy in September." But she also noted uncertainty about the timing of a rate increase. Returning to her cross-country road trip metaphor, Yellen quipped, "The question is whether, on our journey to Manhattan [from San Francisco], we're now in Cleveland or the outskirts of Weehawken [New Jersey]." As the group laughed, she added: "On balance, labor market conditions do seem to be improving somewhat more rapidly than I had expected, and, if faster-than-expected progress continues, I think this does point to an earlier liftoff. . . . I think March is very much on the table as a time when we might begin to tighten."

At the September 16–17 meeting, the FOMC announced plans to end its bond purchases at its late October meeting. It also issued a "Policy Normalization Principles and Plans" document—a detailed road map for markets to determine when the Fed would begin to raise rates well in advance of actual "liftoff."

The FOMC followed through with the termination of the bond purchase program at the October 28–29 meeting. Yellen also delivered a rare scolding to members of the committee for loose lips. Many were talking to reporters about their views of the economy and when the Fed might finally raise interest rates, and they did not all agree, which planted uncertainty in the markets. "While we want to be transparent, I don't think our communications are necessarily clarified by airing a set of conflicting assessments of the policy implications of the latest news," she warned. "Rather, it may just confuse the markets by introducing noise, and for this reason, I would encourage you to avoid publicly drawing firm policy conclusions about the meaning of the latest data before we've had a chance to talk about them here."

At their final meeting in 2014, on December 16–17, Yellen described the economic outlook using her favorite imagery. "If you will forgive me for returning yet again to my cross-country road trip analogy . . . we're in the process of crossing the Allegheny Mountains. There remains some way to go to the Weehawken end of the Lincoln Tunnel, but I'm feeling a lot more hopeful now that we'll make it all the way to Manhattan without hitting any major delay."

Persistently low inflation—below the Fed's 2 percent target—weighed on Yellen, however, and at the January 27–28, 2015, meeting, she said "liftoff" would likely be postponed until June at the earliest. By the March 17–18 meeting, Yellen—wearing a dark green outfit in honor of St. Patrick's Day—felt more confident the Fed could boost rates without waiting for inflation to approach the Fed's target, citing a lag of many months between a rate increase and the impact on the economy. "I consider this a strong argument for an initial tightening with inflation still at low levels, and it's one that I plan to make," she told the group.

At the April 28–29 meeting, John Williams, Yellen's successor as San Francisco Fed president, offered her a gift to help her explain to the public why the Fed was still uncertain whether liftoff would occur in June, September, or December. "So, I've been thinking a little bit outside the box here about how we can . . . get to a more data-dependent approach," he said. "Madam Chair, I have a suggestion for you. I made you a special T-shirt. The message reads 'Monetary Policy Is Data Dependent.'" It was a joke that only Fed officials and staffers could appreciate.

As 2015 progressed, Yellen continued to vacillate about the timing of "liftoff." In July, she said a rate hike in September was still possible. She also noted that the first increase after an extraordinary period of zero rates was mostly symbolic, because the important question for markets was how much and how quickly the Fed would raise rates after that initial increase. She also warned the committee members once again "to refrain from speculating about the time of liftoff."

After delaying "liftoff" at the next few meetings, the FOMC gathered on December 15–16 to do what Yellen had prepared for so meticulously since the start of her tenure as chair. At a time when unemployment had fallen to 5 percent and inflation had crept back up to 2 percent, the committee finally pulled the trigger by announcing a quarter-point boost in the fed funds rate and plans for subsequent but gradual increases as economic conditions warranted. Financial markets, having long expected the move, digested it calmly.

At a news conference to explain the move, Yellen told the assembled reporters: "This action marks the end of an extraordinary seven-year period during which the federal funds rate was held near zero" to support the recovery from what was the worst financial crisis and recession since the Great Depression until the COVID-19 pandemic struck. "It also recognizes the considerable progress that has been made toward restoring jobs, raising incomes, and easing the economic hardship of millions of Americans," she continued. "And it reflects the Committee's confidence that the economy will continue to strengthen. The economic recovery has clearly come a long way, although it is not yet complete."

Indeed, Yellen had much progress to trumpet. The economy had added ten million jobs since 2010, with all racial and ethnic groups showing gains, the Bureau of Labor Statistics reported. Particularly noteworthy was that from 2014 to 2015, median household income adjusted for inflation had increased by $2,800, or 5.2 percent, the largest annual increase on record, according to a White House fact sheet. The poorest 10 percent of households had the biggest gain: nearly 8 percent. It was small progress toward economic equality but still something to cheer.

What Yellen did not realize at the time was that the FOMC would not raise rates again for another year because of an unexpected global economic slowdown. Throughout most of 2016, she counseled her colleagues against moving too quickly to raise interest rates again. She noted that the economy was not in danger of overheating, inflation remained below the Fed's 2 percent target, and there was a social benefit to encouraging employment gains. "A tighter labor market could potentially draw yet more people back into the labor force on a sustained basis," she said at an April 26, 2016, FOMC meeting. "Such a development would be of great benefit to the nation, and we need to be wary of inadvertently blocking it by tightening monetary policy too quickly or too much." She underscored that point at subsequent meetings, saying the Fed should continue to let the economy run a little "hot" to encourage job growth amid scant signs of inflation hitting the Fed's 2 percent goal.

Then, at an FOMC meeting on November 1, a week before the 2016 presidential election, she told the committee that she thought a rate increase would be justified at the next meeting, December 13–14, because of continued progress toward full employment that year, which saw more than two million new jobs created. That's just what the FOMC did. From December 2016 through December 2017, the Fed raised rates a full percentage point in four quarter-point increments. It was a year of decent, if not spectacular growth, as unemployment fell to 4.1 percent by the end of 2017—the lowest level in seventeen years.

On balance, Yellen had guided the economy skillfully, but it was not a time to celebrate. Donald Trump had been elected president, a surprise victory that caused her considerable angst, given his volatile personality, embrace of policies she opposed, and the racist and xenophobic sentiments he had unleashed. On a personal level, she also worried about whether he would give her another four years as Fed chair after her current term expired in February 2018.

As she looked back at how she managed monetary policy as head of the central bank, Yellen took great satisfaction in how well the economy performed, although she would have waited longer to boost interest rates had she known that inflation remained stubbornly below the Fed's 2 percent target. "I initially thought that the forces holding inflation below 2 percent were largely transitory and that inflation was going to quickly pick up to 2 percent. That turned out not to be true," she said. "There were deeper disinflationary forces, I think, than I at first understood. If somebody had told me when I started raising rates that we'd get to 3.5 percent unemployment and inflation would still be running under 2, I would have been really surprised. And if I had known that, I probably would have waited longer to raise rates. But look, I honestly think what I did was very gentle, and it did not stop the economy from recovering and full employment from being achieved."

Yellen recalled being pressured by Fed hawks to raise rates sooner and by doves who thought she acted prematurely. Her hawkish vice chair, Stanley Fischer, all but threw a fit in the summer of 2015 when she resisted a rate hike. Several reserve bank presidents also favored boosting rates then. "I knew there were a lot of people in the FOMC who were not happy with where things were, and they thought we were really behind the curve," she added.

On the other side, Governor Daniel Tarullo thought "liftoff" in December 2015 was too soon but reluctantly went along rather than cast a dissenting vote. "I knew it wasn't going to be an irreversible mistake or an error of history. This was going to be a difference in judgment about the timing," explained Tarullo. "I didn't want to make her job any harder. We got pretty close during that period, and on a personal level I didn't want the difficulties of her job to be increased by a policy difference with a friend."

"I thought I was taking a responsible middle course," Yellen said. "We continued to allow the economy to recover. Unemployment continued to move down." She described her policy as an experiment to see how much unemployment could fall without generating inflation. It showed the economy could produce very low unemployment and inflation at the same time. "It's not like we had a recession or any bad thing happened," Yellen said. "So yeah, there were criticisms on both sides. That's probably a good place to be." Some Republicans complained that Yellen was being partisan by delaying three expected rate increases in 2016 to help Hillary Clinton win the presidential election that year. Yellen countered that the Fed postponed further rate increases in 2016 because the economy had weakened significantly as a result of a sudden devaluation of China's currency in early 2016 that caused a lot of market volatility around the world and a more pessimistic global outlook. "We had a scary period in which it looked like the economy might stall out. Suddenly people thought, 'Well, this is way weaker than we expected,' and they no longer thought it was appropriate to raise rates. So, we held off until the economy was getting back on track. Once that happened, we decided we should get back on the course of gradually raising rates, which we did."

Yellen also planned how the Fed would reduce the trillions of dollars of bonds it had accumulated over the years to boost the economy, an issue of most concern to right-wing Republicans in Congress. "Some members of Congress had said, 'You're never going to be able to get rid of the assets you've put on your balance sheet. It's going to be financial market Armageddon when you try.' We could have just hung on to those assets. It wasn't utterly obligatory to begin to run down our balance sheet," she said. "But I actually thought it was important to show that we could do that in order to be able to use asset purchases as a tool in future episodes. So, we carefully laid the groundwork for gradually running down the balance sheet in the fall of 2017." That was the plan she was forced to alter at the last minute when presented with a better way of doing it.

Bernanke gave Yellen high marks for achieving a difficult task: getting the Fed away from zero interest rates. "She was cautious, well-prepared, and did a good job of running the committee," he said. "I think if you ask progressives today, they'll criticize her for being too hawkish in raising rates, but, of course, she moved much more slowly than was widely expected when she became chair. So early on, she was just following the historic Fed wisdom that, following a period of monetary ease, you need to begin a process of slowly, carefully normalizing rates while making sure inflation stays close to your target."

When the global slowdown occurred in 2016, Bernanke continued, Yellen adopted "a more dovish perspective" and raised concerns that the economy might be weaker than expected, with inflation remaining surprisingly low. That meant a slower pace of rate increases. "Basically, I think there was a shift under her leadership from a strategy of normalization and preemptive strikes against inflation towards a more cautious strategy that took into account the risks and possibility that the economy had shifted into a new normal of lower unemployment, lower interest rates, and lower inflation. She did a good job and certainly got the respect of the FOMC."

Former Richmond Fed president Lacker rated Yellen's performance as one conducted by a very practical and empathetic Keynesian. "She saw monetary policy as capable of doing more to increase employment during the recovery," he said. "It was within the range of reasonable views, but she was at the more optimistic end of the spectrum, and some of us were more pessimistic. I think she wouldn't have been as optimistic if she knew what she knows now about how the recovery ultimately played out," namely that monetary policy alone was limited in its ability to lift low-skilled workers' wages more or stem the growing economic inequality that gnawed at her.

"The other dimension of our differences had to do with the stability of inflation," Lacker continued. "There's a lot of genuine scientific uncertainty about how stable the expectations of businesses and consumers are about inflation, how well anchored those expectations are. For some of us, that incredibly costly experience of getting inflation down in the 1970s and 80s just made us very sensitive to the risks involved in losing control of inflation. And the more dovish Keynesian wing of the committee was more confident that inflation would remain stable even in the face of further monetary stimulus."

Who was right? Lacker conceded that Yellen's view that inflation and inflation expectations would remain in check even when unemployment was low won the day: "I think those of us who were worried in hindsight now can see we were more worried than we needed to be. Her position on the stability of inflation and inflation expectations was borne out."

Former New York Fed president Dudley attributed Yellen's impressive track record in conducting monetary policy to a creative, insightful, and open-minded approach that is the true mark of a Keynesian. "She's not an ideologue. She updates her framework on how the world works based on the incoming information," said Dudley. "It's like the famous line attributed to John Maynard Keynes: 'When the facts change, I change my mind. What do you do, sir?' That's how she performs."

Jay Powell marveled at her performance as chair: "At the end of Janet's term, you could look back and say she made it look easy. There were no major crack-ups because of a lot of very deft footwork; committee management; and thoughtful, insightful decision-making on her part."

# - 11 -

# EMBRACING EMPATHY ECONOMICS

*"The way she changed the institution and pursued the*
*Fed's goals . . . has changed the economics profession"*

RUNNING THE NATION'S CENTRAL BANK INVOLVES MORE THAN setting monetary policy to guide the economy, and Janet Yellen moved quickly to make her mark in other ways. One was to show that the Fed represented the interests of all Americans, not just the financial community. That is why she made a point of giving her first out-of-town speech as chair at the Fed's annual community reinvestment conference in Chicago in March 2014, to discuss ways to help disadvantaged neighborhoods still struggling with high unemployment and homelessness in the wake of the housing crisis. At the time, she had sparked considerable controversy by singling out the plight of two jobless people who subsequently were revealed to be ex-felons. But that experience only strengthened Yellen's resolve to use the Fed's powers to help those in need, including those who spent time in prison and encountered the most trouble finding steady work.

Yellen's empathy with victims of the lingering effects of the Great Recession did not play well with congressional Republicans, who controlled the House when she became chair. They ran the Senate as well after the 2014 midterm elections, which gave the GOP its largest majority in the House of Representatives since the 1928 elections. The Republicans were highly critical of the Fed's easy-money policies, arguing—incorrectly as it turned out—that the central bank would produce a new surge of crippling inflation. To rein in the Fed's independence, several GOP-sponsored bills sought to tie Yellen's hands from conducting monetary policy as she and her colleagues saw fit. The Republicans justified their efforts by accusing Yellen of sacrificing the Fed's cherished independence by becoming too cozy with Democrats in Congress and the Obama administration.

During an acrimonious hearing of the House Financial Services Committee on February 25, 2015, Republicans said they were able to use a *Wall Street Journal* online tool to review Yellen's calendar while chair of the Fed in 2014 and found that of twenty-three meetings or phone calls with members of Congress, sixteen were with Democrats and seven with Republicans. That was enough ammunition for Republicans on the committee to accuse Yellen of running a presumably independent central bank guided by partisan interests. Republican Scott Garrett of New Jersey noted that she also met with Obama the day before the 2014 midterm elections and with liberal advocacy groups on a frequent basis. "So having Congress oversee your agency more thoroughly will not make it more political than it already is," Garrett said.

Republicans were also upset with the Fed's zealous regulation of financial institutions following passage of the Dodd-Frank legislation in 2010. In particular, they vehemently opposed the Consumer Financial Protection Bureau (CFPB), an independent arm of the Fed that advocates on behalf of consumers to promote fairness and transparency for mortgages, credit cards, and other consumer financial products and services.

Yellen pushed back, insisting she met with lawmakers across the political spectrum and never discussed interest rate plans in meetings with Obama administration officials. She also thought the use of her calendar was misleading and a cheap shot. She was keenly aware that her calendar was public information and, as a result, was always careful to try to balance meetings with Democrats and Republicans. The problem was that when her staff had tried to set up appointments with members of Congress, Democrats were more likely to agree than Republicans, who demurred, saying they weren't interested. That was the reason the meetings appeared partisan, she said, thinking back to the calendar dustup. "We always tried to be very careful about reaching out equally on both sides of the aisle, but that was an embarrassment even though it wasn't in any way intentional." A Republican appointee on the Board of Governors backed up Yellen's explanation. "She would have an open invitation out to meet with various Republicans, and they just didn't meet with her," the official said. "And then they were rude to her, which really just made my blood boil in hearing things like that. I thought it was inappropriate."

Yellen and her allies in Congress ultimately prevailed in blocking any of the Republican proposals to curb the Fed's independence from becoming law, but the rupture in relations with the GOP never healed during her tenure. After all, she was a lifelong Democrat who often advocated for the dispossessed in society. But she was hardly the first head of the Fed with a partisan background. Longtime chair Alan Greenspan was a lifelong conservative Republican who served as chair of the Council of Economic Advisers for Republican president Gerald Ford. Yet Greenspan revealed bipartisan tendencies when he endorsed Democratic president Bill Clinton's deficit-reduction package in 1993 and Republican president

George W. Bush's tax cut plan in 2001. And Ben Bernanke, though appointed by Bush, was accused of helping Obama's reelection in 2012 through the huge bond-buying program he had launched. In truth, Fed chairs have long been accused of helping or hurting presidential candidates through interest rate moves close to or during election years. It goes with the territory.

Even so, Yellen highlighted one issue that drove a number of Republicans nuts: the problem of growing inequality in America. It was not a topic Fed chairs traditionally focused on, although Greenspan and Bernanke occasionally mentioned it in speeches. Yellen gave it more prominence, given her decades of work trying to find ways to increase employment and wages of the less fortunate in society.

In November 2006, while president of the San Francisco Fed, Yellen tackled the subject in a speech entitled "Economic Inequality in the United States" to the Center for the Study of Democracy at the University of California, Irvine. She readily admitted that income inequality is not part of the Fed's "dual mandate" to foster stable prices and promote maximum employment. "Nonetheless, this has been an interest of mine for a long time," she said. Yellen then identified the main culprit for growing income gaps in the United States over the past several decades: globalization.

She explained that US exports tended to be high-end goods that required skilled labor to produce, such as aircraft or complex machinery. By contrast, imports tended to be more basic goods, such as steel, clothing, or toys, which easily could be produced by low-skilled workers overseas. Likewise, cars and trucks were designed in the United States but increasingly assembled in Mexico or overseas. The result was increased demand for US workers with higher education and training and a corresponding decline in demand for workers with only a high school diploma or less.

The trend became pronounced during the 1980s, as globalization flourished. Steel and auto workers who made good pay despite limited education and training lost their jobs as their companies moved operations to lower-cost locations or increased the use of automation. The glut of low-skilled labor was worsened by an influx of immigrants willing to take low-paying jobs. A 2019 study by the Federal Reserve Bank of St. Louis found that employment in the US auto industry fell 17 percent between 1994, when the North American Free Trade Agreement took effect, and 2018.

In a prophetic conclusion that might have been written after the Trump-provoked January 6, 2021, insurrection against Congress when it had convened to certify Joe Biden's election as president, she said, "There are signs that rising inequality is intensifying resistance to globalization, impairing social cohesion, and could, ultimately, undermine American democracy." She said the most effective ways to reduce inequality are to improve education, particularly for early childhood, and to construct a stronger social safety net. "Inequality has risen to the point that it seems to me worthwhile for the US to seriously consider taking the risk of making our economy more rewarding for more of the people."

As Yellen noted, inequality is not a task the Fed was set up to tackle, and the solutions she identified are outside the reach of monetary policy. Yet, the Fed is not powerless to address the problem, either. For one thing, it has cast a bright spotlight on inequality through the release of its Survey of Consumer Finances that it conducts every three years. The survey compiles data on the income and wealth of families from the wealthiest to the poorest, and reports the disparities, which have grown substantially. Over time, the survey has dug deeper into what's happening with Black households, Hispanics, and women, to provide a more detailed picture of inequality.

The 2019 survey found that median net wealth for a white family—the value of assets such as savings, investment, and property—was $189,100, compared with $24,100 for a Black family and $36,050 for a Hispanic family, a wide disparity that had barely budged since the prior survey in 2016. The Fed has the ability to help lower-income people at the margins by making it easier for them to obtain bank loans and other financial resources through the community development programs at the reserve banks and the Fed's Division of Consumer and Community Affairs in Washington.

Early in her tenure as chair, at a September 18, 2014, conference on how families of all income levels can build assets, Yellen noted the sobering findings of a 2013 Survey of Consumer Finances: the bottom half of families held a mere 8 percent of all household financial assets, and most lacked the savings to cover an unexpected expense of just $400.

A month later, in an October 17 speech to a conference on Economic Opportunity and Inequality hosted by the Boston Fed, Yellen went into great detail about how bad the problem had become. "The past several decades have seen the most sustained rise in inequality since the nineteenth century after more than forty years of narrowing inequality following the Great Depression," she said. "By some estimates, income and wealth inequality are near their highest levels in the past hundred years. . . . I think it is appropriate to ask whether this trend is compatible with values rooted in our nation's history, among them the high value Americans have traditionally placed on equality of opportunity."

From 1989 to 2013, Yellen explained, the average income of the top 5 percent of households adjusted for inflation grew by 38 percent, compared with less than 10 percent for the other 95 percent. As for wealth, the top 5 percent owned 63 percent of all assets, while the bottom 50 percent owned a mere 1 percent. A main reason for the disparity was stagnating wages for average workers and a steady increase in the value of stocks, predominantly held by the wealthy. Compared with the world's other developed nations, the United States was near the top in both the size of the inequality gap and the speed by which it has grown. Indeed, the gap accelerated noticeably during the COVID-19 pandemic in 2020, as low-wage workers suffered the most job losses and the wealthy benefited from stock prices jumping to new highs.

In her 2014 speech, Yellen offered four partial solutions to narrow the inequality divide: better health care, education, and social services for children; more affordable higher education; more opportunities to start a business; and increased incentives to save and leave inheritances. Much of that agenda became part of President Joe Biden's $3.5 trillion Build Back Better program unveiled in 2021—and shelved later that year—to improve the nation's social safety net.

As she evaluated her own role in combatting inequality as Fed chair, Yellen said she convinced her colleagues to wait a long time until unemployment was low before raising interest rates, and then they did so very gradually. She knew that minorities and low-wage workers were the last to benefit from an expanding economy as new jobs were created and the pool of available labor shrank. That is why she wanted to keep interest rates low and the economy growing for as long as possible without reigniting inflation. In fact, the expansion that began in 2009 and ended with the COVID-19 pandemic was the longest in US history and resulted in record low unemployment and poverty rates for Blacks and Hispanics.

A surprisingly contrary view was made by Yellen's Yale mentor and predecessor as chief White House economist, Joseph Stiglitz. In an interview for a July 13, 2021, PBS *Frontline* documentary called "Power of the Fed," Stiglitz assailed the Fed's bond-buying program under Bernanke and Yellen as "a kind of trickle-down economics" because in pushing down interest rates it sent stock prices soaring. "And so, who owns the stocks? It's the people in the top, not just the top 10 percent, but the 1 percent, the one-tenth of 1 percent," he said. "And so, it increases enormously wealth inequality. We have had increasing inequality really since the late 1970s. And this was putting that on steroids."

The accusation from a longtime friend that the Fed under her watch was contributing to income inequality drew a rare flash of anger from Yellen, who thought it was misguided and a cheap shot. "The Fed has one and only one tool and that's interest rates," she retorted. "And the most important thing is putting people back to work and making sure they have jobs. And the only way to accomplish that is by lowering interest rates." Indeed, it seemed ludicrous to Yellen for Stiglitz to suggest that raising interest rates would reduce inequality by screwing the wealthy more than the poor. Lowering rates resulted in an improved labor market "and that's what the Fed did," she said. "I wouldn't apologize for that."

Yellen acknowledged that lower interest rates also tend to increase the value of assets, such as stocks and real estate, which benefit the wealthy. But lower rates also reduce the rate of return on bonds and other savings wealthy people have. So the Fed's interest rate moves can be something of a mixed bag. Yellen thought it made no sense to raise interest rates to reduce the asset values of the rich because poor people would get screwed as well, and they couldn't afford another setback. The wiser course, she believed, was to focus policy on making life better for the disadvantaged even if that meant the wealthy benefited, too.

❖ ❖ ❖

FED CHAIRS CUSTOMARILY VISIT WALL STREET TO SPEAK ABOUT the economy or meet with financiers from around the world. But in a break from that tradition, Yellen visited an Alcoa forging plant in Cleveland on July 10, 2015, to get a close-up view of what it's like to be a blue-collar worker in the Rust Belt—a region suffering the loss of well-paying manufacturing jobs due to the ravages of global trade and automation. Senator Sherrod Brown, the Ohio Democrat who accompanied her on the visit, recalled vividly six years later how a planned forty-five-minute tour turned into an hour-and-a-half stop.

"She puts on the hard hat, puts on the yellow vest, puts on the safety glasses, and gets into the control booth of this huge, fifty-ton press that stamped out helicopter blades," he said. "She is there moving this lever, pushing that button. I'm sure she wasn't really doing that, since they don't allow untrained workers like Janet Yellen or me to do that. Every time this press came down, the building shook. It might've been the biggest press in Ohio stamping out these huge steel blades. I hate clichés but she really did look like a kid in a candy store. She was so excited about seeing these workers, what they did, the technology and what really made America prosperous over the decades."

"The Fed is still a dark stone building impenetrable from every angle, but I think she humanized it," Brown continued. "She has no arrogance. She has a humility to her that we don't see in these parts all that often. And in that sense, she made people think that the Fed can affect regular people's lives and working families in a direct way. I think she'll be looked on as a pioneer, not just because she's a woman, but because she looked at that Fed job and now Treasury a little differently from her predecessors and she understands Main Street."

Still, to the extent that Yellen gets credit for doing something about inequality as Fed chair, it is at the margins. She didn't use monetary policy to embark on a radical social experiment. In fact, she was quite cautious and pragmatic in raising interest rates during her tenure. True, she allowed the economy to run "hotter" than many economists thought possible without reigniting inflation, but she continued to do so only because inflation remained so dormant. Former Fed governor Daniel Tarullo said the Fed can narrow inequality only modestly by trying to maximize employment: "I think we saw during those last few years of Janet's time as chair a positive impact on income inequality at the bottom. It wasn't huge, but it was there. And of course, Ben deserves credit for that as well."

Using her position to highlight a major social problem plaguing the country, Yellen infuriated congressional Republicans, who already were convinced she was a Democratic activist. "They went crazy over that," recalled a Fed official who remained at the central bank after Yellen left. "They said, 'Stay in your lane. You shouldn't be talking about this.' I mean, now, I would say everybody talks about this. She's obviously right. This was an important issue in the economy, and the Fed chair was in a position to bring it to people's attention. Obviously, at the time it ruffled some feathers, but now even business leaders and Republicans talk about inequality."

"I think she was a little ahead of a lot of the public conversation on this issue. And it was a little jarring for people to hear the Fed chair talk about it," the official continued. "But she knows the economy and is looking at one of the things that's holding it back. That upset some Republicans, but it's not like she had a specific monetary policy to respond to it. She was just pointing to this as a clear issue holding back the full potential of our economy."

Yellen's friend John Williams, the San Francisco and, later, New York Fed president, explained her focus on inequality as a sign of her unrelenting concern with how economic policy affects individuals. "It's about the people. That's what always comes out in conversations with her throughout the time I've known her. So that was always an issue for her," he said. "She was interested in ways to try to help on that, maybe through our work in supervision or community development. It's not like monetary policy is the main driver of economic inequality. At the same time, one of the advantages of a strong economy without inflation pressures is that we can help those who have been disadvantaged."

Jacob "Jack" Lew, who was Treasury secretary while Yellen was Fed chair, recalled how focused she was on the issue of helping everyone earn a decent wage. "I grew up in New York and my father was the first in his family to go to college, so mine was very much a background that reflected the real people in the economy who don't always get a paycheck," said Lew, who is a lawyer by training. "As a labor economist, Janet brought policy debates right down to the basics: What does it mean for jobs? What does it mean for living wages? What does it mean for income distribution? She always thought about financial stability issues and worked on international crisis issues, but for her it wasn't principally a concern about how investors are going to fare. It was a concern of what's going to happen to the underpinning of the economy as the engine for creating jobs for people. It's a set of values that I always considered very admirable, to evaluate whether policies were ultimately the right ones to pursue. But it was never a kind of romanticism. It wasn't pretending that there were any easy solutions or easy villains and heroes. It was getting into the details of how things actually worked and going behind the numbers."

Lew, who spent a lot of time with Yellen during his tenure as Treasury secretary from 2013 to 2017, described a close and comfortable relationship as they discussed difficult economic issues that put him at a disadvantage because he is not an economist. "My background as a lawyer made some of the more technical economic analysis a challenge," he said. "But she would show a respect for looking at the macro issues from a perspective other than that of a trained economist. And having worked with dozens of macro-economists over the years, it's just not a trait that everyone has. I call it a teaching skill and a personality trait that combines a very high level of technical knowledge with respect and humility."

Urban Institute president Sarah Rosen Wartell, who worked with Yellen in the Clinton White House, credited her tenure as Fed chair with bringing about a sea change in how economists think about the economy—less emphasis on Wall Street and Corporate America and more on issues about economic opportunity, disadvantaged communities, and diversity at the Fed. Wartell said Yellen helped encourage greater representation of women and people of color among the regional bank presidents and in the kind of research the banks produce, such as a deeper look at Black unemployment and home ownership or obstacles for businesses started by women. "This makes the Fed open to a broader understanding of what to value and count in the economy," she said.

Pushing the overwhelmingly white and male Federal Reserve System to be more diverse—from the regional banks to the headquarters staff—had been a priority for Yellen. She made a pitch for more diversity in the economics profession at a conference in October 2014. At a September 2016 forum for minority bankers sponsored by the Kansas City Fed, Yellen said the Federal Reserve was committed to a diverse workforce and senior leadership team. Doing so, she explained, provides better understanding of the problems in the communities the Fed serves and a richer mix of solutions. "I hope . . . that in this room today there are individuals who one day may serve as an adviser, director, or even a reserve bank president or member of the Board of Governors," she declared.

Progress toward a more diverse Fed has been slow but noticeable. During her time as chair, Yellen had the satisfaction of seeing the first Black person installed as a regional bank president in the system's history: Raphael Bostic, who became head of the Atlanta Fed in 2017, on the strength of her recommendation. Four years later, in addition to Bostic, three of the twelve presidents were women and one was of Indian descent. President Biden's nominees to the Fed's Board of Governors in Washington in 2022, when confirmed by the Senate, would mark the most diverse seven-member Board in the central bank's history: two white women, one Black woman, one Black man, and three white men. Yellen could take satisfaction knowing she helped shape a Board that finally resembled the nation's population.

"The way she changed the institution and pursued the Fed's goals I think has changed the economics profession," said Wartell. "If we are able to mitigate, if not fully reverse, the forces that have been driving inequality and denying access to opportunity, Janet will have proven to have been a very important author of that changing economic policy and the forces that are fighting against structural as well as political barriers. I feel very lucky that we have her to think about these issues so deeply."

Yellen's focus on inequality also left an impression on her successor, Jerome Powell, who frequently cited it as a concern of the Fed. In his speech at a town hall meeting with teachers on February 6, 2019, Powell called income inequality the nation's biggest economic challenge in the coming decade because of evidence that the mobility responsible for the American Dream—the ability of people from poor families to rise to the middle class or higher—has dropped noticeably in recent decades. Powell would repeat that refrain increasingly during the COVID-19 pandemic, as the inequality gap widened in 2020.

When Yellen raised the volume on the inequality issue, she encountered a lot of pushback, recalled a colleague on the Board of Governors: "People would yell at her and say, 'This is not your business. This is not a society where we talk about inequality. We talk about equality of opportunity, not equality of outcome.' Someone said to her, 'It's all wrong and un-American.'"

Powell did not encounter a backlash when he highlighted the problem, possibly, he figured, because during his tenure, inequality changed from being something that only the left talked about to something mainstream businesspeople raised. After all, it goes to the heart of the American Dream, which is based on fairness, equal opportunity, and people's ability to move up the income ladder. Powell admired Yellen's leadership on the problem and consciously followed in her footsteps to make inequality a signature issue for his time as chair.

Powell eventually encountered pushback for following Yellen's path, in this case for letting inflation increase to a forty-year high in order to push unemployment down and ensure the labor market healed from the crushing loss of jobs triggered by the COVID-19 pandemic. "At present, the Fed is erring too much on the side of maximum employment," Michael R. Strain, an economist at the conservative-leaning American Enterprise Institute, wrote in a November 22, 2021, op-ed in the *New York Times*. "Instead, Mr. Powell must tip the scales back in favor of price stability. If he doesn't, he risks inviting a sluggish economy—or even a recession—in the coming years."

✼ ✼ ✼

WHILE YELLEN WAS ALWAYS LOATH TO CALL ATTENTION TO HER own career of breaking gender barriers, she was an enthusiastic champion of women's rights in the workforce, much as she advocated for narrowing the inequality gap. As far back as her summer internship after college graduation at the Labor Department's Women's Bureau, Yellen had studied endemic job discrimination against women, even though she never felt discriminated against personally.

Barely a month after becoming Fed chair, on March 25, 2014, Yellen acknowledged Women's History Month at a reception at the US Capitol. "It is no coincidence that America's great success in the past century came as women steadily increased their participation in every aspect of society," she began. "Starting with gaining the vote, just a few years before International Women's Day, 'The American Century,' as it's sometimes known, was also a century of progress for women."

"I think our economic success has been due in substantial part to the fuller participation and contribution of women to the economy," she said. "Their increasing participation in the workforce, particularly after 1970, was a major factor in sustaining growing family incomes. Making fuller use of the talents and efforts of women in the workplace has made us more productive and prosperous. . . . Women have made great progress in many occupations and professions, but lag in others. In my own profession, there has been a gradual increase in the share of women in economics, but women still remain underrepresented at the highest levels in academia, in government and in business. There are doubtless numerous reasons for this, and in fact economists themselves are among those engaged in trying to understand the factors that explain why more women aren't rising to higher levels. I hope we continue to seek this understanding, in my field and others where women are in the minority, because the benefits of greater participation for women, it seems to me, are clear and substantial."

Yellen gave a more thoughtful speech on women in the economy three years later, on May 5, 2017, at her alma mater, Brown University, to mark the 125th anniversary of women being admitted to the school. Pembroke College for women, which Yellen attended, did not merge with Brown College for men until 1971. This speech was a Professor Yellen lecture, filled with statistics, historical trends, insights, and even a personal story about husband George's aunt, a

Pembroke graduate who suffered discrimination because she was a woman.

The aunt, Elizabeth "Betty" Stafford Hirschfelder, class of 1923, was a gifted mathematician who embodied "both the opportunities that opened for Pembroke graduates in the decades after she left here and the limitations many women faced and the compromises she, like so many others, was forced to make," Yellen said. A Providence native, George's aunt earned her bachelor's and master's degrees at Brown in mathematics and got her PhD at the University of Wisconsin–Madison, where she taught. George recalled that she originally wanted to be an economist but switched to math because her economics professor told the all-male class except for Betty that he wouldn't let anyone smoke because a woman was present. Math classes had no such restriction.

"Betty married a fellow student and over the next decade coauthored five important papers with him and a well-regarded reference work," Yellen continued. "But, while her husband progressed from instructor to professor at Wisconsin, Betty worked as an instructor on an ad hoc basis. During World War II, while he worked for the government in Washington and New York, Betty stayed in Madison, teaching math to servicemen. When he took a job teaching in California after the war, they divorced, and it was only then that she was a given a position as assistant professor."

George's aunt, Yellen explained, was one example of why women struggled to achieve their professional goals and earned less than men, a disadvantage that had persisted for generations. Yellen then provided a detailed history of women in the labor force, including a surge in the 1970s, when many young women like her got college and advanced degrees to embark on professional careers. Their mass influx into jobs led to workplace protections such as the Pregnancy Discrimination Act of 1978 and recognition of sexual harassment in the workplace. Access to birth control increased, which allowed young women to plan children around career choices. And in 1974, women gained the right to apply for credit in their own name without a male cosigner.

By the early 1990s, Yellen continued, the labor force participation rate of prime working-age women—those between the ages of twenty-five and fifty-four—topped 74 percent, compared with 93 percent for men. Women's share of the traditional fields of teaching, nursing, social work, and clerical work declined as more women became doctors, lawyers, managers, and professors. Their entrance into these male-dominated fields helped narrow the earnings gap with men. Yet, at the time Yellen spoke, women still earned 17 percent less than men overall—10 percent less when adjusted for occupations and experience.

From that set of numbers, Yellen concluded that women continued to suffer from "outright discrimination . . . and an absence of mentors." Women are still poorly represented among corporate CEOs, as partners in top law firms, and as executives in finance. "Even in my own field of economics, women constitute only about one-third of PhD recipients, a number that has barely budged in two decades. This lack of success in climbing the professional ladder would seem to explain why the wage gap actually remains largest for those at the top of the earnings distribution."

Even then, having made such a compelling case for gender discrimination, Yellen still seemed unaware of how much of an exception she represented. Perhaps it was because she never saw her own success to be as remarkable as others saw it. In 2014, shortly after becoming Fed chair, Yellen attended a delayed fiftieth reunion with friends from her 1963 graduating class at Fort Hamilton High School in Bay Ridge. The party was hosted by Bob Levine at his home in Montclair, New Jersey. The seventeen classmates all submitted short bios on their careers that were compiled in a booklet distributed to each attendee. Yellen's submission by email from the

Fed was the shortest, a mere ten words that included a typo: "Janet is an economist, as his [*sic*] her husband and son."

"She was modest in school and she was modest in 2014," said classmate Charles Saydah, the retired newspaper journalist who helped arrange the reunion. Perhaps that modesty had been drilled into Yellen by her mother, or it resulted from the belief that promotions came to her so easily without having to raise her hand—and with a fair amount of luck—that she should not be boastful about her accomplishments.

A few years after that reunion, however, Yellen finally raised her hand for a job. She really wanted to be reappointed to a second term at the Fed. This time, she did not get the tiara.

# - 12 -

## NIGHTMARE ON PENNSYLVANIA AVENUE

*"That [speech] really did snuff out whatever
chance she had for reappointment"*

ALTHOUGH FED CHAIRS ARE SUPPOSED TO BE INDEPENDENT OF
partisan politics, Janet Yellen found herself unwillingly drawn into
the 2016 presidential campaign. Democratic nominee Hillary Clinton refrained from commenting on the Fed, as is traditional, to
insulate the central bank from political influence. However, Republican Donald Trump, who thrived on being a wrecking ball when it
came to every Washington custom and institution, tore into Yellen.

On September 12, 2016, during an interview on CNBC, Trump
accused Yellen of keeping interest rates low to boost the stock market and burnish President Obama's legacy when he left office. Then
she would raise rates and the market would swoon, he predicted.
"She's keeping them artificially low to get Obama retired," he said.
"Watch what is going to happen afterwards. It is a very serious
problem . . . and to a certain extent, I think she should be ashamed

of herself." Trump went on to say that the Fed's easy-money policies were hurting diligent savers who were "practically getting zero interest on their money." As a real estate businessman, Trump added, "I love low interest rates," but for the good of the nation, "rates should be higher."

Yellen had opened herself up for such an attack because the Fed hadn't raised rates since it nudged them up from zero to a quarter of a percent in December 2015. The markets had been expecting three more rate hikes in 2016, but Yellen delayed doing so because of an economic slowdown triggered by financial turmoil and surprisingly weak growth around the world. That gave Republicans an excuse to accuse her of trying to help elect Clinton.

Three days before the election, on November 5, 2016, Trump ran a campaign commercial that Yellen found to be chilling in its subtle anti-Semitism. As Trump spoke, the commercial flashed images of prominent Jews that included Yellen, billionaire financier George Soros, and Goldman Sachs CEO Lloyd Blankfein. Trump branded them as part of a "failed and corrupt political establishment . . . responsible for our disastrous trade deals, massive illegal immigration, and economic and foreign policies that have bled our country dry." The political establishment, he intoned soberly, "has brought about the destruction of our factories and our jobs as they flee to Mexico, China, and other countries all around the world. It's a global power structure that is responsible for the economic decisions that have robbed our working class, stripped our country of its wealth, and put that money into the pockets of a handful of large corporations and political entities. . . . The only people brave enough to vote out this corrupt establishment is you, the American people."

Yellen was stunned that Trump would stoop so low. "It's me and Blankfein and Soros and Hillary, the global elite out to steal your jobs," she recalled. "It wasn't nice," she added with understatement. When Trump pulled an upset by winning the election, a dazed Yellen was appalled.

The antipathy that Yellen and husband George Akerlof felt toward Trump was captured by high school friend Susan Stover Grosart, who remembered having dinner with the pair soon after the start of the Trump presidency. "We were talking about this new administration, and we were all horrified by a lot of what was going on already," Grosart said. "And George looked at me and said, 'They're just so greedy. And they're so mean.' And you know, during all these years that's been my thought: they are so greedy and they're so mean. Sometimes you need a Nobel laureate to get to the heart of the matter, I guess."

Yellen, of course, could not publicly reveal her true feelings about Trump so long as she was head of the Fed. During the course of 2017, she recalled meeting with him only twice. Once for fifteen to twenty minutes early in his presidency, and then in the fall, when he interviewed her about a second term running the central bank. The Fed chair doesn't meet regularly with presidents to maintain the appearance of political independence. Instead, the chair meets weekly with the top economic officials in the administration. In Yellen's case, that meant getting together with National Economic Council director Gary Cohn and Treasury secretary Steven Mnuchin.

Yellen's first meeting with Trump took place at the suggestion of Cohn, who escorted her into the Oval Office. When she met Trump, he apologized for criticizing her during the campaign, saying that's just politics, and that he knew she was a low-interest-rate person like him—except, that is, when low rates seem to help a political adversary like Obama.

Yellen avoided Trump's wrath for the rest of the year, apparently because he really didn't have much to gripe about. The economy was growing, unemployment was falling, and the stock market was rising as the Fed engineered three modest rate hikes without financial disruptions. Yellen sought during this period to keep her personal contempt for Trump in check, though it was not easy. "I think she tried to be a good policymaker and work with whoever is there," explained son Robby. "Trump, of course, is somebody who wasn't into trying to do any of that. He was breaking institutions and creating a nasty, toxic political environment. So, I think it's natural that she was not happy about that."

Despite her antipathy toward Trump, Yellen very much wanted to be appointed to a second term as chair. After all, she was getting universal praise for doing a good job, and there was a tradition of Fed chairs being nominated by presidents of both parties to serve at least two terms as a way of underscoring the political independence of the institution and rewarding successful chairs for their good work. The last Fed chair booted out early was G. William Miller in 1979. President Carter, who had selected Miller, made him Treasury secretary after eighteen months because he proved to be a disaster in trying to control inflation.

A senior Trump adviser familiar with the White House decision-making process for choosing a Fed chair in the fall of 2017 said Trump believed Yellen was very capable and had done a decent job. "He didn't have any particular quarrels with her decisions," said the adviser, who spoke anonymously in order to be candid. "She actually ended the quantitative easing that Bernanke had started and a lot of us didn't like, and she moved rates back a little bit towards normalcy. Sometimes Trump falls in love with people. And sometimes he really doesn't like people. And I would say with Janet he was more neutral."

While Trump was outwardly noncommittal about Yellen, his advisers and Senate Republicans who would have to confirm his nominee were lobbying him to choose a Republican who could be trusted to be loyal, would boost the economy in 2020—when

Trump would be up for reelection—and would relax the Fed's tight supervision of banks required under the 2010 Dodd-Frank law that financial industry lobbyists complained was stifling their activities. Of course, that was the purpose of the law: to limit the kind of reckless trading that caused the Great Recession.

Former Fed governor Daniel Tarullo said he was told by a well-connected Republican strategist at the time that Trump hadn't ruled out renominating Yellen but was being bombarded by advisers and top Republicans in the Senate to name someone who was a friend of deregulation, arguing, "We can't have Janet because she is a strong regulator."

True, Yellen had been a strong regulator her entire career, and she made that clear in a speech on August 25, 2017, at the Fed's annual summer conference in Jackson Hole, Wyoming. She hailed the strict limits on banks that were imposed by the government following the financial meltdown that had begun a decade earlier. "The evidence shows that reforms since the crisis have made the financial system substantially safer," she declared. "The speed with which our banking system returned to health provides evidence of the effectiveness of that strategy."

"Now—a decade from the onset of the crisis and nearly seven years since the passage of the Dodd-Frank Act and international agreement on the key banking reforms—a new question is being asked: Have reforms gone too far, resulting in a financial system that is too burdened to support prudent risk-taking and economic growth?" Yellen asked. The financial industry surely would have responded with a resounding "Yes!" But she stood her ground and said, "Any adjustments to the regulatory framework should be modest."

When Tarullo, who oversaw the Fed's regulation of banks, listened to her speech, he thought, "There goes her reappointment."

He explained why he came to that conclusion: "Talk about a profile in courage. This is August 2017, when most people were thinking, 'Oh boy, it doesn't seem that likely that Trump will reappoint her,' yet it was still thought to be a genuine possibility. She goes to Jackson Hole, where she could have talked about monetary policy in a way that the administration would have loved because she was still being accommodating and all of that. And what did she give? It was that speech on regulatory policy and the importance of what we had done post–global financial crisis."

"That speech was basically saying, 'President Trump, I'd be happy to have you reappoint me and I will do the best I can with your economy, but I'm not going to change my views on what I think is really important in terms of having a robust financial regulatory system,'" Tarullo continued. "This is one where it would have been easy. There was nothing pushing her to address that question, but she chose to do it anyway. That's a level of integrity that even the most decent people in government don't have—to make it so clear to the public, to the president, to everybody. I already admire Janet, as you can tell. I'm enormously fond of her, but my respect and admiration just went up another quantum leap with that speech."

Andrew Olmen, a deputy director of the White House National Economic Council, attended the speech and was not pleased. He saw it as a slap at Trump's efforts to roll back Dodd-Frank. Then Fed governor Jerome Powell, sensing Olmen's displeasure, did a TV interview to say it was not intended as a shot at the administration, and that Yellen had shown flexibility about tweaking onerous regulations.

At the time, the financial industry and the Trump administration were most intent on jettisoning the "Volcker Rule," named after former Fed chair Paul Volcker. It barred banks from using their assets to trade hedge funds and private equity funds, a practice that had been at the center of the 2007 financial crash. Under intense political pressure, the Federal Deposit Insurance Corporation (FDIC) finally agreed to loosen the rule in 2020. But at the 2017 Jackson Hole conference, there was a lot of talk among Republicans about tearing up the rule altogether, a prospect that Yellen found horrifying. So did her vice chair at the time, Stanley Fischer, who gave a speech at the conference bashing the administration's financial deregulatory push.

"So that was already in the air," recalled one senior Fed official in attendance. "Then Janet gives her speech, and it was like a one-two punch. People were talking about Stan's speech, and then she comes in on the back of that. I thought the speech was fine, but it felt to the Trump people like a complete nose-thumbing to deregulation: 'We're not changing it.' I think in hindsight that really did snuff out whatever chance she had for reappointment."

Yellen also suspected at the time that she might be killing her chances to stay on at the Fed. "Some people said, 'That's the speech you give, if you don't want to be reappointed,' but I saw what was happening on regulation, and I didn't like it one bit," said Yellen, who saw Mnuchin undermining the tough rules that had been put in place to rein in risky behavior by the financial community. "I didn't want to see everything we had accomplished on the regulation front dismantled. And I, frankly, thought, 'Over my dead body.' I wasn't going to be a part of that."

✢ ✢ ✢

INSIDE THE WHITE HOUSE AFTER THE JACKSON HOLE CONFERENCE, and unknown to Yellen, a battle was brewing among Trump's top aides over who should succeed her. NEC director Gary Cohn, a former president of Goldman Sachs, wanted the job for himself, according to a Trump adviser and confidant. "He was pushing for it. It was in the newspapers, and Trump would kid him about it publicly," the adviser said. "In an interview with some media outlet while Gary sat in on the interview, POTUS [president of the United States] said something like, 'Well, I know Gary wants the job.' At first POTUS thought it was a good idea, but Cohn and POTUS never really meshed. And then they had differences over Charlottesville, as you may recall that flack."

The reference was to an August 2017 march in Charlottesville, Virginia, by white nationalists and neo-Nazis over the removal of a statue of Confederate Army general Robert E. Lee. One white supremacist rammed his car into a group of counterprotestors, killing a woman and injuring thirty-five other people. Trump, who had courted white nationalists with racist and nativist appeals, had provoked a torrent of criticism when he said of the white marchers, "You had some very bad people in that group, but you also had people that were very fine people on both sides."

Cohn was disgusted by Trump's response, and in his first public comment about the rally, he said, "Citizens standing up for equality and freedom can never be equated with white supremacists, neo-Nazis, and the KKK. I believe this administration can and must do better in consistently and unequivocally condemning these groups and do everything we can to heal the deep divisions that exist in our communities."

Trump never forgave Cohn for his public rebuke and ruled him out quickly as a candidate for Fed chair as the competition heated up. Three serious alternatives to Yellen surfaced. One was John Taylor, a Stanford University economist and former top Treasury Department official in the George W. Bush administration. He was known internationally for creating the "Taylor Rule," a mathematical formula he argued the Fed should follow faithfully to set interest rates instead of using their personal judgment. Many economists, including Ben Bernanke, have criticized the Taylor Rule for putting Fed officials in a straitjacket that prevents them from using discretion in setting interest rates during extraordinary economic periods, such as occurred over the past fifteen years. Numerous studies pointed out flaws in the Taylor Rule that could have led to bad economic outcomes had it been followed. Nonetheless, Taylor had the support among many conservative economists long critical of the Fed's easy-money policies. His White House patron was Vice President Mike Pence, who actively promoted him.

A second candidate was Kevin Warsh, a Wall Street executive who served as an economic adviser in the George W. Bush White House and later as a Fed governor from 2006 to 2011, during the depth of the financial crisis. He was just thirty-five when he was appointed to the Fed, the youngest governor in the central bank's history. His chief backer was Lawrence Kudlow, an outside economic adviser to Trump who had gained celebrity as a host on CNBC shows and as a frequent guest on Fox News. Although he never earned an economics degree, Kudlow served as a financial adviser on Wall Street, became an economic adviser in the Reagan administration, and replaced Cohn as director of Trump's National Economic Council in 2018.

The third candidate was Fed governor Powell, who was being pushed strongly by Treasury secretary Steven Mnuchin. Trump, a superficial narcissist who judged people by appearance and personality more than policies and qualifications, found Taylor too rigid and old—he was seventy at the time. Warsh, who was forty-seven at the time, had the opposite problem, according to a senior White House official. "When Kevin walked in, POTUS said, 'God, you're so good looking. Besides, you're so young.' He didn't look the part of a central banker. It's classic Trump."

Powell was just right for the role. He was sixty-four at the time, classically handsome with a thick head of gray hair and close to six feet tall. "He liked Powell. He thought he looked like a central banker," the adviser said.

Yellen, of course, had everything going against her in the eyes of the misogynist Trump: a seventy-year-old woman who lacked glamour and was barely five feet tall with shoes on. "He would call his billionaire friends and ask, 'Does she look like a central banker to you? Is she too short? Does she lack gravitas?'" said a Fed official who was told about the calls. "I mean, this was so gross. What an embarrassment." Trump never admitted it in public, but word got around that a major reason he had refused to renominate her was that he thought she was too short.

Though he disqualified her on physical attributes and was under pressure to replace her with a Republican friendly to deregulation, Trump actually had a soft spot for Yellen. Her dovish views were in line with his own, and he could not deny that the economy had done very well under her leadership. So, he refused to rule her out initially, even though all of his economic and political advisers were telling him that he should choose his own person going into a reelection campaign in 2020.

Meanwhile, Powell grew nervous by the end of August that Yellen wasn't going to be reappointed. Trump hadn't even interviewed her as news stories carried leaks that described John Taylor and Kevin Warsh as leading candidates. Powell did not want to compete with Yellen for the job, but he was ambitious and wanted to move up in the Fed hierarchy. In 2016, he assumed, like many people, that Hillary Clinton would win the presidential election, and he would have a shot at becoming vice chair of the Fed overseeing bank supervision. He thought that was a possibility even after Trump was elected.

Now, Mnuchin was prodding him to be a candidate for the top job, and Powell pushed back, arguing that Yellen should be reappointed. He said there is a long tradition of presidents from both parties backing effective chairs, and Yellen surely had an impressive track record. But it became clear to him that the Jackson Hole speech had killed her chance at another term. Mnuchin saw it as an affront and a message that "I'm not willing to work with you." So, Powell agreed to seek the job for himself. He had good relationships with the other two candidates but thought Warsh was unqualified and Taylor too rigid. By contrast, Powell figured, he had the experience, temperament, and flexibility to continue leading the Fed along the successful path Yellen had cleared. As a close Yellen ally, he was not a big advocate of deregulation.

Powell's interview with Trump in late September 2017 went smoothly. He told Trump that he had worked closely with Yellen at the Fed for five years, praised her for doing a great job, and vowed to continue her policies. He walked out of the White House thinking the interview couldn't have gone any better.

Trump also interviewed Warsh in late September and then met with Taylor in early October. He had not publicly ruled out reappointing Yellen and finally met with her on October 19. Despite her loathing of Trump, she very much wanted to be reappointed to the Fed and prepared diligently for the meeting.

Yellen recalled that Trump had previously met with a foreign minister from a developing nation, possibly Indonesia, which was growing rapidly at the time, and Trump asked her how rapidly the US economy could grow. This was an obsession with Trump, who kept insisting that the United States could grow 4, 5, or 6 percent a year. It was the rationale for his huge tax cut in 2017, but it failed to supercharge the economy. In reality, growth was limited to 2 to 3 percent at the time because the rate of population and productivity growth—the two key drivers of an economic expansion—were sluggish.

Nevertheless, Trump pressed Yellen to explain why the economy couldn't grow more rapidly like in developing countries. She explained that these countries were starting from a very low level of income and had faster growing populations. By contrast, the United States was experiencing very slow growth in the labor force, so it wasn't possible to grow at the same rate as many developing countries. She talked about the various factors that made it extremely unlikely that the United States could grow that fast. But Trump wanted to argue that his massive tax-cut plan was going to supercharge the economy like nothing that had been witnessed before.

When the conversation turned to how she ran the Fed and how the FOMC worked, Yellen used an analogy that she hoped the former real estate developer could relate to: "I explained to him that the FOMC was a committee. It's not a dictatorship where the chair calls the shots. We got into this because he asked me to offer my view of the other candidates. He said, 'I'm considering X, Y, and Z. Can you offer your views on those people?' I said an important quality to consider is the ability to run a committee and forge a consensus. To be successful, you have to be able to work with others and find a path they all can follow.

"I explained to him that to manage it, you have to be the kind of person who could get a group of people to agree on what color to paint a room when they have all sorts of ideas. You need to find a consensus by seeking a middle ground. So, I told him that this one thinks pink is the most beautiful color and that's the way it should be. The next one thinks turquoise is perfect. And you listen to all of these ideas and say, 'Yeah, I can see how you could think that's an interesting choice and it could be excellent.' When you come to the end, you say something like, 'Well, you know, I've listened to all of your ideas, and I want to suggest that we go with off-white.'"

Yellen, who thought Trump liked that story, recalled being very circumspect during the meeting. She did not want to be too candid in her assessment of the other candidates because she assumed her comments would be leaked into the public domain. After she spoke, Yellen remembered one thing Trump said in response that struck her as ludicrous. He stressed that he was a low-interest guy, which made him a Fed dove like her. To any Fed official, that's a silly thing to say, since a serious policymaker favors low rates only when appropriate, given the state of the economy, not as an unwavering rule. It was an offensive thing to say to Yellen as if she were as simpleminded as Trump when it came to monetary policy. But she kept her mouth shut.

One Trump adviser said Trump thought later that the interview was pleasant and constructive. "He wasn't bowled over, but he wasn't bowled under either," the adviser said. But another official in the room recalled Trump being very impressed with Yellen during the interview—although not enough to reappoint her. Yellen had also concluded that Trump had no intention of reappointing her, but had only interviewed her as a courtesy. She was convinced that he was on the path to appoint somebody else.

She was right about that. Two weeks after her interview, word leaked from the White House that Trump would name Powell to replace her. Trump made it official with a Rose Garden announcement on November 2. "He's strong, he's committed, he's smart," Trump said, as Powell stood at his side. "I am confident that with Jay as a wise steward of the Federal Reserve, it will have the leadership it needs in the years to come." Trump added a few words of praise for the departing Fed chair—"Janet Yellen, a wonderful woman who's done a terrific job"—but he never explained why he had decided to dump her. In words that could have been uttered by Yellen, Powell said, "At the Federal Reserve we understand that monetary policy decisions matter for American families and communities. I strongly share that sense of mission. I'm committed to making decisions with an objectivity based on the best available evidence and the long-standing tradition of monetary policy independence."

Although he thought Yellen deserved to be reappointed, as had all chairs who did a good job, Powell felt his conscience was clear in replacing her because he wasn't competing against her. When it became clear to him that Trump wouldn't keep Yellen as chair, he was willing to pursue the post, aided by Mnuchin's strong backing, particularly because he thought the other two candidates—Kevin Warsh and John Taylor—would be bad choices to lead the Fed.

Ironically, Powell's relationship with Trump peaked the day he was named, and it quickly headed south, while Trump seemed to go out of his way to praise Yellen during her final months as chair before her departure in February 2018.

Trump had called Yellen to deliver the news that he was going to choose Powell as her successor. It was a weird call, she recounted to friends. He sounded incoherent and apologetic for not renominating her. He promised to put her on prestigious commissions as a consolation prize, which struck her as a stupid thing to say for someone who had just denied her the reward she had earned for doing a good job running the Fed. Then he called Yellen again on the eve of the ceremony announcing Powell's appointment. It was another bizarre conversation, as he went on about what a good job she had done and how much he respected her.

And it didn't take Trump long to regret not reappointing Yellen and for Yellen to realize that running the Fed while this idiot was president would be a painful ordeal. The rupture with Powell was triggered by a series of rate increases the new Fed chair engineered during 2018, boosting the federal funds rate from 1.5 percent when Yellen had departed to 2.5 percent by year's end. The Fed raised rates to keep inflation in check because Trump's tax cuts had temporarily boosted growth above 4 percent in the spring. But by late 2018, growth had slowed to less than 3 percent, and Trump was furious. He blamed Powell's monetary policy, not the real reason: the tariffs he had imposed earlier in the year on foreign imports that prompted retaliation from trading partners, a fall in US exports and a drop in US business confidence and investment.

Trump's predecessors going back to Bill Clinton had refrained from attacking Fed chairs in public, but Trump was never one to observe traditions. He excoriated Powell as an "enemy" of the state, said he had "no guts, no sense, no vision," and even raised the prospect of firing or demoting him—something he had no power to do except if Powell had committed a crime or ethical breach. By the summer of 2019, as the economy continued to slow, the Fed began cutting interest rates but that did not stop Trump's tantrums.

One senior White House official recalled witnessing Trump yell at Mnuchin for recommending Powell and then turn to National Economic Council director Lawrence Kudlow and tell him that from then on, Kudlow would be in charge of filling Fed vacancies, a job normally headed up by the Treasury secretary.

Powell stayed in his post and later acknowledged that the Fed had possibly gone a bit too far in raising rates in 2019. As the COVID-19 pandemic hit and sent the economy into a historic tailspin when everything shut down, he provided sound and wise leadership to guide the economy back to recovery.

Powell put up with Trump stoically and in some respects was relieved that he became the target for Trump's rants rather than Yellen, who he thought might have taken Trump's public attacks against the Fed chair more personally than he had. Though bothered at first by Trump's broadsides, Powell tuned them out over time, concluding that the right thing to do was just ignore the volatile guy in the White House; don't take the bait and respond. Powell put his head down, focused on doing what he thought was best for the nation's economy, and started to sleep well at night.

Yellen's husband explained that she felt a responsibility to remain in the Fed job even though she couldn't stand Trump and thought he was a complete dope. "She felt that she had a duty to the American people. She has a loyalty as an economist, and she has a loyalty to the Fed because she thinks it's a very good institution," Akerlof explained. "The reason Trump couldn't reappoint her is because the Fed has its independence, and Janet would have maintained that independence. She wouldn't have felt that it was her duty to get Trump reelected. He knew that. Everybody advising him would have known that she had to do her duty no matter what. But at the same time, she felt that she should put on as good a show as she possibly could when she interviewed with him. And that is what she did."

When she was bypassed for reappointment, Yellen could have stayed on until 2024 to complete her fourteen-year term as a Fed governor, but that would have created an awkward relationship with Powell, so she resigned when he took over, as Fed chairs traditionally have done. Her decision was made easier by the fact that she liked him a lot personally and had trust that he would carry on her policies. He did.

Powell remained in touch with Yellen after she left the Fed based on their mutual admiration and affection. She attended his swearing-in as Fed chair, and the two embraced at the event. Powell knew it must have been painful for her to be denied a second term, but he was confident she didn't blame him as someone down the hall plotting to throw her over the side. Indeed, throughout 2021, she was his ardent supporter for a second term.

Yellen's friend William Dudley, the New York Fed president at the time, said he is convinced that the only reason she didn't get reappointed chair is because she didn't look the part. "My personal view is that Donald Trump wanted someone to look more like his version of a central bank head, and here's this woman who has gray hair, looks grandmotherly, is like five-foot-one," he said. "I'm sure she was disappointed at first. But it all worked out in the end."

❖ ❖ ❖

ALTHOUGH YELLEN'S TENURE AS FED CHAIR WAS UNUSUALLY short, it was indisputably successful based on the economic record during her four years, an assessment shared by colleagues across the political spectrum. With her own characteristic modesty, Yellen credited her strong track record to good timing. "In some ways I feel like I had a relatively easy job in comparison with Bernanke because by the time I got there, the economy was recovering," she said. "My job was to nurture the economy back to health, to gradually get monetary policy in a more normal place, and to do so without in any way threatening the recovery."

"I felt I had to withdraw some monetary policy accommodation. I wanted to do so smoothly, keeping the economy fully on track to achieve full employment—a strong labor market," she continued. "It was technically challenging in various ways. We knew we were going to have to conduct monetary policy using a new set of tools, that we would have to articulate unconventional policies that were going to become standard and would likely have to be used in the future. I basically saw it as my job to get back into a more normal stance and define a new normal of monetary policy. And I think I was pretty successful in doing that."

Princeton economist Alan Blinder, Yellen's Fed colleague in the 1990s, gave her a higher grade. "I think she was great," he exuded. "The only tempering remark is that she was there at a not terribly difficult time. If you compare her years and those in which Ben Bernanke chaired the Fed or now that Jay Powell is chairing the Fed, those were and are, in Powell's case, really tough times to manage the decision-making and more generally to manage the organization. Janet's tenure was easier in that respect, but she did it very well."

San Francisco Fed protégé John Williams, who went on to run the New York Fed, praised his mentor's pragmatism and clear communication during her time as chair. "We weren't following some kind of mathematical formula or theoretical model," he said. "We were using judgment and really trying to weigh all the different factors in coming to the policy decisions. So, it was this wonderful combination of very clear strategic thinking and conceptual thinking driven by her understanding of economics and monetary policy but implemented in a way that was consistent with that framework, not in some kind of intellectual straightjacket."

Randal Quarles, whom Trump appointed as Fed vice chair for supervision during the final months of Yellen's tenure, had been a vocal critic before joining the Board of Governors, based on his belief that she was too slow to raise interest rates and would trigger a new bout of inflation. He took it all back in a confessional at the Brookings Institution on May 26, 2021. "I think one of the biggest things that Janet Yellen did as chair . . . she sort of held back and held back in order to allow the labor market to continue to improve," said Quarles, who resigned from the Fed at the end of 2021. "I thought that was a mistake. I said so at the time from outside the Fed. And I'm very happy to admit now that she was right and I was wrong."

Even Trump's National Economic Council director, Lawrence Kudlow, acknowledged Yellen's successful record at the Fed, although he was highly critical of her support as Treasury secretary for big government spending, higher taxes, and climate change activism: "I'm very disappointed in her as Treasury secretary, but I thought she was a very decent Fed chair."

Perhaps the most objective assessment of Yellen's stewardship came in a report card by sixty-two business, financial, and academic economists surveyed by the *Wall Street Journal* in a December 12, 2017, article, as she prepared to leave office. According to the *Journal* survey, 60 percent of the economists gave her an A, 30 percent gave her a B, 8 percent rated her a C, and a mere 2 percent gave her a D. "She is not given enough credit," the *Journal* quoted Russell Price, senior economist at Ameriprise Financial. "Economic results have been nearly optimal." Bernard Baumohl, chief global economist at the Economic Outlook Group, told the *Journal*, "Her thoughtful leadership to normalize short-term rates and unwind the Fed's balance sheet has impressed investors worldwide." Constance Hunter, chief economist at KPMG, praised her as "a dedicated public servant who put her service to the country above all else" as well as "fair, even handed, intelligent and skilled; we were very lucky to have her at the helm of the Federal Reserve."

Yellen's report card was significantly better than a similar one given to her predecessor, Ben Bernanke, in January 2014, according to the *Journal* article: just 34 percent gave him an A, 45 percent gave him a B, 8 percent a C, 5 percent a D, and 8 percent gave him a failing grade.

Those who downgraded Yellen's performance said her dovish monetary policies, which helped boost the stock market to ever greater heights, would eventually haunt her—either when another asset bubble burst or inflation came roaring back. Neither happened. Four years later, the inflation prediction came true, though caused less by Fed policy than the COVID-19 pandemic that created economic chaos and Russia's invasion of Ukraine, which sent energy prices skyrocketing.

The critics were vastly outnumbered by legions of Fed watchers who applauded Yellen's tenure as she exited. "She can point to a number of accomplishments at the end of her term," the *Journal* concluded in its December article. "The lowest unemployment rate in 17 years (4.1 percent), steady if puzzlingly low inflation (2.1 percent), healthy economic growth (2.7 percent) and progress on the Fed's plan to unwind its crisis-era stimulus efforts by raising short-term interest rates and shrinking its balance sheet."

Undeniably high praise from the nation's preeminent financial publication. Even so, Yellen's mother would surely have asked: Why not all As?

As Yellen was preparing to leave, the New York Fed paid tribute on January 31, 2018, to her signature fashion trademark: "To honor Janet Yellen's extraordinary tenure & accomplishments at the Federal Reserve, her distinction as the first woman Chair, & her inimitable style, we're sharing photos of our colleagues 'popping' their collars–just like she does. #PopYourCollar #WomenInSTEM," the bank tweeted. Male and female Fed staffers around the nation posted photos of themselves with turned-up suit jacket collars to imitate her high-collar look—and to wish her a fond farewell.

On February 2, 2018, her last working day at the Fed, Yellen left a parting gift for the financial deregulators in the Trump administration and Congress who had been so intent on replacing her. In an extraordinary move, the Fed imposed a harsh penalty on Wells Fargo, the nation's third-largest bank, for having deceived customers by opening dummy accounts in their names and forcing some to take out unneeded auto insurance. The Fed barred the San Francisco–based bank from expanding its operations until it corrected its years of misconduct.

As the Fed was announcing its punishment of Wells Fargo, Yellen was packing up her personal things from her Fed office; grabbing a lunch to go and a soda from the cafeteria amid applause from staffers; and making a final walk through the boardroom, where she had participated in dozens of monetary policy decisions. It was all captured by a CBS News film crew for a feature by reporter

Rita Braver that aired on February 4. Asked if it was a bittersweet moment for her, Yellen agreed. "It *is* a bittersweet moment because I really love this job, and it has been the central focus of my life. I enjoy time with my family outside of work. But the work I do here is the core of my existence. And it's been my identity."

At one point during the interview, she ushered Braver into the Portrait Room. "What you see are portraits of all of the former Fed chairs," she explained. Reminded that they are all males, she added with a smile: "They do happen to be men, but I'm hoping to find a place for myself eventually on that wall."

# - 13 -

## A HISTORIC OFFER AND GETTING TO "YES"

*"They needed somebody who was credible
with the markets but not anathema to the left"*

AFTER NEARLY FOURTEEN YEARS AT THE FED, JANET YELLEN, AT age seventy-one, had to ponder where to spend what she assumed at the time would be her more relaxed retirement years. She wound up finding a welcoming home at the Brookings Institution in Washington, DC, one of the oldest think tanks in the United States and arguably the most influential public policy organization in the world.

Brookings was an obvious choice and a perfect perch for Yellen. Its resident scholars included both her predecessor as Fed chair, Ben Bernanke, and her predecessor as vice chair, Donald Kohn. It housed numerous other economics scholars she knew; it had a reputation for being left of center in its viewpoints; and it was a serious research institute, which certainly fit Yellen's philosophy and interests. In addition, Brookings was known as the place where future high-level government officials hung out, waiting to be called back to government service by a new Democratic administration. Yellen, however, didn't have an inkling in 2018 that she would be one of those Brookings scholars recruited for a high-level federal job.

Brookings, one of more than four hundred nonprofit public policy institutes in Washington, is located on Massachusetts Avenue in a section known as Think Tank Row because four other major research organizations are headquartered nearby. It is named after Robert S. Brookings, a wealthy businessman and philanthropist from Maryland who had a keen interest in advancing education and public policy research. In 1916, he became the inaugural chairman of the Institute for Government Research. Later he established the Institute of Economics, and in 1928 started the Brookings Graduate School of Economics and Government in partnership with Washington University in St. Louis. That same year, and four years before his death, the organizations merged into his namesake.

The Brookings Institution's mission is "to conduct in-depth research that leads to new ideas for solving problems facing society at the local, national and global level." Over the years, it has provided intellectual input that has helped shape government economic policy; wartime strategies; and the post–World War II global order, including the Marshall plan. A 2005 study found it to be the most widely cited think tank by news media and politicians.

Yellen immediately found herself in a comfortable environment with people who shared her interests. "It's the most serious public policy institute around, and I thought using it as a base for a blend of activities was something that would work out well for me," she said. "I realized that I would have speaking opportunities and probably would want to take advantage of that."

She had talked to Bernanke before joining Brookings and learned that he had an arrangement under which he would be affiliated with the think tank, get an office, and participate in the organization's activities, but would not draw a salary. That gave him the freedom to earn money on the outside. So, Yellen set up a similar deal.

She quickly discovered that as a former Fed chair, she was very much in demand to speak to financial groups around the world—and for large sums. Yellen was shocked at how much she could earn for a speech: at least $150,000 for an appearance in New York and more if she had to travel to the West Coast or overseas. It was very lucrative and an opportunity to make some big bucks while she was in demand, which she figured would not last long. So she took advantage of that opportunity.

Did she ever. According to her financial disclosure form when she was nominated to be Treasury secretary, Yellen hauled in more than $7 million in speaking fees for dozens of appearances in 2019 and 2020, nearly all of them from large financial institutions such as Citi, Goldman Sachs, City National Bank, UBS, Citadel, Barclays, and Credit Suisse. She received nearly $1 million for nine appearances at Citi and more than $800,000 from Citadel, a giant hedge fund founded in 1990 by billionaire Kenneth Griffin, a major donor to the Republican Party. Occasionally Yellen spoke before other corporate groups, such as Google and Salesforce.

Not bad for someone who had made just over $200,000 a year as head of the Fed. *Forbes* magazine estimated that the blitz of speeches, combined with hefty salaries and honoraria that Yellen and husband George Akerlof pulled down over the years, along with shrewd investing, allowed them to accumulate a net worth of $20 million in 2021. Welcome to the 1 percent.

"She was stunned by the amount of money she was making, and how remarkably easy it was for her to make it. She talked about it quite a bit," recalled a former Fed colleague. "I think she was almost embarrassed by how easy it was for all of this manna from heaven to rain down on her, you know, several hundred thousand dollars to go someplace for an hour or two."

David Wessel, the veteran *Wall Street Journal* Fed reporter and editor who was a colleague of Yellen's at Brookings, said Bernanke had the same initial reaction when he left the Fed. "But Ben looked at it with the cold calculus of an economist," Wessel said. "He figured, 'This is supply and demand, and that's what they want to pay. That's what I'm going to get.' I think Janet felt uneasy about the amount of money. She didn't like the whole game, but it didn't stop her from doing it." She did draw a line, however, on becoming a paid outside consultant to a financial firm, as Bernanke had with Citadel, the hedge fund.

On New Year's Day 2021, Yellen, now the Treasury secretary designate, had filed her financial disclosure form required of cabinet appointees, and it was made public. The revelation of her hefty speaking fees from the same banks that she might be regulating as Treasury secretary drew widespread media coverage—along with criticism about the appearance of a conflict of interest. At the time she was booking appearances, however, Yellen hadn't the slightest clue that she might be returning to government and never found anything unseemly about speaking to financial groups that she had assailed for irresponsible behavior when she was at the Fed. That's because she continued to be tough on some of them as an ex-Fed official.

When she spoke to financial groups, she refused to pander to them. For example, at an event in New Orleans with attendees who engaged in risky finance, she said bluntly that she thought the kinds of transactions they were involved with needed more regulation. But she expressed her criticism in a polite way that wasn't offensive. She never considered it unethical to speak to such groups for six-figure fees, though she occasionally had qualms. After all, some of the people she spoke to were partly responsible for the financial crisis, but she didn't consider everyone who works on Wall Street to be evil.

"I saw the financial crisis as more a matter of allowing structures to exist that are dangerous and that blew up because they weren't properly regulated—not just the result of a bunch of evil doers," she said. "There were, of course, some evil doers who were really ripping off the system. But we allowed an environment to develop in which there was inappropriate regulation. And we didn't realize how dangerous it was until it blew up. I talked a lot about why this blew up, and what we need to do to fix it."

In truth, these gatherings were less about getting a former Fed chair to reveal inside information about what the central bank might do next than to impress clients invited to meet a famous person who had once wielded so much power. Other than their insights from their time at the Fed, former officials have no access to inside information and can only speculate about the future course of monetary policy. "I think some firms think that they can get some edge on how the Fed is thinking by talking to someone who's recently left the Fed," said David Wessel. "I think for most of them, however, it's about their clients being able to take a selfie with Janet or to say, 'You know, I was at a small group dinner with Janet Yellen the other day.' It was all about that."

Yellen's son, Robby, agreed that his mother never said anything in her paid remarks that differed from what she had been saying publicly. "She was very careful about that," he said. "The Biden people scrutinized all of this very carefully before she was appointed as Treasury secretary. She was very upfront about that before they even asked her for the details."

Yellen, who never liked to write speeches, chose to do informal armchair conversations that made preparation easier and created a more intimate atmosphere. "I recognized early on that people who go to conferences wanted to understand me as a person," she explained. "What they're interested in is who is Janet Yellen? They want something light and less canned than the typical 'Fed speech' that you're standing up and reading. My talks were serious but also a bit more entertaining." After accepting a speaking appearance, Yellen would approve of a moderator, who would sit in the other armchair. Then the two would negotiate a set of questions in advance, so Yellen would not be surprised by any questions, and the moderator wouldn't ask about an unfamiliar topic. Then she would prepare by sitting down at her computer and write detailed answers to about ten questions, print them out, read the answers through a couple of times, and then throw the pages away just before the event.

"I engaged in armchair conversations that were unscripted," she said. "But writing my thoughts beforehand helped me think through my views on various topics and helped me organize what I wanted to say. I'd read over my notes, say on the train or on the plane or in the morning before I'd go to the event."

That routine helped her virtually memorize the answers and avoid being asked a question that she couldn't just answer off the top of her head. That's just not her modus operandi. Careful preparation and planning are.

Typically, the topics she signed off on involved trends in the US and global economy; monetary policy; the labor market; cryptocurrencies; and, naturally, factors affecting inequality. Yellen also made a point of talking with women's groups. Often after a big event with clients, the company executives would ask her to get together with senior women in the company to talk to them about issues pertaining to women in the workforce. She led discussions on barriers that hold women back from career advancement, strategies to increase diversity, the importance of programs in which senior women mentor younger female colleagues, and the need for company policies that allow women to balance their careers with family obligations.

While she was on the speaking circuit, Yellen was honored in 2019 by being elected as the president of the American Economic

Association (AEA) for the 2020–2021 term. She joined a distinguished list of economists who headed the organization, founded in 1885. Husband George was a past president, and Ben Bernanke was president at the time of her selection. Aware of how gender-biased the profession was, Yellen and Bernanke established some new committees to advance women in economics, and they hosted association events focusing on women.

A key responsibility of the AEA president is to give a major speech. In Yellen's case, it would be in January 2021. And like everything else she did, she began working on it eighteen months in advance, including during a vacation in the south of France with George, Robby, and brother John and his wife in the summer of 2019. The topic was about threats to financial stability; where the next financial crisis is going to come from; and the need for a new law to update Dodd-Frank, which Republicans had been chipping away since its passage in 2010. It is a speech she completed but never delivered or made public because she had been named Treasury secretary.

"I spent a year and a half working on a major presidential address," she said. "The tentative title was 'Unfinished Business: U.S. Financial Stability a Decade after Dodd-Frank.' What made it especially interesting was that as I was finishing the first draft, the pandemic struck, the financial markets blew up and the Fed had to massively intervene. The crisis pertained to all the things I was discussing in the speech. They were all things that I said could blow up and hadn't been adequately addressed."

For example, she had noted in the speech that money market funds had been overwhelmed during the housing crisis by withdrawals that put them on the verge of collapse and required them to be bailed out. The problem received a great deal of attention after the crisis passed and the Securities and Exchange Commission (SEC) took steps to guard against another run on money market funds when investors are desperate for cash. But Yellen thought the SEC's reforms were inadequate, which is why money market funds were crushed again after the COVID-19 pandemic triggered an economic shutdown in the spring of 2020. Yellen also discussed in her speech the vulnerability of hedge funds, corporate bond funds, and the Treasury securities market during the housing crisis—all problems that had not been adequately addressed by regulators in subsequent years.

"Watching what happened, I was able to revise the speech and use it as a live case study. It's very much relevant to the responsibilities I have now as head of FSOC, the Financial Stability Oversight Council [the interagency group created by Dodd-Frank]. In the speech, I was critical of FSOC's structure and argued that FSOC's powers are insufficient, but I'm currently using all of the powers that FSOC possesses to address the issues that I believe threaten US financial stability." The council spent much of 2021 determining ways to reform financial markets to prevent the kind of crises that had occurred twice in little more than a decade and required massive government bailouts each time to prevent deeper damage to the economy.

The work Yellen was putting in on her AEA speech, her busy schedule of travel for speaking engagements, and the camaraderie she enjoyed with colleagues at Brookings all helped her overcome the disappointment she had felt about being denied a second term as Fed chair. Friends said she buried herself in her work; was buoyed by all the awards admiring groups wanted to bestow upon her; and even began work on a memoir, which she scrapped after a while, even though she had hired her former Fed communications deputy, David Skidmore, to help write it. Skidmore had left the Fed for a post at Brookings, where he had helped Bernanke write his own memoir and a second book.

Despite her historic achievements and substantial contributions to economic prosperity, Yellen thought her life wasn't compelling enough to pen a memoir. She wasn't a rags-to-riches story since she was raised in relative affluence. She hadn't been scarred by some horrific event in her life, and she always was modest about her accomplishments.

"Janet was kind of ambivalent about writing a book herself," recalled Brookings colleague Wessel. "She didn't think she had anything to say. I made a feeble attempt to convince her otherwise, and I think that had she stayed at Brookings, I would've made another run at it arguing that maybe she should do a book for young women. She was very good about meeting groups of either young women who were visiting Brookings or worked there. She really took seriously the role of trying to diversify the economics profession and was aware that she was seen as a role model."

"People would stop right in the hall and talk at length," Wessel continued. "She never seemed to be in too much of a hurry to talk to people. And she did a couple of things for us that are just classic Janet. We had an event on October 3, 2019, on inflation and I asked her to make cursory remarks, but she actually gave a lecture on inflation that was so well-organized and clear. I remember [former Fed vice chair] Donald Kohn saying that's Janet at her best."

Wessel also recalled colleagues kidding Yellen about her height after news stories surfaced that one reason Trump didn't reappoint her was that she was too short. "The stories said she was five-foot-three, and there was a lot of guffawing among the women at Brookings who had worked at the Fed," he said. "All of them knew she was shorter. So, we joked about putting a piece of yarn hanging down over her door that would touch her head as she walked in and out to see how tall she really was. I asked her about it, and she said, 'Wikipedia says I'm five-three. I'm really something like that.' Well, I figured it's someone else's job to correct it." That someone actually was San Francisco Fed president Mary Daly, who had determined years earlier that Yellen didn't even make it to five-even.

Yellen was so busy traveling that she didn't spend a lot of time at Brookings, where she kept her office spare. Occasionally colleagues would see her relaxing with her feet up on the desk, and she would feel embarrassed and quickly put her feet back on the floor. Still, she was very sociable, engaging colleagues in the hallways and looking for lunch partners. "She's a really wonderful person to interact with, completely empathetic on a one-to-one level as well as in her macroeconomic policymaking," said Donald Kohn. "When she was there, she was a very lively, friendly presence, the sort of person who would stick her head in your office and say, 'What'd you think of Jay's press conference at the Fed' or 'If Trump imposes tariffs, how is that going to affect output prices?' I found her to be a good colleague. My only regret was that she wasn't there very often."

❖ ❖ ❖

IN EARLY APRIL OF 2020, WHEN IT APPEARED THAT JOE BIDEN would clinch the Democratic presidential nomination, he asked his closest aide, Ted Kaufman, to form a transition team to begin choosing prospective members of a cabinet should he defeat Donald Trump in November. Kaufman, who replaced Biden as the US senator from Delaware when his boss became vice president in 2009, soon focused on Treasury secretary as a critical post for Biden to be a successful president and advance his economic agenda.

Throughout his long career in the Senate, Biden had worried about growing income inequality and felt government policies favored the wealthy over the middle class and poor during both

Republican and Democratic administrations. As president, a time when the COVID-19 pandemic had widened the inequality gap, Biden wanted an administration that would do more to help reverse that trend. He and Kaufman believed accomplishing that depended on putting the right people in top economic jobs.

One reason they believed the less affluent usually got short shrift from past administrations was the "revolving door" syndrome in which people would eagerly seek a top federal post with the objective of leaving after a short stint for a high-paying private sector job. "If you go back and look at what happened to so many people in previous administrations, that's exactly what happened," observed a Biden adviser. "We weren't very good at figuring out who they were going to be. The people in the Obama administration who we thought would advance income equality turned out to be people who, once they got in, were primarily interested in taking care of the folks on Wall Street. They believed in helping them and then, when they left, they would go to an excellent job."

The adviser did not mention any names, but two from the Obama years that come to mind are National Economic Council director Lawrence Summers, who advised hedge funds and other financial companies both before and after working in the White House, and Treasury secretary Timothy Geithner, who was president of the New York Fed before joining the cabinet and became head of a Wall Street private equity firm after he left the Treasury post.

By the summer, Kaufman and his senior transition team, which included former NEC director Jeff Zients and former US ambassador to Romania Mark Gitenstein, considered fifty potential candidates for Treasury secretary. The others agreed with Kaufman that it would be one of the most consequential appointments Biden would make if he won the election. One by one, the candidates fell by the wayside as the team found problems with them.

Former Fed vice chair Roger Ferguson was a possibility and would be the first Black named to the Treasury post, but his work as a financial industry executive tainted him with the Lawrence Summers/Timothy Geithner problem: being too close to Wall Street. Massachusetts senator Elizabeth Warren, an unsuccessful candidate for the Democratic nomination, had lobbied for the job, but her background was law, not economics—one of Yellen's colleagues called Warren an "economic ignoramus." Plus, with control of the Senate at stake, the transition team couldn't afford having Warren replaced by a Republican chosen by GOP governor Charlie Baker. That was the same problem if they gave Treasury to Senator Bernie Sanders of Vermont, which also had a Republican governor. Besides, the self-described socialist Sanders, the runner-up for the presidential nomination, was too far left for Biden.

Fed governor Lael Brainard, a former senior Treasury Department official in the Obama administration, was highly regarded and also lobbied for the job. But some transition officials claimed she had "sharp elbows" and was not the kind of collegial team player Biden favored. She was also valued as the only remaining Democrat on the Fed Board—and the central bank's leading advocate for tighter scrutiny of the financial industry. She wound up being nominated by Biden to a promotion as Fed vice chair in November 2021. Former White House chief economist and Nobel laureate Joseph Stiglitz had the right background and economic philosophy but at seventy-seven years of age, he was presumed to be in full retirement mode.

Gitenstein said he and Kaufman felt it was important to send a powerful message about Biden's agenda through the person appointed to the job. "We both felt we knew where Biden was coming from, that he felt strongly about income inequality issues," he said. "We wanted someone who had credibility in that space, who could speak for Biden on this and help shape the policies themselves. I started pushing immediately for Janet."

Gitenstein had never met Yellen but was close friends with her older brother, John, dating back decades to when their young daughters were in daycare together. He recalled that years before, when Biden was vice president and Yellen was being considered for Fed chair, John had told him that Yellen had mentioned in a conversation that she had never met Biden. John thought it would be a good idea if they met and asked his friend if he would be willing to try to arrange a meeting, stressing that it was his idea, not Yellen's. Gitenstein agreed to reach out to the vice president's staff. "I remember talking to Biden's people, saying, 'You know, this is somebody who he would be simpatico with,'" Gitenstein said. "I don't think there was any lobbying for the Fed job, but she just wanted to have a relationship with Biden. Not that they wouldn't share values because, of course, they clearly did."

Yellen and Biden, who wound up meeting a few times when she became Fed chair, discovered they shared similar experiences growing up in the 1950s, though from very different perspectives. Biden's family went through financially hard times when his father struggled to find work after World War II. Yellen watched her own father, an affluent physician, treat patients who had lost their jobs. Neither forgot the suffering that molded their political and economic philosophies.

As the transition team went through names, Gitenstein suggested Yellen and urged Kaufman to check her out: "I said, 'You really have to look at this woman's writings and check with all of your experts in the area.' He came back to me and said, 'Wow, she's terrific.'"

Kaufman decided then that Yellen was the one. "She was perfect in so many different ways," he recalled. "Clearly she was a straight shooter. She looked at issues not through some ideological prism but in terms of what's going to benefit the people who are going to be affected by them. Time and again, when she was on the Federal Reserve, that's the way she went. So here was somebody who's going to come into the job who already demonstrated the fact that they were concerned about income inequality, concerned about being evenhanded, and concerned about making sure we benefit the folks who don't have power. She was ideal."

Kaufman knew that previous administration officials' actions didn't always live up to their beliefs. He also was keenly aware after working with Biden for nearly fifty years that the soon-to-be president had always insisted on surrounding himself with advisers whom he trusted to share his values. Biden only knew Yellen from their occasional get-togethers when he was vice president. Kaufman had never met Yellen, but fellow senior transition official Zients knew her well from her time as Fed chair and in subsequent years, so he could vouch for Kaufman's instinct that she was the right choice for Treasury.

Kaufman also recognized a common bond Biden and Yellen share: a capacity to empathize with people very different from themselves. "It's easy to have empathy for your next-door neighbor or your brother or your sister," he explained. "What makes Joe Biden so special is he has empathy for people whose whole life is totally different than his. It really shows in Janet and Joe Biden. She's turned out to be everything that I ever dreamed for. In terms of how she's handled the job; she's just right."

❖ ❖ ❖

As the transition team was meeting, Yellen was busy with her speaking engagements and work on her American Economic Association speech. She had not been involved in any way with Biden's campaign, which had lots of economic advisers. She figured it didn't need any more. Then, out of the blue, she received a call in August from Jake Sullivan, a Biden campaign official who would later be named as the president's national security adviser. On August 11, Biden had chosen California senator Kamala Harris, a rival for the presidential nomination, to be his running mate, and Sullivan asked if Yellen could participate in an economic briefing for the two candidates on August 13.

Yellen remembered the day of the briefing because it was her seventy-fourth birthday. She was planning on taking the day off and doing something pleasant and was puzzled about why she was contacted. Yellen never got to know Biden well when she was Fed chair, although she found him to be warm during their few meetings together. When she was asked to brief him, she wondered why since there were many other economists he might have known better who could do it.

It turns out it was not a tryout for Treasury secretary. The transition team had not gotten to that stage of deliberations yet. Yellen was drafted for the briefing because of her expertise in monetary policy. Still, her participation kept her in mind when the transition team began to narrow its choices for Treasury.

Other briefers on August 13 included economists Jared Bernstein and Heather Boushey, both later named as members of Biden's Council of Economic Advisers. "We were all on Zoom," Yellen said. "My piece of it was to talk about monetary policy and threats to financial stability. We were just in the aftermath of the run on the financial system during the pandemic, and I talked about what the Fed has done." She remembered that Biden must have been told what day it was because he began the briefing by wishing Yellen a happy birthday. That was the last time she had any contact with the Biden folks until after he was elected. "We had a nice meeting, maybe an hour and a half or something like that. And that was it." Then one November day soon after major news organizations had declared Joe Biden the winner of the presidential election, Yellen's phone rang. Jeff Zients, the Obama economic policy director who was now a senior member of Biden's presidential transition team was on the line. Zients and Yellen had met regularly when she was Fed chair and remained friends subsequently, getting together every so often after both left the federal government. "Would you be interested in being on the Biden team?" he asked.

Yellen was surprised by the vague offer, figuring the job he had in mind was Treasury secretary. Returning to public service was the farthest thing from her mind at that point in her life. She was seventy-four years old, had settled into a relaxed routine that included an early bedtime, and she remembered how grueling high-level jobs can be. The thought of returning to a demanding, stressful post was unappealing. When she worked in the White House as chair of President Bill Clinton's Council of Economic Advisers in the late 1990s, presidential aides would think nothing of scheduling a meeting at 10 or 11 o'clock at night. Work was all-consuming, a 24/7 operation.

Yellen told Zients that she was not at a point in her life where she was ready to take on a high-pressured job again. She was in her seventies, and her energy level and physical stamina might not be up to the requirements of a major cabinet post. As an afterthought, she confessed that partisan politics has never been her thing, as she had learned during an often difficult and disheartening two-year stint working in the White House. She felt she wasn't that adept at the political part of the job. She concluded by saying she was content with her current life and that surely there were plenty of qualified people who wanted the job.

Although Yellen never shut the door completely, she figured her negative reaction would be the end of any interest the Biden team would have in recruiting her. She was wrong. Two weeks after

Zients had first called Yellen about joining the administration, Gitenstein called his longtime friend, John Yellen, early one Sunday morning to determine whether his sister was unequivocally disinterested in being Treasury secretary. He explained that after Yellen appeared to turn down the job, the transition team went over the list of other candidates and concluded that she was the perfect person based on Biden's insistence on finding someone who would deal with economic inequality.

John Yellen told his friend that at a recent dinner with his sister, she had sounded clearly negative about joining the new Biden administration. "Gee, you know, I think it would be wonderful for you to be ambassador for some country where you didn't have to work very hard and it might be enjoyable," John told his sister. He got the idea from hearing Yellen and George joke that an ideal government job would be US ambassador to the tiny island nation of Mauritius in the Indian Ocean. Certainly, no pressure there. John Yellen thought they had been serious. They hadn't been, but now Yellen was not joking. She told her brother that she didn't want to be an ambassador, and a return to government as Treasury secretary had no appeal to her at that stage of her life. "Johnny, you have no idea how tough it is being in the White House, the enormous amount of time and stress involved in it," she explained to him. "I just don't want to do that again."

"Janet's very happy with her current life," John told a disappointed Gitenstein, who replied, "They really would like her to do it." After hanging up, John thought to himself, "I guess I ought to get in touch with Janet." He called her a few hours later and relayed his conversation with Gitenstein. "Thanks, Johnny, for telling me," she responded, and her brother assumed that Yellen had firmly ruled out taking the job.

Not so. Later that Sunday afternoon, Yellen called back. Her husband and son were on the phone with her. "Johnny, I'd like you to repeat your phone discussion with Mark as exactly as you can," she said. He related that Biden really wanted her to be his Treasury secretary and that the transition team understood she initially sounded disinterested. Gitenstein had added that a strong deputy Treasury secretary already had been identified and would be able to handle a lot of the workload to make her job more manageable. Yellen listened carefully and then said, "Maybe I really should do this. I feel an obligation."

What changed her mind? Not the power and prestige of the post. Nor the fact that she would be the first woman to occupy the job after more than two centuries of male Treasury secretaries. They seemed secondary considerations to the key issues for her: Was she right for the job, and could she make a difference? As she had done many times before when considering other jobs during her remarkable career, Yellen sat down with two distinguished economists—her husband and son—to hold a family council. They carefully weighed the pros and cons.

George and Robby said they would support her if she decided to turn down the Treasury position, but they argued that it was a very important job; that she could do a lot of good for the country; and if Biden really wanted her, she should take it. She agreed she would be in a position to help nurse the economy back from the shock caused by the COVID-19 pandemic shutdown. After all, that's why she studied economics in the first place: not to construct theoretical models for other academics, but to use economic tools to improve the economy, distribute its gains more equitably, and ensure that everyone who wants to work can find a decent job at a fair wage.

After Yellen's call, John Yellen thought he should get back in touch with Gitenstein, although his sister hadn't asked him to do so. He left a voicemail message that she seemed to have opened the door to accepting the cabinet post. Gitenstein called back fifteen minutes later. "Janet didn't agree to do it, but on the basis of our conversation, I think there's a really good chance that if she were offered the position again, she would take it," John told his friend. Gitenstein sounded excited this time. "Thank you very much, John," he replied. "I'm just about to go into a meeting where this issue will be discussed, and this call is really very important."

A few days later, Zients scheduled another call with Yellen. This time, she knew what was coming. "The president wants you to be Treasury secretary. Can we talk you into doing it?" Yellen still vacillated and said there were surely other suitable candidates. The most likely she had in mind was Fed governor Lael Brainard. "We really want you to do it," Zients persisted. Yellen had already decided her answer if convinced that Biden was intent on naming her. So, she finally said, "I'll do it."

After talking to Yellen, Zients called Gitenstein, saying "You're not going to believe this. She's changed her mind. She's interested." Convinced that he wouldn't be turned down, Biden called her and stressed how important the job was. "We would be thrilled to have you on our team," he said. During their brief conversation, they discussed one of the few policy issues on which they disagreed: Yellen favored a carbon tax as a way to combat global warming; Biden was committed to addressing climate change but opposed a carbon tax as one of the options. "I can live with that," she said.

Getting to "yes" was not an easy process for Yellen. Despite her remarkable abilities and accomplishments throughout her life, she admitted to being riddled with self-doubts about whether she had the energy and skills to handle the job. Was it the fear of falling short of the perfection her mother had demanded? Or was it the inclination of women of her generation to hold themselves back from career advancement—more than men would—if they weren't convinced that they measured up to a new job, as some studies have suggested.

After her initial conversation with Zients, Yellen consulted with a variety of colleagues in addition to her family before agreeing to take the job. Several friends noted that she never turned Zients down flatly, a savvy maneuver that allowed her to keep the opportunity open while she did some soul-searching and sought the advice of those she trusted. "She told me she turned it down but then said she didn't close the door completely," observed a former Fed colleague who did not want to be identified so as to speak more candidly. "It is interesting in how she leaves the door open just a crack, because maybe it's a more complex story than the modest, self-effacing person that we know and love."

"It's a complicated thing," the former colleague continued. "For anyone who's been in public service, if you're in it for the right reason, it's just hard to say, 'no.' If it turns out that you are the best candidate for a variety of reasons, you don't want to take yourself out of the running. And if the person making the decision is the president of the United States and he thinks you're the best person, then for the good of the country you do that."

A friend who discussed the job offer with Yellen said, "I told her she was the perfect choice. They needed somebody who was credible with the markets but not anathema to the left. If they weren't going to give it to Elizabeth Warren, they would give it to someone who they knew Warren could live with and not criticize. So, Janet made total sense from their point of view."

When Yellen sought the counsel of former Treasury secretary Jacob Lew, who worked with her closely when she was Fed chair, he reacted enthusiastically. "When she called me and told me that they asked her whether she'd be open to it, I said I wished I had thought of the idea. That's terrific," he recalled telling her. "And I went through all the reasons why I thought it was a terrific idea."

Still, Yellen expressed concerns about whether she had the political skills for the job. Lew said she had the traits needed to work well with people across the political spectrum. "What could be better than Janet's style of engagement, which is respectful," he said. "She listens, explains but doesn't argue, and teaches." He told her that she possessed great political skills in her ability to make decisions at the Fed, work with the global financial community—those both in government and in the private sector—and explain her decisions in easy-to-understand language. "Everybody knows what her values are and what her policy views are," he said. "But I think everybody also knows that she's going to listen respectfully to people who have different policy views and make the case based on data and analysis and why she thinks that what she's promoting is right. That's a great set of political skills during a very difficult partisan time."

Sounding like a salesman at times, Lew tried to assure Yellen that she could handle the Treasury Department's vast portfolio of issues because of her experience at the Fed. "There are many other things on the Treasury plate. But the international piece is a natural extension," he explained. "She and I sat next to each other for God knows how many hours at international meetings. She knows every central bank governor in the world. She knows all the finance ministers in the world. She knows many of the heads of state in the world. Most Treasury secretaries don't come in with that. And the two primary places where you work with technical financial regulatory issues are the Fed and Treasury."

Lew made the case that a Treasury secretary is not pulled into the kind of chaotic 24/7 pace she observed in the White House as chair of President Clinton's Council of Economic Advisers. Treasury has a huge staff that works around the secretary's preferred schedule, so she would not have to deal with issues erupting at 11 o'clock at night if she needed to be fresh for a meeting at 7 o'clock the next morning. If she had a strong deputy secretary and the right people in other senior positions, she would find the job manageable.

"I think from her perspective, she had to make the hard decision to come back from an interesting, intellectually stimulating life that you control, and go into a world that no matter how you try, you are not in full control," Lew said. "I don't know that I talked her into doing it, but I certainly offered the case why she was the right person."

Yellen also sounded out Lew's predecessor at Treasury, Timothy Geithner, who worked with her at the central bank when he was president of the New York Fed. He offered the same advice as Lew, telling her how much valuable experience and skill she would bring to the job and how much staff help she would have. He concluded with strong encouragement to say "yes."

Son Robby recalled family discussions after Jeff Zients's first call about whether his mother would be well-suited to the job and if someone else were better qualified. "We all felt that she had a set of qualities that did make her pretty well-suited to do this now," Robby continued. "She had developed good skills as a leader of an organization. Another thing is that she had developed good relationships with Congress, and we thought that would probably serve her well. We felt she had clear ideas about what to do regarding the financial system. And she had had good relationships with the people in the White House. We felt she had a lot of qualities that would allow her to do well in this job, and that put to bed some of our worries."

"She wasn't 100 percent certain that she was the best person for the job, which is the appropriate way to be," added George. "You shouldn't take a job if you think that there might be somebody who might do better. Then they called again after Janet's brother got involved, and they said, yes, they wanted her for the job because they thought she was the best person. Then we had to reconsider it." After weighing all the pros and cons over and over again, Yellen, her husband, and her son all agreed: she should take the job.

It also was a smart move for Biden because Yellen had broad support across the political spectrum that would ensure her Senate confirmation, former chief White House economist Laura Tyson noted. Conservatives could support her based on her sound leadership at the Fed, while progressives would like her support for greater economic equality in her role as a central banker. "She wasn't going to be viewed as a threat," Tyson said. "There would have been a number of other candidates for whom that might not be true. Janet was not politically controversial. She clearly had a great track record. She could do the job substantively and politically. She had global recognition. Everything was there for her, unlike the other candidates. The only issue was would she be willing to do it."

"My own view was that if Janet didn't take it, they should give it to Roger Ferguson. He would have been a great Treasury secretary, but Janet was clearly the ideal candidate," Tyson continued. "I know she had serious reservations about doing it. And I know that she chose to do it for all the right reasons. And I know that she's doing a really great job."

As she reflected on her decision to take the post, Yellen said what finally convinced her was the importance of working with Biden to counter a threat to American democracy. "He knows he's got limited time to try to get America back on a more reasonable course," she explained. "I believe this is somebody who is thoroughly committed to doing everything possible to address the enormous challenges that we face in the aftermath of Trump. It's no exaggeration to say the future of American democracy is at stake here. That is a challenge he really sees clearly and feels strongly about. We have to do everything we conceivably can do to make huge changes that will help people and that they'll feel in their everyday lives. When he asked me to be part of that mission, it was something I couldn't say 'no' to."

When the date for the formal announcement had been set for the end of November, Yellen realized she wasn't ready. "Oh my God, I have to get a haircut," she told Brookings colleague David Wessel. He suggested his wife's hairdresser, who had been coming to their home and cutting her hair on their back deck. "I'm sure he'd be happy to come and do yours in your backyard," Wessel offered. But Yellen declined, saying the Biden people insisted that because of COVID, she couldn't be in contact with anybody for two weeks before seeing the president-elect. "So, Robby's going to cut my hair," she said. Wessel replied, "Janet, I can assure you that Jill Biden and Joe Biden are not getting their hair cut by Hunter. I'm sure they got some professional hairdresser." But Yellen insisted, "That's what the rules are." Robby cut her hair.

On November 30, in announcing his historic choice for Treasury secretary, Biden joked that Lin-Manuel Miranda should write another musical about the first woman to head the department. Yellen described the moment with the same reaction she had to being named the first female head of the Fed: touched more by the public reaction than her personal accomplishment in shattering another glass ceiling. "It was really gratifying. I appreciated the fact that I got a lot of support and that people were excited; that made me feel good," she said. "Once I decided I was going to do this, I was totally all in on doing the job."

❖ ❖ ❖

EVEN AFTER HAVING DECIDED IN HER OWN MIND SHE WAS UP for the job, and then accepting when Biden formally offered, Yellen continued to have self-doubts about the challenges that awaited her. The economy was still in bad shape following the shutdown triggered by the coronavirus pandemic, and many federal agencies were broken and dispirited following four years of Donald Trump's self-induced chaos. Privately, she felt terrified at the thought of having a lot of responsibilities for which she had scant expertise. She worried that it would take an enormous amount of work to get up to speed to deal with what awaited her—issues that went far beyond anything she had handled at the Fed.

Adding to the huge challenge before her was concern about what shape the Treasury Department was in after four years of Trump. He regarded career employees as agents of the Deep State, which he wanted to destroy, not as the talented, experienced, and committed civil servants whom Yellen knew are responsible for keeping the government running smoothly and efficiently. He had decimated agencies such as the State Department and the EPA, and Yellen fretted that Treasury would have to be rebuilt at the same time that she would have to get up to speed on a myriad of policy issues. It was a daunting prospect going into the job.

Yellen found some solace in the fact that the transition team was very well-organized and immediately started to provide support to help her assemble a team and prepare for her Senate confirmation. She was particularly delighted when Michele Jolin, her chief of staff at the Council of Economic Advisers who had remained a good friend over the years, had volunteered as an unpaid transition adviser to help guide her former boss into her new post. Jolin also helped the Biden team place other candidates in top jobs. "Michele is fantastic and she immediately offered to support me through the transition," Yellen said. "She dropped everything she was doing and started working full-time with me."

Yellen's description of the amount of work required for her confirmation: "torture and agonizing." First off, she had to prepare to be grilled about topics she knew little about, such as the Internal Revenue Service (IRS), the Mint, the Bureau of Printing and Engraving, and the program aimed at disrupting financing for terrorism.

Equally daunting was the scrutiny of her personal finances that the Senate Finance Committee required before it scheduled her confirmation hearing.

"Essentially you have to undergo a forensic audit of three years of tax returns. It is a miserable and hugely time-consuming activity," she explained. "You have to find documentation for every last thing that is on your tax return down to taxi receipts. Anything that is an error, no matter how small, has to be corrected, and it's easy to make little errors. I had to refile amended returns for two out of the three returns—twice—in some cases to receive small refunds I would have happily forgone." It was pure torture for her to deal with the process.

Yellen had always computed the taxes for herself and George, just as her mother had done when she discovered that Julius Yellen wasn't keeping accurate records. But when Yellen went on the speaker circuit and realized she would have to file twenty state tax returns because of fees she collected for appearances around the country, she hired an accountant, starting with the 2018 tax year. As she went through her finances to prepare for her confirmation hearing, she discovered to her surprise that she had been doing the family's taxes wrong for years: She had listed George's book royalties on Schedule E, which is for rents, royalties, and partnerships. That seemed the logical thing to do, but it was wrong. Book royalties, she discovered, are an exception that go on Schedule C, which is for income from a sole proprietorship business or profession. The correction reduced the couple's tax liability because they could deduct more business expenses. Nonetheless, Yellen had to amend past returns.

The Finance Committee staff went through her returns with a fine-tooth comb, questioning, for example, a $75 charge by United Airlines for a deduction she took for a trip to Buenos Aires in the spring of 2018. She needed to provide documentation for the charge, and after hours of searching her records, she found an email that described the charge as an airport tax. She had to make sure she had a letter acknowledging each charitable deduction she claimed and receipts for every deduction George had claimed. She found the level of scrutiny horrendous and the entire process abusive.

Yellen and her husband also had about $300,000 in individual stocks inherited from their parents that they were allowed to keep in her previous government jobs because they did not pose any potential conflicts of interests. But as Treasury secretary, the couple had to get rid of them by rolling them over into mutual funds. Yellen had to dispose of Office Depot, AT&T, NCR, Raytheon, Pfizer, and Teradata. George had to roll over Conoco Phillips, Dow, Norfolk Southern, Raytheon, Phillips 66, and 21st Century Fox.

On January 19, 2021, the day before Joe Biden was sworn in as the nation's forty-sixth president, the Senate Finance Committee held Yellen's confirmation hearing. It was chaired by Republican Senator Chuck Grassley of Iowa, who would soon surrender his gavel to Democrat Ron Wyden of Oregon now that the chamber was 50–50, though Democrats had the tie-breaking vote in Vice President Kamala Harris in her role as president of the Senate.

On the morning of the hearing, all eight living former US Treasury secretaries issued a statement urging Congress to swiftly confirm her. The group included Republicans George Shultz, James Baker, John Snow, and Henry Paulson, and Democrats Robert Rubin, Lawrence Summers, Timothy Geithner, and Jacob Lew. The current secretary at the time, Steven Mnuchin, would relinquish his post the following day.

The former secretaries warned that the nation faced "unprecedented economic conditions" because of the COVID-19 pandemic that would require the rapid involvement of the Treasury Department. "Any gap in its leadership would risk setting back recovery efforts," they declared. "It is our view—based on personal experience for many of us—that Dr. Yellen's experience, knowledge, judgment, and character make her uniquely qualified for this role. It is hard to imagine a better prepared nominee to meet this great moment of need than Dr. Yellen."

The extraordinary bipartisan endorsement appeared to have its desired effect. As he opened the hearing, Grassley acknowledged Yellen's reputation for trying to work cooperatively with members of both parties, even as he ticked off numerous policy differences with her on issues ranging from global warming to higher taxes on the wealthy and corporations to finance new social programs. "I hope we can move away from partisan divisiveness and personalized attacks against each other," he said. "Dr. Yellen, if confirmed, you can be instrumental in helping generate an environment for bipartisan efforts and reasoned debate."

In her relatively brief opening statement, Yellen reflected all the values that she shared with Biden, thus confirming the transition team's confidence that they were politically compatible. She began by talking about her lifelong career using economics to help people during hard times, a goal she embraced after watching her father treat patients down on their luck. She then talked about how Congress must approve a massive new relief bill to avert even more suffering among those who lost their jobs as a result of the pandemic. "Economists don't always agree, but I think there is a consensus now: Without further action, we risk a longer, more painful recession now—and long-term scarring of the economy later.

"Neither the President-elect, nor I, propose this relief package without an appreciation for the country's debt burden," she continued. "But right now, with interest rates at historic lows, the smartest thing we can do is act big. In the long run, I believe the benefits will far outweigh the costs, especially if we care about helping people who have been struggling for a very long time."

Then she spoke of the problem of economic inequality and how the pandemic was widening the gap by boosting stock portfolios for the wealthy at the same time it was eliminating low-wage jobs. "We have to rebuild our economy so that it creates more prosperity for more people and ensures that American workers can compete in an increasingly competitive global economy," she said. Yellen ended with a political olive branch: "Members of the committee, these are very ambitious goals, and I know we will need to work together. You can count on me to do that in a bipartisan way."

As proof that the transition team had chosen wisely, the Finance Committee approved Yellen's nomination unanimously on January 22 and sent it to the full Senate for a confirmation vote. The committee Republicans said they were putting their policy objections aside to support her, as they believed that she had both the qualifications to lead the Treasury Department and the will to work with Republicans in Congress. That support, Grassley said, "signals an interest by me and I know by all of my Republican colleagues in working cooperatively and in a bipartisan way."

On January 25, 2021, the US Senate confirmed Yellen as the nation's seventy-eighth secretary of the Treasury. The final vote was an impressive bipartisan tally of 84–15, including thirty-four Republicans. Yellen found the bipartisan support gratifying, and it reaffirmed the Biden team's wisdom in choosing someone who had a reputation as a successful Fed chair with good relations with many members from both parties in Congress, notwithstanding the one episode in which she had been accused of being partisan. "I think people on both sides of the aisle thought I had done a credible job as Fed chair and was only interested in doing the best job I could for the American people. I was pleased that people considered me qualified to do this job."

The next day, Yellen was formally sworn in by Vice President Kamala Harris in a simple, one-minute ceremony on the steps of the East Portico of the White House, with the Treasury Department in the background. Yellen raised her right hand and placed her left hand on a Bible held by husband George. Son Robby stood behind them. All four wore black face masks, as Yellen repeated the oath:

"I, Janet Yellen, do solemnly swear that I will support and defend the Constitution of the United States against all enemies foreign and domestic, that I will bear true faith and allegiance to the same, that I take this obligation freely without any mental reservation or purpose of evasion and that I will well and faithfully discharge the duties of the office upon which I'm about to enter, so help me God."

The swearing-in ended with an exchange that was extraordinary because it was a first in US history:

"Congratulations, Madam Secretary."

"Thank you, Madam Vice President. Thank you so much."

On this occasion, the significance of the ceremony, two women who had broken gender barriers together, was very much on Yellen's mind. "I particularly wanted to have her swear me in, and I was very, very aware of the important symbolism of the moment. No doubt about it. She is an incredible first."

Now it was time to get to work. Treasury secretary Janet L. Yellen knew just how much there was to do.

# -14-

# TACKLING AN AMBITIOUS AGENDA

*"I got the sense that she cared not only about*
*Wall Street but also about Main Street"*

JUST HOURS AFTER HER SWEARING-IN AS SECRETARY OF THE Treasury on January 26, 2021, Yellen issued a "Day One Message" to her new department's staff, using the same opening line that colleagues had kidded her about when she began her business school lectures at Berkeley: "My name is Janet Yellen."

"A short while ago, I was sworn in as the 78th Secretary of the Treasury," her message continued. "It's an incredible honor to join this team of 84,000 public servants. I can't overstate that. When President Biden asked if I would accept the position of Treasury secretary, I said 'yes' in large part because I knew who I would be working with."

As she praised the employees' hard work and dedication in handling the 2007–2009 financial crisis, Yellen summoned the staff to take on four new crises: the economic damage from the COVID-19 pandemic, global warming, systemic racism, and income inequality that had been growing for fifty years. "These are ambitious goals, and I am fully aware none of them will be accomplished by working exclusively with a small team out of the secretary's office," the message said. "Ours will have to be an inclusive department. . . . That is why over the next few weeks, I plan to meet with each office and bureau. I want to hear from you about what needs changing and what we can do better."

Following her call for inclusiveness, another career trademark, Yellen referred again to her father's unemployed patients and her desire to become an economist to help those in need. "I know that many of you share this sensibility. You see economic policy as a way to improve people's lives; you see the humanity beneath the data." She concluded by promising to meet her staff virtually at first, then later in person.

Virtual conferences, however, proved to be her first challenge, and a frustrating one. After a quick tour of her new spacious and elegant office, Yellen decided to work from home so long as the pandemic posed a health risk. She assumed she could hold meetings using Zoom, but her predecessor, Steven Mnuchin, had installed a different video system that she found to be unworkable. Participants at meetings might be seen but not heard, some could be heard only when they turned off the video, and some conversations were drowned out by a loud buzzing noise.

"Most of the meeting time was just spent dealing with people who couldn't be heard or seen or both," she said. "To me, it showed a real disregard for the staff at the Treasury to leave such a system in place for so long when so many people are working remotely," Yellen said of her predecessor's treatment of his employees in failing to fix the system. "So, the first week, one of my priorities was trying to put in place a system that would work for all the people who needed to work with one another remotely. It told me what the previous administration's priorities were or weren't." Yellen's

Number Two at Treasury, Deputy Secretary Adewale "Wally" Adeyemo, said her insistence in getting a better videoconference system up and running reflected her desire for personal contact. "She is an inclusive leader who prepares for meetings by making sure that the people who write the memos, the junior staffers, are included in the meetings with her," he said. "She's also been very much focused on the idea of how do I do more town halls and talk to our Treasury people more directly? I think that's part of her wanting to create a sense of morale in a building and government that's had difficulty communicating because of COVID. When we got here the technology was horrible. She was very insistent, 'If I'm going to have meetings with people, I'm going to need to see their faces. We need to figure out a solution.' So, all of a sudden, all these people started to scramble and figured out a way to get Zoom going here. And it changed the whole environment. You could have a conversation and see each other's faces, you can meet people and interact with them as humans in a way that you just couldn't when you're on conference calls all day."

"From her perspective, she's always thinking through the humanity in the way that we operate within the department, she's always thinking about the staff," Adeyemo continued. "While it's been tough to do in a digital environment, it has given us some opportunities for her to speak to the entire workforce in ways that we probably wouldn't have previously. Even a decade ago, when I was working for [Treasury secretary] Jack Lew, we never would have thought about doing a town hall with the entire staff from the Treasury Department."

A simultaneous problem was filling senior positions at the Treasury Department to help Yellen work through all the areas in which she had no expertise. Some were campaign advisers the White House wanted hired and others were people Yellen knew and trusted from previous posts. The only top official selected by the Biden transition team without Yellen's input was Adeyemo, who had been president of the newly formed Obama Foundation. At forty years of age, he was the same age as Yellen's son, Robby.

Adeyemo's background is a classic American success story. Born in Nigeria, where his father was a teacher and his mother a nurse, Adeyemo came to the United States as a child and was raised in southern California. He received his BA degree from Berkeley and his law degree from Yale. He became active in politics in 2004, working for John Kerry's presidential campaign. Adeyemo held several positions in the Obama administration, where he worked at the Treasury Department for Secretary Timothy Geithner and later Jacob Lew. His last job in the Obama administration was deputy National Economic Council director for international economics. He worked at BlackRock, the giant Wall Street investment firm, before running the Obama Foundation in 2019. The former president had great affection for Adeyemo and lamented his departure from the foundation.

When transition team officials were talking to Yellen about being secretary, they informed her that Adeyemo would be her deputy. She had known him slightly, and when she talked to people who knew him well, they all gushed about him and said she was very fortunate to have him as her Number Two, particularly given his knowledge of areas about which she knew little.

Aside from Adeyemo, the White House said Yellen would be able to take the lead on all the other appointments, but it expected to weigh in on her choices. The Presidential Personnel Office plays the leading role in these appointments. It is committed to diversity but also wants to put loyal campaign workers into top jobs. Finding the right people for specialized positions of great responsibility required Yellen and her staff to negotiate with White House officials. "We spent an enormous amount of time evaluating candidates and trying to make these appointments," she said.

For the job of undersecretary for domestic finance, Yellen tapped Nellie Liang, who was her financial stability division head at the Fed and later a colleague at Brookings. For counselor, Yellen selected David Lipton, who had been the Number Two official at the International Monetary Fund for eight years until 2020. He had extensive government experience dating back to the Clinton Treasury Department, where he worked briefly as undersecretary for international affairs. He also worked for Wall Street firms. Yellen knew Lipton from her teaching days at Harvard, where he was a graduate student. She didn't think he would agree to return to the Treasury Department and was thrilled when he did.

Another member of Yellen's close circle of advisers included her chief of staff, Didem Nisanci, a former chief of staff at the Securities and Exchange Commission and staff director of the Senate Banking Committee. As her chief economist at Treasury, Yellen selected Ben Harris, who had served as the top economic adviser to Biden when he was vice president and later a presidential candidate. Harris had been a key player in putting together the series of massive economic packages that Yellen would later try to sell to Congress and the public. From the top on down, it was the most diverse group of senior executives in the department's history.

Even as she assembled her team, however, Yellen had a problem. Most of the high-level jobs required Senate confirmation, and until then, she could not allow them to participate in any Treasury business unless they worked in a less formal capacity as temporary "counselors." That designation allowed them to assist her in limited ways. While waiting for formal nominations and the lengthy confirmation process, Yellen had a lot of pressing—and politically sensitive—issues piling up on her plate. One involved demands by congressional investigators for Donald Trump's tax returns, which are held by the IRS, a division of the Treasury Department. Biden's Justice Department ruled that the IRS had to turn the documents over to Congress, but Trump's lawyers continued to wage a legal fight to block Congress from getting the returns.

An additional touchy issue involved reimposing financial sanctions on Israeli businessman Dan Gertler. During the Trump administration, the Treasury Department had imposed sanctions on Gertler in December 2017, after concluding that he had amassed a fortune "through hundreds of millions of dollars' worth of opaque and corrupt mining and oil deals in the Democratic Republic of the Congo (DRC)." On January 15, 2021, just five days before Trump left the White House, however, the Treasury Department quietly lifted those sanctions without any public announcement. Yellen's Treasury Department, working with the State Department, moved on March 8, 2021, to reimpose sanctions on Gertler.

Working without a confirmed senior staff and from home because of the pandemic, Yellen struggled to get up to speed on other matters that involved urgent decisions. They included tax policy, sanctions against Iran and other countries and foreign officials involved in bad behavior, financing for terrorists, intelligence threats that required Treasury action, and the review of national security implications of bids by foreign companies to purchase American firms. Adeyemo was an expert in many of these issues, but Yellen could not turn to him for help until he was confirmed by the Senate, which happened on March 25. A day later, she personally swore him into office.

Those first months were intense. "There were constant meetings on a wide range of policy issues, and I was spending an enormous amount of time trying to put together a team, working with the White House," she recalled. "Then I'm just thrown full bore into having to handle the full set of Treasury issues, trying to get up to speed on all of them. I had an enormous number of calls with counterparts around the world, briefings on all of the international issues that were on our plate."

Clearly, Yellen was shocked in the beginning over the breadth of issues confronting her and the pace of work—all with very limited senior staff support. She muscled through it, just as she managed to trek mountainous trails and run a half-marathon when she was president of the San Francisco Fed.

"There were nights I went home utterly exhausted and said, 'I don't know how I'm going to go on doing this.' It was just so much work. It was unbelievable," she recalled of those early months. "You know, every single day my team would give me a briefing book to prepare me with background material and talking points to get through the next day. This arrived on my desk at six or seven o'clock at night. On a typical day, it was at least two hundred pages, and I had to read all this material to be able to participate in the meetings and make the calls on my schedule that I saw were set for the next day. My schedule had something almost every half hour, sometimes with fifteen-minute breaks in between meetings in case they ran over."

Amid the crush of work, Yellen found time to perform a task that perhaps is the most indelible mark a Treasury secretary ever makes—literally: preparing her signature to be engraved on all US paper currency printed during her tenure. Naturally, she put extraordinary preparation into the task. First, she reviewed the signatures of all her predecessors who had signed bills. Then she practiced her own signature over and over until she was happy with it. She then provided it for engraving on March 10 but had to wait until a new Treasurer of the United States was named. The treasurer, who oversees the US Mint, the Bureau of Engraving and Printing, and Fort Knox (where gold reserves are stored) had to provide a signature, as well, before the new bills could be printed.

The most demanding issue Yellen had to deal with in her first six weeks on the job was distribution of aid under the massive $1.9 trillion pandemic relief package—called the American Rescue

Plan—that Congress had passed and Biden signed on March 11. The biggest anti-poverty program in a half century, the plan provided $1,400 checks to every member of a family making less than $150,000 a year, extended federal unemployment benefits for another six months, increased the child tax credit, provided subsidies for low-income people to purchase health insurance through Obamacare, expanded the earned income tax credit for low-income adults without children, and offered assistance to those at risk of homelessness.

Yellen had not been involved in putting the package together. That had been done during the transition and negotiations with Congress that took place while she was awaiting confirmation. Privately, as a former Fed chair always worried about accumulating too much federal debt and risking higher inflation, she had concerns that the cost was on the high side and would have preferred something closer to $1.3 trillion, according to colleagues. But given the choice between Biden's full $1.9 trillion package and less than $1 trillion that some in Congress preferred, Yellen believed going big was the better course. She and the rest of the Biden administration had remembered only too clearly the mistake Barack Obama had made at the start of his presidency: agreeing to a stimulus package that proved to be inadequate to leave the Great Recession in the dust. A lackluster economy in 2010 contributed to a Republican takeover of Congress. Yellen also supported a doubling of the federal minimum wage to $15 an hour, even though she previously had expressed concerns that a boost so large might lead to some job losses. Her endorsement of the $15 figure prompted criticism from conservative voices, such as the *Wall Street Journal* editorial page, which accused her of betraying her principles and becoming a political shill.

How did Yellen reconcile her reservations about the size of the relief spending plan? "She realized that there's no simple answer to most big economic questions. There are ranges of uncertainty, like is the $1.9 trillion American Rescue Plan the right dollar figure?" explained a confidant. "She understood that it could cause inflation. She asked herself, 'Is it better to do too little or too much?' And if it turns out to be too much, there are remedies and she got comfortable with it."

"I mean, she might've chosen $1.3 trillion, but it wasn't a relevant choice that was on the table," the confidant continued. "Similarly, with the $15 an hour minimum wage, she might've chosen $13.50, but that wasn't on the table. She got comfortable with the package, given the setting and objectives we had, which were not just about growth, but also about equity, limiting child poverty and making sure that there isn't a wide swath of families struggling."

Yellen embraced the massive aid program and used her credibility as an economist and former Fed chair to urge its passage. She argued that it was essential to help the economy recover a record loss of jobs and that the Fed had the ability to keep inflation in check. The latter claim became a subject of heated debate throughout 2021, led by her longtime sparring partner, Larry Summers. In an op-ed in the *Washington Post* on February 4, Summers became the most prominent Democrat to warn that so much spending, combined with the Fed's program of pumping massive amounts of money into the economy, would spark the biggest burst of inflation since the 1970s. He proved correct, and Yellen admitted in 2022 that she was wrong in predicting inflation would soon subside.

As she reflected on the inflation debate sparked by Summers at the start of the Biden administration, Yellen conceded that the unprecedented nature of the economic collapse caused by the pandemic made it difficult to determine the inflationary dangers lurking in the wake of so much stimulus spending. "That's a big question," she said. Though she had worried that the size of the initial relief package was too big and might prove inflationary, she still preferred to err on the side of doing too much rather than too little. In 2022, she had to grapple with doing too much.

Yellen was angry at Summers for unleashing a broadside against the relief package, even if his warning about inflation proved on target. "He is a public intellectual who says what he thinks is true," she said. "It posed a challenge for us." Having known Summers a long time, she was not surprised by his public attacks, which she found unconstructive. "The package that we enacted was big, no question about it. But there were very good reasons to enact a big package even if it created some risks on the inflation side," she said. "It was far worse to do too little than to do too much." Yellen knew that the Fed would move to combat inflation if prices rose significantly and persisted at high levels. Indeed, that's just what the Fed did in early 2022, although not as aggressively as Yellen would have done had she still been Fed chair. But Summers had created a firestorm that forced the administration on the defensive. Yellen was irritated that he would cause his own party so much grief by arming Republicans and some Democrats—such as Senator Joe Manchin of West Virginia, a conservative by Democratic standards—with a justification for opposing subsequent spending proposals on Biden's agenda.

"I felt the overwhelming need at that point was to address the suffering that the pandemic caused and make sure that there was sufficient demand so that we wouldn't have a weak recovery like we had after the financial crisis that took a decade to get back to full employment," Yellen continued. "The program provided a huge amount of impetus in a short amount of time, but it wasn't permanent. The stimulus would quickly ebb." Yellen had acknowledged that inflation would rise in the short-term. The reason: massive amounts of cash had flowed into the economy to stoke consumer demand at a time of supply bottlenecks caused by the temporary shutdown of the economy in the spring of 2021. "We never had a situation like a pandemic, so it was hard to predict what impact it was going to have," she said. "But I truly felt that the inflation we were seeing would not become endemic."

As Yellen had feared, Manchin cited inflation worries when Biden unveiled a second huge spending package costlier than the $1.9 trillion emergency relief plan. The Build Back Better Act was a package of social benefits totaling $3.5 trillion over ten years. It was a wish list of expanded government benefits that progressives had long dreamed of enacting. It included subsidies for childcare and universal pre-K; dental, hearing, and vision coverage under Medicare; paid family leave; and subsidies to boost green energy. Biden planned to pay for it by boosting income taxes on families making more than $400,000 a year and by raising the corporate income tax slashed under Trump.

Manchin and another recalcitrant Democrat, Kyrsten Sinema of Arizona, voted for the $1.9 trillion relief package but opposed the high price tag of the second one, and they were enough to block passage in a Senate evenly divided between Democrats and Republicans. Manchin insisted on slashing it from $3.5 trillion to $1.5 trillion, forcing Democrats to negotiate revisions of the package well into the fall of 2021. The House of Representatives passed its own version of the Build Back Better Act at a cost of roughly $2 trillion on November 19, 2021, after Yellen provided assurances that it would be fully paid for through a minimum tax on corporations, a surtax on millionaires, and improved tax compliance by the IRS. Nonpartisan budget groups questioned the accuracy of her math, and the bill's fate remained uncertain in the Senate in 2022.

Yellen had tried to make the case that the original $3.5 trillion Build Back Better Act was not inflationary because it would be spread out over ten years—$350 billion a year—compared to the initial $1.9 trillion package that would be spent in the first year. "It has a totally different focus," she said. "It's intended to address long-standing structural problems that have been plaguing our society for decades." She believed it was essential to pass it, but Summers had sabotaged it, even though he agreed it wouldn't worsen inflation.

The debate over inflation dragged into the spring, and Yellen went public with her concerns about the issue in an interview with *The Atlantic* magazine released on May 4. "It may be that interest rates will have to rise somewhat to make sure our economy does not overheat, even though the additional spending is relatively small relative to the size of the economy," Yellen said a tad too candidly. "It could cause some very modest increases in interest rates to get that reallocation."

Her honest admission that inflation was a worry triggered a brief dip in stock prices, prompting her to backtrack during an interview with the *Wall Street Journal* later in the day. "I don't think there's going to be an inflationary problem, but if there is, the Fed can be counted on to address it," she said. That seemed to calm the markets.

By the fall of 2021, as inflation proved to be higher and more persistent than she had predicted earlier, Yellen conceded that it was a bigger problem than she had anticipated. She agreed with Summers that the huge relief package passed in the spring together with the Federal Reserve's massive bond-buying program had injected too much money too quickly into the economy. She concluded that the Fed would reverse course sooner than planned and raise interest rates in 2022 to bring inflation under control. Yet she still defended the original $1.9 trillion relief package as essential to help people in need—her empathy trumping her analytical calculations.

In March 2022, Summers said the Fed's failure to move sooner and more forcefully to curb rising inflation risked a recession. But Yellen believed her successor at the Fed, Jerome Powell, who shared her economic views, would act wisely. That is why she privately lobbied Biden to nominate Powell to a second four-year term as Fed chair and to reject calls by many progressive Democrats, led by Senator Elizabeth Warren, to replace him. Yellen had also recommended that Biden appease the party's left wing by elevating Fed governor Lael Brainard, a policy dove and advocate for tough bank regulation, to the Number Two Fed job: vice chair. Biden took Yellen's advice, announcing on November 22, 2021, both his retention of Powell and promotion for Brainard.

Mentor and colleague Joseph Stiglitz said Yellen's candor about vacillating over the size of the pandemic relief package was a lifelong habit of an academic who can listen to varying arguments before analyzing the data and then reaching her own conclusion. "She has this ability to see different sides of an argument, and actually acknowledges the point that you're making, like in the debate about the risks of doing too much and too little to stimulate the economy," he said. "It's not that she's going to say there's no risk, but she says, 'We have to weigh these risks of doing too little and too much. And here's why I think the risk right now is on one side or the other.' She has a real skill in listening."

❖ ❖ ❖

ONCE THE $1.9 TRILLION RELIEF PACKAGE PASSED ON A PARTY-line vote in Congress, with only Democrats supporting it, Yellen made the rapid distribution of the funds her Number One mission. That job was complicated by the fact that her department was still trying to eliminate bottlenecks that were slowing the department's disbursement of small business loans, rental assistance, and other aid included in the $2.2 trillion emergency Coronavirus Aid, Relief, and Economic Security (CARES) Act that Congress had passed in March 2020 and had reauthorized in January 2021.

"The Trump administration created a large number of new programs that were lodged with Treasury. In some cases, regulations had been written quickly, and we found many that were just unworkable," Yellen explained. "For example, the Consolidated Appropriations Act created an emergency rental assistance program. But the rules promulgated hastily in the Trump administration's final days were so onerous that many families facing eviction just wouldn't be able to get help. We had to make sure all those programs were redone to get help where it was needed."

"Then, when the $1.9 trillion rescue plan was passed in March," she continued, "there were many new programs: state, local, and tribal fiscal relief, more rounds of emergency rental assistance, a broadband program, a homeowners' program, a program to inject capital into CDFI (Community Development Financial Institution) Funds and MDI (Minority Depository Institution) Funds to lend in underserved communities. Treasury was given much of the responsibility to get these programs up and running. We created a new Office of Recovery Programs and appointed a director to oversee all of the programs and insure their effectiveness. The staff at Treasury and at the IRS have played a heroic role in doing all of the extra work entailed. We had to work with the IRS to distribute Economic Impact Payments—the $1,400 checks in the American Rescue Plan. We got the program up and running as we worked with the IRS, and we really wanted to make sure the checks got out quickly to everyone who qualifies. We didn't screw it up. They got out quickly."

That they did. The first checks went out March 12, the day after Biden signed the relief package into law. By March 17, Treasury reported it had distributed 90 million payments by direct electronic deposit totaling $242 billion. By April 7, Treasury had sent out 156 million payments totaling $372 billion. In May, the department began distributing $350 billion in emergency funding for state, local, territorial, and tribal governments.

Deputy Treasury secretary Wally Adeyemo said the key to managing so many aid distribution programs simultaneously was

Yellen's decision to create a completely new structure at Treasury to handle the mammoth task. Mnuchin had managed COVID-related aid programs himself with a small team of aides, according to Adeyemo. "Everything that we'd heard from states and local governments and other recipients was that it was very hard to reach someone at Treasury to give them feedback about what was working and what wasn't. She pushed relatively early on for us to think through how do we staff this in a way where we have people devoted to this work who can engage with the grantees?" he explained. "This was very different from what was happening at Treasury at that point. We built out a structure, brought in somebody to lead the team, and for each program we had a staff member who was assigned to it and focused on it full-time."

"One thing Yellen gets less credit for than she should is her focus on execution," Adeyemo added. "She was very focused on how does Treasury do an exceptional job in executing these programs, such as the child tax credit, which could reduce child poverty by 50 percent if properly executed."

Seeing that program through was a daunting task, but by mid-July, the Treasury Department and the IRS announced that they had distributed the first monthly payment of an expanded child tax credit to thirty-nine million households, covering 88 percent of children in the United States. Eligible families received up to $300 a month for each child under age six and up to $250 a month for each dependent child six and older through the end of 2021. Yellen recalled that Congress insisted on monthly checks rather than a single lump-sum payment, which created a major challenge for the IRS.

"Congress wanted the tax credits advanced on a monthly basis to qualifying households," she explained. "It was a huge task for the IRS, which is the most understaffed, overworked agency in the world. They'd never, ever done anything like trying to pay a monthly check to sixty-four million children. Essentially we were told we've got to figure out how they're going to do that starting July 15. It was a huge job, just one of the enormous headaches I faced when I got there. I was dealing with things of this type every day."

The checks went out smoothly. Not so with the $46.5 billion rental aid program created to help landlords and tenants protected from eviction by a national moratorium—until the Supreme Court shot it down in August of 2021 for exceeding the government's authority. Just before the court's ruling, the Treasury had distributed barely 10 percent of the funds. The problem was all the bureaucratic red tape required: Congress wrote the law in a way that forced states to create agencies to provide the aid received from Washington to distressed renters and landlords. That two-step process frustrated Yellen and her staff. They believed distributing the money directly would have been far more efficient than working through local agencies and that the bottlenecks reflected poorly on the Treasury Department, which was in charge of administering the program, even though it was powerless to change the process. After eliminating many of the hurdles, the department announced on January 7, 2022, that it had distributed more than $25 billion in aid in 2021 to 665,000 landlords and renters.

On September 16, six months after the massive relief bill became law, the Treasury Department announced that it had disbursed $700 billion of the $1 trillion in programs it administered. On January 20, 2022, the department issued a summary of its disbursements in 2021. They included more than 3.1 million payments from the Emergency Rental Assistance Program, nearly $93 billion in monthly child tax credit payments to the families of sixty-one million children, more than $245 billion to state, local, and tribal governments as a part of the State and Local Fiscal Recovery Funds programs, and more than 163 million Economic Impact Payments totaling $390 billion from the American Rescue

Plan. On balance, Yellen was proud to have played a key role in distributing so much aid to people in dire need. She knew the Fed wasn't able to tackle social needs head on and felt she was accomplishing much more in her new role. "I was thrilled to be part of an administration where this was the priority. I didn't have to sell anybody on playing our role and doing it well," she said. "This is what the president wanted to do. This is what I knew I was signing on for. And as soon as I started attending meetings during the transition where policy was being discussed, I saw President Biden's ambition for Building Back Better. I have been totally committed to getting this done: an incredible opportunity to address long-standing problems that require a new New Deal."

To make sure the money flowed smoothly, Yellen and Adeyemo had traveled around the country to meet with groups distributing the aid. On August 4, 2021, Yellen made her first domestic trip as secretary to Atlanta, where she spoke at a meeting of Invest Atlanta, a local economic development agency. There she touted the importance of government assistance during times of crises—including the child tax credit and emergency rental assistance—to lift people out of poverty. During the summer of 2021, Adeyemo checked on rental assistance programs in Houston and Washington, DC, suburbs, and traveled to Yonkers, New York, to visit a child tax credit sign-up program.

Yellen expanded on her belief in the importance of more aggressive government action to combat growing inequality in a virtual speech on May 18 to—of all groups—the US Chamber of Commerce. It was hardly receptive to that message, particularly since she called for higher taxes on corporations and the wealthy to pay for a more activist government. Yet she didn't flinch from making her case.

"We have been the largest economy in the world for over a century and our national income has risen steadily," she began. "Yet in recent decades, a rising share of that income has gone to profits and disproportionate wage gains at the top, while middle-class families have faced wage stagnation." She went on to lament the crumbling US transportation infrastructure, the inability of many families to save enough for college and retirement, and growing discontent about an unfair economic system that increasingly rewards the rich at the expense of the less affluent.

Yellen noted that the United States experienced similar social discontent in the late 1800s, when disparities in financial well-being emerged as a result of the Industrial Revolution and its era of ruthless and greedy robber barons. What followed, she said, was a progressive movement that led to a long list of needed reforms to address flaws in the system. "In the years just before and after World War I, they introduced a progressive income tax, strengthened anti-monopoly laws, created the Federal Reserve, and provided women the right to vote," Yellen explained, as if giving a lecture on American history. "Then, amidst the Great Depression, the New Deal created Social Security, the Securities and Exchange Commission, the Federal Deposit Insurance Corporation, and the Fair Labor Standards Act. That legislation, some of it controversial in its time, continues to provide opportunity, assurance, and stability that Americans count on every day. The question today is whether we, too, can think big and act big.

"It is the time to recommit our government to playing a more active and smarter role in the economy," she concluded. "We're proposing smart investments—to make our economy more competitive and sustainable, to provide opportunities for all families and workers, and to make our tax system fairer. So, let us think big. Let us redouble our efforts to create opportunity, social mobility, and ultimately widespread and sustainable prosperity now and for our children's children. In the hit musical, as Alexander Hamilton approached death, he ponders the question, What is a legacy? He answers: 'It's planting seeds in a garden you never get to see.' Let's build back better together—and build something that lasts for generations. We Americans deserve a better deal."

Yellen's pitch for a bigger role for government was ignored, as news stories focused more narrowly on her call for higher taxes before a hostile business group that had fought every progressive program from the past that she had listed. Yet it defined, as much as any speech she had given, her belief that government, not the private sector, can spread prosperity to more people. It was the counterargument to the crusade for a smaller federal government launched by President Ronald Reagan forty years earlier and embraced by subsequent presidents of both parties.

"This speech laid out a new way of thinking about the role of government," said David Lipton, her Treasury counselor who helped draft it. "It moved away from the idea that government should just be small, providing defense and entitlement spending and doing Keynesian countercyclical policy," he said, referring to Keynes's argument that government needs to boost spending during recessions to revive the economy. "It explained that because we've had basically four decades of Reagan's approach to government, various problems have not been addressed, and some important inequities have arisen. It laid out a logic for thinking about the role of government differently.

"This is what she believes, and if she can help the president do these things—the economic recovery, the infrastructure, spending on climate change, support for families—it would be a tremendous legacy," he continued. "It would, I hope, change the way we think about the role of government, that it should be doing things that will help provide opportunity and protection for the people. That would be quite a change."

Yellen spent much of her early months in office on the phone with members of Congress of both parties trying to sell her vision of government and the need for Biden's massive $3.5 trillion spending plan. As she described her goals: "I tried to do my best to convince them not to waste what is an incredible opportunity. It's so important to address these long-standing problems."

Though she didn't change any minds, she earned a lot of goodwill and respect as someone who knew what she was talking about and was willing to listen to opponents' objections. An adviser who listened to many of the conversations she had with Republicans came away impressed at the cordial exchanges. "I expected that they were just going to bust her ass, you know, complaining, whining," the adviser said. "But they kept it polite, which is a sign of respect. And then they made it clear how much they valued the fact that she's the one at Treasury. Maybe it's a way of saying, 'I don't really trust your president but I'm glad you're there.' They view her as an anchor of wisdom and maturity. The breadth of respect for her from Democrats and Republicans, from the business and financial community to labor is so impressive. It makes her stand out from other Treasury secretaries."

Mark Gitenstein, the Biden transition official who had pushed for Yellen's appointment, said her performance in office vindicated his judgment: "The incredible thing about Janet Yellen is that she has tremendous credibility, not simply with progressives, but with Wall Street. She's a serious expert in so many areas."

Representative Richard Neal, D-MA, chair of the House Tax-Writing Ways and Means Committee, attributed Yellen's broad respect in Congress to both a sharp mind and unassuming manner. "There's a special credibility that's been attached to her performances because of the fact that she's given sound advice and in the magnifying glass of critical analysis, much of that advice has held up," he explained. "I've listened to her deftly handle questions from Republican members of the Ways and Means Committee and Democratic members, and she's done it with great patience and skill. I recall some Republicans who used to question [former Democratic Treasury secretaries] Lew and Rubin pretty vigorously. I thought they were pretty careful with Yellen, and I think part of it is because she's so soft-spoken. Yet she makes her point strongly."

One vital point she made strongly helped avert an unprecedented economic crisis. Republicans had balked at raising the US debt ceiling, legislation required to allow the government to borrow money to cover spending Congress had already approved. Democrats had insisted on a bipartisan agreement to raise the debt ceiling so Republicans would not use the issue against them in the 2022 midterm elections. They knew the public strongly dislikes the government going deeper into debt even while voters enjoy the benefits it pays for. Yellen repeatedly warned in stark—and ultimately persuasive—letters to Congress that failure to raise the ceiling would push the US government into default with its bondholders for the first time and lead to an unparalleled economic "catastrophe." Enough Senate Republicans finally relented and allowed a vote, and Democrats reluctantly raised the ceiling on a party-line vote with just a single Republican joining them. On December 16, 2021, as a never-before default appeared imminent, President Biden signed the legislation that allowed the government to keep borrowing into 2023. Yellen, government bondholders, and the nation could take a deep sigh of relief.

Yellen also learned to make her viewpoint strongly in meetings with top White House officials. Having been shunted aside during policy debates when she worked in the Clinton White House, she was determined to be a player in the Biden White House. Her deputy, Wally Adeyemo, said she integrated herself into the policymaking process to an extent that virtually no other cabinet secretary had. She attended the chief of staff's morning meeting, conferred one-on-one with other White House officials, and helped shape policy positions before formal meetings of the National Economic Council, according to Adeyemo.

"I think she brings a different perspective than anyone else in the administration when it comes to economic policy because she's going to be the spokesperson for the policy," he said. "People often test things against her, because ultimately she is the person who other than the president or the vice president can explain the economic policy of the day." He added that Yellen had significant input in all of the major components of the huge $3.5 trillion package Biden had proposed and was being debated in Congress during the fall of 2021, from the tax proposals to spending for childcare and education subsidies.

While White House officials were focused on strategy for getting the package through Congress, Adeyemo continued, Yellen focused on how the components of the package would produce sustainable economic growth. "I've worked now for three Treasury secretaries, and the most interesting thing about Secretary Yellen is that because of her background as a labor economist, she has views on spending packages that traditionally a Treasury secretary wouldn't weigh in on. I've seen her articulate those views and ask hard questions about the economic impact of different things in ways you wouldn't expect from someone who sits over here at Treasury."

❖ ❖ ❖

TREASURY SECRETARIES TRADITIONALLY HAVE CLOSE TIES TO the financial community, and their first meetings with outside groups upon taking office customarily have been with representatives of big banks and investment firms. Yellen, intent on proving she represented Main Street as well as Wall Street, held her first meeting—two days after being sworn in—with small business owners. Her next meeting, on February 3, was with a group of mayors to discuss the economic needs of their cities. Then she met with the Black Chamber of Commerce on February 5. Having made her point about her priorities, Yellen joined President Biden for a meeting with top CEOs in the Oval Office on February 9. In later months she held meetings with leaders of tribal, Black, and Latino groups.

Clearly, Yellen was not your typical Treasury secretary, noted Lake Charles, Louisiana, mayor Nic Hunter, one of a group of mayors from cities with fewer than eighty thousand residents who met with her on February 25. "I felt it to be a very genuine conversation. I don't think it was just for show or checking a box for her," recalled Hunter, a Republican businessman whose city had been devastated during the previous year by two hurricanes and an ice storm. Hunter, like local officials from both parties, had supported the $1.9 trillion relief package—in contrast to opposition from Republicans in Congress—because of the badly needed aid it would provide to his constituents, who were trying to rebuild from both a pandemic and several natural disasters.

"There was a very authentic back and forth among the group, and I got the sense that she cared not only about Wall Street but also about Main Street and with what we're going through right now in this country," Hunter said. "I think it's important that our federal officials remember that there is a wide range of population in this country that is probably more connected to just Main Street USA than they are to Wall Street, and that was refreshing because when you think about a secretary of the Treasury typically, you might not think of them visiting one-on-one with the mayor of Lake Charles, but that happened and I was very honored by that."

Yellen was described in similar terms by the leader of Jubilee USA Network, a religious group that met with her on March 16. Jubilee is a coalition of more than 750 faith groups focused on alleviating poverty and global conflict and promoting human rights.

"Yellen is absolutely extraordinary because, with all she had on her plate, she prioritized meeting with high-level US religious leaders," said the group's executive director, Eric LeCompte. "Even though I met alone with, I guess, every previous Treasury secretary for the past decade or more, I'm not aware of any meeting previously taking place with the highest-ranking religious leaders in the United States."

"That really says something about Janet Yellen and her understanding that in terms of meeting with the leaders of American life, it's not only world leaders, finance ministers, Fortune 500 companies, it's also these high-ranking religious leaders who represent people who were having an incredibly difficult time during the pandemic crisis," LeCompte said. "What it says is that she understands the need to meet with all types of leaders and groups when forming decisions and moving forward. We actually saw this about Yellen when she was in charge of the Fed, wanting to meet with a variety of different stakeholders. For her to do this so early on in her tenure at Treasury signifies to the entire Treasury staff the importance of meeting with civil society and leaders of America. She's unique in that way. What separates Yellen more than any other meeting I've had with a previous Treasury secretary is that she focuses on the human impact first and the policy numbers second."

In another clear example of how Yellen was not your usual Treasury secretary, her staff issued a report on September 15, 2021, that bemoaned the state of the nation's childcare system, an issue the Treasury Department rarely, if ever, had focused on before. The report concluded that childcare was unaffordable for too many American families, a problem that prevents many families from working and creates a drag on the economy. The report was released to promote Biden's plan for universal preschool and expanded tax credits for childcare. "It's past time that we treat childcare as what it is—an element whose contribution to economic growth is as essential as infrastructure or energy," Yellen said in a statement accompanying the report.

Appearing with Vice President Kamala Harris at the Treasury Department to promote the report, Yellen used her own experience forty years earlier as a new mother who was returning to her teaching job at Berkeley and needed a good caregiver for infant son Robby. Yellen noted that she and her husband, George, could afford to pay more than the going rate to ensure they hired someone who would do a good job. They were fortunate, unlike the vast majority of Americans. "Those who provide childcare aren't paid well, and many who need it, can't afford it," she said. "Most parents need childcare at the exact moment when they can least afford it—at the beginning of their career when their income is lowest.

"The free market works well in many different sectors, but childcare is not one of them," she continued. "Childcare is a textbook example of a broken market, and one reason is that when you pay for it, the price does not account for all the positive things it confers on our society. An enormous body of economic literature finds that kids with access to quality childcare end up in school longer and in higher-paying jobs afterward. When we underinvest in childcare, we forgo that; we give up a happier, healthier, more prosperous labor force in the future."

Yellen differed from her male predecessors in stylistic ways, as well, shunning many of the perks of the post that other Treasury secretaries took advantage of at taxpayer expense. She did not redecorate her ornate office, as many had done, and she took commercial flights for domestic trips, using government aircraft only for official international missions, such as attending meetings of finance ministers in Europe, and then only if the White House signed off on it being an appropriate use of public money. She paid her own way when she flew to her home in Berkeley, California, for a summer vacation in August 2021. "It is highly unlikely that there will be stories out of Treasury about appointees abusing public funds to furnish their offices," Yellen promised. Traveling in lavish style is also something Yellen avoided. She even prefers to carry her own bag and is comfortable flying coach.

By contrast, her predecessor, Steven Mnuchin, became ensnared in a controversy over his excessive use of military aircraft at considerable public expense during his first months in office. A report by the Treasury Department's Office of Inspector General in October 2017 found that he had taken seven flights—sometimes with his wife—at a cost to the government of more than $800,000. A June 15, 2017, roundtrip to Miami cost more than $43,000 for five people—at least ten times the cost of a commercial flight. Mnuchin's explanation was that he needed to make a phone call on a secure line en route home. Though lavish, the trips did not break any laws, the Inspector General's report concluded.

An even starker departure from her predecessors involved the policies Yellen embraced early in her tenure. They included priorities that she had long championed—such as climate change—that had not been the focus of the department before. She had pushed unsuccessfully for action to combat global warming when she was chair of the Council of Economic Advisers more than two decades earlier. This time, she had power to accomplish something.

First, she created the post of deputy assistant secretary for climate and energy economics and gave the job to Catherine Wolfram, a Haas Business School colleague who had joined the Berkeley faculty in 2000. They had been the only women in the school's economic analysis and policy group. Before Yellen arrived, the Treasury Department had had an office of environment and energy, but Mnuchin disbanded it, prompting Yellen to reestablish it with a sharper focus on climate.

In an April 5 speech on her international priorities to the Chicago Council on Global Affairs, Yellen said she would push for action on climate change when she met virtually with her counterparts from around the world at the annual spring meeting of the International Monetary Fund and World Bank, twin groups created after World War II to ensure global financial stability and promote economic development in poor countries. As an aside, Yellen noted her own role as the first female Treasury secretary: "Most noticeably, I will be joined later this week by other female finance ministers, central bank governors, and heads of international financial institutions— not enough, but a start." It was one of the rare times she called attention to her gender breakthrough.

Two weeks later, on April 19, the Treasury Department announced the creation of a Climate Hub and a climate counselor to confront the threat of climate change and to help transform the economy into one with a net-zero emissions future. The office would assess economic and tax policy, financial risks, and lending programs all based on the goal of combatting global warming. In an April 21 speech explaining the policy to the Institute of International Finance, Yellen said the federal government planned to aggressively tackle climate change. "We are committed to directing public investment to areas that can facilitate our transition to net-zero and strengthen the functioning of our financial system so that workers, investors, and businesses can seize the opportunity that tackling climate change presents," she declared.

Toward that goal, Yellen notched an early victory at a meeting of the Group of Twenty (G20) finance ministers in Venice on July 10, when the group endorsed for the first time financial penalties for emitters of carbon into the atmosphere as a way to reduce harmful greenhouse gases.

Another issue of special importance to Yellen, though a far more arcane one, was the issuance of Special Drawing Rights (SDRs) deposited with the International Monetary Fund. SDRs, as noted earlier, are credits that wealthy donor nations provide to needy nations that can exchange them for hard currencies, such as dollars, euros, or Japanese yen. The borrowers pay a small interest rate for tapping SDRs. Ever since she wrote a research paper on the topic while working at the Fed as a staff economist in 1977, Yellen had supported the program as a way for rich countries to share their wealth with poor ones on a modest scale.

On April 1, 2021, the Treasury Department announced it was working with the IMF to help provide up to $650 billion worth of SDRs to aid countries hit hardest by the COVID-19 pandemic. It was the first time the Treasury had supported an SDR allocation since the Great Recession was nearing an end in 2009. Yellen took great pleasure in being able to take that step unilaterally by ensuring that the United States did not exceed the allocation previously approved by Congress. It didn't happen easily.

Career staffers at Treasury were ambivalent about the SDR allocation because it seemed like free money, something the Treasury Department is always leery about. The White House wasn't thrilled either because it worried that members of Congress would be vocal in their worries that bad actors—such as Iran or Venezuela—would get their hands on SDRs and exchange them for badly needed hard currencies. In fact, the IMF has ways to ignore requests for SDRs from governments that it finds objectionable.

An adviser specializing in the issue gave Yellen a detailed briefing on the economic and political pros and cons of the allocation only to learn two months later that she already was an expert on the subject from her work as a Fed staffer. "She sat there during my briefing knowing more about SDRs than I did, as I said, 'Let me mansplain the subject,'" the aide recalled. "I just keep finding that she studied most everything." Yellen ultimately prevailed, and the White House stayed silent, though some Republican critics in Congress howled until the issue quickly dropped from sight.

Just as she worried about the plight of poor nations, Yellen used her new pulpit at Treasury to spread the word that she would remain focused on raising the alarm about economic inequality in the United States, another issue her predecessors rarely raised. She highlighted that concern in a speech on May 26, one day after the anniversary of George Floyd's death. Speaking to the Financial Literacy and Education Commission, she began with a blunt observation: the economy "has never worked fairly for people of color."

"I've been an economist for a long time, and this is one of the areas where I've focused my attention," she continued. "It was probably because I started studying economics during the civil rights movement. I took my first course around 1963. I was a freshman in college, and if you looked at the economic data back then, the average Black family possessed roughly 15 percent of the wealth of the average white family. That is more than a 6-to-1 difference, and it is stark. But perhaps it isn't surprising: Jim Crow laws were still in effect in many places. What is surprising, however, is that it's now more than half a century later, and that 6-to-1 number has barely budged.

"Today, African Americans remain unemployed at roughly twice the rate of white Americans, and that number hasn't much changed in fifty years either. It's as close to a constant as you come in economic data. In fact, if you somehow transported my freshman economics professor to 2021—and you only showed him the employment and the wealth numbers—he would have a hard time guessing that the country has passed the Civil Rights Act or that we'd elected our first Black president or our first Black vice president."

Yellen explained that the economic fallout from the pandemic had hurt Blacks more than other Americans—they were the first to lose their jobs or businesses and last to be rehired when times improved. Her solution: "Big fiscal policy is required to address the inequalities in this country and to build an economy that works for everyone." That was why she worked tirelessly for the massive spending plans that President Biden had proposed during his first months in office. In a small gesture to back up her concern about Blacks left behind, the Treasury announced on June 15 it was issuing grants totaling $1.25 billion to help underserved communities affected by COVID-19.

On October 25, 2021, Yellen followed up on her concern about the economic disadvantages of minorities by taking an unprecedented step as Treasury secretary: naming the department's first Counselor for Racial Equity. The counselor would coordinate Treasury's efforts to advance racial equity by identifying barriers to accessing benefits and economic opportunities and seek ways to reduce them. "The American economy has historically not worked fairly for communities of color. The pandemic threw a spotlight on this inequity; people of color were often the first to lose their jobs and businesses," Yellen said in announcing the new position. "Treasury must play a central role in ensuring that as our economy recovers from the pandemic, it recovers in a way that addresses the inequalities that existed long before anyone was infected with COVID-19."

Yellen underscored her commitment to racial economic equality on January 17, 2022, in remarks on Martin Luther King Jr. Day that Treasury secretaries normally do not utter. "From Reconstruction, to Jim Crow, to the present day, our economy has never worked fairly for Black Americans—or, really, for any American of color," she told the National Action Network, a civil rights group founded by the Reverend Al Sharpton. "Well, since taking office last January, our administration has tried to change that; to ensure that neither the figurative bank of justice—nor any literal economic institution—fails to work for people of color. . . . There is still much more work Treasury needs to do to narrow the racial wealth divide."

The need to help people of color was a common Yellen theme. On November 16, 2021, she pledged to focus Treasury resources on the needs of Native Americans. At a White House Tribal Nations Summit, Yellen recalled meeting struggling small business owners, and was moved by Shayai Lucero, who ran a flower shop, Earth and Sky Floral, on tribal land in New Mexico. "The celebrations of life were how she made her living, and all of them—weddings, proms, Mother's Day gatherings—had been canceled because of the pandemic," Yellen recounted. "One of the reasons her story stuck with our team was that . . . the department has never had a full understanding of how our policies affect Tribal economies."

"Stories of native marginalization are older than the country, and you do not need a PhD in economics to know that our economy has never worked well for Native Americans," Yellen continued. "This is why we're here . . . ensuring that Native communities are counted, that you're heard and that you are represented." On June 21, 2022, to underscore that pledge, Biden appointed Mohegan Tribe Chief Lynn Malerba as the nation's first Native American treasurer of the United States, and Treasury announced the creation of a new Office of Tribal and Native Affairs. The announcements coincided with Yellen's travel to Rosebud Indian Reservation in South Dakota, the first time in history that a Treasury secretary has visited a Tribal nation.

The plight of the Internal Revenue Service (IRS) was another concern that captured Yellen's attention. Whenever Republicans controlled Congress, they often reduced IRS funds and staff, which resulted in fewer audits, less service, and more opportunities for people to evade paying their taxes. Indeed, from 2010 to 2020, the IRS workforce had decreased from 95,000 to 76,000, and the budget fell from $14 billion to $12 billion. The problems of the agency increased significantly during 2021, as the COVID-19 pandemic caused staff shortages and diverted resources to distribute relief money. The result was a record backlog in unprocessed tax returns and inadequate staff to assist the public. Yellen figured that a relatively small investment in improved IRS compliance would produce many times that in higher collections and would also improve tax return processing. The IRS also planned to hire more workers.

In the spring of 2021, the Treasury proposed an $80 billion increase in the IRS budget over a ten-year period. It said the added resources—along with tighter income reporting requirements and tougher penalties for noncompliance—would help close the "tax gap," the difference between taxes owed to the government and those actually paid. According to a Treasury analysis in May, the tax gap totaled nearly $600 billion in 2019 and would rise to $7 trillion over the next decade if left unaddressed—roughly 15 percent of taxes owed. The plan would double the IRS workforce.

On June 9, the *New York Times* published an op-ed by five former secretaries of the Treasury expressing their support for the plan. Entitled "We Ran the Treasury Department. This Is How to Fix Tax Evasion," it was signed by Democrats Timothy Geithner, Jacob Lew, Robert Rubin, and Lawrence Summers, and Republican Henry Paulson. The following month, the nonpartisan Congressional Budget Office (CBO) produced a report that found the payback from bolstering the IRS would be sizable: an $80 billion budget increase over ten years would bring in $207 billion in additional tax revenue, for a net gain of $127 billion. On November 18, 2021, on the eve of the House vote for Biden's scaled-back $2 trillion Build Back Better Plan, Yellen said increased IRS compliance would bring in more than $400 billion over ten years—double the CBO estimate, which did not include some of the new income reporting requirements the IRS sought to crack down on wealthy tax cheats. "The Fact Checker," a *Washington Post* column, accused her in December 2021 of exaggerating the savings and misrepresenting CBO's conclusions.

As part of its move to improve IRS enforcement, the Treasury proposed that cryptocurrency transactions of $10,000 or more be reported to the IRS, just as large cash transactions must. The goal was to rein in the rapidly growing market for digital currencies, such as Bitcoin, which had eluded regulation and was a frequent source of illegal activity, ranging from ransomware to drug smuggling. As the chair of the Financial Stability Oversight Council established by the Dodd-Frank law to avoid another 2007-style crash, Yellen worried about the proliferation of Bitcoin and similar cryptocurrencies that were valued in the trillions of dollars. Her fear was that this burgeoning but still largely secretive business could trigger the next financial crisis—just as exotic and misunderstood derivatives had caused the last one. She would spend considerable time in 2021 and 2022 huddling with other regulators to formulate a broad policy for overseeing digital currencies.

❖ ❖ ❖

WHEN YELLEN WAS NAMED TO THE TREASURY POST, SHE WAS surprised and gratified by the swell of good wishes that flooded in from financial leaders of other countries who had been appalled at how they were treated by the Trump administration. "The United States had really mistreated its neighbors and friends around the world during the Trump years," she said. "They got little or no support for the things they wanted to do and cared about, such as climate change. I think it was, frankly, very destabilizing. So, I had the opportunity to represent the United States in important international forums, including the G7 and G20, and I seized the opportunity to try to turn things around. The issues of importance to them that required our collaboration fit in very well with the Biden agenda. We could see how pleased our neighbors and allies were, how relieved, how supportive they were. It's been a source of satisfaction to me to be able to play that role."

The Biden agenda included rejoining the Paris Climate Accord to fight global warming and strengthening alliances with NATO members that were shredded by Trump. The goodwill that poured in encouraged Yellen to pursue an ambitious and long-elusive goal raised initially by Biden's transition team, one that—if successful—would be a historic accomplishment and seal her legacy as a titan at Treasury: the first major global corporate tax treaty in a century.

Yellen raised the prospect in a letter to her Group of Twenty counterparts on February 25, 2021: "As we know, the changing global economy presents new challenges for corporate taxation. The United States is committed to the multilateral discussions . . . overcoming existing disagreements and finding workable solutions in a fair and judicious manner."

The issue had been the subject of long-standing talks that involved 140 countries under the sponsorship of the Organisation for Economic Co-operation and Development (OECD), a group of wealthy countries that seeks to promote economic progress and world trade. The talks had two goals in mind. The first was to agree on a minimum global corporate tax rate to prevent multinational corporations from sheltering their profits in low-tax countries. The second was to tax a portion of e-commerce profits based on earnings from sales in each country rather than on where the companies are headquartered, as was the current rule. This digital tax would only apply to the largest e-commerce companies, such as Amazon and Google. This approach had long been sought by European countries frustrated that they could not tax US-based giants that made so much of their profits off customers in Europe.

Though seemingly sensible objectives, the tax proposals were highly controversial. Low-tax havens, such as Hungary, Ireland, Estonia, and several small island nations, did not like the idea of losing their advantage in attracting corporations to stash their earnings. The digital tax idea, naturally, sparked vigorous opposition from the affected companies, which could afford to employ legions of lobbyists to mount a counteroffensive in Congress by anti-tax Republicans.

The hundreds of billions of dollars in revenue the proposals could raise, however, were irresistible to finance ministers around the world who were keenly aware that corporate tax revenue was needed to pay for government programs that had been declining for decades. Without an agreed-upon minimum tax, countries had been cutting corporate tax rates to deter companies from moving capital to more favorable havens. It was a race to the bottom. At Trump's urging, Congress cut the US corporate tax rate in 2017 from 35 percent to 21 percent, a move in line with other countries in recent years. The Tax Foundation, a US think tank that examines tax policy, found that the average corporate tax rate globally had fallen from 40 percent in 1980 to just 24 percent in 2021.

The loss of corporate revenue has been a contributing factor in rising budget deficits in the United States for more than half a century, as lucrative tax loopholes granted by Congress allowed some of the most profitable companies on the planet to pay little or no taxes. Historical tables by the White House Office of Budget and Management showed that corporate income tax revenue as a share of the US economy shrank from 6 percent in 1952 to a mere 1 percent in 2019. To help pay for his ambitious spending programs, President Biden had proposed increasing the corporate tax rate to 28 percent, although he signaled that he would entertain a slightly lower figure.

The global talks had gone nowhere under Trump, who had opposed a new tax on digital companies, but the negotiations gained momentum once Yellen indicated a willingness to consider digital taxing and to take a collaborative approach rather than Trump's nationalistic my-way-or-the-highway stance. Negotiators were looking at a tax floor of 15 percent. The minimum tax would not be mandatory but would have incentives to comply: if a country kept a 10 percent tax rate instead of the agreed-upon 15 percent, companies would be subject to paying the 5 percent difference to the country where they are headquartered, thus removing the advantage of sheltering their profits elsewhere.

Yellen took the ball and ran with it. She won support for a tax deal at a meeting of finance ministers from the wealthiest democracies, the Group of Seven (G7), in London in early June. On the plane over, she had spent four hours going over the complex issues with her top international tax expert, grilling him down to the minutiae. A tentative agreement was reached by 132 countries on July 1 and endorsed at a meeting of the Group of Twenty finance ministers in Venice and then by finance ministers from the European Union in Brussels later that month.

The accord—expected to take effect in 2023—established a global minimum tax of 15 percent on multinational corporations with more than $900 million in revenue. The largest multinationals, those with more than $24 billion in revenue, would start paying taxes where their sales are recorded, not just their home base. In other words, Apple would pay less US taxes but more overseas, while Sony would pay more US taxes and less in Japan. Financial, energy, and mining companies were excluded from the arrangement to get most countries on board.

An adviser who attended the meetings with Yellen recounted how she employed her negotiating skills to the fullest to forge an agreement. She would patiently listen to each of her colleagues' reservations, then say she understood why those issues were so important to them before laying out her own constraints. "Then she would say, 'Given what you have said and what I've said, maybe here's a way forward.' And time after time after time, she managed to move people to a conclusion," the adviser said. "A lot of these were alpha-male foreign minister types and—pardon the overuse of the metaphor of herding cats—she really got people with very different and initially quite incompatible approaches to come together. She found the way through that." EU Economy Commissioner Paolo Gentiloni singled Yellen out as the linchpin for reaching the historic agreement.

The adviser who attended the meetings with Yellen had seen past efforts at a tax accord fail over the decades because of intransigence among finance ministers in Europe who said tax policy was strictly a national concern and none of the business of international groups like the OECD. So, he was shocked that a tentative deal came together so quickly. "My first surprise was how much she knows. Then my second surprise was how well she interacts and negotiates. And my third surprise is how much respect people have for her," he said. "At the EU finance ministers meeting, people said the nicest things about Yellen. Someone said something about how great it was that the planets had aligned again so that the transatlantic cooperation between America and Europe could resume. And then [European Central Bank president] Christine Lagarde, when it was her turn to speak, said, 'Well, the planets may be aligned, but Janet's the star.' And everybody applauded."

Representative Richard Neal, the chair of the House Ways and Means Committee, which would try to shepherd the accord through Congress, was also surprised that a deal came together so soon: "Let's be honest. It's been tougher for women along the way in economics than it has been for men. But I thought her performance at the G7, the G20, and the OECD was outstanding."

Wally Adeyemo was particularly impressed with how Yellen forged a consensus at the G7 meeting in London. She studied up on each of her counterpart's particular concerns so she could address them and demonstrate how the group could find common ground.

"She understood where the French, the British, the Germans were coming from, and then was able to help them move towards a consensus," he said. "Once the G7 was aligned, you had a sense of momentum to the point where an entire deal appeared likely to come together before the end of 2021."

Yellen acknowledged the historic nature of the agreement—though the needed approval by Congress was anything but certain. Yet, with typical modesty, she refused to take credit for tackling the issue in the first place. "I didn't dream up the idea of an international treaty to establish minimum global taxes. This was a project that had been going on at the OECD for many years," she said. "But it seemed to reach a dead-end during the Trump years in the absence of US support. The Biden transition team identified it as an important opportunity. They understood that we've had a race to the bottom in corporate taxation for decades. Corporations enjoyed a huge tax cut under Trump, and corporate revenue had greatly declined. It was a giveaway to the rich. The transition team understood that an international agreement could enable a rise in taxes to a more reasonable level, and, more generally, it could end a global race to the bottom in corporate taxation that served only to shift more of the tax burden onto workers. My role has been to help close the deal. I have been honored to participate."

Dealing with the concerns of 140 different nations, however, was a mammoth task, Yellen admitted, but one that meshed with her patented skill: superpreparation. When India balked at part of the agreement, Yellen had to call Finance Minister Nirmala Sitharaman. "I didn't understand India's issue and concern. I couldn't understand how to address it without the people involved explaining the background so I understood exactly the issue the Indians had encountered. I knew I had better read that memo before I got on the phone with her or else I was going to screw up this OECD negotiation. I was both exhausted and thrilled to have an opportunity to contribute."

After a virtual meeting with her G7 counterparts on September 9, Yellen hailed the historic achievement that had now been supported by 134 countries representing more than 90 percent of the world's economic activity. She urged participating nations to adopt the new rules swiftly. "The new international tax system would meet the needs of the 21st century global economy by providing governments with resources to invest in their workers and economies, as well as improving the standing of U.S. businesses by leveling the playing field in which they compete," she said in a statement released by the Treasury Department.

On October 8, Yellen could celebrate her biggest victory in her first nine months in office: 136 nations agreed to the biggest overhaul of international tax rules in one hundred years, a deal made possible when holdouts Ireland, Estonia, and Hungary threw their support behind a 15 percent minimum corporate tax. Kenya, Nigeria, Pakistan, and Sri Lanka remained opposed, but they lacked the economic clout to thwart an agreement. "When this deal is enacted, Americans will find the global economy a much easier place to land a job, earn a living, or scale a business," Yellen declared. Then she added an observation that once again underscored her determination to make economic policy—even trade—work to the benefit of everyone: "President Biden often talks about a 'foreign policy for the middle class.' Today, is what foreign policymaking for the middle class looks like in practice."

It would be up to Congress to make the accord a reality by 2023. Lawmakers would have to ratify the agreement—signed by 137 nations as of the end of 2021—and agree to a new minimum 15 percent tax rate on foreign earnings of US corporations.

It was a once-in-a-lifetime opportunity that very likely would play a major role in determining how enduring a legacy Janet Yellen would have as the first female successor to a well-established icon whose face adorns US currency—Alexander Hamilton, the nation's first Treasury secretary.

In 2022, Yellen would use her skills and goodwill with other world financial leaders to oversee another issue with far more worrisome consequences: economic sanctions against Russia to punish it for its unprovoked and brutal invasion of neighboring Ukraine. The sanctions she and her staff identified and imposed in coordination with allies were the toughest ever imposed. More nations worked in unison with the United States than in any such previous effort.

# EPILOGUE

*"I have been incredibly fortunate.*
*I have lived a life of Big Joys and Small Sorrows."*

LEGACIES TAKE YEARS—OFTEN DECADES—TO FORM, AS THE passage of time helps determine just how enduring a person's mark on history is. So, in 2022, it is premature to discuss Janet Yellen's legacy without asking a number of key questions about the future.

Did she help guide the economy toward a golden post-pandemic era during her tenure as Treasury secretary as she had done as Fed chair, or did she preside over an ugly revival of stagnation—sluggish growth and inflation—as her intellectual rival and occasional tormentor, Lawrence Summers, prophesied? Did she pull to the finish line congressional approval of a once-every-century international tax accord that brought order to the global tax system and increased corporate tax revenue for all nations? Was she successful in using her people skills and intellect to bring Democrats and Republicans together behind sensible programs that laid the foundation for future growth, prosperity, and greater economic equality?

We will have to wait for future events to render answers to these questions. Still, Janet Yellen already has laid down indelible markers that allow for an early assessment of her as both a remarkable public servant and one who made the lives of countless millions of Americans better off as a result of the policies she embraced.

For starters, her ability to break glass ceilings multiple times as the first woman to climb to the top of the economic policymaking world will remain as historic achievements, even though she insists on being judged based on her performance without regard to her gender. On that point, her former colleague on the Fed Board of Governors, Laurence Meyer, agrees: "I hate to think of her as the first female secretary of the Treasury. She's tremendously qualified under any circumstances. It was an inspired choice by Biden, and a pretty obvious choice to be head of the San Francisco Fed, as she was to be chair of the Fed, as she was to be chair of the Council of Economic Advisers."

"Janet never thought of herself as someone breaking glass ceilings, she never thought of herself as gender first," added former chief White House economist Laura Tyson. "She is a serious macroeconomist. She became devoted to serious economic analysis of policy issues. That is what drove her. She was confident because she was good at what she does. She had rigor, she had commitment and was so passionate about the work. She's an incredibly hard worker who agonizes over every speech and every single data point. It's a no-nonsense approach. And those are all things that I would attribute to her success. It turns out that there were glass ceilings shattered along the way, but that isn't what was motivating her. And other people recognized over time that she's the right person for these jobs, not because she's a woman. It's not a case of 'Let's put her into this place because she might do the right job.' No. It's that she's the right person for this job, period. That's how I think about it."

Still, it's hard to ignore the many glass ceilings she shattered and how long it took someone to break through them—nearly two-and-a-half centuries in the case of Treasury secretary. And despite so many historic accomplishments, she always keeps her ego in check with a modesty that is an exceedingly rare trait in a power- and status-obsessed city like Washington. "You never get the feeling that she finds someone isn't worth her time," observes David Wessel, the former *Wall Street Journal* reporter and editor who worked with Yellen at the Brookings Institution. "She's not one of those people who go to a Washington cocktail party and look over your shoulder at the next more important person in the room."

Her pleasing personality made Yellen all the more effective when added to her ability to communicate complex economic concepts with down-to-earth clarity and her knack for winning the respect of peers, subordinates, and all manner of politicians. That combination made her a unique figure in Washington's supercharged environment.

"She models how it is to be an economist and succeed in a world that really is not set up for a woman to succeed, particularly someone of her generation," said Claudia Sahm, a senior macroeconomist who worked at the Fed for more than a decade until leaving in 2019. "Just watching her and seeing how she navigates it, how she brings such incredible policy advice and policymaking to the job is an example for all economists, especially women. It's definitely been an important example for me. On some level it's telling us Janet has done it so it can be done. We can learn from her. That's the piece that is inspiring."

Sahm, who is thirty years younger than Yellen, said her former boss also has a gift in being able to bring out the best in her staff. "She has an ability to look out for her people, nurture them, encourage them," added Sahm. "She leads without throwing elbows. She believes in pulling people up behind her and holding everyone to extremely high standards. When I brought work to Janet and it wasn't good enough, you got the response, 'I know you can do better. Here's this to think about. Come back to me,' as opposed to someone bringing in work and being told, 'What is this? This is wrong,' and you send a person off demoralized. With Janet, you go back and do your best work."

As a working mother, Sahm, a self-described "Macro Mom," recalled being touched one day at the Fed when Yellen, then chair, happened to be in the elevator as Sahm and a female colleague were talking about how hard it was to balance work with raising young children. Yellen jumped into the conversation, recalling how she had to go through the same problems at Berkeley when her son, Robby, was young. "You don't have to bake cookies, just go to the grocery store," Sahm recalled her saying. "It's tough but don't be hard on yourself."

"She didn't have to say anything, but she shared an experience from her life that showed you can do this, and your kid's school will be fine with store-bought cookies," Sahm continued. "She didn't have to step in and be supportive. She's the chair of the Fed. It is not her job to make people feel better in the elevator on the way to the cafeteria. There's no way she remembers that conversation in the elevator, but things like that meant so much to me. That was Janet being Janet. She does the little things. And then she does the huge things."

One of those huge things is Yellen's career-long focus on combatting global warming and economic inequality, which have gotten unprecedented propulsion as a result of her tenure at the Treasury Department. One signature achievement involves climate change: for the first time, she made it the focus of every aspect of the financial world that the Treasury supervises. Another is the unprecedented scale of federal subsidies she directed to those most in need of government help to live happy and productive lives.

"There was a lot of discussion prior to her arrival about the importance of finance to climate change," said deputy Treasury secretary Wally Adeyemo. "I'd worked for Secretary Lew and Secretary Geithner, and they both spent a bit of time on it. But I think that during her tenure, we will see more centrality of finance, including regulation, tax policy, and fiscal policy, towards addressing the climate crisis in a way that's never been seen before. That'll be largely because the president is focused on it, and you have a Treasury secretary with unique skills who spent a great deal of time thinking about these issues and understands each in a way that few others before her did. And I think we'll probably see while she's secretary one of the biggest investments in both human capital and infrastructure in the United States in more than a generation to address some of the long-term challenges we've had. A big piece of that will be in not just the programs but their implementation."

Notwithstanding some news stories in mid-2022 suggesting Yellen had lost clout and confidence among White House officials as inflation worsened, Brian Deese, director of Biden's National Economic Council, described Yellen as a unique and powerful voice in the administration. "No one in modern American history brought more experience and perspective around the core economic challenges facing the country, the core regulatory questions facing the financial system and the international ramifications," said Deese, a colleague and friend of Yellen. "As a result, she has commanded a unique degree of deference to her views. The president and our entire economic team have relied on her to bring that experience and wisdom to guide our path through what has been one of the most significant and complicated economic periods in modern American history. She's a person uniquely suited for such a complicated period."

She also proved to be a person perfectly suited to get along with Biden on a personal level. White House aides observed two septuagenarians who developed a warm, comfortable relationship. "The president's got enormous respect for her and is quite deferential to her views of the economy," said one aide, who added that Biden was particularly enamored of Yellen's legendary ability to explain arcane issues in down-to-earth language. "He can understand her, and she speaks in a way that helps him explain these issues publicly."

Son Robby believes his mother and Biden embarked jointly on a bold agenda to reverse the growing economic inequality that poses risks to the well-being of millions, the values on which the United States was founded, and even the country's social and political stability, which have been tested so deeply in the past year.

"Major economic problems are intermixed with political and sociological issues," said Robby, who has explored the connection in his research, as has his father. "There are a lot of people who are struggling for identity and purpose and meaning in their lives, and their growing disaffection creates worries for our political system." He cited the 2020 book *Deaths of Despair and the Future of Capitalism* by Anne Case and Angus Deaton. It focuses on the declining opportunities and growing despair of blue-collar families, as growing corporate capitalism redistributes wealth from the working class to the wealthy.

Capitalism used to bring prosperity to all, though unevenly, a trend that gave rise to the American Dream. Now it is doing the opposite: the top 1 percent have accumulated as much wealth as the bottom 90 percent, a disparity that keeps growing to an extent unseen in a century. That is why Yellen's embrace of empathy economics is so timely and necessary in today's divided and contentious times. Yellen was determined to use her high-level government posts to resurrect an economic system that distributes prosperity more fairly. "This is a moment when we have a window where maybe we can do something," said Robby. "I think we're all concerned that if we don't take the right steps now, we may lose a critical opportunity. I think it's exciting that my mother and Biden are trying to do bold things because it is so important."

For Yellen, using her Treasury post to do "bold things" is simply a continuation of a half-century-long crusade to use the tools of government to advance the public welfare. It is her core belief, reinforced by Yale mentor James Tobin, that big government can be a force for good when it is run by people who are talented, hardworking, and dedicated to improving society for all.

"Fundamentally, I feel that government can make a huge difference to people's everyday lives, including existential problems like climate change, and I want to be part of those solutions," Yellen said, as she reflected on why she had devoted her life to public service. "That's how I felt at the Fed. Good policy can really make our lives better, and I want to contribute. I found my work at the Fed exceptionally satisfying. I understood that the Fed didn't have the full set of tools to address society's concerns, but we could make a difference. A full-employment economy is very important."

At Treasury, Yellen finally had the full set of tools—influence over spending and tax programs that can go further to enhance people's lives. How does she see her own legacy? "I hope people will see me as someone who was always willing to contribute to the solution of societal problems, and that I have, to the best of my ability," she said in her typically understated way. Then she diverted attention away from her own achievements to pay homage to the legions of government workers with whom she has worked for so many decades.

"I think that a cadre of experienced and dedicated public servants is a huge resource. It's important to cultivate, value, develop, and nurture a civil service with the expertise to craft policy and make it work," she said. "I've seen throughout my career in government, the deep motivation, talent, and resourcefulness of our civil servants. I have also seen how much we depend on them. I recognize their contributions, and I try to motivate and inspire public service."

This is a welcome contrast to the anti-government views espoused by President Ronald Reagan and other politicians who denigrate civil servants as lazy, self-serving, and corrupt. That has hurt the morale of dedicated federal workers and discouraged many talented young adults from seeking public service careers.

"I want people who work at the Treasury—at all ranks—to feel as motivated as I do. I want them to work hard and feel they're doing something important and that their contributions are appreciated. Leadership can make a big difference. At Treasury, I try to do everything I can to be inclusive and to listen, so that everyone knows that they are part of the team. The mission of that team is service to our country. As it's said in the Marines: Semper Fidelis. Always Faithful."

Yellen best summed up her life, her contributions, and her belief in public service during a moving and highly personal commencement address to graduates of her alma mater, Fort Hamilton High School, on June 23, 2021, nearly six decades after she left Bay Ridge for a storied career. It was an address that in many ways brought her full circle from the little girl growing up in postwar America to great political power in Washington.

"The Fort provided the foundation for my life's journey," she began. "It has been a half century since my graduation but I retain the values that I learned here. And I am confident that they will serve as the same solid foundation for your lives that they have for mine."

She then recounted two stories that illustrated how the school provided that foundation for her. "The first story," she said, "is about being open to what life throws at you, rolling with the punches." Yellen then talked about working on the school newspaper, *The Pilot*, under the tutelage of her caring and inspiring faculty adviser, Jacob Salovay. He told the students that they could not always choose their assignment. "He taught us that you should look for the joy in every assignment, in every story, big and small. And, furthermore, those presumably small stories might be the ones that ended up as your favorites."

"Mr. Salovay—and his big lesson about journalism—slipped to the back of my mind. It was not until I was around 30, and starting a new job, that I began thinking about *The Pilot* again," she continued. "I had been denied tenure at my first job, which was at a university. I confess that failure was a real disappointment. I took a new job, at the Federal Reserve. And my previous disappointment vanished from my mind. My respect for the incredible Federal Reserve staff, and the important work of the Federal Reserve became the heart of my life. I had discovered a new joy." And it was there she met her future husband, George, she told the graduates. "I have been incredibly fortunate. I have lived a life of Big Joys and Small Sorrows. There's really no accounting for what assignment life will hand you next, but as Mr. Salovay taught me, it is important to find the joy in what you do."

After noting that she had kept tabs on *The Pilot* and read about how students were coping with the pandemic, Yellen continued: "My second lesson is about this community, Bay Ridge—and keeping a piece of it with you. A few years ago, I met with a dozen close friends for an informal Fort Hamilton reunion. It was our 50th, give or take a few. We were a bit surprised at how gray we had all become. But we were much more surprised that all of us had chosen careers involving public service, such as in education, in social work, in health care, in journalism, in other forms of government.

"Was it all a coincidence? Or was there a common reason we all chose working on behalf of the public—and loved the jobs, too? My classmate Jackie Leo gave the answer: 'Growing up in Bay

Ridge,' she said, 'was a gift.' . . . It was clear: Bay Ridge was home to people of many different backgrounds, but there was a mutual respect, an abiding desire to make the neighborhood work. That was the gift my friend Jackie had been talking about, and it was the reason, I think, so many of us went into public service. The lesson Bay Ridge taught us was that a happy and successful life—like a happy, successful community—depends not just on others' love and respect for you, but, even more, on your love and respect for them."

Then the latest secretary of the Treasury referred to the first secretary, the high school's namesake: "When I became Treasury Secretary, quite a few people mentioned Alexander Hamilton. That made sense. The man helped establish the Treasury Department, and even now he is having a moment. The Broadway show is a hit. But I confess: The Hamilton association I am proudest of—the one closest to my heart—is my association with this school. Because if any institution deserves to bear the name of our first Treasury Secretary—of Alexander Hamilton—it's this one.

"This school, this place, and all the people in it are living monuments to the man and what he represents: that a community isn't just something that happens, it's not just a group of people living in proximity to one another. A community—like a country—has to be made. And made by people, people who come here and pour their heart and their soul into building it. So, that is the piece of this place I especially hope you take with you. Take it with you wherever you go and in whatever form it works."

Yellen quoted from a poem by Jacob Salovay that she had kept for so many years. It ended, "Wisdom is living, but where you live determines wisdom, too."

"I am so lucky to come from Bay Ridge and to be a graduate of Fort Hamilton High," she concluded. "My heart will always be here. Fifty years from now you will be saying the same thing. And, as you know, your heart will be here, too."

Indeed. Fifty years from now, the sons and daughters of Fort Hamilton High will surely be saying many of the same things that Janet L. Yellen said on this early summer day in 2021. But in 2071, they may well speak fondly about another notable Treasury secretary closely associated with the school, one who had a positive impact on their lives—and those of so many millions of others across the United States of America.

# ACKNOWLEDGMENTS

AN AUTHOR WHO WRITES A BIOGRAPHY ABOUT A LIVING PERson who refuses to cooperate faces a daunting challenge to produce a credible account. Fortunately, I was able to chronicle the remarkable career of Janet Yellen with her full support. I am deeply grateful that she made the time during her hectic first two years as secretary of the Treasury to talk to me about her life with thoroughness and a level of candor rare among public officials I have covered as a journalist in Washington, DC, for forty-five years. I also appreciate that she made it possible for me to interview her husband, George Akerlof; her son, Robert "Robby" Akerlof; her brother, John Yellen; and countless friends, colleagues, and subordinates who might well have declined interview requests without her approval. They were generous with their time and keen in their analysis. I thank the entire Yellen family for their help in producing an authoritative biography, as well as many dozens of current and former colleagues in academia and government who provided insightful comments about Janet Yellen's life, personality, and character traits, and her professional accomplishments and challenges.

Some of those I interviewed offered additional assistance: Henry Stewart, the Bay Ridge historian, and Valerie Hodgson, president of the Fort Hamilton High School Alumni Association, who took me on a walking tour of the neighborhood where the Yellens lived. A thanks, as well, to Kaye Houlihan, Fort Hamilton High's principal, who showed me around the school. Several childhood friends were very helpful: Jim Brochu, Jackie Leo, Charles Saydah, Barbara Schwartz, Julie Lippmann, and Mary Jacobson, who provided photos, clippings from their high school newspaper and literary magazine, and other resources that assisted my research. I want to add my appreciation to rapper Dessa and her assistant, Becky Hoffman, for granting permission for reprinting lyrics from "Who's Yellen Now" in this book.

Former Federal Reserve vice chair Donald Kohn was immensely helpful in reviewing the sections of the book about the Fed's history and operations to ensure I produced an accurate account. Joanne Lipman, my former editor in chief at *USA Today* and an expert on gender bias in the workplace, provided valuable context about the barriers women have encountered since the 1950s and how they have changed over the years. Rebecca Blank, the former chancellor at the University of Wisconsin–Madison (now president of Northwestern University), was very helpful in explaining the gender bias in the field of economics that persists today. Former Commodity Futures Trading Commission chair Brooksley Born explained the controversy over regulating derivatives in the 1990s.

Two good friends provided valuable help and support. David Vogel, whom I first met in 1969 when we were roommates sharing a New York City apartment, coincidentally became a colleague of Yellen's decades later at the Haas School of Business at Berkeley, where he is a professor emeritus of business ethics. David shared numerous insights about Yellen, provided contacts to interview at Haas, and encouraged me to write this biography. Barry Wood, a fellow economics journalist I have known and admired for many years, boosted my morale at key moments when I struggled to complete this biography. And as a member of the Cosmos Club, Barry was able to show me the side entrance Yellen was forced to use when she got married at the then male-only club in 1978.

A number of my sources patiently fielded numerous requests and questions while I was working on this project throughout 2021. I thank Janet Yellen's longtime friend Vivian Nash; Treasury press secretary Calvin Mitchell; Biden transition volunteer Michele Jolin; Federal Reserve press secretary Michelle Smith; and Smith's former deputies, David Skidmore and Susan Stawick. Brown University archivists Mary Murphy and Jennifer Betts helped me track down materials and alumni I sought. Heidi Hartmann showed me copies of the legendary notes her former Yale classmate took as a graduate student.

This book would have remained just an idea had it not been for my agent, Gail Ross of Ross Yoon Agency in Washington, DC. Gail was my agent for a biography I wrote in 1986 about former Reagan budget czar and wunderkind David Stockman. Gail had encouraged me ever since to write another book. It only took me thirty-six years to come through. I am so grateful that Gail never gave up on me.

Every writer needs a strong editor, and, to my good fortune, I found one in John Mahaney at PublicAffairs. John's editing was thorough and precise, and his suggestions were spot on. His guidance and support were invaluable as I worked on this biography. Barb Pearson, another strong editor and a former colleague at *USA Today*, did a superb job scrutinizing my manuscript for factual errors. And a shout-out to Melissa Veronesi and her team of sharp-eyed copy editors for cleaning up my manuscript of the many mistakes I made.

I could not have made it through this project without encouragement—and friendly taunting—from my fellow "amigos," Dave Beckwith and Tom DeFrank, veteran journalists who mentored me when I first arrived in Washington four decades ago to cover the Big Leagues of politics. They reminded me to avoid writing a hagiography, sage advice I took to heart.

I save my final thanks and gratitude for two special people in my life. The first is my longtime friend of fifty years, Zane Lumelsky, my best man at my wedding. Zane served as both my researcher—finding obscure documents and seemingly untraceable sources—and my manuscript reader, offering helpful suggestions and corrections that made for a better book. Early on, when I fretted that I would never finish this project on time, he advised me repeatedly, "Just remember that it's like eating an elephant; you take a little bite every day until you're done." That analogy actually calmed me down.

Lastly, I thank my wonderful wife for the past forty-five years, Lois Kietur, who held my shaking hand from my initial contract talks through the publication of this book. Lois was the first reader and editor of my manuscript, making numerous wise changes and offering suggestions for improving the clarity and flow of the narrative. She boosted my confidence when I needed it and was there for me whenever I needed her—which was often. My gratitude and love are boundless.

# *BIBLIOGRAPHICAL ESSAY*

THE PEOPLE I QUOTE THROUGHOUT THIS BIOGRAPHY COME from 150 interviews I conducted by telephone or Zoom conferences in 2021 and 2022. I conducted nine Zoom interviews with Janet Yellen that lasted a total of more than fifteen hours between April 27 and November 14, 2021. We also had numerous email exchanges and telephone conversations. Interviews in 2021 with Yellen's family included her brother, John Yellen, on January 12 and September 21; her husband, George Akerlof, on February 13 and 20 and September 25; and her son, Robert "Robby" Akerlof, on April 6 and 8. John and George had follow-up exchanges with me.

Most of those I interviewed allowed me to quote them by name. Some declined to be identified at all, and others asked that only selective comments be quoted anonymously so that they could speak candidly about sensitive issues involving Yellen, her colleagues, and events in her life. These anonymous quotations are sprinkled throughout the book. All quotations from interviews I conducted are from transcripts of the recorded conversations. They have been edited for grammar, clarity, and brevity.

Some have been changed slightly at the request of sources who had asked me to clear their quotes in advance. No comments have been altered in any substantive way. Several sources said I could use the information from our interviews but not in direct quotations or attribution.

## INTRODUCTION

Yellen's March 31, 2014, speech in Chicago is posted on the Federal Reserve's website, which maintains an archive of all former Fed officials' speeches. Numerous authoritative sources have estimated that one-third of the adult working-age population has a criminal record, including a November 17, 2015, article by Matthew Friedman on the Brennan Center for Justice website. It's worth noting that most individuals with criminal records have not been convicted of serious crimes. The controversy over Yellen's singling out of former felons is detailed in numerous news accounts, including an April 2, 2014, *Washington Post* article, "Yellen Gave a Shout Out to Two Ex-Offenders in a Speech This Week. So What?" Yellen's conversation with Sam Bell on the Amtrak train to New York was recounted by Yellen and her former press aide, David Skidmore.

Former Fed governor Daniel Tarullo was interviewed on June 7, 2021. Comments about Yellen by Adam Posen, president of the Peterson Institute for International Economics, were published in the Fall 2020 issue of *The International Economy* magazine, of which I am executive editor. Former Yellen aide Michele Jolin was interviewed on May 7, 2021. Brookings Institution colleague and former *Wall Street Journal* reporter and editor David Wessel was interviewed on May 25, 2021. San Francisco Fed president Mary Daly was interviewed on May 3, 2021. Former *USA Today* editor in chief Joanne Lipman is the author of *That's What She Said: What Men Need to Know (and Women Need to Tell Them) About*

*Working Together* (William Morrow, 2018). She was interviewed on May 28 and August 16, 2021.

Rapper Dessa talked about Yellen in a January 29, 2021, interview with Jill Riley of *The Current*, a listener-supported website that covers music. Former Fed governor Laurence Meyer, founder and chairman of Monetary Policy Analytics, Inc., in Washington, DC, was interviewed on February 16, 2021. Yellen's record as an economic forecaster was detailed in Jon Hilsenrath's and Kristina Peterson's July 28, 2013, article in the *Wall Street Journal*, "Federal Reserve 'Doves' Beat 'Hawks' in Economic Prognosticating."

Other quotes in the Introduction are from interviews in 2021 with Haas School of Business professor James Wilcox (March 24), former Fed vice chair Donald Kohn (January 20), Haas global business professor David Teece (January 21), Haas professor emeritus Michael Katz (January 30), and economist Joseph Stiglitz (February 15). The views of president-elect Joe Biden's transition "brain trust" were explained to me in interviews with former US ambassador Mark Gitenstein (May 2), and Biden confidant Ted Kaufman (August 24).

Yellen's January 26, 2021, "Day One Message" was in a Treasury Department release posted online. Several news organizations described the size of the $1.9 trillion American Rescue Plan as the biggest social welfare expansion in "recent history." A March 9, 2021, column by Jason L. Riley in the *Wall Street Journal* called it "arguably the largest expansion of the welfare state since Lyndon Johnson's Great Society."

## CHAPTER 1

My description of the history of Bay Ridge is based on *How Bay Ridge Became Bay Ridge* (Henry Stewart, 2019) by local resident Henry Stewart, and *Bay Ridge: Images of America* by Peter

Scarpa, Lawrence Stelter, and Peter Syrdahl, of the Bay Ridge Historical Society (Arcadia Publishing, 2001). My description of the neighborhood where Yellen grew up is based on a walking tour I made with Henry Stewart on September 23, 2021.

I interviewed Yellen's longtime friend Susan Stover Grosart on January 29, 2021. The description of the Yellen home is based on my interviews with John and Janet Yellen and a personal visit that I made. They also discussed the background of their parents, Julius and Anna Ruth Yellen. I obtained additional information about their parents from Ancestry.com, geni.com, US Census data from 1910 and 1940, and the Archives & Special Collections at the University of Glasgow, Scotland. Yellen's husband, George Akerlof, told me that she bought her trademark high-collared jackets from the boutique Nina McLemore in Chevy Chase, Maryland.

I interviewed Yellen's childhood friends Barbara Schwartz on February 1, 2021, Jim Brochu on January 5, 2021, and Rich Rubin on February 8, 2021. John Yellen provided me copies of the letters that his mother wrote to him while he was in college. I interviewed Mary Azzara Jacobson on February 4, 2021; Florence Capaldo Kimball on February 1, 2021; Carol Overfelder Kleinman on January 6, 2021; Charles Saydah on February 2, 2021; Adele Corradengo Wilson on January 26, 2021; Julie Cohn Lippmann on February 2, 2021; and Jackie Leo on January 27, 2021. My description of Fort Hamilton High School, the motto on the wall of its entrance, and Yellen's photo on the school's Hall of Fame are from a personal visit I made to the school on September 23, 2021, with Valerie Hodgson, president of the Fort Hamilton High School Alumni Association. Yellen's poems and short story from *The Anchor* are from a copy of the magazine provided by Charles Saydah. Clippings of Yellen's editorials in *The Pilot* were provided by Mary Jacobson.

CHAPTER 2

Details of Pembroke's parietal rules protest are based on an interview with Phyllis Santry on May 7, 2021, articles in the *Pembroke Record*, and oral histories in Brown University's archives. "An Analysis of Out-of-Wedlock Childbearing in the United States," by George Akerlof, Janet Yellen, and Michael Katz, was published in the *Quarterly Journal of Economics* 111, no. 2 (1996): 277–317, https://doi.org/10.2307/2946680. Background material on James Tobin came from the Tobin Project, a research group dedicated to continuing his economic research and policies. Yellen provided me a copy of her eulogy at Tobin's memorial service.

Gary Smith's comments are from an email he sent me on February 18, 2021. I interviewed Yale classmate Heidi Hartmann on May 13, 2021. She showed me a complete set of notes on Tobin's lectures that Yellen took and Hartmann retained over the years. The 1969 Black Panther murder trial mentioned in passing was detailed in numerous media stories at the time. I interviewed Vivian Nash on January 14, 2021. A copy of Yellen's Senior Honors Thesis at Pembroke was provided by Jennifer Betts, archivist at Brown's John Hay Library. I conducted the following interviews in 2021 about Yellen during her Yale and Harvard years: Edwin "Ted" Truman (June 24), Robert "Robby" Akerlof (April 6 and 8), Michael Katz (January 30), Benjamin Friedman (February 1), Jerry Green (February 17), Gail Pierson Cromwell (May 25), Joseph Stiglitz (February 15), William James "Jim" Adams (February 24), Claudia Goldin (April 7), and Andrew Rose (January 19). Some friends and colleagues asked that certain quotes be attributed anonymously so they could speak frankly.

Details about Pierson and the Red Rose Crew are from the book *The Red Rose Crew* by Daniel J. Boyne (Hyperion Press, 2000). "Commodity Bundling and the Burden of Monopoly," by

William James Adams and Janet Yellen, was published in the *Quarterly Journal of Economics* 90, no. 3 (1976): 475–498, https://doi.org/10.2307/1886045.

## CHAPTER 3

A description of the Federal Reserve Act is based on content from the Fed's website and additional analysis provided by Donald Kohn, a former Fed vice chair. Details of the Special Drawing Rights (SDR) allocation are in an April 1, 2021, Treasury news release. CNBC posted a video of Yellen's exchange with Senator John Kennedy on March 23, 2021. I conducted the following interviews in 2021 with Yellen's friends and colleagues: economists Alicia Munnell (January 22), Laura D'Andrea Tyson (October 11), Richard Lyons (January 26), and Lawrence Summers (May 18). The description of the Cosmos Club comes from the club's website, a personal visit, and interviews with club staff members. Background on George Akerlof's father, Gösta, comes from George and an obituary published in the *New York Times* on May 11, 1966.

Yellen's paper "Efficiency Wage Models of Unemployment" was published in the *American Economic Review* 74, no. 2 (1984): 200–205. The paper "East Germany in from the Cold: The Economic Aftermath of Currency Union" was written by George Akerlof, Andrew Rose, Janet Yellen, Helga Hessenius, Rudiger Dornbusch, and Manuel Guitian for *Brookings Papers on Economic Activity* no. 1 (1991): 1–105. Andrew Rose and Yellen examined how trade imbalances affect currency exchange rates in the paper "Is There a J-Curve?" in the *Journal of Monetary Economics* 24, no. 1 (1989): 53–68.

## CHAPTER 4

Yellen's description of herself as a "non-ideological pragmatist" when nominated to the Federal Reserve Board in 1994 was in an April 23, 1994, *Los Angeles Times* article, "Clinton Names 2 Economists to Fed Board," by James Risen. Background on former Fed governor Susan Phillips is on the Fed website. The history of the Fed is explained on the Fed's website, with elaboration provided by former vice chair Donald Kohn. The description of the exterior and interior of the Fed headquarters in Washington, DC, was provided by Susan Stawick, a member of the Federal Reserve's press office.

All quotes from Federal Open Market Committee meetings come from official, verbatim FOMC transcripts that the Fed posts on its website five years later. I conducted interviews in 2021 with former Fed vice chair Alan Blinder (March 10), former governor Lawrence Lindsey (March 24), and former chair Alan Greenspan (February 25). I learned of the rivalry between Greenspan and Blinder over policy and their jockeying to be named chairman in 1996, when Greenspan's term expired, from interviews I conducted with Greenspan, Blinder, and other Fed officials while I was a senior editor at *Business Week* magazine. Their rivalry was an open secret early on, as reported in a September 9, 1994, *New York Times* article, "Fed Deputy Denies Rift with Chief," by Keith Bradsher.

Yellen provided a copy of the twelve-page memo she wrote and sent to Greenspan. It is dated June 10, 1996, and titled "Job Insecurity, the Natural Rate of Unemployment, and the Phillips Curve." Greenspan's dovish stance toward inflation because of his "insecure workers" theory was widely reported, including in a *New York Times* article, "Job Insecurity of Workers Is a Big Factor in Fed Policy," by Louis Uchitelle, on February 27, 1997. Fed chair Ben Bernanke announced an explicit inflation target of 2 percent at a news conference following an FOMC meeting on January 25, 2012. Laurence Meyer explains a key 1996 meeting when he and Yellen lobbied for a rate increase in his 2004 memoir, *A Term at the Fed*, published by HarperCollins.

CHAPTER 5

Several senior officials who knew the details of Yellen's selection as CEA chair and her subsequent work were willing to talk about her tenure there only anonymously. Michele Jolin, whom I interviewed on May 7, 2021, described GOP efforts to eliminate the CEA. I also interviewed CEA colleagues Jeffrey Frankel on March 22, 2021; Rebecca Blank on March 15, 2021; and American University president Sylvia Mathews Burwell on June 16, 2021. Gene Sperling did not respond to multiple requests for an interview. Yellen was among seven cabinet and other appointments that President Clinton made on December 20, 1996, for his second term, according to a video of the event posted online by C-SPAN. A video of Yellen's CEA chair confirmation hearing before the Senate Banking Committee on February 5, 1997, is posted on C-SPAN.

Several news stories documented divisions among President Clinton's advisers over whether he should support EPA administrator Carol Browner's push for tougher clean air standards, including "Clinton Backs EPA's Tougher Clean Air Rules" by Jo Warrick and John F. Harris in the *Washington Post* on June 26, 1997.

Blank expounded on her belief about sexism in economics in an essay, "What Should Mainstream Economists Learn from Feminist Theory," for the book *Beyond Economic Man: Feminist Theory and Economics*, edited by Marianne A. Ferber and Julie A. Nelson (University of Chicago Press, 1993).

Discussion of gender bias at the American Economic Association's annual meeting in Philadelphia is described in the January 10, 2018, *New York Times* article, "Wielding Data, Women Force a Reckoning over Bias in the Economics Field," by Jim Tankersley and Noam Scheiber. Details about the Clinton-Lewinsky affair, from the first report through the president's acquittal of impeachment charges, are thoroughly covered by multiple media accounts and historical records. Detailed activities of the CEA and its members each calendar year are listed on the US Government Publishing Office website. Yellen's March 4, 1998, testimony before the House Commerce Committee on the economic costs of the Kyoto Protocol is posted on the same federal government website. A Treasury Department news release announced the creation of a Treasury Climate Hub and counselor position on April 19, 2021. The department's press office released Yellen's speech at an international summit on climate change in Venice on July 11, 2021.

A description of derivatives and the concerns of the Commodity Futures Trading Commission in the 1990s was provided by former CFTC chair Brooksley Born, whom I interviewed on June 17, 2021. Clinton signed the Commodity Futures Modernization Act on December 21, 2000. In "The Mellowing of William Jefferson Clinton," a May 26, 2009, *New York Times Magazine* article by Peter Baker, Clinton said critics had a valid argument in complaining that "I should have raised more hell about derivatives being unregulated" when he was president. The CFTC website provides a detailed description of the Dodd-Frank Wall Street Reform and Consumer Protection Act of 2010.

## CHAPTER 6

The book *The Fabulous Decade: Macroeconomic Lessons from the 1990s* by Alan Blinder and Janet Yellen was published by the Century Foundation in 2001. A text of George Akerlof's 2001 Nobel Banquet speech on December 10, 2001, is posted on the Nobel website, as is the text and video of his formal lecture on December 8, 2001, at Aula Magna, Stockholm University. Interviews I conducted include Roger Ferguson (May 11, 2021), David Tang (July 14, 2021), and Jerome "Jay" Powell (August 19, 2021). Numerous past and present Fed officials who worked with Yellen asked that some of their observations be quoted anonymously so that they could be more candid.

Karen Horn's biography, which notes that she was the first female president of a Federal Reserve Bank, is posted on the Fed's website, as are the states that comprise the San Francisco Fed region and the salary of the regional bank's president. The Community Reinvestment Act of 1977 is explained on the Fed's website. Yellen's speech, "Economic Inequality in the United States," to the Center for the Study of Democracy, 2006–2007 Economics of Governance Lecture, University of California, Irvine, on November 6, 2006, is posted on the San Francisco Fed's website. Powell's comments on November 30, 2018, announcing the creation of the Janet L. Yellen Award for Excellence in Community Development are posted on the Fed's website.

Background on Washington Mutual savings and loan and French bank BNP Paribas was compiled from numerous news accounts about them at the time of the unfolding financial crisis in 2007. Likewise, background on Countrywide Financial Corp. was compiled from numerous news accounts from 2004 through 2016. Background on Countrywide founder Angelo Mozilo was compiled from numerous news accounts at the time, including a February 17, 2011, *New York Times* article, "Long After Fall, Countrywide's Mozilo Defended His Legacy," by Ben Protess.

## CHAPTER 7

Direct quotes from FOMC meetings and conference calls are contained in official Fed transcripts posted on its website, as well as Fed statements released the same day. The emergency Term Securities Lending Facility (TSLF) announced by the Fed on March 11, 2008, is explained on the Fed's website. Details on the collapse of Lehman are provided in numerous news articles and books. Details of the $700 billion Troubled Asset Relief Program (TARP) created by the Treasury Department in October 2008 are explained on the department's website. I interviewed former Fed chair Ben Bernanke on June 10, 2021, and former New York Fed president and Treasury secretary Timothy Geithner on February 19, 2021. The Obama adviser who arranged for Yellen to brief the candidate before his economics speech at Cooper Union on March 27, 2008, asked to remain anonymous so as to speak more candidly. A video of Obama's speech at Cooper Union is posted on YouTube. A transcript of the speech was posted on several news websites, including that of the *New York Times*.

## CHAPTER 8

Salaries of Fed governors are listed on the Fed website. Yellen told me how much she made as vice chair in 2010. President Obama's remarks in nominating Yellen, Sarah Bloom Raskin, and Peter Diamond to the Fed Board of Governors on April 29, 2010, are in the White House archives posted online. The US Government Publishing Office posted a transcript of the July 15, 2010, confirmation hearing for Yellen, Raskin, and Diamond. Yellen's speech on October 11, 2010, to the National Association for Business Economics in Denver is posted on the Fed website. An audio recording of Yellen's interview with the staff of the National Crisis Inquiry Commission in November 2010 was posted online by the commission.

Background on the Fed's move toward more openness is detailed in "A Short History of FOMC Communication" by Mark A. Wynne, the Federal Reserve Bank of Dallas Research/Economic Letter 8, no. 8 (2013). Details about the Fed leak were compiled from numerous news articles and senior Fed officials at the time who had direct knowledge of the incidents and the follow-up investigations. Some current and former Fed governors would speak about the leaks and other sensitive issues only if quoted anonymously. Jeffrey Lacker's resignation from the Richmond Fed was detailed by former colleagues and numerous news articles at the time, including an April 4, 2017, *New York Times* article, "Richmond Fed President Resigns, Admitting He Violated Confidentiality," by Binyamin Appelbaum. The Fed's new ethics rules were described in the October 21, 2021, *New York Times* article, "Fed Unveils Stricter Trading Rules Amid Fallout from Ethics Scandal," by Jeanna Smialek. Jeremy Stein was interviewed on May 24, 2021.

## CHAPTER 9

Numerous current and former officials in the Clinton and Obama administrations and the Fed offered their views of Lawrence Summers on condition that they not be identified by name. Cornel West described his conflict with Summers in the article "Why I Left Harvard University" in the *Journal of Blacks in Higher Education* no. 47 (Spring, 2005): 64–68. Summers's comments suggesting that women may have less aptitude than men in science and math were made at a January 14, 2005, academic conference and first reported by the *Boston Globe* in the January 17, 2005, article "Summers' Remarks on Women Draw Fire" by Marcella Bombardieri.

I interviewed Senator Sherrod Brown, D-OH, on October 5, 2021. His office provided a copy of the letter he wrote in support of Yellen as Fed chair that was sent to the White House on July 25, 2013. Heidi Hartmann provided a copy of the letter she and eight hundred other economists signed in support of Yellen's selection as Fed chair. I interviewed Senator Jeff Merkley, D-OR, on August 5, 2021. His office provided a copy of a letter he sent to the White House on January 14, 2009, complaining about provisions of the Troubled Asset Relief Program (TARP).

The September 15, 2013, announcement by the White House that Lawrence Summers was withdrawing his name as a candidate for Fed chair is from the White House archives posted online and a *Washington Post* article of the same date. President Obama's announcement of Yellen's nomination as Fed chair on October 9, 2013, comes from a video of the event from the White House archives. C-SPAN posted a video of Yellen's Senate Banking Committee hearing on November 14, 2013. Details on Yellen's Senate confirmation as Fed chair on January 6, 2014, came from multiple news accounts at the time. California senator Barbara Boxer commented on Yellen in an email. Videos and transcripts of Yellen's official swearing-in on February 3, 2014, and her ceremonial swearing-in on March 5, 2014, are posted on the Fed's website.

## CHAPTER 10

The example of Fed chair Alan Greenspan's "Fedspeak" occurred in testimony from the Federal Reserve Board's semiannual monetary policy report to Congress before the Senate Banking Committee on February 13, 2001. It is one of several examples of Greenspan's "Fedspeak" listed on the website of the Federal Reserve Bank of Dallas. A video and transcript of Yellen's first news conference as Fed chair is posted on the Fed's website. A *Financial Times* story, "Markets Rattled as Fed Points to Earlier Interest Rate Rises," by Robin Harding, posted March 19, 2014, said she "stumbled" at her rookie news conference. Other media stories posted online that cited her "gaffe" and "blunder" included Reuters, Bloomberg, Forbes, MarketWatch, and CNBC.

A February 2017 study of FOMC dissents by the St. Louis Federal Reserve Bank is posted on its website. Description of the economic progress made in 2015 comes from the Bureau of Labor Statistics' online archive and a January 6, 2017, White House report "Eight Years of Labor Market Progress and the Employment

Situation in December," by Jason Furman, chair of the Council of Economic Advisers. Several Republican economists and former Fed members told me that it was a common view among Republicans that Yellen was helping Hillary Clinton's presidential election campaign in 2016 by postponing rate increases, but they did not want to be identified by name.

## CHAPTER 11

An archive of elections maintained by the US House of Representatives shows that the Republican majority achieved in the 2014 midterm election was the largest since 1928. A transcript of the House Financial Services Committee hearing on February 25, 2015, when Republicans accused Yellen of being partisan, is posted on the committee's website. Yellen's November 6, 2006, speech "Economic Inequality in the United States" to the Center for the Study of Democracy at the University of California, Irvine, is posted on the San Francisco Federal Reserve Bank's website. Evidence of loss of well-paying manufacturing jobs in the Midwest includes a finding that as of 2018, employment in the US auto industry was 233,700 workers, a 17 percent decline since 1994, according to an April 15, 2019, study, "The U.S. Auto Labor Market since NAFTA," by the Federal Reserve Bank of St. Louis.

The report "Disparities in Wealth by Race and Ethnicity" in the 2019 Survey of Consumer Finances was posted on the Fed's website on September 28, 2020. Yellen cited the 2013 Consumer Finance Survey findings on September 18, 2014, at the 2014 Assets Learning Conference of the Corporation for Enterprise Development, Washington, DC. A prerecorded video of her remarks is posted on the Fed website. Her October 17, 2014, speech to the Fifty-Eighth Economic Conference on Economic Opportunity and Inequality, hosted by the Boston Fed, is also on the Fed website. Record low unemployment rates for Blacks (5.5 percent) and

Hispanics (3.9 percent) were set in September 2019, according to a Bureau of Labor Statistics report on October 4, 2019. A Census Bureau report on September 15, 2020, said poverty rates for Blacks and Hispanics fell to record lows in 2019.

A video of Joseph Stiglitz's interview in the PBS *Frontline* documentary, "Power of the Fed," which aired on July 13, 2021, was posted online by PBS. Yellen promoted diversity on October 30, 2014, in welcoming remarks at the National Summit on Diversity in the Economics Profession in Washington, DC. She spoke about the need for more minority bankers, by videoconference on September 29, 2016, at "Banking and the Economy: A Forum for Minority Bankers," an event sponsored by the Federal Reserve Bank of Kansas City. Both speeches are posted on the Fed website. Fed chair Jerome Powell called inequality the biggest economic challenge, in response to a question at "A Conversation with the Chairman: A Teacher Town Hall Meeting" in Washington, DC, on February 6, 2019, according to a February 7, 2019, news story, "Federal Reserve Chair Calls Income Inequality the Biggest Challenge in Next 10 Years," by Heather Long in the *Washington Post*. Yellen's March 25, 2014, remarks on Women's History Month at a reception at the US Capitol are posted on the Fed website, as is her May 5, 2017, speech at "125 Years of Women at Brown Conference," sponsored by Brown University. Yellen's email on her career for the 2014 Fort Hamilton High School reunion, including her typo, was provided by classmate Charles Saydah.

## CHAPTER 12

Donald Trump's September 12, 2016, interview on CNBC attacking Yellen is posted on CNBC's website. Yellen provided a link to the November 5, 2016, Trump campaign commercial that Yellen found to be chilling in its subtle anti-Semitism. Her speech on financial regulation on August 25, 2017, at the Fed's annual summer conference in Jackson Hole, Wyoming, is posted on the Fed's website. Then Fed governor Powell said in an interview with me that he did a TV interview at the 2017 Jackson Hole conference to say Yellen's speech was not intended as a shot at the Trump administration.

Trump's comments about the August 11–12, 2017, march in Charlottesville, Virginia, by white nationalists and neo-Nazis were widely reported by news outlets. Between October 28 and November 1, 2017, numerous news organizations—including CNBC, the *Washington Post*, *New York Times*, and *Wall Street Journal*—reported that Trump would name Powell as Fed chair. His comments in nominating Powell as Fed chair in the Rose Garden on November 2, 2017, are posted on the White House archives website. Trump's attacks on Powell from 2018 through 2020 as an "enemy" of the state and that he had "no guts, no sense, no vision" are among numerous tweets from his now suspended Twitter account that news organizations reported at the time.

Powell's admission that the Fed raised rates too much in 2019 is based on a *Washington Post* article, "The Year the Federal Reserve Admitted It Was Wrong," by Heather Long on December 11, 2019. Fed vice chair Randal Quarles's comments about Yellen were made at a Brookings Institution event, "The Economic Outlook: A Conversation with the Fed's Randal Quarles," on May 26, 2021. A video of the interview is posted on the Brookings's website.

## CHAPTER 13

The Brookings Institution discusses its founding, history, and mission on its website. Details on Yellen's speeches and the income she received for them are listed in the publicly released financial disclosure form she filed when nominated to be Treasury secretary. The history of the American Economic Association, including a list of current and past presidents, is detailed on its website.

Videos of Biden's nomination of Yellen as Treasury secretary on November 30, 2020, were posted online by numerous news organizations. A video of Yellen's January 19, 2021, confirmation hearing before the Senate Finance Committee is posted on C-SPAN's website. A January 19, 2021, news article by *The Hill* provided a detailed account of the letter that eight former secretaries of the Treasury wrote to support Yellen's nomination to the post. Multiple news outlets reported on Yellen's unanimous approval as Treasury secretary by the Senate Finance Committee on January 22, 2021, and the 84–15 vote to confirm her by the full Senate on January 25, 2021. A video of Vice President Kamala Harris swearing in Yellen as Treasury secretary on January 26, 2021, is posted on C-SPAN's website.

## CHAPTER 14

Deputy Treasury secretary Adewale "Wally" Adeyemo's background is detailed in a biography posted on the Treasury Department's website. I interviewed Adeyemo on September 13, 2021.

A Treasury Department release on December 21, 2017, announced that on that date "the Trump administration launched a new sanctions regime targeting human rights abusers and corrupt actors around the world." The list included Dan Gertler, described in the release as "an international businessman and billionaire who has amassed his fortune through hundreds of millions of dollars' worth of opaque and corrupt mining and oil deals in the Democratic Republic of the Congo (DRC)." On January 15, 2021, Andrea M. Gacki, director of the Treasury Department's Office of Foreign Assets Control, issued without public announcement a notice to the law firm Arnold & Porter Kaye Scholer LLP that it was issuing a license to Gertler that lifted restrictions imposed by the prior sanctions, which had frozen Gertler's assets in the United States. The license was to expire on January 31, 2022.

On March 8, 2021, Ned Price, a State Department spokesman working for the Biden administration, issued a press statement on the "Revocation of License Granted for Dan Gertler" that said, "Today, the Department of the Treasury, in consultation with the Department of State, revoked the license that was issued to Specially Designated National Dan Gertler on January 15, 2021. The license previously granted to Mr. Gertler is inconsistent with America's strong foreign policy interests in combatting corruption around the world, specifically including US efforts to counter corruption and promote stability in the Democratic Republic of the Congo (DRC). As the original designation of Mr. Gertler under the Global Magnitsky sanctions program in 2017 and subsequent designations in 2018 made clear, Mr. Gertler engaged in extensive public corruption." On December 6, 2021, the Treasury Department issued a release stating that its Office of Foreign Assets Control had sanctioned Alain Mukonda "for providing support to sanctioned billionaire Dan Gertler." The release also said, "As a result of Gertler's actions, between 2010 and 2012 alone, the DRC reportedly lost more than $1.36 billion in revenues from the underpricing of mining assets that were sold to offshore companies linked to Gertler."

Yellen admitted that her 2021 inflation forecast was wrong during a May 31, 2022, interview with Wolf Blitzer on CNN's *The Situation Room*. *The Atlantic* magazine and *Wall Street Journal* posted their interviews with Yellen on May 4, 2021, and May 5, 2021, respectively, on their websites. They showed how she shifted her explanation about inflation and the Fed's likely response. Yellen's May 18, 2021, speech to the US Chamber of Commerce was released by the Treasury Department. A video of Yellen's visit to Invest Atlanta on August 4, 2021, is posted on the Treasury Department's website. The department's report on childcare needs and Yellen's comments about the issue on September 15, 2021, were contained in a department news release. The creation of the

Treasury's Counselor for Racial Equity on October 25, 2021, was announced in a Treasury Department news release. Treasury secretary Steven Mnuchin's extensive air travel at public expense was detailed by the Treasury Department's Office of Inspector General, as reported in the October 5, 2017, *New York Times* article, "Seven Flights for $800,000: Mnuchin's Travel on Military Jets," by Alan Rappeport. Yellen's April 5, 2021, speech on her international priorities to the Chicago Council on Global Affairs; the April 19, 2021, announcement of the creation of a Climate Hub and a climate counselor; and Yellen's comments to the Group of Twenty finance ministers in Venice on July 10, 2021, were detailed in Treasury Department news releases. On April 1, 2021, the Treasury Department announced it was working with the IMF to help provide up to $650 billion worth of Special Drawing Rights (SDRs) to aid countries hit hardest by the COVID-19 pandemic. Yellen's speech on May 26, 2021, one day after the anniversary of George Floyd's death, to the Financial Literacy and Education Commission, was in a Treasury news release, as were her remarks at the White House's Tribal Nations Summit on November 16, 2021. Details on the partisan divide in Congress over raising the debt ceiling in the fall of 2021 and Yellen's role in averting a default are chronicled in numerous news stories.

The size of uncollected taxes estimated by the Treasury was contained in a report issued in May 2021, called "The American Families Plan Tax Compliance Agenda." The proposal to increase IRS funding was in a news release issued by the department on May 20, 2021. The Congressional Budget Office (CBO) said in a September 2, 2021, post by CBO director Phillip L. Swagel that an $80 billion budget increase for the IRS over ten years would bring in $207 billion in additional tax revenue for a net gain of $127 billion. Yellen estimated in a November 18, 2021, statement released by the Treasury Department that $400 billion in additional revenue would come from increased IRS compliance efforts. Glenn Kessler, who writes "The Fact Checker," a *Washington Post* column, awarded her two out of four "Pinocchios" in the December 5, 2021, print edition for exaggerating the savings and misrepresenting CBO's conclusions. The IRS announced on March 10, 2022, that it would hire five thousand more people to help deal with its backlog of returns.

Background on the international tax treaty talks came from news sources, interviews with Treasury officials—some who would only discuss the issue speaking anonymously—and fact sheets from the Organisation for Economic Co-operation and Development (OECD). A December 9, 2020, Tax Foundation report, "Corporate Tax Rates Around the World, 2021," by Sean Bray, found that the average corporate tax rate globally had fallen from 40 percent in 1980 to just 24 percent in 2021. Corporate tax revenue as a share of the US economy shrank from 6 percent in 1952 to 1 percent in 2019, according to historical tables compiled by the White House Office of Management and Budget (OMB). The July 1, 2021, tax agreement endorsed by the Group of Twenty finance ministers in Venice and finance ministers from the European Union in Brussels was detailed in Treasury Department statements and multiple news media accounts.

## EPILOGUE

*Politico* published "Yellen, Biden's Not-So-Secret Weapon, Sees Clout Diminished," by Kate Davidson and Victoria Guida on May 26, 2022. Bloomberg News published "Janet Yellen Is Struggling at the Treasury Job She Never Wanted," by Saleha Mohsin on June 15, 2022. Yellen's commencement speech at her alma mater, Fort Hamilton High School in Bay Ridge, New York, on June 23, 2021, was posted online. National Economic Council director Brian Deese was interviewed on February 3, 2022.

# INDEX

**Owen Ullmann**'s five-decade career in journalism began as a reporter for the Elizabeth, New Jersey, *Daily Journal*; more recently, he has held senior management and editorial positions

at *USA Today*. Prior to *USA Today*, he spent six years at *Business Week* magazine, where he managed the Washington Bureau as senior news editor. From 1983 to 1993, he worked in the Washington Bureau of Knight-Ridder Newspapers, covering economics, the White House, and the State Department. He won two awards from the White House Correspondents' Association for his coverage of the Reagan presidency. Owen worked for the Associated Press from 1973 to 1983, as automotive writer in Detroit and later as labor writer and chief economics correspondent in Washington. He currently serves as executive editor and Washington columnist for *The International Economy*, a quarterly written for central bankers, finance ministers, financiers, and academics. He has also taught journalism at the University of Wisconsin–Madison and lectures on a variety of current affairs topics. He previously wrote a critically acclaimed biography of David Stockman, President Ronald Reagan's brilliant and brash budget director.

PublicAffairs is a publishing house founded in 1997. It is a tribute to the standards, values, and flair of three persons who have served as mentors to countless reporters, writers, editors, and book people of all kinds, including me.

I. F. STONE, proprietor of *I. F. Stone's Weekly*, combined a commitment to the First Amendment with entrepreneurial zeal and reporting skill and became one of the great independent journalists in American history. At the age of eighty, Izzy published *The Trial of Socrates*, which was a national bestseller. He wrote the book after he taught himself ancient Greek.

BENJAMIN C. BRADLEE was for nearly thirty years the charismatic editorial leader of *The Washington Post*. It was Ben who gave the *Post* the range and courage to pursue such historic issues as Watergate. He supported his reporters with a tenacity that made them fearless and it is no accident that so many became authors of influential, best-selling books.

ROBERT L. BERNSTEIN, the chief executive of Random House for more than a quarter century, guided one of the nation's premier publishing houses. Bob was personally responsible for many books of political dissent and argument that challenged tyranny around the globe. He is also the founder and longtime chair of Human Rights Watch, one of the most respected human rights organizations in the world.

·　　·　　·

For fifty years, the banner of Public Affairs Press was carried by its owner Morris B. Schnapper, who published Gandhi, Nasser, Toynbee, Truman, and about 1,500 other authors. In 1983, Schnapper was described by *The Washington Post* as "a redoubtable gadfly." His legacy will endure in the books to come.

Peter Osnos, *Founder*